CAVALIERS
&
ROUNDHEADS

By the same author

Christopher Hibbert

CAVALIERS
&
ROUNDHEADS

The English Civil War,
1642–1649

A ROBERT STEWART BOOK

CHARLES SCRIBNER'S SONS
New York

Maxwell Macmillan International
New York Oxford Singapore Sydney

For Jack and Alison
with love

Copyright © 1993 by Christopher Hibbert

Charles Scribner's Sons
Macmillan Publishing Company
866 Third Avenue
New York, NY 10022

Macmillan Publishing Company is part of the Maxwell Communication Group of Companies.

Library of Congress Cataloging-in-Publication Data

Hibbert, Christopher, 1924–
    Cavaliers and roundheads : the English Civil War, 1642–1649 / by Christopher Hibbert.
        p.   cm.
    "A Robert Stewart book."
    Includes bibliographical references and index.
    ISBN 0-684-19557-7
    1. Great Britain—History—Civil War, 1642–1649.   I. Title
DA415.H43   1993
941.06′2—dc20   92-42669
                                                                                CIP

Macmillan books are available at special discounts for bulk purchases for sales promotions, premiums, fund-raising, or educational use. For details, contact:

Special Sales Director
Macmillan Publishing Company
866 Third Avenue
New York, NY 10022

10   9   8   7   6   5   4   3   2   1

Printed in the United States of America

CONTENTS

MAPS

TABLE OF
PRINCIPAL EVENTS

1625
27 Mar: Accession of King Charles I
11 May: King Charles marries
Henrietta Maria, sister of
King Louis XIII of France

1628
28 May: Petition of Right elaborates
Parliament's grievances
23 Aug: Murder of Duke of
Buckingham

1629
3 Mar: The King dissolves
Parliament

1633 William Laud appointed
Archbishop of Canterbury

1635 John Hampden refuses to pay
Ship Money

1639
28 May: The King, leading army
against the Scots, arrives in
Berwick

1640
13 April: Short Parliament assembles
3 Nov: Long Parliament summoned

1641
12 May: Earl of Strafford executed
23 Oct: Rebellion breaks out in
Ireland

22 Nov: Grand Remonstrance details
Parliament's further
grievances

1642
4 Jan: King attempts to arrest the
Five Members of Parliament
10 Jan: King leaves Whitehall
Long Parliament issues
Militia Ordinance
1 June: The Nineteen Propositions
issued by Parliament
22 Aug: King raises standard at
Nottingham
23 Sept: Prince Rupert's victory at
Powick Bridge
23 Oct: Battle of Edgehill
12 Nov: Prince Rupert attacks
Brentford
13 Nov: Defence of Turnham Green

1643
19 Jan: Sir Ralph Hopton's victory at
Braddock Down
2 Mar: Lord Brooke killed at
Lichfield
19 Mar: Lord Northampton killed at
Hopton Heath
30 Mar: Sir Thomas Fairfax defeated
on Seacroft Moor
16 May: Battle of Stratton
18 June: John Hampden mortally
wounded at Chalgrove Field
30 June: Battle of Adwalton Moor

5 July: Sir Bevil Grenville killed at
              Landsdown
13 July: Battle of Roundway Down
13 July: King and Queen reunited at
              Edgehill
26 July: Royalists take Bristol
18 Sept: Rupert and Essex clash at
              Aldbourne Chase
20 Sept: First Battle of Newbury
25 Sept: Solemn League and Covenant
              signed
10 Oct: Roundhead cavalry rout
              Cavaliers at Winceby

1644
6 Jan: Hopton recaptures Arundel
19 Jan: Scottish army invades
              England
25 Jan: Battle of Nantwich
21 Mar: Prince Rupert occupies
              Newark
29 Mar: Battle of Cheriton
29 June: Battle of Cropredy Bridge
2 July: Battle of Marston Moor
2 Sept: Battle of Lostwithiel
27 Oct: Second Battle of Newbury

1645
10 Jan: Archbishop Laud executed
Feb: Establishment of New Model
              Army
3 April: House of Lords passes Self-
              Denying Ordinance
30 May: Sack of Leicester
14 June: Battle of Naseby
10 July: Battle of Langport
11 Sept: Parliamentarians capture
              Bristol
13 Sept: Royalists routed at
              Philiphaugh
24 Sept: Battle of Rowton Heath
15 Oct: Sack of Basing House

1646
30 Jan: Chester surrenders
21 Mar: Lord Astley defeated at Stow-
              on-the-Wold
20 June: Royalists sign articles of
              surrender at Oxford
5 May: The King surrenders to Scots
              at Newark

1647
2 June: The King seized at Holdenby
17 July: Army accepts the *Heads of the
              Proposals*
28 Oct–   The Army and the Levellers
8 Nov: engage in the Putney Debates
26 Dec: The King signs the
              Engagement with the Scots at
              Carisbrooke

1648
17 Jan: Parliament breaks off
              negotiations with the King by
              the Vote of No Addresses
June–Aug: Siege of Colchester
17–19 Aug: Battle of Preston
20 Nov: *Remonstrance of the Army* laid
              before Parliament
6 Dec: Colonel Pride purges
              Parliament

1649
30 Jan: Execution of the King

1650
3 Sept: Cromwell defeats Scots at
              Dunbar

1651
3 Sept: Battle of Worcester

1653
4 July: The Parliament nominated by
              Cromwell, 'Barebone's
              Parliament', assembles

1655
Mar: Penruddock's Rising
          suppressed
          Institution of Major-generals

1658
3 Sept: Death of Cromwell

1660
4 April: Charles II issues Declaration
          of Breda
29 May: Charles returns to London

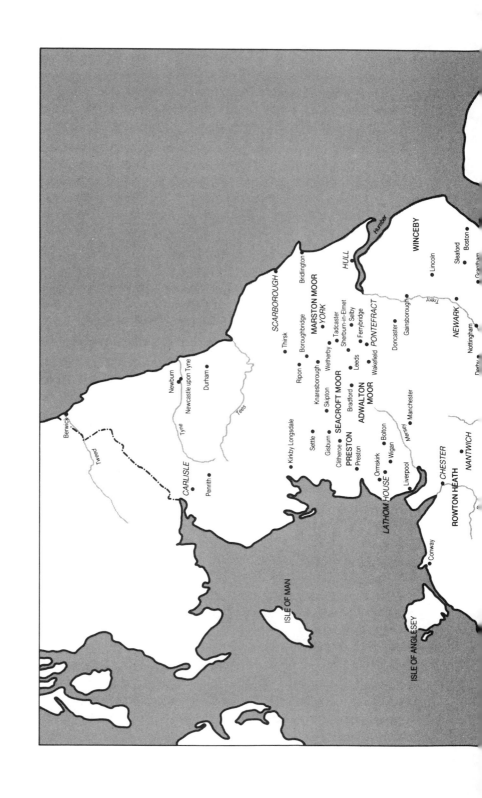

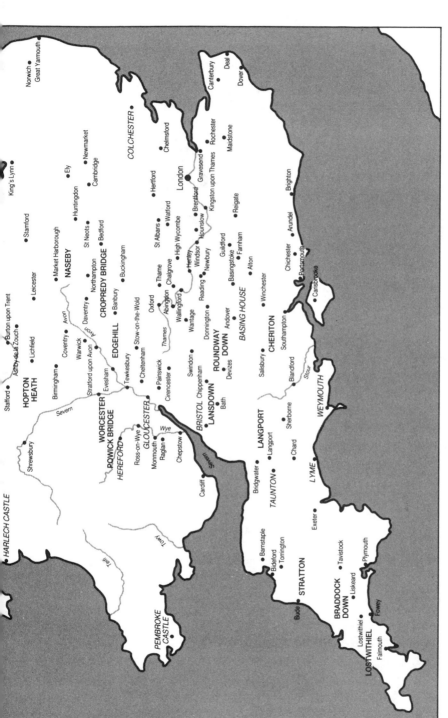

Civil War Locations

Names in bold type represent battle sites. Names in italic represent sieges.

HARLECH CASTLE

PEMBROKE CASTLE

Norwich
Great Yarmouth
King's Lynn
Stamford
Ely
Huntingdon
Newmarket
Cambridge
Market Harborough
St Neots
Bedford
COLCHESTER
Chelmsford
Canterbury
Deal
Dover
Rochester
Maidstone
NASEBY
CROPREDY BRIDGE
Banbury
Buckingham
Northampton
Daventry
Leicester
Stow-on-the-Wold
Oxford
Thame
Chalgrove
St Albans
Watford
High Wycombe
Hertford
London
Gravesend
Brentford
Hounslow
Kingston upon Thames
Reigate
Burton upon Trent
Ashby-de-la-Zouch
Stafford
Lichfield
HOPTON HEATH
Coventry
Avon
Warwick
Avon
EDGEHILL
Stratford upon Avon
Evesham
Tewkesbury
Cheltenham
Painswick
Cirencester
Swindon
Wantage
Abingdon
Wallingford
Thames
Henley
Windsor
Newbury
Reading
Donnington
Andover
Guildford
Basingstoke
Farnham
Alton
BASING HOUSE
Chichester
Arundel
Brighton
Portsmouth
Carisbrooke
Shrewsbury
Severn
WORCESTER
PQWICK BRIDGE
HEREFORD
GLOUCESTER
Ross-on-Wye
Monmouth
Raglan
Chepstow
Wye
Cardiff
Severn
BRISTOL
Chippenham
LANSDOWN
Bath
Devizes
ROUNDWAY DOWN
Salisbury
CHERITON
Winchester
Southampton
Blandford
Stour
WEYMOUTH
Teifi
Towy
Towy
Bridgwater
LANGPORT
Langport
TAUNTON
Chard
Sherborne
LYME
Barnstaple
Bideford
Torrington
Exeter
STRATTON
Bude
BRADDOCK DOWN
Liskeard
Tavistock
Plymouth
LOSTWITHIEL
Lostwithiel
Falmouth
Fowey

Oliver Cromwell

Miniature by Samuel Cooper

AUTHOR'S NOTE AND ACKNOWLEDGEMENTS

This is a narrative history of the Civil War in England concentrating upon what happened rather than upon what brought it about, upon the minor engagements and sieges – in which most of the war's casualties were incurred – rather than upon the major battles, and upon the impact which the fighting had upon the civilian population. I have at the same time introduced as much little-known, curious and illuminating detail as I have been able to find.

It is intended for the general reader not the student, although I hope the student to whom the field is new may perhaps find it a useful introduction to the works of those scholars listed in the bibliography to whom I am myself deeply indebted. No references to sources are given in the text; but, for any readers who might be interested in consulting them, annotated copies of the book have been deposited at the library of the National Army Museum, Royal Hospital Road, Chelsea and the Mugar Memorial Library, the University of Boston, Massachusetts.

For their help in a variety of ways I must express my thanks to Margaret Lewendon, Alison Riley, Dr Francis Sheppard and to Dr Peter Boyden who kindly arranged for me to study the Civil War Papers of Brigadier Peter Young in the National Army Museum. I am much indebted also to the staffs of the London Library, the British Library, the Bodleian Library, Oxford, and the County Record Offices of England and Wales, in particular to Michael Farrar, Cambridgeshire County Archivist; Richard Childs, Principal Archivist, Sheffield City Council; Mrs J. Challinor, Derbyshire Library Service; H. A. Hanley, Buckinghamshire County Archivist; the staff of the Surrey Record Office; Miss S. J. Lewin of the Hampshire Record Office; Jim Grisenthwaite and D. M. Bowcock, Assistant County Archivists, Cumbria Record Office; R. P. Jenkins, Senior Assistant Keeper of Archives, Leicestershire Record Office; Mrs

Patricia Gill, County Archivist, West Sussex Record Office; Miss Rachel Watson, Northamptonshire County Archivist; Miss Jane E. Isaac, Assistant Archivist, Suffolk Record Office; Miss Monica Ory, Deputy County Archivist, Warwickshire Record Office; Adrian Henstock, Principal Archivist, Nottinghamshire Archives Office; Mrs M. M. Rou, Devon County Archivist; James Collett-White, Bedfordshire County Record Office; Miss Kathleen Topping, Manager, Centre for Kentish Studies, West Kent Archives Office; A. M. Carr, Deputy Head of the Record and Research, Shropshire Cultural Services; and Miss J. T. Smith, Principal Archivist, Essex County Archives; to my agents Bruce Hunter and Claire Smith; to Richard Johnson of HarperCollins and to Charles Scribner's, Sons, New York.

   I am also most grateful to Hamish Francis for reading the proofs, to Katherine Everett for her help in choosing the illustrations, to Robert Lacey, my editor at HarperCollins, and to my wife for having compiled the index.

   Finally I want to say how much I am indebted for his generous help to John Morrill, Fellow of Selwyn College, Cambridge and to Donald Pennington, sometime Fellow of Balliol College, Oxford, for having read the typescript and having given me so much useful advice.

                                                    Christopher Hibbert

PROLOGUE

*'It is called superstition nowadays for any man
to come with more reverence into a church than
a tinker and a dog into an ale-house.'*

Archbishop Laud

On a winter's day in 1624 Lord Kensington, England's 'wooing Ambassador' as he called himself, rode into Paris to present as alluring a portrait as he could of the twenty-three-year-old Prince of Wales. Without recourse to the hyperbole which envoys on such a commission as his had commonly to employ, Kensington, himself an extremely handsome man 'of a lovely and winning presence', was confident that he could draw a picture sufficiently appealing to recommend the Prince as a husband for the King of France's daughter, Henrietta Maria.

He could honestly describe a courteous young man, kind and considerate, rather delicate, even feminine in appearance, it was true, and by no means tall, no more than 5 feet 4 inches in fact, but healthy, with limbs made strong by vigorous exercise, by riding, tennis and golf, a curious Scottish game, as Kensington had to explain, which required both skill and strength in wielding a crooked club to drive balls made of hard leather stuffed with feathers into certain holes made in the ground. The Prince was meditative and studious; he read often from a little book, written out by hand and containing – though Lord Kensington had never looked closely inside it – noble sentiments and spiritual advice; he was most regular in his religious observances. Yet he was a young man of action, too, and of physical courage; he hunted with splendid spirit and took a keen interest in military affairs, having once even asked his father for permission to go off and fight in the service of the Doge of Venice. He was renowned for his temperate tastes: he had a good appetite but never ate greedily, preferring plain food to rich; he enjoyed a glass of wine or ale but never drank to excess, often, indeed, contenting himself with a glass of water or fruit juice; there had never been the least suspicion of his misbehaving with any young ladies of the English Court.

Lord Kensington took care not to emphasize this demure chastity, which seemed to some of the more uncharitable gossips in England to suggest that the Prince might be 'less than a man'. Nor did Kensington find cause to lay too much emphasis on the solemnity of his nature, the rarity of those occasions upon which a smile of amusement lit up his small, pale, wistful face or brought a gleam of pleasure into his sad, rather prominent eyes, the even rarer occasions upon which he had been heard to laugh. There was certainly no need to mention his flashes of petulant temper, his occasional obstinacy, his disconcerting reserve, the stammer that sometimes impeded his speech, Scottish in accent like his father's, though not so strongly so.

He had been born in Scotland on 19 November 1600, twelve miles outside Edinburgh, in a bedroom overshadowed by the great stone tower of Dunfermline Abbey. His father was King of Scotland then, and although – as the son of the Queen of England's cousin, Mary, Queen of Scots, and as the great grandson of King Henry VIII's sister, Margaret – King James was generally accepted as the rightful heir to the English throne, Queen Elizabeth had not yet nominated him as her successor. Nor had she done so until she was on her deathbed in March 1603 when, brought the long-awaited news at Holyroodhouse, King James rode fast for the English border, followed by his lively and handsome Danish wife Anne, and accompanied by numerous courtiers and retainers who hoped to share with him some of the profits of his inheritance. Prince Charles was left in the care of nurses and servants. He was three years old by then, but he had not the strength to walk and he could not speak.

His father suggested that he might walk if his weak legs and ankles were placed in irons, and that he might perhaps talk if a surgeon were to cut the ligament at the base of his tongue. But the child's

kindly Cornish nurse warned that these drastic measures might well
do more harm than good. If he were left in her care, living in the
country, nature and love would do their work; and so they did. His
legs admittedly were still rather bowed, his stammer was troublesome in times of stress, but he had grown, as Lord Kensington
assured the French King, into a man of presence and worth. He was
not as clever as his father, Kensington might have added; he did not
have his father's political judgement, though he shared to the full his
belief that monarchs ruled their kingdoms by divine right, as God's
lieutenants on earth. Yet while King James was slovenly in manner,
unprepossessing in appearance and argumentatively dogmatic in
speech, Prince Charles was, above all, the very personification of
courtliness. 'He is grown a fine gentleman,' one of Lord Kensington's friends observed, 'and beyond all expectation I had of him
when I saw him last; and, indeed, I think he never looked nor became
himself better in all his life.' In earlier years he had occasionally
revealed his jealousy of his elder brother, Prince Henry, a clever,
handsome, athletic boy, their mother's favourite, but this paragon
had died at the age of eighteen twelve years before; and Prince
Charles was now the undisputed heir to the English throne.

Complimentary as were the reports which Lord Kensington gave
of the Prince of Wales in Paris, they were no more enthusiastic than
those he sent back to London about the fourteen-year-old Princess,
'the loveliest creature in France and the sweetest thing in nature'. She
was certainly too vivacious to be considered plain; her face, always
expressive of some emotion, of excitement, sorrow, happiness or
anger, was appealing in its responsiveness and childish candour; yet
it had to be admitted that, for all Lord Kensington's excited pronouncements, she was no great beauty. Her eyes, so most of her
portraits seem to suggest, were hooded by heavy lids; her upper lip,
as even Van Dyck was to indicate, was noticeably protuberant in
consequence of her projecting teeth. Her complexion was sallow;
she was so small that the fringe of tight, black rings of hair that
framed her face would scarcely reach her intended bridegroom's
shoulder. She walked about her rooms with the quick, sudden movements of a sparrow; she spoke quickly, too, and had a quick temper.
She was a determined and uncompromising Roman Catholic.

Her marriage was celebrated on a platform outside the west door
of Notre-Dame on May Day 1625, the duc de Chevreuse standing

in for the absent Protestant bridegroom to whom he was distantly related. The next month at Canterbury her second wedding took place. Her father-in-law had died some weeks before on 27 March, so her husband was now King Charles and she was the Queen of England.

The people of London were ready to welcome her as such. Two days after her wedding she and her husband set out by barge from Gravesend followed by hundreds of boats whose numbers grew ever greater as they approached the roaring cannon of the Tower. The King and Queen, both dressed in green, stood by the open windows of the barge, bowing and waving to the cheering crowds. All the way from the Tower to Somerset House in the Strand, which was to be the new Queen's London home, the cheering and shouting continued as the crowds of people jostled each other on the riverside stairs, peered down from the windows of the buildings on London Bridge upon the royal barge, clung to the sides of the surrounding boats.

The people's enthusiasm for their young Queen Henrietta Maria did not, however, last long. It was soon noticed that she responded to their acclamations, if at all, with a sulky ill grace. When they crowded round her and stared at her, she turned away or even scowled at them. Particularly she disliked being watched with gaping curiosity when she had her meals at Whitehall Palace. 'Divers of us being at Whitehall to see her being at dinner,' reported one of the sightseers traditionally admitted to this intriguing spectacle, 'and the room somewhat overheated with a fire and company, she drove us all out of the chamber. I suppose none but a Queen could have cast such a scowl.'

She took no trouble to learn English; she showed no inclination to talk to anyone except the French women who constantly surrounded her; she even refused to attend her husband's coronation, choosing instead to peer down on the King from a window in Old Palace Yard as, under a dark and threatening sky, wearing white, not purple – the robes of innocence rather than of majesty – he walked towards the Abbey accompanied by his dear friend, the Duke of Buckingham.

It was only too clear that the Queen disliked England and the English people, that in particular she disliked the Duke of Buckingham, who patronizingly treated her as though she were a little inex-

perienced girl in need of his worldly advice, and that she shrank
from a husband whom she could not yet begin to understand or even
to like. Unhappy and homesick, she took a perverse pleasure in being
so obviously a foreigner, in flaunting her Catholicism in the face of
Protestant susceptibility.

Her husband's reaction to her pert, combative and sometimes
almost hysterical self-will, was a cold disapproving silence, occasionally broken by sudden flashes of rage. He complained to Buckingham
of 'all her various neglects', the way she tried to avoid being alone
with him, how he had to communicate with her through a servant.

Convinced that the cause of the unhappiness of his marriage was
the 'maliciousness' of her French attendants, the King – who had
conceived an aversion to foreigners which was never entirely to leave
him – determined to be rid of them and, on the afternoon of 26 June
1626, accompanied by the Duke of Buckingham, he walked into the
Queen's room at Whitehall Palace. Her attendants watched in awed
silence as he sharply told her to come outside with him for a moment.
The Queen replied that if he had anything to say to her he could do
so where they were. Angrily he took hold of her hand, pulled her
after him to his own apartments, pushed her inside, locked the door
and told her that he had had quite enough of her French friends: all
of them were to be sent home. She burst into tears, then fell to her
knees in supplication, then, losing her temper, ran to the window,
smashed her fist through the glass and began to shout to the people
gathered in the courtyard below. The King pulled her back, bruising
her hands and tearing her dress.

The King's unhappy marriage was but the most personal of the
depressing problems that faced him on every side. The country had
drifted into a war with Spain which dragged on for four years; and,
before it was over, England was at war also with France. Then, in
the summer of 1626, the Duke of Buckingham as Lord High Admiral
led a disastrous expedition to relieve Huguenot rebels in La Rochelle
who were being besieged there by the Catholic forces of the French
King. The Duke brought his badly mauled army back to Plymouth
'with no little dishonour to our nation, excessive charge to our treasure, and great slaughter of our men'. Distressed as he was by foreign
affairs, the King was as deeply troubled by affairs at home.

His father had never disguised his impatience with Parliament, or rather with the country gentry, professional men and merchants who constituted the House of Commons. After dissolving one particularly difficult assembly, the so-called Addled Parliament of 1614, King James had declared that he was surprised that his 'ancestors should have permitted such an institution to come into existence'. He could not govern indefinitely without Parliament, since he needed the money that only Parliament could provide; but he had always been insistent that the Commons had no right to question his policies, to interfere with his inherited prerogative powers. These privileges depended upon *him*, he had told the Speaker, denying that the Commons had any business meddling with matters of state; and when they had entered in their journal a protestation that their privileges did not depend upon the King but were the 'ancient and undoubted birthright of the subjects of England', he had dissolved Parliament, torn the protestation from the book with his own hand and ordered the arrest of those Members whom he took to be the troublemakers. Yet persistently as King James had maintained that his powers were absolute, laboriously as he had set them out in treatises on the Divine Right of Kings, regularly as he had informed Parliament that he was outside or above the law, he was shrewd enough never to lay claims to authority which the laws of the country or the Church of England would have good cause to deny him. Although he had frequently declared his belief that he had no duty to communicate with Parliament at all unless he wished to do so, in practice he had been in almost constant communication with it whenever it was sitting. His relations with the Commons, while often strained, had never reached breaking point; indeed, with the last of his Parliaments they had been perfectly agreeable.

His son had been brought up in the belief, as propounded in a little manual, *Basilikon Doron*, which King James had written for him, that kings, like fathers, derived their authority from God and from Him also derived their right to demand obedience and honour. A few months before his accession Charles had heard his father tell Parliament – and he himself clung resolutely to the belief throughout his life – that the King of England sat on Jesus's throne on 'this part of the earth'.

But Charles was neither so shrewd as his father nor so wary; he did not appreciate just how possessively Parliament regarded its right to approve taxation. He affronted Parliament by virtually ignoring it. Whereas it had been his father's practice to make long speeches to both Houses, to send them frequent messages, to remind them constantly of his theory of kingship, he himself addressed them in the briefest, curtest way. He left them in no doubt that he regarded it as Parliament's duty, as it was all his subjects' duty, to recognize his absolute authority, to trust him to do what was best for them of his own goodwill. Miserable in his marriage to an unhappy and highly-excitable wife, dependent upon the wayward advice of the volatile and forceful Duke of Buckingham, he seemed driven by a nervous insecurity and sense of personal inadequacy to arrogate to himself privileges and rights which his father would never have claimed. 'This King,' wrote Lucy Hutchinson, daughter of the Lieutenant of the Tower of London and wife of a Nottinghamshire gentleman, 'was a most excellent judge and a greate lover of paintings, carvings, gravings and many other ingenuities . . . But a worse encroacher upon the civill and spirituall liberties of his people by farre than his father.' Grave, reserved and fastidious as was his usual demeanour, those close to Charles learned to beware of the sudden outbursts of anger which erupted when he felt his authority or dignity questioned, to dread the obstinacy which was to bring about his downfall.

Moreover, he was wholly lacking in the bonhomie which had attracted men to his great-great-grandmother's brother, Henry VIII, and which his father had often carried to such excess. For all his gentleness and constancy, the exquisite courtesy of his manner, his innate goodness, he was a man more revered and respected than liked. His constraint and lack of humour were barriers to intimacy that all but a very few found it impossible to cross. His slight stammer, which in another man might have been appealing, was in him merely a defect which made it the more difficult for him to put strangers and Members of Parliament at their ease, seeming to emphasize the atmosphere of melancholy that surrounded him.

This atmosphere was reflected in the normally sad expression of his face, an expression so well conveyed in Van Dyck's *Charles I in Three Positions* that when Bernini saw it he described the countenance depicted as 'doomed'. 'Never,' the sculptor said, 'never have I beheld features more unfortunate.'

Underlying the melancholy there was a certain lack of sympathy in the King's responses, a defensive rejection of an intimacy that might reveal him as less assured than he tried to be. Few men ever

felt that Charles really liked them. Few servants ever felt that their
services were truly appreciated; if they did not do their duty they
were politely dismissed; if they did do their duty they were merely
doing what was expected of them. They were treated well but rarely
with a hint of warmth or affection.

Charles was a diligent man rather than an intelligent one; he
understood books better than people, though he did learn and gain
experience from people: as Philip Warwick, later to be one of his
secretaries, said, like King Francis I of France he learned more by ear
than by study. Moreover, he seemed incapable of making that sort
of contact with his subjects which was to ensure for his eldest son,
despite all his manifest faults, a far greater personal popularity and
following.

The first Parliament of King Charles's reign, in 1625, failed to provide him with the financial support he had asked of it, declining to
grant him for more than a single year the right to collect those
customs duties which his predecessors had been granted for life.
Displaying more interest in religion at home than in the King's differences with dynasties abroad, its members went on to urge stronger
measures against Roman Catholicism, fresh support for Puritanism,
and the public disgrace of a clergyman who had denied that the
Pope was Antichrist. Charles replied by dissolving Parliament and
appointing the clergyman one of his own chaplains.

The King's second Parliament, in 1626, proved no more satisfac-
tory than the first. In order to make it more tractable, he had rendered
those Members who had previously proved most tiresome ineligible
for election by appointing them sheriffs. This manoeuvre, however,
merely resulted in the elevation to the leadership of the Commons
of a Member far more dangerous than the relatively moderate men
who had been excluded, Sir John Eliot, son of a rich Cornish squire.
Emotional and vehement, Eliot harangued the Commons in a loud,
harsh voice, protesting that he and his fellow Members were not
creatures of the King elected to approve his policies and vote him
supplies but men with individual consciences and a duty to act only
in accordance with what they knew to be right. He demanded an
inquiry into the conduct of his erstwhile friend and patron, the Duke
of Buckingham, and went so far as to urge his impeachment.

Charles reacted as though in panic. He had Eliot arrested and

imprisoned in the Tower. But when the House, refusing to be intimi-
dated, declined to do any further business until Eliot was released,
the King gave way, releasing Eliot, yet at the same time despatching
a curt and provocative message to the House enjoining its Members
to lose no more time in voting him the money for which he was
tired of waiting.

On his return to the Commons, Eliot immediately returned to the
attack. In the middle of a violent storm that dashed the rain against
the windows of the chamber and hurled the waters of the Thames
across the river steps, he demanded that the complaints of the Commons should be heard and registered before financial matters were
discussed, at the same time attacking the Duke of Buckingham in
the most extravagant terms. Eventually the Duke was impeached by
the Commons. The King responded by dissolving Parliament in 1626
before the proceedings against Buckingham had been completed.

Unable now to raise money through the House of Commons, the
King was reduced to finding other, more direct means of support.
Disregarding Parliament's refusal to grant him the Crown's traditional customs duties, he ordered their collection; he imposed a
capital levy, had those who refused to pay it imprisoned, and dismissed the Lord Chief Justice for questioning its lawfulness.

The immensely expensive failure of the Duke of Buckingham's
expedition to France in 1627, however, obliged the King to summon
Parliament again in the hope that its Members would recognize the
common danger. But the danger, as the Commons saw it, came not
from the country's enemies abroad but from what they took to be
the tyranny of the King at home. They refused to grant money
to him until they had set out their grievances, in particular their
condemnation of taxation without Parliamentary consent and imprisonment without due legal process. They incorporated their grievances in a Petition of Right of 1628 which they presented to the King
for his assent as though it were a statute. Declining to bestow such
authority upon it, the King said that he would be graciously pleased
to accord it his 'royal word'. The Commons, unwilling to trust his
word, expressed their dissatisfaction with the formula and returned
with renewed vigour to the condemnation of the Duke of Buckingham, whom they saw as the chief source of all their misfortunes. In
an attempt to save his dearest friend, Charles gave way and, calling
upon the Commons to attend him in the House of Lords, he signified

his formal assent to the Petition, adding with petulant self-justification, 'This I am sure is full, yet no more than I granted you on my first answer. And I assure you that my maxim is that the people's liberties strengthen the King's prerogative and that the King's prerogative is to defend the people's liberties . . . I have done my part, wherefore if the Parliament have not a happy conclusion the sin is yours. I am free of it.'

Overlooking his ill grace and overcoming their irritation at his implied rebuke, the Commons rose to their feet and accorded him 'such an acclamation as made the House ring several times'. Their cheers were repeated in the streets outside where 'a general joy in all faces spread itself suddenly and broke out into ringing of bells and bonfires miraculous'. Yet, if the King was forgiven for the time being, the Duke of Buckingham was not; and the campaign against him, both inside and outside Parliament, gathered momentum. Hundreds of handbills were printed and passed from hand to hand in the streets: 'Who rules the Kingdom? The King. Who rules the King? The Duke. Who rules the Duke? The Devil.'

As week passed week that summer of 1628 the rage of the people against Buckingham grew more and more intense. In June a physician and astrologer whom he was known to consult was battered to death in the street; and in August the Duke himself was murdered at Portsmouth by a lonely and embittered officer, John Felton, to whom he had refused promotion.

Charles was at prayers when the grievous news was given him. He remained kneeling, his pale face drawn and tight, as his chaplain continued with the service. When it was over, he went to his room and threw himself sobbing across his bed. He could never forgive the man whom he blamed for his death, that 'wicked rebel' Sir John Eliot who had so viciously attacked Buckingham in Parliament, comparing him to Sejanus, the evil counsellor of the Emperor Tiberius. The King ordered that Buckingham's murderer should be 'put to the question' to force him to reveal his accomplices. The lawyers declined to sanction the use of torture, and Felton was executed at Tyburn, protesting that he had acted alone, 'not maliciously but with love of his country'. Yet, in the King's mind, Felton remained Eliot's creature; Eliot's was the ultimate responsibility. He would soon be made to pay for it.

Eliot took his seat in Parliament again in the January following the Duke's death, determined to maintain the principle that the Commons had a right to criticize the King's incompetent or misguided counsellors; but, sensing the advantages of allying the growing Puritan enthusiasm in the country with demands for political change, he and his friends changed the emphasis of their attack. They now moved against the King on religious grounds.

They had numerous and varied complaints: he had presented to a Crown living a clergyman who had declared that refusal to pay the King's forced loans was not merely a crime against the state but a sin against God; he had transferred one of his High Church chaplains to the see of Chichester; he had appointed William Laud, a well-known opponent of the Puritans and advocate of the scandalous doctrine that the Roman Church was one of the true churches of Christendom, Bishop of London; he had appointed one of Laud's closest allies, William Juxon, who was to succeed Laud as Bishop of London, Dean of the Chapel Royal; and he had given intolerable provocation to the Puritan gentry in the Commons by declaring that the affairs of the Church of England were nothing to do with Parliament.

Charles's own position was clear enough. He had read with approval and admiration the Bishop of Chichester's *Appelo Caesarem* which identified Popery with tyranny and Puritanism with anarchy, and which concluded, 'poperie is originall of Superstition; puritanisme, the high-way into prophaneness; both alike [are] enemies unto piety.' This stated his own views precisely. They were much like those of his father and of his father's predecessor, Queen Elizabeth. In a speech to Parliament, in which he condemned the doctrines of the radical Puritans, he called for the Church's return to the 'purest times of Queen Elizabeth's days'. He had abhorred the behaviour and beliefs of his own Queen's priests; but he regarded with even more distaste the opinions of the Puritan landowners and merchants in the House of Commons and of the Puritan preachers whose disrupting, provocative sermons could be heard all over London. It was his firm belief, as it had been his father's, that attacks on the bishops were attacks on the King, and that insults to the Book of Common Prayer must not be tolerated. When, in a later year, an unruly congregation in Essex knocked the Prayer Book out of the hands of their curate and kicked it about the church, he undoubtedly hoped, on turning to the House of Lords to condemn the outrage, that they would do more than merely insist upon the submission of the 'poor and silly men' who had committed it.

As Eliot and his friends in the House of Commons belaboured in ever stronger terms the High Church bishops for poisoning the purity of the true faith, accusing the Bishop of Winchester in particular of preaching 'flat popery' and refusing to confirm the Crown's right to its traditional revenues until they had debated a resolution that 'the affairs of the King of Earth must give way to the affairs of the King of Heaven', the King decided he must take a firm line.

He sent orders to the Speaker to ask the House to adjourn. Its militant Members refused to accept the request, shouting defiantly 'No! No!' in the Speaker's face. Sir John Eliot rose to insist that it was for the Commons to adjourn themselves. But, protested the Speaker, it had been the King's command: the House must adjourn, there could be no more speeches, and if there were he would leave the chair. So saying, he stood up and prepared to leave the chamber; but immediately two of Eliot's supporters sprang at him and forced him back into his seat. 'God's wounds!' one of them, Denzil Holles, a childhood friend of the King and now the impetuous Member for Dorchester, bellowed above the roar, 'God's wounds! You shall sit till we please to rise.' Another Member locked the door and put the key in his pocket.

In growing pandemonium, which on occasions came close to hysteria, the House passed resolutions against the religious policy of the Government and against both the levy and the payment of the customs duties, known as tonnage and poundage, without Parliamentary sanction. Each resolution was met by deafening shouts of 'Aye! Aye!' Then the doors were unlocked and the Members emerged, some of them elated by their bold defiance, many others, who would have slipped away earlier had the door not been locked, in evident apprehension.

Charles was at once appalled and indignant. Condemning the 'undutiful and seditious' behaviour of the Commons, and referring to its most unruly Members as 'vipers', he ordered the arrest of Sir John Eliot who was left to languish in the Tower where, suffering from tuberculosis, he died three years later, his pleas for release denied or ignored.

If few others could share the strength of the King's feelings against Eliot and his indignation at the behaviour of his supporters in the

Commons, there were those, even among the Puritans, who agreed with the diarist Simonds D'Ewes that 'divers fiery spirits in the House' had been 'very faulty'. For D'Ewes himself the day of this fateful clash between King and Parliament in 1629 was the 'most gloomy, sad, and dismal day for England that [had] happened in five hundred years'.

The Parliament which dispersed in such tumult in 1629 was the last which was to meet for eleven years; and the King contrived to persuade himself that his political troubles were over. So, too, were the unhappy years of his marriage. There had been a slight improvement in his relations with his wife after her French attendants had been sent home in 1626 and her household had come under the direction of kindly, sensible English ladies whose rooms were frequently visited by the tactful and attractive French ambassador who helped to bring the King and Queen closer together. The reconciliation had become surer and firmer when the Duke of Buckingham's military campaigns had deprived Charles of his friend's companionship for a longer period than he had ever had to bear. In his loneliness he had been driven to seek the consolation of his now less cantankerous wife. And, after Buckingham's murder, in the agony of his grief was conceived a new love. Formerly the Queen had displayed a physical aversion to a husband without either the imagination or the humour, the experience or the sensuality to overcome the nervousness and shrinking reluctance of an unawakened and underdeveloped girl; now they had reached 'such a degree of kindness', the court jester, Archie Armstrong, told the Earl of Carlisle, that the king was 'a wooer again'. He gazed at his wife with soulful desire, repeatedly gave her presents, evidently felt restless and unfulfilled when they were apart, and when they were together, so an ambassador reported to his government, kissed her 'a hundred times' in an hour.

Her first baby died within an hour of its christening; but the mother soon recovered and her husband was so kind and considerate that she felt not only 'the happiest princess', but 'the happiest woman in the world'. A few months later she was pregnant again, with a pre-natal craving for shellfish. The baby, born on 12 May 1630, another boy, was big and healthy. He was christened Charles. Other children followed him with the most satisfying regularity, a princess, Mary, the next year; another son, Prince James, in 1633; a second daughter, Princess Elizabeth in 1635; then a third daughter in 1636; and a third son in 1640. They were all healthy children, and their mother, her years of unhappiness now far behind her, settled down to a life of full contentment. Year by year the King's affection for her deepened; and her influence over him was to have the most fateful consequences in the future. He made no public protest when various people at court were converted to Roman Catholicism under her influence, nor when she took her two elder sons to mass. Edward Hyde, later first Earl of Clarendon, then a successful young lawyer who was to know them both well, observed, 'the King's affection to the Queen was of a very extraordinary alloy; a composition of conscience and love and generosity and gratitude . . . insomuch as he saw with her eyes and determined by her judgement.'

The country being at peace, the King was able to pay his way without the necessity of calling Parliament, resorting to all manner of devices for raising money – some of doubtful legality, all of them unpopular – for the ordinary costs of government. Customs duties were collected as of right; obsolete laws were resurrected to extract money from those who had breached their provisions; Crown lands were managed with the utmost severity, and royal forests extended; monopolies were sold to companies and corporations since the law forbade their sale to individuals; fines were imposed upon all owners of freehold land worth £40 a year or more who had not applied for knighthood at the King's coronation; and Ship Money, a tax which had been levied by ancient right upon maritime towns and counties to meet naval expenses, was extended to inland areas also.

As in the past when advised by Buckingham, the King was not so widely blamed for these impositions as were his ministers and advisers, in particular Thomas Wentworth, the future Earl of Strafford, and William Laud, who was appointed Archbishop of Canterbury in 1633, the one a hard, intelligent, impatient and energetic man, the son of an ancient family and owner of huge estates in Yorkshire, whose great wealth had been increased by none too scrupulous methods, the other the son of a Reading clothier, a 'little low red-faced man of mean parentage', in Sir Simonds D'Ewes' description. Overworked, fussy, unimaginative and outspoken, sometimes irritable and often rude, William Laud had made many enemies. He was scholarly and devout, withdrawing seven times a

day, however pressing his business, to kneel in prayer; yet those
who had seen the eyes in his alert, flushed face flash with sudden and
alarming anger, who had been shouted down by him in argument,
who had suffered at his hands in the Star Chamber or in the Court
of High Commission, had good cause to fear and dislike him.

To him Puritans were like wolves 'to be held by the ears'; and,
while introducing measures which effectively reduced the number
of those who propounded what he took to be their heretical doctrines, he appointed to vacant sees bishops who were prepared to
endorse his own and the King's views on conformity, the use of
the Prayer Book, surplices and organs, the proper position of the
communion table as an altar at the east end of the church rather than
as a mere slab of wood in the middle, the need to make services
more reverent and churches more beautiful. 'It is called superstition
nowadays', he once indignantly complained, 'for any man to come
with more reverence into a church than a tinker and a dog into an
ale-house.'

Very insular in his outlook, he set great store by the Englishness
of the established Church which was beginning to be called Anglican,
the Church which had kept itself free from the deviations of the
medieval popes, which remained the true Church of Christendom,
which must be steered in that 'middle way', as the King described
it, 'between the pomp of superstitious tyranny and the meanness of
fantastick anarchy'.

This view of the meaning and importance of the English Church
offended both Catholic and Puritan, yet it could not be said that the
jointly held views of the King and Archbishop were imposed upon
a wholly antagonistic people: there was much in 'Laudism', and not
only its nationalistic overtones, which appealed strongly to all
classes. While enemies of the established Church ranted against
bishops, many parishes presented petitions in support of them and
later organized demonstrations in favour of altar rails and organs.
Indeed, during these eleven years when the King ruled the country
without reference to Parliament, there were numerous people to be
found who believed the country in general, as well as the Church in
particular, was set upon a fair and encouraging course. New roads
were being built and old ones improved, canals dug and swamps
drained; a postal service was started; attempts were made to improve
local government and to find work for the unemployed. The country

was prosperous and remained at peace. Edward Hyde went so far as to suggest that in 1639 'England enjoyed the greatest measure of felicity it had ever known. But then,' Hyde continued, 'in the midst of this scene of happiness and plenty, a small, scarce discernible cloud arose in the North, which was shortly after attended with such a storm, that even rooted up the greatest and tallest cedars of [the country]; blasted all its beauty and fruitfulness; brought its strength to decay, and its glory to reproach.'

PART ONE

I

THE GATHERING STORM

'Lord, what work was here! What clattering of glasses! What beating down of walls! What tearing up of monuments! What tooting and piping on the destroyed organ pipes!'

Bishop Joseph Hall

The distant rumblings of the storm had first been heard in Scotland, where the King had offended not only the nobility by taking back into royal hands estates which had once belonged to the Crown and had since been alienated, but also the Presbyterian congregations of the Kirk by his evident determination to impose upon them the popish practices of the detested Englishman, William Laud. When a new prayer book designed upon Anglican lines was introduced there was a riot in St Giles's Cathedral in Edinburgh, and a bishop suspected of concealing a crucifix beneath his vestments was chased through the streets by a mob of three hundred angry women. A representative of the King's Government in Edinburgh, who ran to the bishop's assistance and was himself attacked, reported to London that the King must choose between abandoning his prayer book and forcing it down the Presbyterians' throats with the help of a well-equipped army of forty thousand men. The Marquess of Hamilton, the King's Commissioner in Scotland, warned the King that his countrymen were 'possessed by the Devil', and that if his Majesty used his army in this way he would not only provoke rebellion in England but risk the Crown in his other two kingdoms of Scotland and Ireland as well.

In defiance of this prescient advice, an English army was raised; but, far from being the powerful force recommended, it was a tawdry array of discontented raw recruits, special levies, trained bands and militia, neither inspired by their cause nor encouraged by the prospects of good pay, whereas the army raised by the Scots, fired by patriotism and religious faith and commanded by a wily, though barely literate old professional soldier, Alexander Leslie, was largely composed of clansmen trained to battle and troops experienced in Continental warfare, backed up by hundreds of men and women ready to fight on the barricades with knives and pitchforks in defence of a National Covenant which, signed by all classes, pledged resistance to 'papistry'.

The English army which the King in person led against the Scottish rebels in March 1639 was numerous enough, being over twenty thousand strong. Yet, apart from the regiments raised in those far northern areas where men were always ready to fight their traditional enemies across the border, the rank and file remained dispirited and their equipment so limited and primitive that many of the trained bands had to make do with bows and arrows until supplied with pikes which proved inadequate. 'Our army is but weak,' lamented Edmund Verney, Knight Marshal of the King's Palace, 'our purse is weaker; and if we fight with these forces . . . we shall have our throats cut.' Sir Jacob Astley, the King's Sergeant-Major recalled from retirement to command the infantry, felt obliged to concur. 'Our men are very raw,' he reported, 'our arms of all sorts naught, our victuals scarce, and provisions for horses worse.' The Earl of Essex, another veteran of Continental wars and for a time commander of the cavalry, was no more confident of success; nor was that charming courtier and 'wooing ambassador' Lord Kensington, recently created first Earl of Holland, whom the King was unwisely persuaded to put in Essex's place by Holland's friend, the Queen; nor were the regimental commanders, many of whom resented the King's having resorted to an ancient and, for them, most inconvenient tradition by calling upon his tenants-in-chief to attend upon him with an appropriate number of men. 'We have had a most cold, wet and long time of living in the field,' wrote Thomas Windebank, one of the many sons of the King's Secretary of State, Sir Francis Windebank, when the war was over, 'but kept ourselves warm with the hope of rubbing, fubbing and scrubbing those scurvy, filthy, dirty, nasty, lousy, itchy, scabby, shitten, stinking, slovenly, snotty-nosed, logger-headed, foolish, insolent, proud, beggarly, impertinent, absurd, grout-headed [daft], villainous, barbarous, beastial, false, lying, roguish, devilish, long-eared, short-haired, damnable, atheistical, puritanical crew of the Scottish Covenant.'

As the Scottish rebel army advanced purposefully towards the border, the English forces began to crumble away; and at Berwick in June the King, who – always reluctant to recognize that his authority was limited by what it was possible to achieve – had declared that he would 'rather dye than yield to these impertinent and damnable demands' of the Scots, was now obliged to come to terms and to agree to a meeting of a General Assembly of the Church of Scotland and to the election of a Scottish Parliament to negotiate a peace. The differences between the two sides, however, particularly on the question of bishops, were too marked for settlement. The Scottish Parliament was adjourned and war seemed inevitable once more.

Thomas Wentworth, soon to be created Earl of Strafford, came over from Ireland to give his advice in 1639. The King's principal Secretary of State at this time was Sir Henry Vane, an assiduous courtier of the Queen, a 'busy and bustling man', smooth, cunning, evasive and equivocal. His views, when he could be prevailed upon to express them, contrasted sharply with those of the Earl of Strafford, whom he much disliked and by whom he was much distrusted in turn. It was Strafford's opinion that prompt, vigorous and if necessary ruthless action was essential. For far too long the government of the country had been drifting along indecisively, uncertainly directed by such incompetent and procrastinating ministers as Vane who told the King what he wanted to hear rather than what he ought to know. In pain, limping from gout and weakened by dysentery, Strafford was blunt and irritable, his 'soure and haughty temper' as Philip Warwick described it, much exacerbated. To resolve the country's problems, he said, a very large sum of money would be needed; therefore a new Parliament must be called.

The King had always found it difficult to like Strafford. So had the Queen. But both recognized in him, as did William Laud, a man of forceful authority whose thoroughgoing policies had brought order and some measure of prosperity to Ireland and might extricate England from its present troubles. Strafford's advice was accepted: in April 1640 the Members of what was to become known as the

Short Parliament assembled in the chamber of the House which had remained empty and silent for so long.

Most of these Members, elected for the first time, were inexperienced in the ways and customs of the House. They gazed about the chamber, one of them said, wondering 'who should begin'. Some looked towards John Hampden, Member for Buckinghamshire, who was described by Edward Hyde, Member for Wootton Bassett, as 'the most popular man in the House'. The eldest son of a Buckinghamshire landowner of ample fortune, Hampden had first been elected to Parliament in 1621, and had since achieved national fame by undergoing a term of imprisonment for refusing to pay Ship Money. Respected as Hampden was, though, he was not much of an orator and had always shown more aptitude for committee work than for public debate.

It was left, therefore, to an older member who had first entered Parliament in 1614 to take the lead. This was John Pym, a thickset, scholarly-looking man, intense and studious, with a rough and shaggy appearance which gained him the nickname 'Ox'. Like Eliot and Hampden and so many other Parliamentary leaders of his time, he came from an old country family. The son of a gentleman from Somerset, he had been at Oxford before entering the Middle Temple; and, though he was never called to the bar, his speeches were those of a clever lawyer, precise, considered, telling, quite without the frantic rhetoric of Sir John Eliot's harangues.

He had earned the dislike of the King by his speaking against the Duke of Buckingham, and he now alienated his erstwhile friend the Earl of Strafford by advising his fellow Members of the Commons to refuse to vote any money for the King's war against the Scots until the country's grievances had been considered and satisfied. Strafford reacted characteristically to this provocation: he advised the dissolution of Parliament and, since an army strong enough to subdue the Scottish rebels could not be raised in England, the use against them of an army from Ireland. The situation, Strafford insisted, was getting out of hand: there was rioting in the City; south of the river a mob had surged towards Lambeth Palace, forcing the Archbishop to seek shelter in Whitehall; apprentices, dock hands and watermen were marching through the streets with drums, waving staves at passers-by and shopkeepers. 'Unless you hang up some of them,' Strafford warned the King, 'you will do no good with them.' Several rioters were accordingly imprisoned; two of the ringleaders were hanged; and the rack was brought out for the last time in England to torture one of them. Order for a time was restored. But the City Aldermen continued to refuse to contribute to the loan which was essential to a successful prosecution of the Scottish war.

The English army which marched north that summer against the Scottish rebels was consequently both underpaid and ill-supplied as well as ill-disciplined: two Roman Catholic officers were murdered by their men, who then deserted. Nor did it have the undivided support of the civilians it left behind. Before it marched two of its soldiers fell into conversation with two clothiers in the Green Dragon Tavern in Bishopsgate Street. The clothiers expressed sympathy for the Scots, whereupon one of the soldiers said they must be Puritans. One of the clothiers asked if 'he could tell what a Puritan was, whereat [the soldier] flew into such a rage he threw a trencher, and hit him on the head'.

The English army, defeated at Newburn on 28 August, met the fate which all sensible men had predicted; and the terms to which the King was obliged to agree were deeply humiliating: the Scottish army was to be paid £850 a day until its claims were settled; and it was to be left in control of Northumberland and Durham. The Scottish provincial government was also to be paid its expenses. So yet another Parliament would have to be called in London, and it was not likely to accept dissolution as tamely as had its predecessor, nor to rest until the King's 'evil counsellors' had been removed from office.

The Members of this new Parliament, which, summoned in November 1640, was to become known as the Long Parliament, directed their attack first against Strafford, whom they had arrested and taken away to the Tower. Then William Laud was impeached and sent to join him there. Several less courageous counsellors slunk abroad.

The Queen took it upon herself to stiffen her husband's resolve. Distressed by the death of their little daughter Anne, frequently in tears, sleeping badly and feeling ill, she pleaded with the King to stand firm against the demands of Parliament, not to disband the Irish army, at one moment plotting to rescue Strafford from the Tower, at another trying to placate John Pym and his fellow Puritans by reducing the number of Roman Catholics in her household and by arranging for the marriage of her eldest daughter Mary to the

Protestant Prince of Orange, whose requests for the hand of her second daughter Elizabeth had previously been rejected with scorn, constantly badgering the King not to give way to the Commons' demands.

The King's policy, such as it was in these alarming months, was to wait upon events, promising and prevaricating, standing his ground as long as possible, then reluctantly giving way, endeavouring to persuade the Commons that their revolutionary demands threatened to bring the whole country to disaster, and that, as he put it to them himself, a skilful watchmaker might improve the working of a watch by taking it to pieces and cleaning it, provided that, when he put it together again, he left 'not one pin out of it'.

Yet the determination of Strafford, endorsed by the Queen, to remain in the Tower for ever rather than to advise the King to surrender to Parliament in exchange for his freedom made a reconciliation with the Commons difficult to achieve, while the need to pay the Scottish rebels to prevent them advancing south made a break with Parliament impossible to contemplate.

The King, therefore, felt unable to resist a whole series of measures which declared monopolies and taxes levied without Parliamentary consent illegal, required the calling of Parliament every three years, reversed the judgements in several Ship Money cases, abolished prerogative courts, settled the limits of the royal forests, roundly condemned Laudism, and, in March 1641, demanded that the Earl of Strafford should be brought to trial on a charge of High Treason.

The conduct of this trial in Westminster Hall demonstrated only too painfully to the King's friends how far his Majesty had fallen in public esteem. Sitting in a small curtained room at the back of the throne, he was 'little more regarded' than the guards upon the doors. There was 'loud clattering', so a witness recorded, and 'much public eating not only of confections but of flesh and bread, and bottles of beer and wine going from mouth to mouth without cups, and all this in the King's eye'.

The accused looked tired and ill, his beard grey, his back bent, though he was not yet fifty. But he answered the questions that were put to him quickly, calmly, occasionally with contempt, gaining much support by his skill and courage, obliging his accusers to conclude that a charge of High Treason would not serve their purpose and that instead they should bring in a Bill of Attainder which, if

Parliament would pass it and the King assent to it, would secure the prisoner's execution on the grounds that it was necessary for the safety of the state.

Mobs paraded about the streets demanding Strafford's death. Robert Baillie, the Scottish Presbyterian divine who was in London at the time, recorded that 'on Monday some thousands of citizens and prentisses awaited all day at Westminster, cryed to every Lord as they went in and in a loud and hideous voyce for justice against Strafford and all traitors . . . On Wednesday a sudden bruite ran through the Citie that the Papists had set the Lower House on fyre and had besett it with armies; in a clapp all the Citie is in alarum: shops closed, a world of people in armes runnes down to Westminster.'

The Commons passed the Bill by a majority of 204; the Lords' majority was seven. Strafford's life now depended upon the King, who had given him his word that he would never let his minister suffer 'in life, honour or fortune'. With the mob shouting for the traitor's death beneath the windows of Whitehall Palace and threatening to break down the doors, Strafford wrote to the King to release him from his promise, urging him, 'for the prevention of evils' which might result from his refusal, to give his assent to the Bill. For two days the King hesitated, listening to conflicting advice. But, warned that the lives of the Queen and their children might be endangered by his stand, and advised by the Bishop of Lincoln that a monarch had two consciences, one public and one private, and that while the private conscience might find the condemnation of Strafford abhorrent, the public conscience must be concerned with the danger of further bloodshed, the King eventually persuaded himself that it was his duty to submit. He signed the commission with tears in his eyes.

On 12 May Strafford walked with firm step to the scaffold on Tower Hill, passing beneath a window where his old friend Archbishop Laud looked down piteously upon him through the bars. Strafford bowed to him. 'My Lord,' he asked, 'your prayers and blessings.' Laud raised his hand in benediction and murmured a prayer, before falling back fainting from the window. 'Farewell, my Lord,' said Strafford, marching on. 'God protect your innocency.'

'I sinned against my conscience,' the King told the Queen after the axe had fallen. 'It was a base, sinful concession.' He believed that he would never forgive himself for what had happened that day, and he never did. Yet he also came to believe that Strafford's death was due not to his having made concessions too late but to his ever having made any concessions at all.

The execution of Strafford seemed to excite the appetite for revolutionary measures of those Members of the Long Parliament who were eager for further reform, who were determined upon what the nonconformist preacher Edmund Calamy described as a 'second Reformation'. According to one observer, 'reformation [went on] as hot as toast', while noncomformist sects proliferated and the extreme amongst them grew ever more outlandish, though few so *outré* as the Muggletonians, who condemned both prayer and preaching, and the Adamites, peculiarly hysterical descendants of the Brethren and Sisters of the Free Spirit, who conceived themselves as being in that state of innocence obtaining in the Garden of Eden before the Fall and believed it appropriate to worship God in Adam and Eve's condition of nakedness. Inspired by preachers and pamphleteers, by female preachers leading congregations in extempore prayers, and by Puritan writers like John Milton who castigated the clergy of the Church of England for stumbling into 'new-vomited paganisme', their prayer book for being 'the skeleton of a Mass-book' and their communion table for being 'pageanted about like a dreadful idol', apprentices chased Anglican parsons down the streets, calling them 'Abbeylubbers' and 'Canterbury Whelps' and tearing the gowns from their backs.

From all over the country, now and later, there came reports of altar rails being torn down and altars overturned, of prayer books being thrown about churches and graveyards, of vestments being stripped from the backs of Laudian clergy, of attacks upon those opponents of Calvinist doctrines known as Arminians, and of bishops menaced by gangs of women who threatened to hang them with their lawn sleeves. In one church some wild sectaries, provoked by the curate's kneeling as he administered the sacrament to his parishioners, kicked the communion bread up and down the chancel; in others candles were trampled underfoot, crucifixes and organs broken and stained glass windows smashed. At the Church of the Holy Sepulchre without Newgate, a woman encouraged her child to urinate on the communion table; in Newcastle women were said to be tearing up surplices as well as prayer books; in Kidderminster there was a riot when some members of the parish objected to the churchwardens' removal of a crucifix from their churchyard cross. The sectaries 'make such havoc in our churches,' wrote one observer, 'by pulling down ancient monuments, glass windows and rails, that their madness is intolerable.'

At Norwich the Bishop, Joseph Hall, was driven out of his palace which was left without 'so much as a dozen of trenchers or the children's pictures', and his chapel and the cathedral were desecrated and wrecked:

> Lord, what work was here! What clattering of glasses! What beating
> down of walls! What tearing up of monuments! What pulling down
> of seats! What wresting out of iron and brass from the windows
> and graves! What defacing of arms! What demolishing of curious
> stonework! . . . What tooting and piping on the destroyed organ
> pipes! And what a hideous triumph on the market day before all
> the county, when in a kind of sacrilegious procession all the organ
> pipes, vestments, copes and surplices, together with the leaden
> cross which had been newly sawn down from the Green Yard
> pulpit, and the service books and singing books were carried to the
> fire in the public market place, a lewd wretch walking before the
> train in a cope trailing in the dirt, with a service-book in his hand,
> imitating in impious scorn the tune, and usurping the words of the
> Litany.

Later there were similar scenes at Canterbury, where a Puritan clergyman made use of a guide book to the cathedral to demolish 'many window-images', 'many idols of stone', 'seven large pictures of the Virgin Mary' and a window dedicated to 'their prime cathedral saint, archbishop Becket with cope, rochet, mitre, crozier . . . Now it is more defaced than any window in that cathedral. Whilst judgement was executing on the idols in that window, the cathedralists cried out . . . "Hold your hands, holt, holt, heer's Sir, etc." The minister [carrying out the desecration] being then on top of the city ladder, near 60 steps high, with a whole pike in his hand rattling down proud Becket's glassy bones . . . to him it was said, "'Tis a shame for a minister to be seen there" . . . Some wished he might break his neck, others said it should cost blood.'

By the time the work of desecration in Canterbury was finished, a catalogue of the damage done there made sorry reading:

> The windows, famous both for strength and beauty, so generally battered and broken down as they lay exposed to the injury of all weathers; the whole roof with that of the steeples, the chapter-houses and cloister extremely impaired and ruined, both in the timber work and lead; the water tables, pipes and much other of the lead in almost all places cut off . . . The choir stripped and robbed of her goodly hangings, her organ and organ loft.
>
> The communion table [stripped] of the best of her furniture and ornaments. Many of the goodly monuments of the dead shamefully abused, defaced, rifled and plundered of their brasses, iron-gates and bars; the common Dorter (affording good housing for many members of our Church) with the Dean's private chapel and a goodly library over it, quite demolished, the books and other furniture sold away . . . Our very common seal, our registers and other books, together with our records and evidences seized, many of them irrecoverably lost; the Church's guardians, her fair and strong gates, turned off the hooks and burned.

Everywhere self-appointed preachers, 'cobblers, tinkers and chimney-sweepers', women as well as men, were haranguing congregations and inciting them to further excesses, talking for hours on end, often unintelligibly. A button-maker had to be dragged from the pulpit of St Anne's, Aldergate where he had been drawing out 'his words like a Lancashire bagpipe and the people could scarce understand any word he said'. The leatherseller Praise-God Barebone, whose two brothers were stated to have been named Christ-Came-Into-The-World-To-Save Barebone and If-Christ-Had-Not-Died-Thou-Hadst-Been-Damned Barebone, preached a sermon reported to have lasted five hours of a winter's afternoon to a congregation 'about the number of an hundred and fifty'.

Distressed by such reports and by the speeches of the more vehement and progressive Members of Parliament, a group of more moderate men began to emerge. Among them were Lucius Cary, son of the first Viscount Falkland, an accomplished, impulsive, learned and delightfully good-natured young man, Member of Parliament for Newport; John Hampden's cousin, Edmund Waller, a vain poet with an exceptional gift for declamation, who confessed that he had a 'carnal eye' and that he wished only to enjoy his wealth and popularity in peace; Sir John Culpeper, Member for Kent, a 'man of sharpness of parts and volubility of language', in Edward Hyde's description, a persuasive orator, though short-tempered and irresolute; and Edward Hyde himself, 'a fair, ruddy, fat, middle-statured, handsome man', with 'an eloquent tongue' and a 'dexterous and happy pen', who was then Member for Saltash. The devotion of these men to the Church of England was rarely as fierce as their opponents' dislike of it: as one of them, Lucius Cary, 'was wont to say, they who hated bishops hated them worse than the devil, and they who loved them did not love them so well as their dinner'. Yet, as the Puritans became ever more zealous and uncompromising, so these more reasonable Members of Parliament and their adherents showed themselves increasingly prepared to defend the established Church and to support the King. Before the King could take advantage of this change in his fortunes, however, in October 1641 a rebellion broke out in Ireland, the third of his troublesome kingdoms, now released from Strafford's firm rule; and the tide turned once more.

The rebellion, in which thousands of British settlers were massacred by native Irishmen, became known as the Queen's Rebellion. For it was she, her enemies protested, who was behind it all, who was in secret correspondence with the Catholic Irish, who now dominated the conscience of the King and would persuade him to make use of the army, which would have to be raised for the suppression of the rebellion in Ireland, to crush opposition at home.

The Commons were determined to ensure that the King did not gain control of this army. Under pressure from Pym, they sent him a message demanding the dismissal of his present advisers and their replacement by Ministers who enjoyed the confidence of Parliament. They also sent him a petition, calling for the bishops to be denied their votes in the House of Lords, as well as their Grand Remonstrance, a critical document which, in two hundred clauses debated for weeks, set out their complaints and listed the grievances they intended to have redressed.

The King, insisting that he had no unworthy advisers – and commenting privately, 'The Devil take him, whomsoever he be, that had a design to change religion' – publicly replied that the Church of England had no need of the reforms for which the Commons pressed. Encouraged by reports of deep divisions in the Commons and believing he had the support of the House of Lords, he decided not merely to stand firm but to attack: he ordered firm action to be taken against the mobs parading the London streets and swarming about Westminster Hall shouting, 'No Popery! No bishops! No popish Lords!' He dismissed the Puritan Lieutenant of the Tower and replaced him with Captain Thomas Lunsford, a swashbuckling desperado who had, some years before, narrowly escaped being put on trial for murder and was said to roast the flesh of babies. The appointment of Lunsford to so important a post occasioned further tumults. There were renewed demonstrations against bishops in Westminster, where coaches were held up and roughly searched and their occupants questioned by rowdy gangs. John Williams, the Welsh-born Archbishop of York, collared an apprentice who was loudly shouting, 'No bishops!' and endeavoured to drag him into the Lords, but 'the rest of the fellows came jostling in upon the Archbishop in such a rude manner that the Archbishop escaped very hardly with his life'.

Over the next few days there were violent clashes in Westminster Hall where Captain Lunsford and his swaggering Royalist friends, mostly unemployed army officers, marched up and down with drawn swords, threatening to 'cut the throats of those roundheaded dogs that bawled against bishops'. There was trouble, too, around Westminster Abbey, where stones were hurled from the roof at a crowd of apprentices trying to break into the building to rescue some of their friends being held inside for questioning, and in Whitehall where there was fighting in the nearby streets in which several men were killed and wounded.

Although the King dismissed Lunsford, he continued to provoke his opponents. He appealed for volunteers for an expedition to Ireland; and, when the Commons impeached twelve bishops and were reported to be threatening to impeach the Queen, he ordered the arrest on vague but wide-ranging charges of Lord Mandeville, the Earl of Manchester's son and the leading Puritan agitator in the House of Lords, and of five of the most vexatious Members of the House of Commons: Pym, Hampden, Denzil Holles and two men who had been most active in the proceedings against Strafford, William Strode, the young Member for Beeralston, and Sir Arthur

Haselrig, a Leicestershire baronet, in the opinion of Edward Hyde an 'absurd, bold man', who was used as a stalking horse by his cleverer though less forceful colleagues.

To order the arrest of these men was a simple matter; to have them actually taken into custody was not, since the King could not get the order confirmed and the Commons refused to acknowledge its legality. The Queen and a young friend of hers, Lord Digby, son of the Earl of Bristol, urged the King to go down to the Commons with an armed guard and to arrest the men himself. 'Go, you poltroon,' the Queen is alleged to have cried out furiously when her husband hesitated to adopt so drastic a course. 'Go and pull those rogues out by the ears, or never see my face again.'

She had made such threats before: she would go back to France, she had said, or retire to a convent if he would not show his enemies who was master of his kingdoms. Obediently he agreed to go. He kissed her and told her he would be back within the hour.

Sending a message to the Lord Mayor forbidding him to take any action in defence of Parliament, and calling upon the Inns of Court to have all lawyers and students capable of bearing arms ready to take action against his enemies, the King left in his coach on 4 January 1642 for New Palace Yard, accompanied by several courtiers, and followed by a crowd of excited Londoners wondering what was afoot, and by four hundred armed men described by a young lawyer whose sympathies lay with Parliament as 'desperate soldiers, captains and commanders, papists, ill-affected persons, being men of no rank or quality . . . panders and rogues'. The King entered the House of Commons and, courteous as always, took off his hat as he walked towards the Speaker's chair, nodding as he went to various silent Members whose faces he recognized.

'Mr Speaker,' he said, 'By your leave, I must for a time make bold with your chair.'

He sat down, explained his presence, and asked for the five Members to come forward. There was no response. The House remained perfectly quiet.

'Is Mr Pym here?'

Still there was silence. He turned to the Speaker, and repeated the question. The Speaker fell upon one knee before him and said, 'Sire, I have neither eyes to see nor tongue to speak in this place but as the House is pleased to direct me.'

''Tis no matter. I think my eyes are good as another's.'

The King looked along the benches; and at length was forced to admit his attempted coup, on which his whole future depended, had failed. 'Well!' he said with an air of reproach, 'since I see all my birds have flown, I do expect that you will send them unto me as soon as they return hither.'

Having gone so far he was determined not to retreat, as convinced that these five men were at the heart of a conspiracy to undermine his authority as they and their supporters were convinced that the King had now shown himself in his true colours as a tyrant. Issuing a proclamation ordering the City to surrender the five Members who had sought sanctuary within its walls, he marched to the Guildhall himself to demand at a meeting of the Common Council that they should be handed over to him. His words were greeted with shouts of 'Privileges of Parliament! Privileges of Parliament!' to which he responded, 'No privileges can protect a traitor from legal trial!'

He returned to Whitehall, his coach surrounded by people shaking their fists at him as they shouted abuse through the windows, and by others no less loudly crying out, 'God bless the King!' and cursing 'that rogue' Pym. One of these averred that he 'would go twenty miles to see Mr Pym hanged and would then cut off a piece of Mr Pym's flesh to wear about him in remembrance of him'.

London was now in uproar. Shops had closed their doors; people had come out into the streets in their thousands; women collected stones to throw at soldiers who might be sent into the City to drag out the five Members variously reported to be in hiding in Coleman Street, Cornhill or Red Lion Court; stools and tables were thrown into the roadway to hinder approaching horsemen; Royalists, who a few days before had been chasing citizens about Westminster with their swords, now prudently chose to stay indoors. Rumours flew from mouth to mouth: the King's supporters were going to launch an attack on the City and planned to hang Mr Pym outside the Royal Exchange. Barricades were erected, chains pulled across the streets, cannon dragged towards crossroads, cauldrons taken to the top of buildings so that boiling water could be poured down upon the heads of advancing troops. The Inns of Court regiments declared their support of the House of Commons, as the government of the City had already done. Volunteers poured into the City to offer their services in its defence, apprentices from the brickfields at Bethnal

Green and Spitalfields, iron workers from Southwark, watermen from Bermondsey and Shoreditch, silk workers from Spitalfields. The houses of Roman Catholics were attacked.

> In the dead of night [6 January 1642] there was great bouncing at every man's door to be up in their arms presently and to stand on their guard [wrote Nehemiah Wallington, a Puritan turner, in his diary], for we heard (as we lay in our beds) a great cry in the streets that there were horse and foot coming against the City. So the gates were shut and the cullises let down, and the chains put across the corners of our streets, and every man ready on his arms. And women and children did then arise, and fear and trembling entered on all.

The Lord Mayor was called upon to summon the Trained Bands, those companies of armed citizens originally raised to maintain order in the City and to suppress riotous behaviour. But the Lord Mayor at this time was Richard Gurney, a former silkman's apprentice who had been left a fortune by his master and had subsequently married a very rich wife; and, as a zealous Royalist, Gurney refused to issue the summons. The Trained Bands mustered anyway, by whose orders no one was sure; and soon six thousand citizens were standing ready to withstand any troops the King might bring against them.

The officers of the Trained Bands were mostly members of the Fraternity or Guild of Artillery of Longbows, Crossbows and Handguns. Later to be known as the Honourable Artillery Company, this was an ancient regiment of gentlemen much interested in military affairs, several of whom left London from time to time to gain experience of warfare in foreign countries. Their men, musketeers and pikemen, were citizens elected for such duty by the aldermen of their wards and called upon to provide themselves with the necessary equipment. In addition to his immensely long pike, the citizen choosing to become a pikeman had to appear on parade with a breastplate and backplate, a gorget to protect his throat, tasses to guard the thighs, and a helmet. The musketeer also had to have a helmet as well as a musket, musket rest, powder flask and 'bandeleers with twelve charges, a prymer, a pryming wire, a bullet bag and a belt two inches in breadth'. The cost to a musketeer was reckoned to be £1 3s. 4d., to a pikeman £1 2s. od. In addition both had to arm themselves with swords. Pikemen considered themselves superior to musketeers not only because their weapons had a more ancient and respectable lineage, but also because anyone could fire a musket, whereas it took considerable strength and a decent height to handle a pike effectively.

The amount of training the men undertook depended largely upon the energy of their officers. Some colonels called their men out infrequently between general musters, a few scarcely ever, so that it came to be said of their bands, as it was of some Trained Bands in the counties, that the instruction they most commonly received was training to drink. Other officers, such as Captain Henry Saunders of Cripplegate, demanded that their men parade at six o'clock in the morning for an hour in the summer months, insisting that this unwelcome discipline was 'no hindrance to the men's more necessary callings, but rather calls them earlier to their business affairs'. At least Captain Saunders did not require the men to practise shooting at that time in the morning, 'neither to beat drumme nor display Ensigne but onely exercise their Postures, Motions and formes of Battell' so that those still abed near their training ground were not unduly disturbed.

Traditionally, the London Trained Bands could be summoned for service only upon the orders of the Lord Mayor. But after Richard Gurney's refusal to call them out that January night, the House of Commons declared that the authority for their summons would no longer rest with the Lord Mayor alone but in future must reside with a committee comprising members of the Court of Common Council and of the Court of Aldermen as well as the Mayor himself. At the same time a Committee of Safety was formed, consisting of six Aldermen and six members of the Court of Common Council, to supervise London's warlike preparations; and, more significantly yet, Philip Skippon was appointed commander of all London's Trained Bands at a salary of £300 a year.

Philip Skippon had been a soldier all his adult life since leaving home in Norfolk. He had fought on the Continent, been wounded more than once, and had returned to England some years before as a captain in the Dutch service. A good and brave man of devout and simple religious faith, which was later to find expression in three books of devotion addressed to his fellow-soldiers, he was respected by men and officers alike. His strong Puritan views were well known, his courage as undoubted as his administrative abilities. In conjunction with a newly formed Committee for London Militia, he reorganized the Trained Bands into six regiments known by the colours of their ensigns – Red, White, Blue, Yellow, Green and Orange – the regiments having six or seven companies with two hundred men in each company. The nominal colonels of the regiments were influential citizens, mostly leading Parliamentary Puritans, appointed for political, family or business reasons rather than for their military capacity, but the lieutenant-colonels and junior officers had experience if not of warfare at least of training and drilling with such units as the Guild of Artillery. Care was taken to ensure that the companies comprised men drawn from the same wards of the city, so that Portsoken men served with Portsoken men, for instance, and Farringdon with Farringdon. The friendly rivalry of the Trained Bands, whose various traditions dated from the reign of Queen Elizabeth, was thus preserved. In the hands of Philip Skippon they were a formidable force.

On 10 January, the day upon which Skippon's command of the Trained Bands was confirmed, the King left Whitehall for Hampton Court, fearing that the life of his wife was in jeopardy even more than his own. He drove through streets thronged with people crowding round his carriage and waving placards on which was scrawled the single word *Liberty*. The next day the five Members of Parliament whom he had tried to arrest came out of their hiding places in Coleman Street and, accompanied by numerous watermen and cheered by crowds on both banks, were taken by barge upriver to Westminster. Here they were met by Philip Skippon and his London Trained Bands, their ensigns flying in the winter air, wearing in their hats or waving on the points of their pikes, 'like a little square banner', a copy of *The Protestation*, a document remonstrating against the policies of the King and the Church but vague enough to be accepted by all other than extreme Royalists.

From Hampton Court, where – since no preparations had been made for their arrival – 'the princes were obliged to the inconvenience of sleeping in the same bed with their Majesties', the royal family moved on to Windsor. From here the Queen and Princess Mary, who was to join her new husband in Holland, left for Dover with 'small attendance and pomp', accompanied by the household's tiny dwarf, Jeffrey Hudson, who in happier days had been picked up by the gigantic porter at the palace gate as a tasty morsel between the two halves of a loaf of bread. The Queen also took with her urgent messages for military help addressed to the Prince of Orange and the King of Denmark, a large selection of the crown jewels which she hoped to sell or pawn, and a code in which she was to write forceful letters to her husband urging him to be resolute in dealing with his enemies and to remember 'that it is better to follow out a bad resolution than to change it so often', warning him against 'beginning again [his] old game of yielding everything', and, in her fear that she or her friends might be sacrificed as Strafford had been, reminding him of the promise he had made to her at Dover – 'that you would never consent to an accommodation without my knowledge and through me . . . If you do not take care of those who suffer for you, you are lost.'

2

TAKING SIDES

'I have heard foul language and desperate quarrelings even between old and entire friends.'

Henry Oxinden

Immediately upon landing on the Continental shore the Queen set about enlisting help in her husband's cause, attempting to persuade foreign princes that it was in their own interest to support a fellow-sovereign in his hour of need, cajoling money from the Prince of Orange, doing all she could to induce Charles's uncle, King Christian IV of Denmark, to come to his nephew's aid, raising money for weapons and for the pay of volunteers, complaining of persistent colds and coughs and intermittent headaches, yet tireless in her endeavours and firm in her resolve.

She met with little success. King Christian was preoccupied with the protection of Danish interests in northern Germany and with the prevention of Swedish encroachments. The Prince of Orange was hampered by his Protestant people's support of the English Parliament. Everywhere she went or looked to for help the Queen was made aware of the reluctance of foreign courts to come to the aid of a King who had lost the support of his capital and largest seaport and who was likely to lose the support of his fleet, whose principal naval dockyard at Chatham was already in the hands of Parliament and most of whose captains and crews were soon to declare their allegiance to the Puritan Earl of Warwick, the Lord High Admiral, a forthright, level-headed man of 'a pleasant and companionable wit and conversation, of an universal jollity', as Edward Hyde described him, who in turn declared for Parliament and was to make an incalculable contribution to the success of its cause.

Faced with the prospect of losing control of the land forces of the country as well as of the navy, the King dug in his heels. Months before, a Militia Bill, which would have effectively transferred military command from the King to Parliament, had been proposed. It was now pressed upon him again. He would never accept it, he protested. 'By God! Not for an hour! You have asked that of me which was never asked of any King.'

The House of Commons declined to accept the King's refusal. They issued the Bill on the authority of Parliament as an Ordinance, providing for the safeguarding of the realm, revoking military appointments previously made by the King, and taking it upon themselves to appoint the Lords Lieutenants of counties who were to be responsible for the recruitment of troops. It was a provocation which the King could not accept, his determination never to lose his right to command his army being just as fixed as his resolve never to lose the right to choose his own advisers. Much to the unconcealed pleasure of extremists on both sides, the battle lines were now drawn: the time for talking and compromise had passed; the struggle was about to begin.

Indeed, it had, in a sense, already begun. In almost every county where beacons were being set and postboys galloped down the roads with urgent messages, there were quarrels and occasional fights; men walked about armed and shouted insults to each other across the streets. Even in the closest families there were deep divisions. In the Verney family, for example, a family described by the King as 'the model he would propose to gentlemen', the father, Sir Edmund Verney, Knight-Marshal of the King's Palace, although prompted in the past by 'his dislike of Laudian practices' to vote steadily in the House of Commons in opposition to the King's wishes, felt in duty bound to stand by his master when called upon to do so. His third son, Edmund, who was to die fighting in Ireland, also sided with the King. But Edmund's eldest brother, Ralph, Member of Parliament for Aylesbury, threw in his lot with Parliament, much to the family's distress. 'I beseech you consider,' Edmund wrote to him, 'that majesty is sacred; God sayeth, "Touch not myne anointed."

Although I would willingly lose my right hand that you had gone the other way, yet I will never consent that this dispute shall make a quarrel between us. There be too many to fight with besides ourselves. I pray God grant a sudden and firm peace, that we may safely meet in person as well as affection. Though I am tooth and nail for the King's cause, and shall endure so to the death, whatever his fortune be; yet, sweet brother, let not this my opinion – for it is guided by my conscience – nor any other report which you can hear of me cause a diffidence of my true love to you.'

Their father confessed that he did 'not like the Quarrel' and heartily wished 'the King would yield and consent to what they desire'. But his conscience was concerned 'in honour and in gratitude'. He had eaten the King's bread and 'served him near thirty Years', and he would 'not do so base a Thing as to foresake him' now.

The Cornish squire Sir Bevil Grenville, grandson of Queen Elizabeth's admiral, 'a lover of learning and a genial host', who had many friends amongst the Parliamentarians and was to die fighting bravely against them, said much the same thing: 'I cannot contain myself within my doors when the King of England's standard waves in the field, the cause being such as to make all that die in it little inferior to martyrs . . . I go with joy and comfort to venture a life in as good a cause and with as good a company as ever Englishman did; and I do take God to witness, if I were to choose a death it would be no other but this.'

For men like Edmund Verney and Bevil Grenville it was not only that the King's majesty was sacrosanct, there was also the belief that the King was the defender of the true Church; and although religion became of much more importance later in the struggle than it was in the beginning, it was even now of grave concern. Moreover, while it was never primarily a class struggle, there was an undeniable fear amongst many of the King's supporters that the lower classes would use this opportunity to turn upon their masters, that the predominantly Puritan merchants and shopkeepers of the towns were intent on upsetting the structure of power to their own advantage, that the King's opponents represented rebellion and chaos as opposed to law and order. Sir Thomas Gardiner, the Recorder of London, told Ralph Verney that he had overheard the most anarchic speeches being made in Oxfordshire, working men announcing, 'The gentry have been our masters for a long time and now we have a chance to master them.' 'Now they know their strength,' Gardiner added, 'it shall go hard but they will use it.'

Many of those who sided with Parliament spoke of their cause with a passion equal to that of Sir Bevil Grenville's protestation of loyalty to the King, proclaiming their readiness to fight for freedom and justice, to die in a just cause, to defeat the machinations of those whom Simonds D'Ewes called 'the wicked prelates and other like looser and corrupter sort of the clergy of this kingdom who doubtless had a design by the assistance of the Jesuits and the Papists here at home and in foreign parts to have extirpated all the power and purity of religion and to have overwhelmed us in ignorance, superstition and idolatry.'

There were many, of course, who chose not to take sides, who considered local problems more important than national ones, just as there were thousands who were drawn into the conflict on the side that their landlords and masters elected to support, or who accepted orders from one side or the other merely for the sake of a quiet life. Most of these fought without any sense of mission, as was later to be shown by the ease with which Royalist prisoners were induced to come over to Parliament's side after their capture and Parliamentary captives to join the ranks of the Royalists. Although religion certainly played an important part in determining allegiances, men like Lord Brooke, one of the King's most obstinate opponents and, in Milton's opinion, 'a right noble and pious Lord', who urged a crusade 'to shed the blood of the ungodlie', were not numerous on either side.

It has been estimated that there were about 1,300,000 boys and men in England between the ages of sixteen and fifty in 1642, and that well over a quarter of them were to take an active part in the struggle. And of those who succeeded in remaining observers rather than participants there were few who escaped the war's consequences. Even so, there were many who were not too sure what all the fuss was about, or, as Sir Arthur Haselrig said, did not really care what government they lived under, 'so long as they may plough and go to market'. Some did not even know there was a conflict at all. Long after the war had started and the first battles had been fought, a Yorkshire farm labourer, when advised to keep out of the line of fire between the King's men and Parliament's, learned for the first time that 'them two had fallen out'.

There were also those who shilly-shallied, disguising such convictions as they had, like the Earls of Clare and Kingston. The former of these, in the dismissive words of Lucy Hutchinson, whose husband had been appointed Parliamentary Governor of Nottingham, 'was very often of both parties and never advantag'd either'; while as for the Earl of Kingston, 'a man of vast estate, and not lesse covetousnesse', he 'divided his Sonns betweene both Parties and conceal'd himselfe'. Then there were those, of course, who changed sides as opinions were modified and as the fortunes of war favoured first one side then the other.

The Verneys were far from being the only family broken by the quarrel. When, for instance, a convoy of treasure was being carried to the King's headquarters through East Anglia, Henry Cromwell, a first cousin of Oliver Cromwell, Member of Parliament for Cambridge, brought out fifty men to protect it on its way, while Valentine Walton, who was married to Oliver Cromwell's sister, ordered two hundred men to seize it. The resultant fight was witnessed by a crowd of impartial, though fascinated villagers. There were similar disagreements in the family of Stephen Goffe, Rector of the parish of Stanmer in Sussex. One of his sons, a zealous Puritan, decided to join Parliament's army when the moment came; another became chaplain to the King and a spy in the Royalist cause. John Hutchinson's family was also divided, his Byron cousins fighting for the King and one of them, Sir Richard Byron, serving in the Royalist force which was to assault Nottingham in 1643. When the Royalists seemed close to taking the town, Hutchinson ordered his men to take Byron 'or shoote him and not let him scape though they cut his leggs off'.

Sir Henry Slingsby, a Yorkshire squire, described a savage fight 'between two that had been neighbours and intimate friends':

> At another part of the town of York, Lieutenant Collonel Norton enters with his dragouns, Captain Attkisson encounters him on horseback, the other being [on] foot; they meet; Attkisson misseth with his Pistol, the other pulls him off his horse by the sword belt; being both on the ground Attkisson's soulgiers comes in, fells Norton into the ditch with the butt ends of their musketts; then comes Norton's soulgiers and beats down Attkisson and with blows at him broke his thigh bone, whereof he dy'd.

Slingsby himself was a characteristic example of a man who dismayed many of his friends by choosing what they took to be the wrong side. An opponent of Laudism, he thought 'it came too near idolatry to adorn a place with rich cloaths and other furniture', and was equally critical of the extravagance and superficiality of the King's court, yet, while considering it 'most horrible that we should engage ourselves in a war one with another [having] lived thus long peaceably, without noise of shot or drum', he became a dedicated Royalist, refused to take oaths which would have allowed him to continue in possession of his estate, and, having taken part in a Royalist conspiracy, was beheaded on Tower Hill.

John Hutchinson, the Nottinghamshire squire, who much resembled Slingsby in his tastes and outlook, was quite as firm in his support of Parliament. So was his wife, though she did regret that her husband – who, she was pleased to say, had declined to marry an heiress, the granddaughter of his family's doctor, because he 'could never stoupe to think of marrying into so meane a stock' – had now to associate with 'factious little people (by whom all the Parliament Garrisons were infested and disturb'd) insomuch that many worthy gentlemen were wearied out of their command, some opprest by a certeine meane sort of people in the House whom, to distinguish from the most Honorable Gentlemen, they called *worsted stocking* men'.

Other wives, and mothers and daughters, were often dismayed by conflicting loyalties: Frances Devereux was married to the Marquess of Hertford, a staunch Royalist and Governor to the Duke of York; her brother was to command the forces of Parliament.

Nor was it only friends and members of the same families who were distressed to find themselves in opposing camps, but also men of different generations. Younger men with less experience of the King's deviousness, and influenced by the opportunities presented by royal absolutism abroad for such as they, tended to be Royalist. Certainly this was so in the House of Commons, where half the Members were under forty years of age and where, as Professor Lawrence Stone has observed, of those under thirty twice as many chose to support the King as fought for Parliament. In the Upper House, of peers in their twenties and thirties who took part in the war, four out of five did so on behalf of the King.

'Parents and children, brothers, kindred, I and dear friends have

the seed of differences and divisions abundantly sowed in them,'
Henry Oxinden, a member of an old Kentish family, wrote home
to a cousin from London. 'I find all here full of fears and void of
hopes . . . Sometimes I meet with a cluster of gentlemen equally
divided in opinions and resolution, sometimes three to two, sometimes more odds, but never unanimous. Nay more, I have heard
foul language and desperate quarrelings even between old and entire
friends.'

Another country gentleman, Thomas Knyvett of Norfolk, wrote
to his wife:

> Oh sweet hart I am nowe in a great strayght what to do . . .
> Walking this other morning at Westminster, Sir John Potts [a
> Member of Parliament] . . . saluted me with a commission from
> my Lord of Warwick [appointed by Parliament, Lord Lieutenant
> of Norfolk] to take upon me (by virtue of an ordinance of parlia-
> ment) my company and command again. I was surprised what to
> do, whether to take or refuse. 'Twas no place to dispute, so I took
> it and desired some time to advise upon it. I had not received this
> many hours, but I met with a declaration point-blank against it by
> the King . . . I hold it good wisdom and security to keep my
> company as close to me as I can in these dangerous times and to
> stay out of the way of my new masters till these first mutterings
> be over . . . I do fancy a little house by ourselves extremely well,
> where we may spend the remainder of our days in religous tranquil.

The King was on his way north. From Hampton Court he had gone
to Greenwich, then on to Royston and Cambridge where he was
shown round Trinity College and St John's. From Cambridge he
had ridden on to Huntingdon, to the manor house at Little Gidding
where the quiet orderliness of the kindly Ferrar family soothed his
distressed spirit. He went out shooting and bagged a hare and in the
evening, playing cards, he won £5, which he presented to his hostess
for her charities; and the Prince of Wales, now eleven years old, was
given apple pie to eat in the pantry. 'Pray,' the King said on taking
his leave, 'Pray for my speedy and safe return.'

Urged by Edward Hyde, until recently one of the Crown's opponents, now one of its chief advisers, to do or say nothing which might
hinder a compromise settlement, the King from time to time on his

northward progress issued a conciliatory statement, but gained little support. People flocked to see him in their thousands. As many as thirty thousand, so it was estimated, came to Lincoln from the surrounding countryside. Few, however, were prepared to join him in arms. There were rumours that most of those who did were papists, rumours that the King did his best to scotch. At Stamford he published a proclamation enjoining the enforcement of the laws against Roman Catholics; and at York he announced his 'zealous affection to the true Protestant profession and his resolution to concur with Parliament in any possible course for the propagation of it and the suppression of Popery'. He denied that help was being sought in other countries, while still actively seeking it, and assured his people that he longed for the 'peace, honour and prosperity of the nation'. While he spoke of peace, however, he prepared for war; and, suspecting this, Parliament despatched a committee to York, ostensibly as a diplomatic mission, in reality to keep a close watch on him. The committee found the city far from being the pleasant place which the indefatigable traveller Celia Fiennes was to describe fifty years later. There were scuffles in the streets and rowdy arguments in alehouses. Rival groups 'ran foul of each other with rough words and rough handling'. Two inoffensive priests, one of them almost ninety years old, whose only offences were their Roman Catholic ministrations, were hanged.

On 22 April 1642 the King sent a party of courtiers to Hull, a town with a strong castle which held a large store of ammunition and artillery in its magazine and a port which the Queen had persistently advised him to seize for the unloading of the supplies she hoped to send him. Among the men who rode out of York on this mission to discover the feelings of the authorities and people of Hull were the King's eldest nephew, the Elector Palatine, a dull man and compulsive fornicator, whose attachment to Protestantism could not be doubted, and Charles's younger son, the eight-year-old Duke of York, who had been brought from London by the Marquess of Hertford.

The Governor of Hull was Sir John Hotham, whose natural bad temper was exacerbated by his anxiety not to do anything which might harm his family's standing in Yorkshire. He had been imprisoned some years before for refusing to collect a forced loan, but his loyalty to Parliament was not thereby taken on trust; and since the Mayor of Hull as well as 'a goodly number of the townsfolk' were Royalist in sentiment, Peregrine Pelham, one of the Members of Parliament for the place, spent as much time there as he did at Westminster to ensure that control of the port was not lost.

Since the King's young son had come to Hull supposedly on a social visit, Hotham decided that he could not very well refuse the party admittance; but when he heard that the King himself intended to visit the town, and was, indeed, on the way with a troop of cavalry, he made excuses, prompted by Pelham, for his inability to receive him at such short notice.

The King arrived at dinner time to find the gates closed against him. There was a shout from the top of the wall. His Majesty, Hotham called down, could not enter. One of the King's companions shouted back instructions to the people of the town to throw the Governor off the wall and open the gates themselves. No one moved to do so; and, after a time spent in angry remonstrance, the King's party were obliged to withdraw to York, followed by the Duke of York and the Elector Palatine who, complaining that he had been duped into taking part in the ignominious enterprise, and unwilling to be on what he now felt would be the wrong side in the coming struggle, sailed home to the Continent.

At York the King was able to hold court in reasonable style thanks to the generosity of Edward Somerset, the unpractical Welsh Roman Catholic Earl of Glamorgan, and his son, Lord Herbert, who presented him with £22,000 of their family's fortune, soon to be followed by a further £100,000. Yet although he could offer some of the pleasures that might have been enjoyed at Whitehall, few guests were entertained at his table. The royal musicians were sent for, but they declined to come, explaining that their salaries had not been paid and the expenses of the journey were consequently beyond them. Several noblemen whom the King hoped would join him also declined to do so, among them the Lord Chamberlain, the Earl of Essex, and the Earl of Holland, Groom of the Stole and First Lord of the Bedchamber. Others, like the Earl of Leicester, complaining of unpaid expenses and debts, made it clear that they might have supported the King more readily had he settled them. As it was, several of the few Privy Councillors who joined him at York did so with evident reluctance, while a quarter of those of their colleagues who had been in office in 1640 chose to side with Parliament. Nor was the King able to win over Lord Fairfax, who had represented the county of York in the Long Parliament and was sent as one of a committee of five to represent Parliament's interests in York, to report upon the King's actions and to see what could be done to frustrate his recruitment of troops. Lord Fairfax's son, Thomas Fairfax, who had been born on the family's estate at Denton in Yorkshire thirty years before, made it known that he was as ready to defend the rights of Parliament as was his father.

Thomas Fairfax was an attractive man, reticent and reserved, though ruthless when he felt he had to be, slim and so dark in complexion he was known as 'Black Tom'. His expression was generally mournful in repose, though in battle he became 'so highly transported', in Bulstrode Whitelocke's words, that he 'seemed more like a man distracted and furious than of his ordinary mildness and so far different temper'. He was 'of as meek and humble a carriage as ever I saw in great employments,' Whitelock added, 'and but of few words in discourse or council; yet when his judgement and reason were satisfied he was unalterable . . . I have observed him at councils of war that he hath said little, but hath ordered things expressly contrary to the judgement of all his council.'

'A lover of learning,' so John Aubrey said, he had matriculated at St John's College, Cambridge at the age of fourteen and had later brought out a volume of poems and translations entitled *The Employment of my Solitude*; but he had decided early upon a military life and he was not yet eighteen when present at the siege of Bois-le-Duc. On his return to England in 1632 he had announced his intention of joining the Swedish army in Germany. As a young officer he was remarkable for his courage; as a commander he was renowned for the forcefulness rather than the subtlety of his occasionally imprudent attacks and for the discipline he imposed upon his troops, who held him in high regard.

Several Yorkshire noblemen, including Lord Savile, Treasurer of the Household, decided to throw in their lot with the King, but many gentlemen who had left Westminster for Yorkshire repaired to their country estates rather than to York; and when on 12 May Charles formally called upon the gentry of the county to attend him in arms, several of the most influential, Sir Philip Stapleton, Member for Boroughbridge, and Sir Hugh Cholmley, Member for Scarborough, among them, strongly objected to his doing so. They also protested when the King rode to Heyworth Moor to attend a demonstration of loyalty which had been organized by Lord Savile. Hundreds of anti-Royalists appeared from the surrounding villages to spoil the occasion and to present their own petitions to the King. Savile tried to prevent them approaching his Majesty but Thomas Fairfax evaded him and managed to get close enough to push a petition onto the King's saddle. Charles ignored it and, in riding on, almost knocked Fairfax to the ground.

For his behaviour this day Savile was declared by Parliament to be a public enemy no longer of their number. Alarmed by this verdict, he withdrew to his house, Howley Hall, where he tried to come to an accommodation with those whom he had offended through the mediation of relatives of his in London. On 5 April the King, deserted by Savile, was presented with a petition from the Yorkshire nobility and gentry, asking him to come to terms with Parliament.

In London, Parliament now reigned supreme. There were occasional demonstrations in favour of the King whose supporters, encouraged by several of the richer merchants, wore red ribbons in their hats as a token of their allegiance and one day gathered in sufficient numbers to chase a mob out of St Paul's where they were trying to pull down the organ. Another day a drunken Royalist, brandishing a dagger, forced a pious citizen to kneel down by Cheapside Cross and say a prayer for the Pope. But for the most part Londoners seemed perfectly content to follow Parliament's lead, to turn out on parade in Finsbury Fields, to lend plate and money at 8 per cent, and to obey the injunctions of the various emergency committees set up by the supporters of John Pym, including a Committee of Defence comprising five peers, the Earls of Essex, Northumberland, Pembroke and Holland and Viscount Saye and Sele, and ten Members of the House of Commons, John Hampden, Denzil Holles and Pym himself prominent amongst them. To lend the weight of incontestable legal authority to his own injunctions and proclamations, Charles ordered the Lord Keeper, Lord Littleton, to send the Great Seal to York and to follow it himself. Parliament retaliated by declaring that no orders or proclamations other than those issued in its own name were valid. This provocative declaration was followed in a few days by the Nineteen Propositions which required Parliamentary control not only of the army, but of the Church, the royal children, the law and

of all officers of state. They were, in effect, tantamount to a demand
that the King must surrender all executive power. Outraged, he
immediately rejected them, condemning their authors as raisers of
sedition and enemies to 'my sovereign power', as would-be
destroyers of 'rights and properties, of all distinctions of families
and merit', persuading many waverers that Parliament had, indeed,
presented him with an ultimatum that could be accepted only with
dishonour.

He continued to protest that he intended no violence against Parliament, that all would be settled peaceably. But it could no longer be
doubted that he had resolved upon war. The Lords Lieutenant of
counties throughout England were ordered to read his Commission
of Array, a counterblast to Parliament's Militia Ordinance.

All over the country unrest was growing and sides were being
taken in bitterness, sadness and anger, as castles were fortified, sentry
boxes installed by the gates in city walls, trained bands ordered to
keep watch on magazines, as posterns and bridges were barred at
night, as horsemen were put through their paces, gentlemen studied
such textbooks as Henry Hexham's *Principles of the Art Military as
Practised in the Wars of the United Netherlands*, and farm workers and
yeomen were drilled in town squares and country fields. In Leicester
the Mayor was sternly warned not to read the King's Commission
of Array by the Puritan Lord Willoughby of Parham, who had been
appointed by Parliament to a military command in the area and who
proclaimed Parliament's Militia Ordinance instead, provoking the
Earl of Huntingdon's son, Henry Hastings, to attempt to capture the
city with a company of colliers he had called up from the mines on
his family's estates. In London the Royalist Lord Mayor did manage
to read the King's Commission of Array but soon found himself
in the Tower for his pains. Elsewhere the publication of the rival
proclamations was attended by uproar and violence. At Cirencester
the Lord Lieutenant was chased out of the town when he tried to
read the King's Commission; in Cambridgeshire the Lord Lieutenant
was similarly maltreated and the palace at Downham of the Bishop
of Ely, 'one of the greatest Papists in the Kingdom', was invaded
and ransacked; at Watlington in Oxfordshire the Royalist Earl of
Berkshire was silenced by John Hampden, and his coach was
smashed to pieces. There were clashes in Somerset where a Puritan
hurled a stone at a crucifix – in a gesture of hatred for symbols of

popery common to nearly all counties – and where the Marquess of Hertford, the Lord Lieutenant of the county, was driven out of Wells by Sir Edward Hungerford and forced to retreat into Dorset and then into Wales, while his second-in-command Sir Ralph Hopton, with less than two hundred men, was obliged to withdraw to Cornwall. There was trouble in Wolverhampton where a crowd of men and women had already chopped up communion rails and tables which had been made 'an idol of'. There was fighting, too, in Worcestershire where a rabble of other would-be inconoclasts, wild in their hatred of what they took to be idolatrous, had been driven across the county boundary; and in Shropshire crowds pelted effigies of Parliamentarian soldiers, already known as Roundheads because of their close-cropped hair which – like that of apprentices who cut their hair short to demonstrate their contempt for lovelocks – was in marked contrast to the flowing tresses of the Royalist Cavaliers, the *cabaleros*, who were derided for their supposed attachment to the ways of foreign Catholics. And 'from the Puritanes' custome of wearing their haire cut close round their heads with so many little peakes as was something ridiculous to behold,' Lucy Hutchinson explained, 'that name of roundhead became the scornefull terme given to the whole Parliament party; whose Army indeed marcht out so, but as if they had only bene sent out till their haire was growne: two or three years after, any stranger that had seen them would have enquir'd the reason of that name.'

In Gloucestershire a vicar of severely Puritan views and extremely short temper fell with fury upon a constable who dared to ask him for a loan for the King, pulling out his hair and kicking him into a ditch. In Dorchester there was an equally savage brawl when Lady Blanche Arundell's chaplain, who had been arrested as he was boarding a ship for France, was hanged and his fellow-Roman Catholics, in attempting to seize relics from his body, were set upon by Puritans. Later there were riots in the countryside when mobs, mostly of unemployed workers, attacked the houses of those whom they accused of being Royalists or papists, tore down enclosure fences and killed deer in parks and woods. From Norwich came rumours of 'a virgin troop' of virtuous maidens formed for the protection of members of their sex and for revenge upon 'papists and Cavaliers' who had committed outrages against them.

The fear of attack by foreign papists was widespread. In many of the petitions which had been addressed to Parliament by the counties of England since December 1641 this fear seemed to be uppermost in the petitioners' minds. They were alarmed by the vulnerability of the English coasts to invasion from abroad by papist armies supported by papists at home, the 'drawing of swords' and 'a war between Protestants and papists which God forbid'. 'At Westminster there was a sense of outright confrontation with the Crown from which there could be no turning back,' the historian Anthony Fletcher has observed. 'We find this entirely absent in the petitions. During the weeks they were being written and circulated many town councils looked to their defensive arrangements. But they were preparing not for civil war but for a national state of emergency based on the papist conspiracy.'

In some counties in these early days of the conflict the Royalists, and such papists as there were among them, achieved small triumphs. In Cheshire, at Nantwich, they rode about the town, preventing Sir William Brereton, one of the Members of Parliament for Cheshire, from recruiting there. In Hampshire, at Portsmouth, the extravagant, ambitious and unreliable roué Colonel George Goring, who had been appointed Governor of the port by Parliament, suddenly declared his allegiance to the King. In Oxfordshire, the Earl of Northampton succeeded in carrying off the guns which were being sent through the county to fortify Warwick Castle. In Oxford itself scholars had formed Royalist troops, much to the annoyance of a majority of the citizens; and when the two Members of Parliament for the town tried to put an end to their drilling the scholars turned upon them and chased them off. In the north, Newcastle upon Tyne was seized for the King by the Prince of Wales's former Governor, the Earl of Newcastle; and Lord Strange, soon to become Earl of Derby on his father's death, took over several stores of arms and ammunition in the King's name in Lancashire, and advanced upon Manchester, described by the antiquary John Leland a century before as 'the fairest, best builded and most populous town in Lancashire' and by now a centre of the clothing industry and a hotbed of Puritans. The Puritan Lord Wharton, a most handsome and elegant young man extremely proud of his beautiful legs, whom Parliament had appointed Lord Lieutenant of Lancashire, also advanced upon Manchester. Lord Strange arrived first and, as the son of a powerful man who owned thousands of acres in the county, he was asked to dinner by the leading citizens of Manchester. Enraged by this welcome afforded to one of the King's most loyal supporters, some of the more militant clothiers and weavers of the town attacked the Royalist party. There was a short and savage fight in the pouring rain; several of Strange's men were wounded; and one Mancunian, a linen weaver named Richard Percival, was killed, the first fatal casualty of the war, so it was alleged by his accusers when Strange was proclaimed a traitor by the House of Commons. Strange himself was nearly shot as he rode away to Ordsall.

In York, where young desperadoes eagerly looked forward to the real fighting, the King prepared new plans for the seizure of the crucially important port of Hull. Already the Earl of Newcastle had tried to take the place. 'I am here at Hull,' he had written to the King, 'but the town will not admit me by no means, so I am very flat and out of countenance.'

The King himself now advanced upon the town and made as if to lay it under formal siege, digging trenches and erecting batteries, hoping that this display of preparations for an assault would induce Sir John Hotham to surrender the town into his hands. Indeed, Hotham had promised as much. Not long before, the Royalist Lord Digby had been captured aboard a ketch in the Humber estuary and had been sent as a prisoner to Hull, where he had persuaded Hotham that by delivering up the town to the King's forces he might not only prevent the war, but earn honour as well as riches for himself. The Governor was persuaded. He released Digby and undertook that 'if the King would come before the town but with one regiment, and plant his cannon against it and make but one shot, he should think he had discharged his trust to the Parliament as far as he ought to do, and that he would then immediately deliver up the town'. But Hotham was now not alone in command in Hull. To stiffen his resistance Parliament had sent Sir John Meldrum, an experienced Scottish soldier who had served for years in various armies on the Continent, including that of Gustavus II Adolphus of Sweden. Led by the resolute Meldrum, upon whose advice the surrounding fields had been flooded, the defenders of Hull made two sallies against the Royalists' works, 'the first blood, as some say, that was shed in these unnatural wars'.

Impatiently standing before the troublesome town, the King was approached by the Earl of Holland, who brought one final plea from Parliament that he should abandon his preparations for war and return to London. The King replied that Parliament should first instruct Sir John Hotham to open the gates of Hull as 'an earnest of their good intentions'. Holland refused to consider such a bargain. Then, said the King, deeply affronted by this offensive challenge to his kingly dignity, 'Let all the world now judge who began this war.'

With Hull and Manchester and several other strategic places in the north in the hands of his enemies, and with no help to be expected from Scotland, the King began his march on London, hoping that the small army he had so far attracted to his standard would be reinforced as he marched through the Midlands. Men would surely come in from the estates of the Earl of Northampton, Lord Lieutenant of Warwickshire, from those of the Earl of Lindsey in Nottingham-shire and Lincolnshire, and from the Earl of Huntingdon's lands in Leicestershire. But few men did join him. It was harvest time, for one thing, and for another the King was rumoured to be still making overtures to Parliament as though he intended, even now, to reach a compromise. Men were reluctant to jeopardize their future by openly declaring their support of a cause which might at any moment be abandoned or betrayed. They were also in fear of Parliament. Upon the King's entering Leicester on 22 July 1642, he was received with 'warm expressions of loyalty' from 'ten thousand of the gentry and better sort of inhabitants of that county', but he received little practical help from any of them because, so it was said, 'if the King was loved as he ought to be, Parliament was more feared than he'. When he entered Nottingham in the third week of August he had scarcely more than a thousand men at his command.

The weather was windy and rainy; the people of Nottingham, a town of market traders, tanners and silk workers, were unwelcom-ing; the news of Royalist fortunes elsewhere was dispiriting. The Royalist standard, attached to a tall red pole, was unfurled in a field in the town – the spot is now marked by a tablet on Standard Hill. It had taken twenty men to carry it into the field, and several of these had to hold it upright in an insufficiently deep hole dug with daggers and knives. A proclamation, denouncing the Commons and their troops as traitors, was haltingly read by a herald. It had been prepared some time before, but at the last minute the King had decided to alter its wording, which he did so clumsily that the herald could hardly read it and stumbled through it with painful hesitation. Later the wind blew stronger than ever and threw the standard down.

These were miserable days at Nottingham. A 'general sadness covered the whole town'; and so few were the King's supporters that one of his commanders warned him that, if an attempt were made to capture him, it might prove impossible to save him. The King became so depressed that emissaries were twice sent to London to seek terms for peace, and on both occasions were rebuffed.

In September, however, volunteers began to arrive in increasing numbers. On the sixth of that month Parliament had declared that all men who did not support it were 'delinquents' and that their property was to be handed over to sequestration committees. This meant that many of those who would have been happy to remain neutral were virtually obliged to fight in their own defence; it meant, as the Parlimentarian Sir Simonds D'Ewes admitted, that 'not only particular persons of the nobility', but 'whole counties' became 'desperate'. Men who feared that their fortunes might well be lost if Parliament won now undertook to fight for the King, in whose victory their own salvation might be secured; while gentry, whose income from land was declining and whose fortunes depended upon the rich perquisites which only the court could offer, needed no further persuasion to fight.

Well-to-do landowners, having made up their minds to support the Royalist cause, raised troops at their own expense, sometimes going so far as to threaten tenants with eviction if they did not come forward, while the promise of money in the King's own Commission of Array encouraged others to join his side. Many of those who offered their services were obviously incapable of controlling a horse in battle and had to be enlisted as infantrymen. For the most part they looked unpromising material. But the cavalry seemed sound enough, and in the opinion of at least one captain of a Parliamentary troop of horse, they were certainly superior to those on his own side. They were, he said, 'gentlemen's sons, younger sons and persons of quality', rather than the kind of troopers being enlisted in the Parliamentary cause who were mostly 'old decayed serving-men and tapsters, and such kind of fellows'. 'Do you think that the spirits of such base and mean fellows,' he asked, 'will ever be able to encounter gentlemen that have honour and courage and resolution in them?'

By the end of the second week in September two thousand horse-men and about 1,200 infantry had been enlisted by the King's officers. Many of these had come down from Yorkshire and some were described as 'the scum' of that county; but those who had more recently joined were considered of better mettle, and their commanders capable men.

Chief of the infantry commanders was Jacob Astley, a sixty-three-year-old soldier from Norfolk who had had much experience of Con-tinental warfare and was deemed as fit for the office of Major-General of the Foot as 'any man Christendom yielded'. Also with the King at Nottingham, as his Colonel-General of Dragoons, was Sir Arthur Aston, a Roman Catholic from 'an ancient and knightly family' who, like Astley, had seen much service abroad in the service of the Kings of Poland and of Sweden. These two officers were soon to be joined by another senior professional soldier who had served on the Conti-nent, Patrick Ruthven, recently created Earl of Forth, a Scotsman almost seventy years old, gouty, hard-drinking and deaf, who had won the respect of the King of Sweden, in whose army he had served, by being able 'to drink immeasurably and preserve his under-standing to the last'. He had also preserved into old age his quickness of perception and strategic skill.

Respected as Forth was, however, his fame was shortly to be eclipsed by a man a third his age. This was the King's nephew, Prince Rupert, the twenty-three-year-old son of the King's sister Elizabeth and her husband Frederick V, the Elector Palatine, one of the leading Protestant princes of Germany. Born in Prague in 1619, Prince Rupert had entered the University of Leyden at the age of ten, already familiar with the pikeman's eighteen postures and the musketeer's thirty-four, and recognized as a rider of marvellous accomplishment. When he was barely fourteen he had gone off to join the armies in the Low Countries and although his mother had summoned him back on that occasion, he had ridden off again in 1637 as commander of a cavalry regiment to fight the Holy Roman Emperor in the Thirty Years' War. Within a few months he had been taken prisoner at Lemgo, but by then he had impressed all who came into contact with him with his bravery and resource. He had trained his men to understand that a good regiment of cavalry was not a mere collection of individual horsemen, able to go through the parade-ground movements of thrusting, guarding and parrying with chosen rivals in single combat, but a kind of battering-ram that should thunder down upon its opponents in a powerful mass, over-throwing them and driving them back by the sudden, irresistible force of its impact.

To many who met Prince Rupert for the first time he seemed an intolerable youth. Arrogant, ill-tempered and boorish, he appeared to have no manners and no taste. Before he had left Holland for England he had quarrelled with both Henry Jermyn and George Digby and most of the Queen's other friends who were in exile with her. Henrietta Maria herself wrote to warn Charles: 'He should have someone to advise him for believe me he is yet very young and self-willed . . . . He is a person capable of doing anything he is ordered, but his is not to be trusted to take a single step of his own head.'

It was true that he was impulsive and impatient; it was true, too, that his innate reserve and sensitivity led him to hide behind a mask of dismissive hauteur, that his irritation with the mannered *politesse* of court behaviour induced him to adopt the manners of the tough sailors and dockers with whom, disguised in old canvas clothes, he had chosen to mix as a student in the taverns of The Hague. As Sir Philip Warwick said of him, 'a sharpness of temper and uncommuni-cableness in society or council (by seeming with a pish to neglect all another said and he approved not), made him less grateful than his friends wished; and this humour soured him towards Counsellors of Civil Affairs who were necessary to intermix with him in Martiall Councils. All these great men often distrusted such downright sol-diers, as the Prince was, tho' a Prince of the Blood, lest he should be too apt to prolong the warr, and to obtain that by a pure victory, which they wished to be got by a dutiful submission upon modest, speedy and peaceable terms.'

Yet Rupert was far more than a rough, handsome soldier of for-tune with a taste for fancy clothes, fringed boots, feathered hats, scarlet sashes and long curled hair; he was more than a cavalry leader of undeniable skill and courage. He was highly intelligent, a remark-able linguist, an artist of uncommon merit, a man with an inventive skill and curiosity of mind that was to give as much pleasure to his later years of sickness and premature old age as the several mistresses who visited him in his rooms at Windsor Castle. Above all, he was a commander whose men obeyed and trusted him. If he was apt to be reckless in the heat of battle, he was 'as capable of planning a campaign as he was of conducting a charge'.

Henrietta Maria had exaggerated his failings: he may have been far less capable of directing a full-scale battle than leading a cavalry charge; he was certainly incapable of restraining his own excited enthusiasm after an initial success; but he was an inspiring leader of men and the King's trust in him was not misplaced. His tall, thin figure, 'clad in scarlet very richly laid in silver lace and mounted on a very gallant Barbary horse', became as inspiring a sight to his own cavalry as it was alarming to his enemies. His life seemed charmed; pistols were fired in his face, but he escaped with powder marks; when his horse was killed under him he walked away 'leisurely without so much as mending his pace' and no harm came to him. The Roundheads accused him of being protected by the devil. They said that the white poodle – which accompanied him everywhere, which would jump in the air at the word 'Charles', and cock his leg when his master said 'Pym' – was a little demon that could make itself invisible, pass through their lines and report their strength and dispositions to its master.

Although there were capable officers in the King's army more than twice Prince Rupert's age and with far greater experience, he was immediately appointed his Majesty's Lieutenant-General of Horse, a demonstration of royal favour and trust which, combined with his arrogant manner and foreign birth, discountenanced the King's civilian advisers and his military commanders alike. Prince Rupert did not get on well with either Sir Edward Hyde, now largely responsible for writing the King's speeches, or with Hyde's friend Lucius Cary, Viscount Falkland, who had been appointed Secretary of State a few months before. Nor were Rupert's relations easy with the haughty, able though unreliable Lord Digby, who was as ambitious to be recognized as a fine general as he was to be seen as an astute statesman. Rupert's arrival at Nottingham also displeased Henry Wilmot, Commissary-General of Horse, who had to be content to serve as Rupert's second-in-command, although considerably older than his superior and a seasoned campaigner in Scotland and in the Dutch service. Moreover, the Prince's commission, which gave him a command independent of the elderly Earl of Lindsey, the King's Commander-in-Chief, was bound to lead to trouble in the future.

Prince Rupert's stock with fellow-officers fell even lower when it was decided to leave Nottingham for Shrewsbury where there were better hopes of attracting more recruits. On their way the Prince and his brother Maurice, who had come with him from Holland, made no scruple in clattering up the drives of country houses of known Parliamentary supporters and demanding money with menaces, a practice common enough on the Continent but not to the taste of English gentlemen. It was regarded as a particularly bad example to troops whose discipline was quite lax enough as it was and whose behaviour in houses in which they were quartered was much condemned. Certain other Royalist commanders followed Prince Rupert's example. Lord Grandison, for instance, rode into Nantwich with his troop and forced his way into several houses belonging to Parliament's supporters and supposed supporters: it became a saying amongst Royalist soldiers that 'all rich men were Roundheads'. In Yorkshire a party of Royalists broke into George Marwood's house at Nun Monkton, near York. 'It was done in the day-time and by 24 horse or thereabout,' a Parliamentary pamphlet recorded. 'They threatened Mrs Marwood and her servants with death to discover where her husband was and swore they would cut him in pieces before her face and called her Protestant whore and Puritan whore. They searched all the house and broke open 17 locks. They took away all his money . . . and all his plate they could find . . . And, though it be Mr Marwood's lot to suffer first, yet the loose people threaten to pillage and destroy all Roundheads, under which foolish name they comprehend all such as do not go their ways.'

Although plundering expeditions were far from general in all counties, and in many areas successful efforts were being made to maintain tranquillity, the behaviour of the Royalists at Henley-on-Thames was not exceptional. Here a regiment under Sir John Byron was quartered at Fawley Court, a large house just outside the town which belonged to Bulstrode Whitelocke, a rich young lawyer and Member of Parliament for Marlow. Whitelocke, who was in London at the time, had sufficient warning of the Royalists' approach to tell one of his tenants, William Cooke, to hide as many of his valuable possessions as he could. The tenant and his servants 'threw into the mote pewter, brasse and iron things and removed . . . into the woods some of [Whitelocke's] bookes, linnen & household stuffe, as much as the short warning would permit'. But enough remained in the house and outbuildings for the 'brutish common soldiers' to indulge in an orgy of plunder.

> There they had their whores [Whitelocke recorded in his diary]. They spent and consumed in one night 100 loade of Corne and hey, littered their horses with good wheate sheafes, gave them all sorts of Corne in the straw, made great fires in the closes, & William Cooke telling them there were billets and faggots neerer to them [than] the plough timber which they burned, they threatened to burne him. Divers bookes & writings of Consequence which were left in [the] study they tore and burnt & lighted Tobacco with them, & some they carried away [including] many excellent manuscripts of [my] father's & some of [my own] labours. They broke down [my park fencing] killed most of [my] deere & lett out the rest. Only a Tame Hinde & his hounds they presented to Prince Rupert.
>
> They eate & dranke up all that the house could afforde; brake up all Trunkes, chests & any goods, linnen or household stuffe that they could find. They cutt the beddes, lett out the feathers, & tooke away the courtains, covers of chayres & stooles, [my] Coach & 4 good Coach horses & all the saddle horses, & whatsoever they could lay their hands on they carried away or spoyled, did all that malice and rapine could provoke barbarous mercenaries to commit.

Soon afterwards, at another of Whitelocke's houses in Henley, Phyllis Court, Parliament's soldiers 'did much spoyle & mischiefe, though he was a Parlem[en]t man, butt bruitich soldiers make no distinctions. Major G[eneral] Skippon directed Phyllis Court to be made a Garryson, & it was regularly fortefyed and strong, & well manned because Greenland [at Hambleden] hard by it was a Garryson for the King, & betwixt these two stood Fawley Court, miserably torn and plundered by each of them.'

General as pillaging became, it was, however, felt that Prince Rupert's activities were peculiarly unacceptable as those of a foreign interloper, and characteristic of a man who cockily demonstrated his marksmanship in Stafford by shooting the weather-vane off the steeple of St Mary's Church. In Leicester he threatened to plunder the town unless the inhabitants gave him £2,000, to 'teach them that it was safer to obey than refuse the King's commands'. They collected £500 and fearfully presented it to him. The King disavowed his nephew's conduct; but he kept the money all the same.

Yet, if the depredations of the Royalists were reprehensible, those of the Parliamentarians were quite as bad, if not worse. Sir Philip Warwick recalled that when a Puritan praised the sanctity of the Roundhead army and condemned the faults of the Cavaliers, a friend of his replied: 'Faith, thou sayest true; for in our army we have the sins of men (drinking and wenching) but in yours you have those of devils, spiritual pride and rebellion.'

The vandalism of the Parliamentarians was not as indiscriminate as Royalist propaganda later suggested. The west window, stone angels and ironwork of Edward IV's tomb in St George's Chapel, Windsor, for example, were spared, even though the castle was a Roundhead garrison; and the stained glass in King's College Chapel, Cambridge, was also untouched, though the chapel itself was used as a drill hall. Yet in Canterbury, Parliamentary troops shot at the crucifix on the South Gate leading to the cathedral, rampaged about the aisles and transepts, jabbed pikes into the tapestries and tore the illuminated pages from the service books. Norwich Cathedral might have suffered in the same way had not a force of five hundred armed men poured into the building to help the members of the choir protect the organ from a mob which had succeeded in tearing out the altar rails. In Rochester Cathedral Parliamentary troops smashed glass and statues, and kicked the precious library across the floor. In many other churches effigies upon tombs were hacked about and inscriptions in Latin, 'the Language of the Beast', defaced. In Colchester, where the vicar of Holy Trinity narrowly escaped hanging, the house of the Lucas family was invaded, their chapel ransacked, its glass destroyed and the bones from the family tombs thrown from wall to wall. The house of their friend Lady Rivers was similarly attacked and pillaged and robbed of property worth £40,000.

Letters written by Nehemiah Wharton, an officer in Parliament's army, give numerous examples of similar depredations committed by his troops as well as of the countless sermons the men attended before and after their pillaging expeditions:

Tuesday [9 August 1642] early in the morninge, several of our soldiers inhabitinge the out parts of the town [Acton] sallied out unto the house of one Penruddock and . . . entred his house and pillaged him to the purpose. This day also the souldiers got into the church, defaced the auntient glased pictures and burned the railes. Wensday: Mr. Love gave us a famous sermon . . . also the souldiers brought the holy railes from Chissick and burned them . . . At Hillingdon, one mile from Uxbridge, the railes beinge gone, we got the surplesses to make us handecherchers . . . Mr. Hardinge gave us a worthy sermon . . . We came to Wendever where wee refreshed ourselves, burnt the railes and one of Captain Francis his men, forgettinge he was charged with a bullet, shot a maide through the head and she immediately died . . . sabbath day morning Mr. Marshall, that worthy champion of Christ, preached unto us . . . Every day our souldiers by stealth doe visit papists' houses and constraine from them both meate and money . . .They triumphantly carry away greate [loaves] and [cheeses] upon the points of their swords . . . Saturday I departed hence and gathered a compliete file of my owne men and marched to Sir Alexander Denton's parke, who is a malignant fellow, and killed a fat buck and fastened his head upon my halbert, and commaunded two of my pickes to bring the body after me to Buckingham . . . Thursday, August 26th, our soildiers pillaged a malignant fellowes house in [Coventry] . . . Friday several of our soildiers, both horse and foote, sallyed out of the City unto the Lord Dunsmore's parke, and brought from thence great store of venison, which is as good as ever I tasted, and ever since they make it their dayly practise so that venison is as common with us as beef with you . . . Sunday morne the Lord of Essex his chaplaine, Mr. Kemme, the cooper's son, preached unto us . . . This day a whore, which had followed our campe from London, was taken by the soildiers, and first led about the city, then set in the pillory, after in the cage, then duckt in the river . . . Wensday wee kept the Fast and heard two sermons . . . Our soldiers pillaged the parson of this town [Northampton] and brought him away prisoner, with his surplice and other relics . . . This morninge our soildiers sallyed out about the countrey and returned in state clothes with surplisse and cap, representing the Bishop of Canterbury . . . Saturday morning Mr. John Sedgwick gave us a famous sermon . . .

Not content with plundering civilians, the soldiers plundered each other:

This morning [7 September 1642] our regiment being drawne into the fields to exercise, many of them . . . demanded five shillings a man which, they say, was promised to them . . . or they would surrender their armes. Whereupon Colonell Hamden, and other commanders, laboured to appease them but could not. So . . . we feare a great faction amongst us. There is also great desention betweene our troopers and foot companies, for the footmen are much abused and sometimes pillaged and wounded. I myselfe have lately found it, for they took from me about the worth of three pounds . . . A troope of horse belonging unto Colonel Foynes met me, pillaged me of all, and robbed mee of my very sword, for which cause I told them I would [either] have my sword or dye in the field and I commaunded my men to charge with bullet, and by devisions fire upon them, which made them with shame return my sword, and it being towards night I returned to Northampton, threetninge revenge upon the base troopers.

Of all the towns which Wharton passed through during his military service few suffered more severely at the hands of plunderers than Worcester. He thought the county of Worcestershire a 'very pleasaunt, fruitfull and rich countrey, aboundinge in corne, woods, pastures, hills and valleys, every hedge and heigh way beset with fruits, but especially with peares, whereof they make that pleasant drinke called perry wch they sell for a penny a quart, though better than ever you tasted in London'. But the town of Worcester, though 'pleasantly seated, exceedingly populous, and doubtless very rich . . . more large than any city' he had seen since leaving London, was 'so vile . . . so bare, so papisticall and abominable, that it resembles Sodom and is the very emblem of Gomorrah, and doubtless worse'. It was more sinful even than Hereford whose people Wharton later discovered to be 'totally ignorant in the waies of God, and much addicted to drunkenness and other vices, principally unto swearing, so that the children that have scarce learned to speake doe universally sweare stoutlye'. Worcester, indeed, was 'worse than either Algiers or Malta, a very den of thieves, and refuge for all the hel-hounds in the countrey, I should have said in the land'.

It was certainly treated as such. The cathedral, conceded by Wharton to be a 'very stately cathedrell with many stately monuments', was ransacked, the organ pulled to pieces, images and windows smashed, books burned, vestments trampled underfoot and kicked about the nave or put on by Roundhead soldiers who pranced in them about the streets. The aisles and choir were used as latrines; campfires were lit; horses were tethered in the nave and cloisters where the traces of rings and staples can still be seen.

In parish churches in Worcester the clergy were required to give their pulpits over to Puritan army chaplains – who harangued soldiers and civilians alike – and were presented with demands to pay money to have their churches spared the punishment inflicted on the cathedral. An entry in the accounts of St Michael's church reads: 'Given to Captain and Soldiers for preserving our church goods and writings, 10s. 4d.'

Valuable goods from private houses were seized and sent to London as booty; the Mayor and one of the Aldermen were also despatched to London as prisoners; and some lesser citizens were hanged in the market place as suspected spies.

Outside the town, in the village of Castlemorton, the house of one Rowland Bartlett was invaded by a party of Roundhead soldiers commanded by a Captain Scriven, the son of a Gloucester ironmonger.

In a confused tumult they rush into the house [in the words of a Royalist publication describing an outrage similar to numerous others committed elsewhere]. And as eager hounds hunt from the parlour to the kitchen, from whence by the chambers, to the garrats . . . Besides Master Bartlet's, his wives, and childrens wearing apparell, they rob their servants of their clothes: with the but ends of musquets they breake open the hanging presses, cupboards, and chests: no place was free from this ragged-regiment . . . They met with Mistress Bartlets sweat-meats, these they scatter on the ground: not daring to taste of them for feare of poyson . . . Except bedding, pewter, and lumber, they left nothing behind them, for besides two horses laden with the best things (Scrivens owne plunder) there being an hundred and fifty rebells, each rebell returned with a pack at his back. As for his beere, and perry, what they could not devour they spoyle.

Nor was this the only unwelcome visit Rowland Bartlett had from plundering Roundhead soldiers. On a later occasion they took away 'good store of bacon from his roofe, and beefe out of the powdering tubs'. They stole his 'pots, pannes and kettles, together with his pewter to a great value'; they seized 'on all his provisions for hospitality and house-keeping' and then broke his spits. They 'exposed his bedding for sale and pressed carts to carry away his chairs, stooles, couches and trunks' to Worcester.

It was near Worcester, in September 1642, that Prince Rupert was to have his first experience of English warfare.

3

TRIAL OF STRENGTH

'My Lord, we have got the day, let us live to
enjoy the fruit thereof.'

Lord Wilmot

While the King's forces were withdrawing from Worcester towards
Shrewsbury in the late summer of 1642, the Parliamentarians were
on the march towards them. They were commanded by Robert
Devereux, third Earl of Essex, the son of that gifted, wayward Earl
who had so fascinated Queen Elizabeth I and been beheaded for
attempting a *coup d'état* against her Council. It was difficult to con-
ceive of a son less like his father. Handsome, reckless and opinion-
ated, exasperatingly conscious of his considerable talents, the father
had marched about the Queen's court, his tall figure leaning forward
like the neck of a giraffe as though he were a prince of the blood,
beguiling women, carelessly offending or carefully charming men.
The son, born in London in 1591, was now fifty-one years old, a
stolid, stout, retiring man, plodding, honest and taciturn, often to
be seen puffing ruminatively on a pipe. He had been married at the
age of thirteen to Frances Howard, the sultry, sensual and unbalanced
daughter of the Earl of Suffolk, who was the same age as himself.
This young bride had soon afterwards become the mistress of Robert
Carr, Viscount Rochester, and, with the help of her powerful family,
had managed to obtain an annulment of her marriage to Essex on
the grounds of his impotence. Essex then married Frances, daughter
of Sir William Paulet. This marriage too was unhappy and, so it was

whispered, unconsummated. Like her predecessor, Frances took a lover, Sir Thomas Uvedale. Soon afterwards she became pregnant. Essex resignedly acknowledged as his own the resultant baby who died soon after its birth. The parents then separated; and Essex went to live with his sister, wife of the Earl of Hertford, at her house in the Strand.

By then Essex had seen a good deal of active service on the Continent. He had not much distinguished himself, but his amenable, dutiful reliability and the loyalty he inspired among his subordinates recommended him to Pym and his friends who had, after all, a very circumscribed field of talent from which to make their selection. At least, silent though he so often was behind those thick clouds of smoke from his pipe, Essex seemed to have a good knowledge of the military manoeuvres practised on the Continent by the commanders of the armies in which he had served; and who else, it was asked in London, could be found with Essex's authority and reputation?

Essex's orders were 'to rescue His Majesty's person, and the persons of the Prince and the Duke of York out of the hands of those desperate persons who were then about them'. It was still convenient to suppose that it was not the King himself who was at fault but his advisers, that Parliament was taking up arms to protect the King from them, and indeed from himself, rather as though, in the words of an unnamed Member of Parliament, he were a man contemplating suicide, or 'as if he were at sea and a storm should rise and he would put himself to the helm, and would steer such a course as would overthrow the ship and drown them all'. In obedience to his orders to 'rescue his Majesty's person', Essex presented himself before Parliament to take his leave of its Members. Ignoring the Commons, he addressed a few words to the Lords then left abruptly, declining to wait for a reply. Several Members of the House of Commons went to look for him, 'hoping to obtain some word of recognition'. Eventually they found him sitting in the Court of Wards puffing on his pipe. He stood up, acknowledged their presence in silence, his hat in one hand, his pipe in the other, and left the room without speaking.

On 9 September he left London for Northampton. He was cheered as he passed through the streets, though some spectators looked askance upon his troops, 'ragged looking and marching out of step', ten thousand of whom had gone on before him, rather more than half of them mounted. Few of them had had any more than the briefest drilling; many were evidently intent upon plunder; and certainly, before they reached Northampton, they had pillaged villages and ransacked houses all along the way, several companies threatening to turn back unless they received their overdue pay. 'We are perplexed with the insolence of the soldiers already committed,' one of his officers warned Essex, 'and with the apprehension of greater. If this go on, the army will grow as odious to the country as the Cavaliers.'

The Earl of Essex himself had good cause to complain of his men's conduct, but good reason, too, to hope that order would soon be brought into the ranks, since he had many seasoned officers under his command, both British and foreign. Sir William Balfour, a Scottish professional soldier of strong Protestant views, who had once whipped a priest for trying to convert his wife to popery, was with him as Lieutenant-General of the Horse. Essex could also rely upon Sir James Ramsay, another Scottish professional of proved accomplishments, soon to be commended for his gallantry. To give advice in gunnery there was a French expert, on cavalry tactics a Croatian and a Dutchman, Hans Behre, who had his own troop of Dutch mercenaries and was appointed Commissary-General. Moreover there were men of high social rank among Essex's officers as well as distinguished Members of Parliament. Denzil Holles, Member for Dorchester, commanded a regiment of foot. John Hampden, Member for Buckinghamshire, also raised a regiment of foot whose men wore green coats and were soon recognized as among the best soldiers on either side. Sir Arthur Haselrig, Member for Leicestershire, commanded a troop of horse; so did Oliver Cromwell, Member for Cambridge. Other commanders of regiments included Henry Mordaunt, second Earl of Peterborough, whose father had been Essex's General of the Ordnance until his death in June; William Fiennes, first Viscount Saye and Sele; Henry Grey, first Earl of Stamford; Robert Greville, second Baron Brooke; Edward Montagu, Viscount Mandeville, heir of the first Earl of Manchester. William Russell, fifth Earl and later first Duke of Bedford, was appointed Lord-General of the Horse under Sir William Balfour's watchful eye.

As Essex's army advanced towards him, the King continued his withdrawal towards Shrewsbury, pausing on the way near Stafford to address his assembled forces: 'Your consciences and your loyalty have brought you hither to fight for your religion, your King and the laws of the land. You shall meet with no enemies but traitors, most of them Brownists [followers of the Puritan, John Brown], Anabaptists and Atheists, such who desire to destroy both Church and State and who have already condemned you to ruin for being loyal to us . . . [I promise, if God gives us victory,] to defend and maintain the true reformed Protestant religion established in the Church of England, to govern according to the known laws of the land [and to] maintain the just privileges and freedom of Parliament.'

At Shrewsbury, as the King had hoped, volunteers flocked to his camp from Wales and the north in ever increasing numbers. So also did they at Chester. Money came in, too. In the recent past money had been one of the King's most nagging worries. Before these present troubles the resources of the Crown had been badly affected by both inflation, which had presented a problem to all the governments of Europe since the middle of the sixteenth century, and by the economic depression of the early seventeenth century; and after the war had begun the King's finances, already close to breakdown when he came to the throne, and indeed long before that, sunk to such a parlous state that when he had arrived in York it was estimated that he had as little as £600 left. But thanks to rich well-wishers like his cousin, the Duke of Richmond, and the Earl of Newcastle, whose losses in the struggle were said to amount to an enormous sum, the King was soon able to pay for rapidly growing forces. The Earl of Glamorgan continued to supply the King with immense sums of money, as did his son, Lord Herbert. Between them they raised no less than £117,000, which today would be worth well over £2 million; and when the Prince of Wales was sent to visit the Somersets at Raglan Castle he was presented with several pieces of the family plate.

The universities of Oxford and Cambridge were not so generous. Little of the college plate which was set aside for the King at Cambridge actually reached him; and, for fear of Parliamentary punishment, not much was offered anyway, several colleges ignoring the King's repeated request, much to the satisfaction of the city's Member of Parliament, Oliver Cromwell, who marched a party of soldiers to King's College with drums beating to prevent any treasure from that rich college falling into Royalist hands. Other colleges collected varying amounts of plate, but hardly any was sent, and most of what did leave Cambridge never reached its destination.

These were sad says for Royalists in Cambridge. Three heads of colleges were arrested and carted off to London to be imprisoned there; other members of the University known to support the King were insulted as they walked the streets; the University preacher was attacked and forcibly prevented from giving a Latin sermon; the Vice-Chancellor and several of his colleagues were locked up on a particularly cold night without food or fires for declining to pay the taxes the Parliamentary Commissioners demanded of them; eventually twelve heads of colleges and 181 Fellows and other senior members of the University were deprived of their positions, sent away to earn their livings as best they could, and replaced by acknowledged Puritans. The Fellows of Queens' College were purged in their entirety. 'The whole Corporation of Masters and Fellows,' so it was reported, 'were ejected, imprison'd or banish'd thence'; and, according to Thomas Fuller who had entered the college at the age of thirteen in 1621 when his uncle was President, there was not a single scholar left in the college either. The President, Edward Martin, who suffered several years' imprisonment, was replaced by Herbert Palmer, a well-known Puritan and reputed author of *Scripture and Reason Pleaded for Defensive Arms*, a book justifying the use of force against the King.

At Queens' the Parliamentary ordinance for 'the utter demolishing, removing and taking away of all Monuments of Superstition or Idolatry', the destruction of altar rails, candlesticks and crucifixes, and the removal of communion tables to the body of the church, was obeyed with particular ruthlessness. 'We beat downe about 110 Superstitious Pictures besides Cherubims and Ingravings,' wrote Parliament's agent for implementing the ordinance in East Anglia. 'And we digged up the steps for 3 hours and brake down 10 or 12 Apostles & Saints within the Hall.'

Elsewhere in Cambridge there were similar depredations. Colleges, purified of their papist excrescences, the stained glass in their chapels smashed, were turned into barracks or prisons; collections of ancient coins were appropriated and sold; a review of soldiers was held in King's College Chapel; avenues of trees in college gardens were cut down for fortifications; several bridges were destroyed; and on Cromwell's orders in St Mary's Church, where the Book of

Common Prayer was torn to shreds, the wood carvings were destroyed though there was evidently 'not one jot of imagery or statue work about them'.

William Dowsing, the son of a Suffolk yeoman, who was commissioned with the task of demolishing superstitious monuments, ornaments and pictures in Cambridgeshire and Suffolk, kept a detailed journal of his work, minutely recording his depredations in the churches and chapels of East Anglia. At Haverhill, for example, in the process of working what he called his 'godly thorough reformation', he claimed to have broken down 'about an hundred Superstitious Pictures; and seven Fryars hugging a Nunn; and the Picture of God and Christ; and divers others very superstitious'. '200 had been broke down before I came,' he added. 'We took away two popish Inscriptions . . . and we beat down a great Stoneing Cross on the top of the Church.'

At Peterhouse, Cambridge, so Dowsing said, he was responsible for the demolition of 'two mighty great angels with wings and divers other angels and the four Evangelists and Peter with his Keys over the chapel door . . . and about 100 cherubims and divers superstitious letters in gold, and six angels in the windows . . . and 60 superstitious pictures, some Popes and some crucifixes, with God the Father sitting in a chair and holding a globe.' An eyewitness described Dowsing going about 'like a Bedlam breaking glasse windowes, having battered and beaten downe all our painted glasse . . . mistaking perhaps the liberall Arts for Saints . . . and having defaced and digged up the floors of our Chappels, many of which had lien so for two or three hundred years together, not regarding the dust of our founders and predecessors, who likely were buried there; compelled us by armed Souldiers to pay forty shillings a Colledge for not mending what he had spoyled and defaced, or forthwith to go to Prison.'

Such plate as did reach the King from Cambridge was mostly handed over for melting down to Thomas Bushell, an ingenious and enterprising engineer and entrepreneur, who managed with notable success the royal mines of Wales. As the King himself acknowledged in a letter of thanks, Bushell performed 'manie other true services' in the Royalist cause: 'Your providing us with one hundred tonnes of leadshot for our army without mony, which ws paid before twentie pounds per tonne; and your helpinge us to twenty-six pieces of ordinance . . . and your contracting with merchants beyond the seas for providing good quantities of powder, pistol, carabine, musket and bullen . . . and your cloathing of our liefe guard [of miners] and three regiments more with suits, stockings and shoes when we were ready to march in the feild.'

With Bushell's help a mint was established at Shrewsbury and recruits were soon being paid 4s.4d. a week, more than many were earning in civilian life. Later that year musketeers were being paid at the rate of 6s. a week and horsemen as much as 17s.6d. But these rates had to be lowered as the months went by, and by the spring of 1644 the pay of ordinary soldiers had dropped to 4s. a week; corporals had 7s., sergeants 10s.6d., lieutenants £1 8s., and captains £2 12s.6d. But these amounts, roughly the same in both armies, were often no more than notional. In the ranks of Royalists and Parliamentarians alike there were frequent complaints about pay being late or not forthcoming at all, and in the areas through which their armies passed there were just as angry charges that soldiers pillaged what they could not or would not buy. A soldier was supposed to receive every day from the commissariat two pounds of bread, one pound of meat or cheese, and an allowance of either wine or beer. But in these early days of the conflict he very rarely did so, and was driven to living as he could off the country, or as it was sometimes termed 'at free country', much to the distress of the people at large. A characteristic petition from the 'inhabitants of Middlesex and other south-eastern counties' complained of the 'intolerable oppression of Free Quarter' which rendered them 'no better than mere conquered slaves [of the soldiers] who like so many Egyptian locusts fed so long upon [them] at free cost'.

In the Royalist army colonels of horse were ordered 'to quarter and billet their respective regiments in such places as we have assigned, and there to take up such necessary provisions of diet, lodging, hay, oats and straw as shall be necessary for them. And if there shall not be sufficient for such supply in their quarters then they are to send out their warrants to the several parishes adjacent, requiring the inhabitants to bring in all fitting provisions for their daily supply. For all which, as for that taken up in their quarters, they are to give their respective tickets, and not to presume upon pain of our high displeasure, to send for greater quantities than will suffice for their numbers of men and horses.'

Tickets were, however, not always given for the provisions taken:

and, when given, were not always honoured. Civilian people consequently 'carried away or hid all their provisions, insomuch as there was neither meat for man or horse: and the very smiths hid themselves, that they might not be compelled to shoe the horses, of which in those stony ways there was great need'.

A sergeant recorded at about this time, 'At Aynhoe we were very scanted for victuals; at Chipping Norton our regiment stood in the open field all night having neither bread nor water to refresh ourselves, having also marched the day before without any sustenance.' Outside Swindon his regiment came upon some thousand sheep and sixty head of cattle. Persuading themselves that they belonged to 'malignants and papists', they immediately rounded them all up. Such behaviour was common enough in both armies.

Warned of Essex's approach towards Worcester, the King ordered Prince Rupert to take half the cavalry which had so far assembled under the royal standard to intercept him. By 23 September, the Prince's horse were about two miles south of Worcester near the village of Powick where the river Teme flows into the Severn. As he approached the Severn he was told that a body of Parliamentary horse, some thousand strong, had crossed the Teme at Powick Bridge behind him. They were advancing up a narrow lane between thick hedges which gave them no room to manoeuvre. Prince Rupert immediately saw his opportunity. Drawing his men up in the open field at the end of the lane, he prepared to charge as soon as the enemies' leading horsemen had emerged from it. Waiting until a goodly number had appeared from behind the hedge, the Cavaliers galloped forward at their commanders' order, overthrowing those Parliamentary horsemen who had come out into the field and throwing the rest into the utmost confusion as they rode this way and that, incapable of understanding, still less of carrying out, such orders as were given them. 'Our wounded men they brought into the city,' so Nehemiah Wharton recorded, 'and stripped, and stabbed and slashed their bodies in a most barbarous manner and imbrued their hands in their blood. They also met a young gentleman, a Parliament man – his name I cannot learn – and stabbed him on horseback with many wounds, and trampled upon him, and also most maliciously shot his horse . . . All night we had small comfort, for it rained hard. Our food was fruit, for those who could get it; our drink, water; our beds, the earth; but we pulled up hedges, pales and gates and made good fires . . . Thus we continued singing of psalms until the morning. Saturday morning we marched to Worcester [which Prince Rupert had abandoned as being indefensible] the rain continuing the whole day, and the way so base that we went up to the ancles in thick clay; and, about four of the clock after noon, entered the city where we found twenty-eight dead men, which we buried . . . We shortly expect a pitched battle, which, if the Cavaliers will but stand, will be very hot; for we are all much enraged against them for their barbarisms, and shall show them little mercy.'

The Royalists claimed a great victory at Powick Bridge. So also did the Parliamentarians, who were in the habit of claiming victory even in battles which had never been fought. But Essex recognized that his cavalry would have to be far better trained before they engaged the Cavaliers again. They must, he instructed, practise the ceremonious forms of military discipline so that in future they would know how to 'fall on with descretion and retreat with care'.

Encouraged by this victory and by the reputation which his nephew had gained from it, the King welcomed the recruits, who continued to come to him at Shrewsbury from the surrounding areas, in much improved spirits. By the beginning of October he had six thousand foot soldiers at his command, in addition to the horsemen whom Prince Rupert was training as assiduously as were Essex's officers the Parliamentary cavalry; and by the middle of the month he was ready to march upon his recently abandoned capital, convinced, as Edward Hyde said, that it was owing to 'the wonderful providence of God that from the low despised condition [he] was in at Nottingham, after the setting up of his standard there, he should be able to get men, money and arms and, within twenty days of his coming to Shrewsbury, to march, in despite of the enemy, even towards London'.

The King set out for London on 12 October, following the course of the Severn down to Bridgnorth, where the people came out into the streets to cheer him on his way, then turning east for Kenilworth, gathering more recruits *en route* until he had over fifteen thousand infantry and some eight thousand horsemen, more troops than he was ever to command again. They were not as well armed as his officers would have liked, some of the Welshmen who had joined him at Wolverhampton having to be content with pitchforks and even scythes and sickles; but he had twenty field guns and the men appeared to be in as good spirits as he was himself. They had been much encouraged by their cavalry's victory at Powick Bridge and were already congratulating each other upon the superior merits of the young commander, Prince Rupert, who, for all his squabbles with his fellow-commanders, had undoubtedly instilled confidence into their men. He had found a 'very thin and small army' at Nottingham, as Sir Philip Warwick, one of his officers said, 'and the Foot very meanly armed'. But he had soon 'ranged and disciplined them' and 'put such spirit into the King's army that all men seem'd resolved'.

The Earl of Essex, impeded by a large artillery train which he always insisted upon, marched slowly towards Warwick, a coffin and a winding sheet packed amongst the baggage in his wagons. When he reached the village of Kineton, intent upon intercepting the King's march on London, his guns were a day's march behind him on the road from Worcester. It was the late afternoon of 22 October when he rode into Kineton. The next day was a Sunday; and as he was on his way to matins that morning at the parish church of St Peter, he was told that the Royalist army had been sighted less than three miles away, across the road to London on the rising ground of Edgehill above the little village of Radway.

Prince Rupert had occupied this ground with his cavalry the night before, and had waited there for the infantry to join him. As soon as they did so there was trouble once more between the commanders, who had already differed as to the route the army had followed from Shrewsbury. Prince Rupert, whose commission exempted him from receiving orders from anyone other than the King, laid down in his most high-handed manner a plan of battle for the infantry as well as the horse. The Earl of Lindsey objected to it. They quarrelled, too, about the disposition of the pikemen and musketeers; and when the King came down on his nephew's side, Lindsey lost his temper, hurled his baton to the ground and, declaring that if he was 'not fit to be a general he would die a colonel at the head of his regiment', he stormed off to the troops he had raised in Lincolnshire. The King asked the old Earl of Forth to take over the command from him.

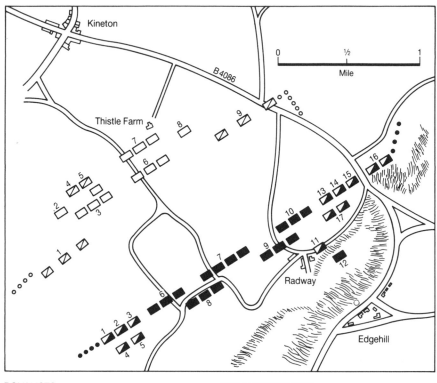

ROYALISTS

■ Cavalry   ■ Foot   ●●● Dragoons

1   Lord Wilmot
2   Lord Grandison
3   Earl of Carnarvon
4   Lord Digby
5   Sir Arthur Aston
6   Henry Wentworth
7   Sir Richard Fielding
8   Sir Nicholas Byron
9   John Belasyse
10   Charles Gerard
11   Gentlemen Pensioners
12   William Legge's firelocks
13   Prince Maurice
14   Prince Rupert
15   Prince of Wales
16   King's Life Guard
17   Sir John Byron

PARLIAMENTARIANS

▱ Cavalry   ▱ Foot   ∘∘∘ Dragoons

1   Lord Feilding
2   Sir William Fairfax
3   Sir John Meldrum
4   Sir Philip Stapleton
5   Sir William Balfour
6   Charles Essex
7   Thomas Ballard
8   Denzil Holles
9   Sir James Ramsay

The Battle of Edgehill

The army was then drawn up in line of battle largely as Prince Rupert had proposed, the infantry in the centre, three brigades in the front rank, two in the second, pikemen in the middle, musketeers on the wings. Prince Rupert's brigade of horse was on the right wing, with Sir John Byron's horse in reserve. Beside them were the King's Life Guard of cavalry under his cousin, Lord Bernard Stuart. The King's standard was held by Sir Edmund Verney, still unwilling to desert the King but reluctant to fight for him. In command of the cavalry on the left, with Lord Grandison, Robert Dormer, Earl of Carnarvon and Lord Digby, was Prince Rupert's second-in-command and rival, Henry Wilmot. On either flank were the dragoons, support troops riding horses much inferior to those of the cavalry and, at £4 each, costing less than half the price commanded by cavalry horses. When engaging the enemy, dragoons dismounted to fire their muskets and carbines on foot.

Behind the lines of musketeers and pikemen were the heavy guns waiting to fire over their heads; while the lighter guns were placed between the infantry brigades in the front rank. To the rear of the fighting men stood the surgeons, four or five of them attached to headquarters, the rest regimental surgeons, assisted by surgeons' mates, few of them qualified, most as inexpert in the use of their crude instruments as those who tended the wounded knights at Agincourt in 1415.

Facing the Royalists the Parliamentary army was drawn up on the lower ground in a similar manner, infantry brigades in the centre, cavalry on either wing, Sir James Ramsay's brigade on the left, with a reserve commanded by Denzil Holles. Sir William Balfour and Sir Philip Stapleton, a Yorkshire gentleman of moderate estate, were on the right with Basil, Lord Feilding, whose old father, the first Earl of Denbigh, was serving as an ordinary soldier in the opposing army, 'with unwearied pains and exact submission to discipline, engaging with singular courage in all enterprises of danger', until he was mortally wounded the following year.

Both armies presented a colourful appearance, beneath the bright, emblazoned standards of their various troops. The men in some regiments were clothed in red coats, in others blue or green, grey or buff or russet. Officers and sergeants, who provided their own clothes, were dressed as their fancy dictated, in some cases more flamboyantly than was deemed appropriate by the more sober minded, with velvet hats, fringed silk scarves about their waists, and cloaks 'laden with gold and silver lace'. 'The daubing of a coat with lace of sundry colours, as some do use them,' wrote one disapproving observer, 'I do neither take to be soldierlike nor profitable for the coat.'

Several officers in Parliament's army were quite as flamboyantly dressed and wore their hair quite as long as their Royalist counterparts, as luxuriantly indeed as the Parliamentary Colonel John Hutchinson who, as his wife proudly related, had 'a very fine thicksett head of haire, a greate ornament to him'. Even Roundhead sergeants were not above dressing extravagantly. One of these was happy to make use of a gift of his 'mistress's scarfe and Mr Molloyne's hatband, both of which came very seasonably for [he had just had made] a soldier's sute for winter, edged with gold and silver lace'. Later in the war coats became even more showy, with linings of a contrasting colour, and crosses or swords embroidered in red or blue silk on white sleeves. Brightly coloured scarves and sashes also became commonplace, usually crimson silk for Cavaliers, orange silk for Roundheads; and men on both sides wore field-signs in their hats, bits of white paper or sprigs of oak, so that they could recognize each other in the confusion and smoke of battle.

In the best-equipped infantry companies the men were provided with outer coats of thick, buff-coloured leather and steel back and breast plates. They also had, as well as their beaver hats or monteros, steel helmets, known generally as 'pots' which they were all too ready to take off and throw away, together with their even heavier 'backs' and 'breasts', when on the march in hot summer weather. For carrying their provisions they were issued with what were known as 'snapsacks' of leather or canvas. They were also given bandoleers for their cartridges and, for their powder, bags to hang from their belts.

They were told to take good care of their powder. Much of it had to be imported; the rest came from powder mills in England which might fall into the hands of the enemy, as those at Chilworth in Surrey and Lydney in Gloucestershire subsequently did. Moreover, saltpetre, an essential ingredient, was never in large supply. It had been a royal monopoly before the war; and, since it was a byproduct of bird droppings and human urine, government officials had authority to enter any properties they chose to dig in henhouses and privies. In 1638 'saltpetre men', as they were known, had sought permission to extend their activities to the floors of churches 'because women pisse in their seats which causes excellent saltpetre'.

Most soldiers carried short swords or axes as well as matchlocks, clumsy firearms which were as difficult to load quickly as they were to fire accurately. Until paper cartridges came into more general use, the requisite amount of powder had to be poured down the barrel, then rammed home with a rod before the ball was inserted, followed by a wad to ensure that it did not fall out again. To light the powder, the musketeer carried his match, a length of flax impregnated with saltpetre or cord boiled in vinegar, and this he lit at both ends when the time for firing came. Accidents were common. It has been calculated that three hundred men were killed by accident before the war was over, and hundreds more were injured. A Royalist officer commented, 'We bury more toes and fingers than we do men.' The open flame of the match could not, of course, be tolerated near large stores of powder; so infantry guarding the artillery train were equipped with flintlock muskets, a far superior weapon which was too expensive to be supplied to the infantry generally. Nor were cavalry troops usually supplied with the flintlock carbines which later became standard equipment. A few had wheel-locks in which the powder was fired by the friction of a small clockwork wheel, wound up by a spanner, against a piece of iron pyrites. But most had to be content with a pair of flintlock pistols which were even less reliable than flintlock muskets. They also had swords, often none too sharp, and they wore the same back and breast plates as the infantry, as well as high boots of thick leather which offered some protection to their legs. One or two regiments were supplied at their commanders' expense with the kind of articulated plate armour to be seen in Continental cavalry regiments and with helmets designed to protect the neck and nose as well as the skull. Sir Arthur Haselrig's cuirassiers from Leicestershire were issued with such comprehensive armour that they were nicknamed 'the Lobsters'.

Even the most sophisticated armour, however, offered little protection against a determined pikeman armed with a pike sixteen to eighteen feet long, the hilt of which he would hold firmly in the earth beside his instep while the sharp steel point was levelled at the chests of the oncoming horse.

Men who had served in armies on the Continent argued endlessly as to the merits of the cavalry tactics favoured in the contending armies. There was, for example, the tactic known as 'the Dutch', in which a troop of horsemen came on at a quickish trot in about six ranks, firing their pistols as they advanced upon the infantry, then wheeling to one side to reform and charge again, brandishing their swords. Advocates of this tactic tended to deride the practice, perfected in the Swedish army of King Gustavus II Adolphus, in which the cavalry charged in not more than three ranks, the troopers riding so close together that their knees were interlocked, and holding their fire until the crash, or just before the crash, of impact.

Gustavus Adolphus himself had devised a drill for infantrymen to withstand these cavalry charges: they were to form up in three ranks, the first kneeling, the second crouching, the third standing, so that all could fire in the same instant, waiting until the last possible moment to do so, it being impossible for even the most skilled marksman to be sure of hitting his target at distances greater than sixty yards. After firing they were to retire quickly to reload, while another three ranks took their place. In the confusion of battle such drill, practised on the parade ground, was rarely performed satisfactorily. More often, once the infantrymen's matchlocks had been discharged they lashed out with their swords or axes or the stocks of their firearms in the ensuing mêlée, inflicting as many savage wounds on horses and riders as they could until the survivors retreated from the field or rode away for another charge, disappearing into the sulphuric gunpowder smoke of the battlefield.

Pikemen were drawn up closely packed in square, rectangular or circular 'hedgehogs', sometimes protected by 'swines' feathers', stakes with metal tips driven into the ground at an angle of 45 degrees. If steady and well-trained, pikemen could be relied upon to resist a cavalry charge, since horses would shy or turn away from an apparently immovable and dangerous obstacle. But the sight of thundering, shouting troops of horse would unnerve all save the most resolute man; and once a 'hedgehog' had begun to waver it could rapidly disintegrate, and was more than likely to do so when the pikemen comprising it were also being engaged by enemy infantry. Often the two sides were so closely interlocked that it was scarcely possible to raise an arm in defence or attack; men mortally wounded remained upright in the crush; and brave men could be carried off willy-nilly in a surge of terror-stricken soldiers struggling to escape the conflict, as was to happen to both Sir Thomas Fairfax and the King in the days to come.

The King, wearing a black velvet coat lined with ermine, addressed his senior officers in his tent: 'The foe is in sight. The best encouragement I can give you is this. Come life or death, your King will bear you company, and ever keep this field, this place, and this day's service in his grateful remembrances.' He then rode down the line, accompanied by his sons and his senior commanders and preceded by a scarlet standard 'larger than ordinary so that it might be known in what part of the Army the person of the King was'. His long hair partially concealed by a steel cap covered with velvet, he 'rode to every Brigade of Horse and to all the Tertias of Foot to encourage them to their Duty, [speaking] to them with great Courage and Cheerfulness which caused Huzza's thro' the whole Army'.

Prince Rupert meanwhile 'passed from one Wing to the other', one of his men recalled, 'giving positive Orders to the Horse to [charge] as close as was possible, keeping their ranks with Sword in Hand, to receive the Enemy's Shot, without firing either Carbine or Pistol till we broke in amongst the Enemy, and then to make use of our Fire-Arms as need should require'.

Sir Jacob Astley contented himself with a brief and moving prayer: 'O Lord, thou knowest how busy I must be this day. If I forget thee, do not thou forget me.'

At about one o'clock in the afternoon the Earl of Essex's heavy artillery opened fire. Soon afterwards the King himself ignited the charge that sent the first shot from his own guns hurtling over the narrow stretch of open land that separated the two armies. For an hour or so the cannon on both sides roared at each other to little effect, the less well-trained of the gunners managing only to fire a round every seven or eight minutes, palls of smoke slowly rising into the air. Then, shortly before three o'clock, a trumpet sounded and Prince Rupert and his cavalry suddenly charged headlong against the enemy's left wing. The troopers obeyed their orders to hold their fire until close enough to the moment of shattering impact to be sure of their targets; and, when they did fire their pistols, the result was devastating: Sir James Ramsay's troopers, shocked by the sudden clash, waited only to discharge their own pistols, and in some cases drop them to the ground, before galloping off the field. Joined by several companies of frightened infantry, they rode helter-skelter through their own reserve, Denzil Holles bravely 'planting himself in the way and doing what possibly he could to make them stand'.

A less impetuous and more experienced body of cavalry would now have rallied and, leaving the scattered enemy to gallop off, would have wheeled round to attack the Roundhead centre; but Prince Rupert could not prevent most of his excited, shouting men from pursuing the fleeing enemy across the fields to Kineton. They thundered through the village and way beyond it, coming upon the enemy's baggage train and thoroughly plundering it, burning wagons, killing wagoners, drawing to a halt only when John Hampden was seen approaching with the staunch tenants of his Buckinghamshire estate, with the Parliamentary reserve and the rest of Essex's guns.

When Prince Rupert at length returned to the field of battle, he discovered that Henry Wilmot's brigade on the Royalist left had also charged at the opposing cavalry, had driven them back and recklessly pursued them, as well as several companies of infantry, out of sight. One of his more capable officers, Sir Charles Lucas, the Earl of Newcastle's brother-in-law who had served as a cavalry officer in Flanders, did his best to hold the men back, as Denzil Holles had done on the army's other flank. Yet, for all his efforts, he managed to rally fewer than two hundred, and the Royalist infantry in the centre of the line were consequently left dangerously exposed. Sir William Balfour and Sir Philip Stapleton, on the right of the Parliamentary line, made the most of their opportunity. They had managed to keep their men together in reserve when the leading ranks of horse were thrown back by the force of Wilmot's charge. They now took them round, concealed by hedges and folds in the ground, to fall upon the Royalists' guns and the infantry beside them. Encouraged by the success of this attack, the Roundhead infantry advanced and came to blows with the main body of the King's infantry, now moving forward to meet them, led by Sir Jacob Astley crying 'March on Boys!' and moving forward, so the Duke of York observed, 'with a slow, steady pace and a vary daring resolution'.

The subsequent hand-to-hand fighting was savage and confused. The King's standard, the Banner Royal, was captured; its bearer, Sir Edmund Verney, was killed, his severed hand still grasping the staff;

and John Smith, the brave Roman Catholic Royalist officer who recaptured it, was himself almost slain in the attempt. 'They shall have me with it, if they carry it away!' he cried, rushing rapier in hand upon the men endeavouring to make off with it. 'Traitor, deliver the standard!' Although wounded already, he killed one of the men and drove the others off, retrieving the precious emblem. He survived to be knighted next day, only to be mortally wounded in a subsequent battle. Lord Feilding was captured; Sir Jacob Astley and Sir John Byron were both wounded; so were two other infantry commanders, Charles Gerard, later Earl of Macclesfield, and John, Lord Belasyse. Many of the King's Life Guard were killed. Lord Taaffe was shot in the mouth; Lord d'Aubigny died of his wounds. The King's own life was threatened and one of his footmen was shot in the face; while the action came so close to the Prince of Wales that he cocked his pistol and crying, 'I fear them not!' would have joined the fight had his attendants not pulled him away.

True to his word, the Earl of Lindsey fought at the head of his own regiment, swearing that he would never serve with such boys as Prince Rupert again. He was badly wounded and taken prisoner. His son tried to save him, 'standing undauntedly with his pike in his hand bestriding his father'; but he was captured too, and watched helplessly as his father died.

When dusk began to fall the fighting slackened as the Parliamentary infantry, exhausted by their exertions, gave ground before Prince Rupert's returning horsemen. A determined charge might have secured an uncontested Royalist victory, as Lord Falkland suggested; but Wilmot would not agree. His men could face no further effort. 'My Lord,' he said, 'we have got the day, let us live to enjoy the fruit thereof.' Yet after the sun had set no one could be sure who had won. Both sides claimed to have triumphed, and, declining to leave the field, they encamped for the night where they were, exhausted and hungry, lying amongst the dead and dying in a darkness 'as cold as a very great frost and a cold northerly wind could make it'.

'The night after the battle our army quartered upon the same ground,' wrote Edmund Ludlow, son of Henry Ludlow, Member of Parliament for Wiltshire, and a member of Essex's bodyguard. 'No man nor horse got any meat that night and I had touched none since the Saturday before, neither could I find my servant who had my cloak, so that having nothing to keep me warm but a suit of iron, I was obliged to walk about all night which proved very cold by reason of the sharp frost . . . [When I did at last get] meat I could scarcely eat it, my jaws for want of use having almost lost their natural faculty.'

All around him in the darkness plunderers furtively crept about from body to body, searching the pockets of those no longer able to resist them, and stripping the clothes from the bodies of both the dead and the wounded. William Harvey, the physician and discoverer of the circulation of the blood – who told John Aubrey that he had been in attendance upon the Prince of Wales during the battle and had passed the time by reading a book under a hedge until a bullet had grazed the ground by his side – now calmly pulled a corpse over him for warmth. Around him the Welsh troops, miserable and far from home, muttered incomprehensibly. Later the balladeers sang a gloomy song about them:

> In Kineton Green,
> Poor Taffy was seen,
>   O Taffy! O Taffy!
> Taffy [he] stood
> To [his] knees in blood,
>   O do not laugh ye . . .
> [His] sword and spear
> Did smell for fear
> And [his] heart were
> In a cold plight;
> Made Taffy outright,
> His poor britches beshite
>   O Taffy! O Taffy!
> The guns did so fart
> Made poor Taffy start . . .
>   O Taffy, poor Taffy.

After the King's cavalry had marched 'almost to Warwick and found the coast clear from the enemy', Edward Hyde reported, 'they returned to the field to view the dead bodies, many going to enquire after their friends who were missing, where they found many not yet dead of their wounds, but lying stripped amongst the dead. Amongst them, with others, [was] an old gentleman of great fortune in Lincolnshire.' This man, Sir Gervase Scrope, had 'fallen with sixteen wounds in his head and body, and had lain stripped among the dead from that time, which was about three of the clock in the afternoon on Sunday, all that cold night, all Monday and Monday night and till Tuesday, for it was so late before his son found him, whom with great pity he carried to a warm lodging, and afterwards in the march to Oxford where he wonderfully recovered. The next morning after, being Wednesday, there was another gentleman (one Bellingham, of ancient extraction in Sussex, and the only son of his father) found amongst the dead and brought off by his friends with twenty wounds . . . The surgeons were of opinion that both these gentlemen owed their lives to the inhumanity of those who stripped them, and to the coldness of the nights, which stopped their blood better than all their skill and medicaments could have done, and that, if they had been brought off with any reasonable distance of time after their wounds, they had undoubtedly perished.'

4

THE SPREAD OF WAR

'Come on my boys, my brave boys, let us pray heartily and fight heartily and God will bless us.'

Philip Skippon

The day after the battle at Edgehill, the Earl of Essex moved off towards Warwick. His army was still a formidable force, far from the devastated rabble which those of his officers who had fled to London after Prince Rupert's first charge had reported it to be. But it had been badly mauled, suffering 1,500 casualties. His baggage train was lost; so were several of his guns and large stores of arms and ammunition as well as his private coach and fifty of his colours. More wagonloads of stores were captured when Prince Rupert's cavalry fell upon his rearguard on the road to Warwick next day.

Prince Rupert pressed the King to advance fast on London and forcibly dissolve Parliament without delay now that the road was clear. So did the Earl of Forth. But others more cautious, including the Earl of Bristol, advised him to hold back. Charles wavered, unwilling to commit himself irrevocably, yet reluctant to appear incapable of doing so. Before the fighting at Edgehill he had seemed glad that the time of debate was over, that the problems which beset him were not his to settle now, but in the hands of God. His hesitations and waverings had appeared to be resolved, his self-confidence increased by the knowledge that all must be decided by the savage but simple remedies of force. Yet the sudden experience of violence, the fearful sights, smells and sounds of battle now brought him once more to doubt and indecision.

The Parliamentarians, too, were uncertain how next to proceed. They were strongly supported, as they always had been, in virtually all the larger towns. They still held London and, so long as the King failed to take this, by far the largest centre of population and by far the most important commercial centre in the country, they could feel secure in their control over the Home Counties and the south-east, over East Anglia and much if not most of the Midlands. But in the north, except in those areas of west and south Yorkshire which the Fairfax family stolidly held for Parliament, the Royalists were in control. So were they in Cheshire, except in those towns held for the Roundheads by Sir William Brereton and his friends. So were they, too, in most of Lancashire apart from those strongly Puritan towns centred upon Manchester. The Royalists prevailed also in most of Wales and along the Welsh marches and, increasingly so, in the south-west, despite the long tradition in those counties of resistance to autocratic tyranny as recently demonstrated by Sir John Eliot, born in Cornwall, and John Pym, born in Somerset.

Anxious not to lose the south-east, Essex withdrew from Warwick towards London, leaving the Royalists free to take Banbury and to restock their army from its supplies of clothes and food. He was much concerned by the turn of events. Numerous deserters from the Roundhead ranks had wandered off after the battle at Edgehill, taking their weapons with them. An appeal for money in the City met with a discouraging response, despite the widely reported arrest of several citizens who refused to meet the demands. The mood of the people of the capital was disquieting: the Trained Bands remained reliable and resolute, and scores of citizens came out into the streets to work on the defences, while an emergency ordinance released apprentices from their indentures should they go to join the Parliamentary army. But there were muttered grumbles against Parliament and repeated demands for a truce. It was decided to suggest to the King that representatives of both sides should meet to discuss terms for a treaty; and the King's two younger children, Princess Elizabeth, now eleven years old, and Prince Henry, four, were brought from St James's Palace to the City for use as hostages.

The offer of peace negotiations was accepted by the King, but neither side abided by the agreement for a 'cessation of arms'. Parliament, having recalled the Earl of Warwick from the fleet to direct the defence of London, advanced the Trained Bands out of the City towards the scattered villages beyond the suburbs of Westminster, where some of them saw open country for the first time, like the London apprentices whom Captain Robert Harley later saw running into the fields 'to see what manner of things cows were'.

As the Trained Bands marched out of London the Royalists moved down through Oxford and Reading towards Brentford, which Rupert's cavalry surprised on the misty morning of 12 November, clattering through the rough and muddy streets of the little town, brandishing their swords and shouting threats.

Parliament's troops in Brentford were commanded by Denzil Holles and Robert Greville, second Lord Brooke, a severe and obstinate Puritan who was to be shot in the eye and killed a few months later. Greville's men, 'all butchers and dyers' as their opponents derided them, were not as staunch as he. At the approach of the Cavaliers they ran away almost to a man, with the notable exception of one of their captains, a young brewer and political agitator named John Lilburne who was, however, soon captured as he tried to rally his men around an abandoned standard.

Denzil Holles fought on as he had done at Edgehill; but his men could not withstand the relentless blades of Prince Rupert's horse who cut them down in the High Street and by the banks of the river, driving those who surrendered into the pens where animals were kept awaiting sale in the market, then forcing their way into the houses of the town, helping themselves to food and drink in larders, stealing what they fancied, and throwing furniture and bedclothes out of the broken windows.

> Poor Brentford is made a miserable spectacle [reported the Puritan tanner, Nehemiah Wallington of Little Eastcheap] for they have taken from the inhabitants all the linen, bedding, furniture, pewter, brass, pots, pans, bread, meal, in a word all that they have, insomuch that when the Parliament's army came into the town on the Lord's day at night, the innkeepers and others begged of the soldiers a piece of bread. They have taken from divers of the inhabitants, some to the value of four hundred pounds . . . some more . . . and from the poorer sort all that ever they had, leaving them not a bed to lie on, nor apparel, but what they have on their backs, nor a pair

of sheets, nor a piece of bread, and what beer they drank not, they
let run out in their cellars. Divers families of repute, with their
wives and children, were driven to such extreme poverty thereby,
that they have begged ever since. And [the Royalists] took divers of
the townsmen (who never opposed them) after they had plundered
them, putting them in irons, and tying others with ropes, and so
led them away like dogs . . . Who can read this without a sad heart
and a mournful eye?

When exaggerated accounts of the looting of Brentford reached the
capital, Essex's soldiers and the Trained Bands united in their determination to prevent the Cavaliers advancing further down the road
to London. Thousands upon thousands of citizens, apprentices,
tradesmen, peers and Members of Parliament were ranged across the
road at Turnham Green, upriver from Putney, to block the Royalists'
advance, shoulder to shoulder with troops who had fought at
Edgehill. There were in all about twenty-four thousand armed men
well placed behind hedges and ditches, in orchards and gardens,
standing in the doorways of stables and barns, gazing in nervous
defiance from tavern windows. Behind them there were cannon in
the main streets of the City and at every gate. There were barricades
across the roads in Westminster and in the northern suburbs,
fieldworks in the parks, armed ships in the river.

To shouts of 'Hey for old Robin!' the still much-liked and
respected Earl of Essex rode from regiment to regiment, while the
Puritan veteran Philip Skippon, in command of the Trained Bands,
went 'all along with his soldiers', according to Bulstrode Whitelocke,
who was serving with John Hampden's regiment, 'talking to them,
sometimes to one company, sometimes to another', calling out
'Come on, my boys, my brave boys, let us pray heartily and fight
heartily. I will run the same fortunes and hazards with you. Remember the cause is for God and for the defence of yourselves, your wives
and your children. Come, my honest, brave boys, pray heartily and
God will bless us.'

There were, however, no hazards to be run that day. The hours
– it was a Sunday – passed slowly and quietly by. Neither army
moved. Each stood warily facing the other, the Londoners being fed
in the afternoon from carts stacked high with 'an hundred loads of
all manner of good provisions of victuals, bottles of wine and barrels

of beer' which had been loaded up outside taverns and houses after morning service. Large crowds of spectators who had ridden out of London to watch the battle sat uneasily in their saddles waiting for the performance to begin, galloping away when it seemed or was rumoured that the Royalists were about to attack and, with each stampede, carrying off with them a number of nervous recruits, several of whom decamped for good after every panic. Essex wisely refrained from putting this well-fed though ill-assorted army to the test of battle; the Royalists, for their part, tired, hungry and out-numbered by more than two to one, dared not use their cavalry in such confined country against so large a force.

The King had no alternative but to turn back. He withdrew towards his palace at Hampton Court, then to Oatlands and Reading; while Essex moved to Windsor where the castle had been seized for Parliament by Colonel John Venn and his dragoons after the fighting at Edgehill. From Windsor – where most people were predisposed in Parliament's favour because of the Crown's strict imposition of forest laws, its enclosure of land and numerous prosecutions for poaching – Essex with a large force of some nineteen thousand men marched west. Having already taken Henley-on-Thames where in a skirmish in Duck Street, now Duke Street, a party of Royalist troops were scattered with some loss of life on both sides, he made for Reading, Archbishop's Laud's birthplace, an important centre of the clothing industry on the banks of the Thames where the Kennet joins the main river.

Reading had been strongly fortified by the Royalist Governor, Sir Arthur Aston, an unpleasant, vindictive and widely disliked Roman Catholic whom other Catholics denied was of their faith. 'Much esteemed where he was not known,' Edward Hyde wrote of him, 'he was much detested where he was . . . A man of a rough nature, and so given to an immoderate love of money that he cared not by what unrighteous ways he exacted it.' He was also notoriously cruel, 'adjudging that a soldier against whom he bore a grudge, should have his right hand sawn off'.

Bullying soldiers and townspeople alike, Aston had had Reading surrounded by deep ditches and high embankments made from earth and from high blocks of stone carted over from the Abbey church, the nave of which had been blown up for the purpose. Strong as Reading's defences were, however, the town was not expected to hold out for long: the small garrison of little more than three thousand men was reported to be so unruly and dispirited that the Governor, in characteristic fashion, had hanged several of the worst offenders. The people of the town, disgruntled by having to work on the fortifications, were additionally aggrieved by the Royalists' incessant demands for provisions and money 'to pay those great charges which [were] now laid upon the Borough concerning cloth, apparel, victuals and other things for His Majesty's army'. They were required to supply money for wood and coal for the fires in the garrison's guardhouses, as well as sacks stuffed with wool to protect musketeers on the embankments; they were asked for loans which were not repaid; their houses were occasionally plundered by Aston's troops who, as mercilessly as their enemies, pillaged the surrounding countryside. On one occasion they demanded eight carts to be filled with firewood and bedding at Wokingham and destroyed four houses when the people refused to obey the order; on another they threatened similar violence when removing five cartloads of wheat and 150 sheep from angry villagers at Wargrave.

Having captured a Royalist outpost there, Essex took up position on Caversham Heights to the north of Reading and opened fire on the town below with his heavy guns, concentrating upon the defences around St Peter's Church, which guarded the way to the bridge, and so battering it with his shot that the spire was knocked down and the north side reduced to ruins. The Royalists' response was initially brisk, but soon became intermittent. They had scarcely forty barrels of powder, and a young ensign sent for more to a Royalist ammunition store at Henley-on-Thames failed to return. This young officer, Rupert Flower, succeeded in getting through the Parliamentary lines, swimming across the Thames and clambering through the branches of the trees in Caversham Park above the heads of Roundhead soldiers bivouacked on the grass below him. He delivered his message at Henley; it was agreed that the powder should be sent upriver by barge under cover of darkness; but on his return journey Flower was spotted as he swam back across the river by a patrol keeping watch upon a bridge. He was dragged out of the water and tortured. He revealed the plan in his agony and the barge was captured that night.

In Reading the garrison had more to worry about than their lack of powder. The Parliamentary forces had swept down from Caversham Heights, crossed the Thames by Caversham Bridge and established themselves on the Berkshire bank of the river where they were gradually advancing their lines, reinforced by a further three thousand infantry, five hundred horse and three more heavy cannon under Lord Grey of Werke. These reinforcements were mostly frightened recruits who ran away when the garrison made an unexpected sortie from the town; yet, even so, Essex was able to extend his lines south of Reading and to open fire with his heavy artillery on the defences on this side of the town where the steeple of St Giles's Church was almost as badly damaged as that of St Peter's. Worse than this, Sir Arthur Aston, while standing in a guardroom on the fortifications, was hit on the head by a cannon shot. He was knocked senseless and was so confused when he regained consciousness that the command had to be transferred to Colonel Richard Feilding, son of the first Earl of Denbigh who was killed while fighting for the King, and brother of the second Earl who was one of Parliament's senior officers. Far less resolute than the unpopular Aston, Feilding despatched an apprehensive message to Oxford informing the Royalist headquarters there that Reading would have to be relieved within a week, otherwise he would be obliged to surrender it.

The King left for Reading immediately, having already sent a supply of powder and five hundred infantry with instructions to endeavour to get through the enemy lines and into the town. The King's troops clashed with a party of Parliamentary horse at Dorchester where, after a short and savage fight in the narrow streets of the little town, the Royalists were driven off. The King himself halted at Nettlebed where he was informed that Colonel Feilding, unaware that relief was on its way, had undertaken to surrender Reading to the Earl of Essex, provided the garrison could march away to Oxford with their arms and baggage.

Joined now by Prince Rupert, the King marched on towards Reading and from Caversham Heights his troops charged down against the Parliamentary garrison guarding the bridge, rushing past a large mud-walled barn from which Roundhead musketeers opened up a devastating fire, knocking down Cavalier after Cavalier as a sudden storm hurled rain and hailstones into the Royalists' faces.

Hearing the noise of gunfire, some officers in the town urged

Feilding to lead a sally in support of the King's troops. But he declined to do so: he had already ordered a white flag to be hung out; hostages, three officers on each side, had been exchanged; the final terms of surrender were already being discussed. In honour, Feilding said, he was bound to keep the peace. If the King himself were to knock at the gate and command him to break his word he would disobey him.

So the Royalists retreated, unaided, up the hillside, leaving many men lying wounded in the scattered barns and houses outside the town walls and numerous corpses on the hillside to be buried next day by the local people on the Earl of Essex's orders.

On 27 April 1643 the articles of surrender were signed. Sir Arthur Aston was borne out of the town in a horse litter. Behind him marched the garrison, their colours flying and drums beating, escorting fifty carts of baggage and sick and wounded men. They 'marched to the King – who stayed for them – and then with him to Oxford', Edward Hyde later recorded. 'But at their coming out of Reading, and passing through the enemy's guards, the soldiers were not only reviled and reproachfully used, but many of them were disarmed, and most of the waggons were plundered, in the presence of the Earl of Essex himself and the chief officers, who seemed to be offended at it but not to be able to prevent it, the unruliness of their common men being so great. And as this breach of the treaty was so notorious and inexcusable, so it was made the rise, foundation and excuse for barbarous injustice of the same kind throughout the greatest part of the war, insomuch as the King's soldiers afterwards, when it was their part to be precise in the observation of agreements, mutinously remembered the violations at Reading, and thereupon exercised the same license.'

Colonel Feilding was brought before a court martial. The King strongly suspected him of treachery, and intimated that he should suffer accordingly, even though he was a nephew of the Duke of Buckingham. The court obediently found him guilty and sentenced him to death. He was saved only by Prince Rupert's intervention.

As the Royalist and Parliamentary armies marched away from each other, Parliament formulated proposals for a peace treaty which they knew the King would have to reject; and, in a successful attempt to raise contributions from rich merchants and property owners who had hitherto been reluctant to part with money for their cause, they also broadcast the contents of an intercepted letter from one of the Queen's entourage who wrote of the prospect of help soon coming from foreign countries for the subjugation of London. The King, 'distracted in thought', rode on to Oxford, thereafter his headquarters and his court.

5

LONDON AND
OXFORD

'At the windows the sad spectacle of war,
sometimes of plague, sometimes sicknesses of
other kinds by reason of so many people being
packed together.'

Ann Fanshawe

At the outbreak of the war Oxford, a prosperous town of some ten thousand inhabitants, had been divided in its loyalties, the University generally supporting the Royalists, the town for the most part favouring the Parliamentarians, a difference of view which exacerbated the long-standing resentment which many citizens felt for the University and its presumption in controlling so many aspects of the city's life, issuing rules for the conduct of the market, licensing alehouses, and charging what were often considered excessive rents for the many properties the University and colleges owned. When Royalist troops approached the city in August 1642 under the command of Sir John Byron, an energetic officer with an immense moustache and a reputation for engaging the enemy 'when he needed not', a group of citizens attempted to close the gates against them, while the Vice-Chancellor and others of the King's friends in the University gathered on Magdalen Bridge to greet them with shouts of 'Welcome, gentlemen!' And, as townsmen looked on disapprovingly, Royalist sympathizers blocked the main road to the south 'with longe timber logges to keep out horsemen' and carried 'loades of stones up to Magdalen Coll. Tower to flinge downe upon the enemie'. A crooked trench was dug outside Wadham College to help guard the road from the north; sentinels were posted, 'four squadrons were formed whereof two of them were musketeers, a third was a squadron of pikes, the 4th of halberdes'; and, so recorded Anthony Wood, the future antiquarian, then a ten-year-old pupil at Magdalen College School, 'the schollers and priviledged men [persons granted the privileges of the University without being students] to the number of 400 or (as some saye) to the number of 450, repayred [to the Parks] where they were instructed in the wordes of command & their military postures, and trained up and downe in the exercise of armes in a very decent arraye, and no less delightsome prospect to behold the forwardness of so many proper yonge gentlemen, so intent, docile and pliable to their business.' When Byron's men marched out of the city to join the King, several of these young gentlemen left with them, together with three Fellows.

Soon afterwards Parliament's troops entered the city to take their place. They were under the command of the influential Lord Saye and Sele, who had worked hard to bring the area round his country home, Broughton Castle near Banbury, under the influence of Parliament. A Fellow of New College and a man, in Clarendon's words, of 'a close and reserved nature, of a mean and narrow fortune, of great parts and the highest ambition', his nickname was 'Old Subtlety'. His men arrested the Vice-Chancellor and the Warden of New College who had drilled his Royalist scholars in the quadrangle; searched the houses of suspected Roman Catholics; armed the citizens while disarming the members of various colleges which they simultaneously searched for plate; and, finding popish books in some of the libraries, threw them onto bonfires in the streets. They would also have burned the pictures in Trinity College chapel had not the ancient President, Dr Ralph Kettell, insisted that no one ever took the slightest notice of them. 'Truly, my Lord', he told Lord Saye and Sele, 'we regard them no more than a dirty dishcloth.'

Many of the Roundhead soldiers, 'very untractable and undocile in their postures', came into Christ Church, Anthony Wood recorded, 'to viewe the church and paynted windowes, much wondereinge at the idolatry thereof; and a certaine Scot being amongst them, said that "he marvayled howe the schollers could go to their bukes for those painted idolatrous wyndowes" . . . [After a search] they founde out Christ Church plate hid in walles behinde wainescote & in the seller, and they carried it awaye in the night in a greate cowle [a large wooden tub carried on a pole] betwixt 2 men to my Lord's [Lord Saye and Sele's] lodging at the Starre.'

Day by day ill-feeling intensified not only between Parliament's men and Royalist sympathizers but also between rival factions in the Parliamentary army. 'Many of the soldiers fell out amongest themselves,' wrote Anthony Wood, 'and fought with their naked swordes one with another in the highe streete at Carfaxe & about the Starre, some having their thumbes cut of, and some their fingers. The quarrell arose amongst some of them in drinke, & castinge out wordes to this purpose, that "when they came to fight, if it were against the Kinge they would take his part rather than fight against him" . . . The quarrell was betwixt the blewe coates and russett coates & their captaines.'

Yet, fight as they would amongst themselves, the Roundhead soldiers turned immediately upon civilians who presumed to join their quarrels: two citizens 'were apprehended in a most violent manner by the soldiers for utteringe certaine wordes to this effect "that they should saye *a poxe on all Roundheds that goe to fight against the Kinge.*" They were drawn with halters up to Yeild [Guild] Hall from whence, after some examination, they were had to Bocardo prison.' One company of dragoons from London considered it as well to go armed to church because of the enmity of town and scholars alike.

On leaving the city with his companions to join the Parliamentary army, one of Lord Saye's soldiers was outraged beyond endurance by the Baroque porch of the University church of St Mary which had recently been rebuilt by William Laud's chaplain, Dr Morgan Owen. 'The Lundon troopers went out about noone,' Anthony Wood said, 'and as they came alonge downe the high streete, Mr Mayor presented them with wyne at his doore freely; and passing by St Marie's church, one of them discharged a brace of bulletts at the stone image of Our Lady over the Church porch, and at one shotte strooke off her hed and the hed of her child which she held in her right arme; another discharged at the image of our Saviour over All Soules gate, and would have defaced all the work there had it not byn for some townesmen who entreated them to forebeare.'

When the King first entered the city on 29 October 1642, riding at the head of his men 'with about 60 or 70 colours borne before them which they had taken at Edgehill', it seemed that the inhabitants had had quite enough of Parliamentary occupation. Both citizens and scholars cheered him as he rode by and listened with evident approval to protestations of loyalty from the heads of colleges and the Mayor. As a precaution, the citizens were disarmed, but they parted with their weapons without undue complaint and acquiesced in the arrest of their Member of Parliament, an avowed supporter of Parliament. At first they even appeared eager to assist in helping to erect the extensive fortifications of ditches, ramparts, palisades, gates and drawbridges which were eventually to stretch all around the city, under the supervision of a Dutch engineer, Bernard de Gomme, who instructed them in the art of placing sharpened stakes known as storm poles in the sides of ramparts to act as a kind of *chevaux de frise*. But the early enthusiasm soon waned; and within a few months men were being fined for not turning up for work and women penalized for not sending substitutes. On one day, of 122 citizens ordered to the fortifications, only twelve appeared.

There was also widespread reluctance to make the financial sacrifices which were demanded of citizens and University alike, though tradespeople were doing well with so many rich people clamouring to buy in Oxford what they had once bought in London and looking none too carefully at the price. By the beginning of the following year the University had contributed £1,500 to the Royalist cause; yet more was urgently required. In the early summer the King asked for a further £2,000 from both University and city as well as gold and silver plate for his new Oxford coinage. Over two thousand pounds were melted down in all, St John's College offering £800 in lieu of their plate. The King took the money, but he also took the plate. As well as plate, brass kitchenware was collected, not very successfully, to be melted down for ordnance; the city's cornmarket was demolished so that its lead roof could be used for bullets and its timber for military engines; church bells were added to the materials in store.

In addition to lump sums, regular assessments were levied, some colleges providing as much as £100 a week. Certain households were allowed to quarter troops or stable horses instead of paying the levy; others had to provide cattle or food or fodder for horses. The surrounding villages were also called upon for supplies and what was not offered readily was liable to be taken by force. According to Wood, upon one occasion, 'a drive of fat great oxen . . . were driven into Christ Church quadrangle early in the morning'. It transpired, however, that these animals belonged to one of the King's supporters, so they had to be returned to him. But, fortunately for the garrison, 'upon the Wednesday or Thursday after this there came to Oxford another drove of oxen and about 300 sheep, which were true pillages from his majesty's enemies'.

Such pillaging helped to ensure that there was never a serious food shortage in Oxford, and soldiers received fairly regularly their pound of bread and half-pound of cheese every day. Hearing rumours of 'scarcitie of vittells' in Oxford, several of those who came to the city from outside 'brought store of vittels with them, as fowles and bottels of wine on sumpter horses'. One such arrival was the Earl of Pembroke whose servants, 'findinge it otherwise here at Oxford (God be thanked)', took the provisions off to sell 'to the huxters etc'.

The King established himself at Christ Church. Around him in other colleges, in lodging houses, taverns, rented rooms and garrets, cavalry officers and secretaries, chaplains and servants, musicians and ladies of the court made new homes for themselves in what cramped quarters they could find in the still largely medieval and Tudor town. Many were dreadfully uncomfortable. 'My father commanded me to come to him at Oxford where the court then was,' wrote the eighteen-year-old daughter of Sir John Harrison who was shortly to marry an officer on the staff of the Prince of Wales. 'But we that had till that hour lived in great plenty and great order found ourselves like fishes out of water . . . For from as good a house as any gentleman in England had, we came to a baker's house in an obscure street, and from rooms well furnished to lie in a very bad bed in a garret; to one dish of meat, and that not the best ordered; no money, for we were as poor as Job [her father had lent the King a large amount in 1641], nor clothes more than a man or two brought in their cloath bags . . . At the windows the sad spectacle of war, sometimes of plague, sometimes sicknesses of other kinds by reason of so many people being packed together.'

Prince Rupert, who lived in a house in the High Street with his brother, Prince Maurice, for a time moved into St John's College at which he had been nominally entered as an undergraduate during a visit to England in 1636 and which was also the temporary home of the French Ambassador. All Souls was turned into an arsenal, the cloisters and tower of New College into a magazine, Frewin Hall into a cannon foundry, the tower of Brasenose and the town hall into food stores, the Law and Logic Schools into granaries, the School of Rhetoric into a store for rope bridges and scaling ladders, the Astronomy and Music Schools into workrooms for the tailors who stitched together the uniforms for the King's troops. Jesus College provided accommodation for persons of quality from Wales. Pembroke College was reported as holding seventy-nine men, twenty-three women and five children as well as Sir Edward Nicholas, the new principal Secretary of State. Soldiers and their wives and women were lodged wherever accommodation could be found, principally in the parishes of St Ebbe, St Michael and St Mary Magdalen and in the church of St Peter le Bailey. Many of them were Welsh who could not make themselves understood and who were believed to be largely responsible for the constant pilfering. Prisoners were held in the churches of St Giles and St Thomas the Martyr and in the castle where they were starved and beaten by the Governor in an effort to persuade them to join the King's army, as several did rather than endure the frightful conditions there. The main quadrangle of Christ Church was used as a cattle pen.

Beyond the city walls a mill was established at Wolvercote for grinding sword blades forged at Gloucester Hall; at Osney the corn mills were reconstructed for the making of gunpowder; a large house at Godstow was fortified as an outpost; wood was carted in from Shotover for the construction of the defences as well as white clay for the soldiers' pipes. The executive committee of the Privy Council was based at Oriel. When, in January 1644, the Oxford Parliament was formed it met at Christ Church, the Lords later moving to the Upper Schools and the Commons to the Great Congregational Hall.

A mint was established at New Inn Hall where the Master of the London Mint set up the dies which he had brought with him from the Tower and the King's medallists, Thomas Rawlins and Nicholas Briot, were put to work not only on designs for new coins but also for medals to be awarded to soldiers for brave and distinguished service.

On the advice of George Digby, a Royalist news-sheet entitled *Mercurius Aulicus, communicating the Intelligence and Affairs of the Court to the rest of the Kingdom* was printed in Oxford to be distributed in London and elsewhere as a counterblast to the defamatory pamphlets which

were issued so regularly by the London presses. It was published
weekly at a penny – though reprinted and sold in London at as much
as 1s.6d. – and contained not only news of events but ballads mocking
the Parliamentary leaders, derisory accounts of them and their actual
or supposed policies, and contentious rebuttals of items printed in the
Parliamentary news-sheet, *Mercurius Britannicus*. Much of the material
in *Mercurius Aulicus* was inspired or written by its editor, John Birken-
head, a Fellow of All Souls, who was, according to John Aubrey, a
man 'of middling stature, great goggly eyes, not of a sweet aspect . . .
exceedingly confident, witty, not very grateful to his benefactors' and
ready to tell the most damnable lies. Copies of his publication were
evidently taken to London by women who, disguised as beggars, hid
them in their skirts, distributing some on the way and picking up
others at places where they had been left for delivery.

By January 1643, Oxford was more like a garrison than a university
town. While some scholars and Fellows of colleges were working
on the fortifications, others, like Peter Turner, Savilian Professor of
Geometry, joined the colours and were drilled on Port Meadow, in
the Parks and in college quadrangles. Noble students sought leave
to don the gleaming armour of the King's Life Guard. Soldiers
brawled when off duty to such an extent that the sale of drink had
to be prohibited after nine o'clock at night. Duels were so commonplace that scarcely a day passed without an officer being wounded,
and Prince Rupert once had to part two furious contestants with a
pole-axe.
   At the same time the life of the court continued as though its
denizens were still in Whitehall. A Master of Revels was appointed
and the King's Sergeant Painter, William Dobson, was summoned
to Oxford where he was so overwhelmed with commissions for
portraits that he asked for half his fee before beginning work. There
were musical entertainments and plays; new sonnets and satires were
published; new fashions were paraded through the streets and copied
by citizens' wives; love affairs were conducted by the river bank
and beneath the secluded walls of college gardens; fashionable ladies
appeared in Trinity College chapel, 'half-dressed like angels', defying
the 'terrible gigantique aspect' and 'sharp, grey eies' of Ralph Kettell,
who had already been President for over forty years and who, it
was supposed, 'might have lived some years longer and finished his

century, had not those civil wars come on; which much grieved him that was wont to be absolute in the college to be affronted and disrespected by rude soldiers'.

In London there were those who contrived to lead as boisterous a life as many of the courtiers in Oxford. Sir Henry Blount, the celebrated traveller who had fought with the King at Edgehill, decided he had had enough of a soldier's life and returned to London to enjoy the pleasures of his old haunts and of the whores whose company he liked so well.

He was pretty wild [said John Aubrey], especially addicted to common wenches . . . Drunkenness he much exclaimed against, but he allowed wenching . . . [Upon his return to London he] walked into the Westminster Hall with his sword by his side. The Parliamentarians all stared upon him as a *Cavalier*, knowing that he had been with the King. He was called before the House of Commons where he remonstrated to them that he only did his duty [as a Gentleman Pensioner] and so they acquitted him.

In those days he dined most commonly at the Haycocks ordinary [inn], near the Palsgrave Head tavern in the Strand, which was much frequented by Parliament men and gallants. One time Colonel Bettridge being there (one of the handsomest men about the town) and bragged how much the women loved him. Sir H. Blount did lay a wager with him that 'let them two go together to a bordello; he only (without money) with his handsome person, and Sir Henry with a twenty-shilling piece on his bald crown, that the wenches should choose Sir Henry before Bettridge'. Sir H. won the wager.

Sir Humphrey Mildmay, rich, gregarious and jovial, the second of whose fifteen children was Master of the King's Jewel House, was also in London enjoying himself at this time, drinking cheerfully in taverns with his brothers and other Parliamentarians, as well as with fellow-Royalists, going to the theatres which were not yet closed, larking about with bawds and harlots, 'a-playing with punks [whores] on the Thames till towards midnight', taking pleasure in ignoring the fast days appointed by Mr Pym.

★

As the weeks passed, however, the prevailing mood in London grew more grim. Shops were poorly stocked; the houses of suspected Royalist sympathizers were regularly searched; food was expensive, and with a population of over 350,000 to feed, often in short supply. Moreover, since Newcastle was blockaded, coal was almost unobtainable except at exorbitant prices, well above those fixed by Parliamentary ordinances. 'Some fine-nosed city dames,' one Londoner wrote sardonically, 'used to tell their husbands: "Oh husband! we shall never be well, we nor our children, whilst we live in the smell of this city's seacoal smoke. Pray, a country house for our health, that we may get out of this stinking seacoal smell." But – how many of these fine-nosed dames now cry, "Would to God we had seacoal! O the want of fire undoes us! O the sweet seacoal fire we used to have."'

Not only did citizens have to pay more for coal and food, but they were repeatedly being asked for money for the furtherance of the Parliamentary cause and the war's unfortunate victims. They were also asked to pay two shillings for passes to move in and out of the city. Outspoken opponents of Parliament were imprisoned without trial, and their property confiscated. At the beginning of December 1642 there was a noisy demonstration outside Haberdashers' Hall where a Parliamentary committee was discussing methods of taxation. Crowds of people, angered by the disruption in trade and loss of employment which the war was bringing, called out for peace, insulting and jostling known supporters of Parliament. Four days later there was an even rowdier and more violent demonstration outside the Guildhall. To repeated shouts of 'Peace! Peace!' and threats to cut the throats of the Lord Mayor and various prominent Aldermen, a mob attacked the soldiers on guard, wounded several of them and, grabbing hold of their swords, bade the rest go off to a nearby tavern. 'Spend the money you got from the state,' they shouted at them, 'for you shall have no more from us.' Order was restored only when a detachment from one of the city's Trained Bands – upon whose help Parliament and Parliament's staunch Puritan supporter, Isaac Penington, the rich fishmonger and landowner, Gurney's successor as Lord Mayor, could always rely on in times of crisis – marched into Guildhall Yard and dispersed the demonstrators.

In the House of Commons, much reduced in number, Pym and

his supporters, while doing what they could to curb the demands of extremists who were crying out for ever harsher measures, did their best to encourage those who were losing heart and proposing a negotiated settlement. From time to time there came from Oxford a Declaration or Proclamation from the King condemning the unpopular measures of the truncated Parliament, denouncing all who paid duties not imposed by him as guilty of treason, and exacerbating the concern and discontent of Londoners.

But as the weather improved, and as food supplies became more plentiful, the mood of Londoners grew more cheerful and confident; and, as the weeks went by, the city's fortifications became more and more impressive. A ditch nine feet deep and nine feet wide with a rampart nine feet high stretched round the city. There were twenty-four star-shaped forts of rammed earth and stout timber at intervals and, between the forts, there were redoubts, redans and counterscarps. Between them these strong points contained well over two hundred cannon. At all hours of the day, even on Sundays, men could be seen working on forts and ramparts under the direction of Dutch engineers. When they were finished the defences, several miles in length, surrounded not only the city of London but also the areas to the east known as Tower Hamlets and the built-up area south of the river in Southwark, as well as Westminster. William Lithgow, the Scottish traveller who was in London at the time, described how the Londoners were 'wondrous commendable in marching to the fields and outworks (as merchants, silk-men, Macers, Shopkeepers etc) with greate alacritie, carrying on their shoulders iron Mattocks and wooden shovels, with roaring Drummes, flying collours, and girded swords; most companies also interlarded with Ladies, women and girles . . . carrying buckets to advance the labour . . . The greatest company which I observed to march out were the [guild of] Taylours, carrying fourtie six collours, and seconded with eight thousand lusty men. The next in greatest number were the Watermen, amounting to seven thousand Tuggers, carrying thirty-seven collours. The Shoemakers were five thousand . . . The Porters marched forth one day towards Tayburne fields carrying twenty three collours and upon that same day a thousand Oyster wives advanced from Billingsgate through Cheapside to Crabtree field all alone with drummes and flying collours and in a civil manner, their goddess Bellona leading them in a martial way.'

Ladies of rank appeared as well as fishwives, the Lady Mayoress, Abigail Penington, prominent amongst them, brandishing an entrenching tool as a popular ballad described her. Samuel Butler, then a young clerk, and the later author of the satirical poem *Hudibras*, wrote of these women who

> March'd rank and file with drums and ensign,
> T'entrench the City for defence in.
> Raised rampiers with their own soft hands
> To put the enemy to stands;
> From Ladies down to oyster wenches
> Labour'd like pioneers in trenches,
> Fell to their pick-axes and tools,
> And help'd the men to dig like moles.

It was estimated that the members of over fifty trade guilds with their wives and families vied with each other in their zeal as engineers and labourers. As well as the tailors, watermen, shoemakers and porters observed by Lithgow, there were feltmakers and cappers to the number of five thousand and almost the entire company of Vintners. Members of Parliament rolled up their sleeves with lawyers from the Inns of Court who paraded in Covent Garden at seven o'clock in the morning with 'spades, shovels, pickaxes and other necessaries'. At one time, it was estimated that as many as twenty thousand people were at work without pay, drawing only their rations if required.

Since the men of the Trained Bands were reluctant to spare time from work to man the fortifications, seven regiments of Auxiliaries were raised for the purpose, the men in these new regiments being paid by subscription from the citizens at large. By the end of that summer there were more than twenty thousand officers and men under arms in London in the Trained Bands and Auxiliaries, besides two regiments of City Horse.

6

FIGHTING IN THE
WEST COUNTRY

*'They fell to plunder very cruelly for the space
of four hours, insomuch that the poor women
and children did make such a lamentable cry
that they might have been heard half a mile
off, crying, "Murther! Murther!", and yet
could find no pity.'*

Nehemiah Wallington

From beyond London's fortifications – which were never to be of
any use and which have now completely disappeared – there had
come intermittently dispiriting reports of Parliamentary defeats, of
towns upon which the capital relied for supplies being lost to the
enemy. In the north, in Yorkshire, Sir Thomas Fairfax had been
defeated at Tadcaster by the Earl of Newcastle and obliged to retreat
to Selby, eventually being driven back and cut off from the Puritan
towns of the West Riding from which he had been receiving supplies.
In Lancashire, the conceited and heavy-handed James Stanley, the
former Lord Strange, now, since his father's death in September, the
seventh Earl of Derby, had rampaged about from one village to
the next, enforcing the people to what he insisted was their proper
obedience both to the King and, just as imperatively, to the Stanley
family, lords of these parts since the time of Edward II. In the west
the Parliamentary commander, Henry Grey, first Earl of Stamford,
had been obliged to withdraw from Hereford to Gloucester. At Marlborough in Wiltshire, 'a town the most notoriously disaffected of all

that county', Royalist dragoons had burst into the wide high street before dawn on 5 December 1642 and, so the Puritan chronicler Nehemiah Wallington was told, 'ran through the streets with their drawn swords, cutting and slashing those men they met with, whether soldiers or not'.

> They set their houses on fire [Wallington added]. And at the same time their soldiers breaking up of shops and houses, and taking away all sorts of goods, breaking of trunks, chests, boxes, cabinets, bedsteads, cupboards, presses, coffers, and many that were not locked, but yet they would break and dash them all to pieces; and thence rifled and carried away all kinds of wearing apparel, all money or plate they met with, all sorts of shoes and boots, stockings, hats, and woollen and linen cloth of all sorts, sheets, beds, bolster cases, cutting up the cases and scattering the feathers in the streets to be trampled on by horses and men; also searching men's and women's pockets for money, and threatening them with pistols and swords to shoot, or run them through, if that they would not give them money, by which means compelling many men to lead them to the places where they had hid their money.
>
> In their plundering they had no regard to rich or poor, to Roundheads (as they call them) and those that were of the like disposition as themselves, for they pillaged even poor men that live on alms of the town, and beg their bread.

In Cornwall four of the county's leading gentry, including Sir Bevil Grenville, had been joined by the Royalist professional Sir Ralph Hopton from Somerset, and another Somerset gentleman, the ingratiating Sir John Berkeley, later first Baron Berkeley of Stratton. And here in Cornwall at Braddock Down between Liskeard and Lostwithiel, on 19 January 1643, a sprightly force of Cornishmen whom they had raised between them had suddenly appeared from the gorse bushes after a well-directed cannonade. They had driven the Parliamentary troops down to Lostwithiel and through it on the road to Saltash and Plymouth, capturing wagonloads of supplies, hundreds of muskets and four cannon, before withdrawing to Tavistock.

A few weeks later Prince Rupert and the Marquess of Hertford advanced upon Cirencester, intent upon opening up a supply route

to Oxford from the Cotswolds and denying London both its supplies
of wool and its payments of money from the Cotswold towns. As
at Marlborough, the Cavaliers swept into the town; and, although
it was bravely defended by Parliament's soldiers firing from the
upper windows of the houses as well as from the barricades of
wagons and casks pulled across the streets, Cirencester also fell,
together with large stores of arms and provisions and many prisoners
who were marched off to London tied together in pairs.

> Among them was a proper handsome man [recorded Bulstrode
> Whitelocke] with a very white skin, where it could be seen for the
> blood of his wounds. He not being able to go, was set naked on
> the bare back of a horse, his wounds gaping and his body smeared
> with blood; yet he sat upright upon his horse with an undaunted
> countenance, and when a brawling woman cried out after him,
> 'Ah, you traitorly rogue, you are well enough served.' He, with a
> scornful look towards her, answered, 'You base woman,' and
> instantly dropped off dead from his horse.

Prince Rupert followed up his success at Cirencester by advancing
north against Birmingham while the Earl of Northampton, the
former Master of the Robes, advanced upon Stafford. Northampton
was a very rich man who, in Edward Hyde's words, had passed his
life up till now in that 'ease and plenty and luxury which was then
thought necessary to great fortunes'. 'From the beginning of these
distractions', however, as Lord Lieutenant of Warwickshire, he had
'been awakened out of his lethargy. All distresses he bore like a
common man and all wants and hardnesses as if he had never known
plenty or ease.' Having occupied Stafford, he rode out to challenge
a Parliamentary force which was commanded by two baronets from
the Midlands, Sir John Gell and Sir William Brereton.

The two armies clashed outside Stafford around the coal-pits of
Hopton Heath on 19 March. After a fierce fight the Earl of Northampton's troops captured eight of the enemy's guns and drove the
enemy horse off the field; but, leading his men in pursuit, Northampton had his horse killed under him and his helmet was struck
from his head. Surrounded by Roundhead soldiers, he refused to
accept the mercy they offered him. 'I scorn,' he said, 'to accept
quarter from such base rogues as you are.' Provoked by such disdain,

one of the soldiers 'slew him by a blow with a halberd on the hinder part of his head' while another struck him across the face.

The eldest of the Earl's six sons asked for their father's body back, but Gell and Brereton replied that they would comply with the request only in exchange for their captured guns. That Brereton should have behaved so badly caused some surprise. No one, however, expected anything better of Gell. Nor did anyone know what had prompted him to take Parliament's side in the first place, since, according to Lucy Hutchinson, 'he had not understanding to judge the equity of the cause, nor piety, nor holiness, being a foul adulterer all the time he served the Parliament, and so unjust that without any remorse he suffered his men . . . the most licentious, ungovernable wretches that belonged to the Parliament . . . to plunder both honest men and Cavaliers'.

A fortnight after the Earl of Northampton's death on Hopton Heath, Prince Rupert fell upon Birmingham, a small, staunchly Puritan town, 'echoing with the noise of anvils', where swords were made for Parliament. So decidedly, indeed, were its inhabitants on Parliament's side that two Royalist agents who came to Birmingham with ready money to buy swords for the King were immediately arrested and thrown into gaol. Prince Rupert's force consisted of six to seven hundred foot and 1,200 horse, among them, serving as a volunteer though in his sixties, the Earl of Denbigh, soon to be mortally wounded. They charged into the place 'like so many Furies and Bedlams', shouting and singing, shooting at the windows of the houses, leaping over hedges and ditches in pursuit of their prey, galloping down 'the long pretty street called Dirtey [now Deritend], cursing and damning, threatening and terrifying the poore Women most terribly, setting Naked Swords and Pistols to their breasts'. The Birmingham men, led by an intrepid clergyman, responded bravely, returning the Cavaliers' shouts with cries of their own, 'Cursed dogs!' 'Devilish Cavaliers!' 'Popish traitors!' Their resistance, however, was soon overcome and, in the words of a Parliamentary tract which does not differ essentially from Royalist admissions, 'they fell to plundering all the Town, picking purses, and pockets, searching in holes and corners, Tiles of houses, Wells, Pooles, Vaults, Gardens and every other place they could suspect for money or goods, forcing people to deliver all the money they had'.

They beastly assaulted many Womens chastity [this tract continued], and impudently made their brags of it afterwards, how many they had ravished; glorying in their shame . . . were outrageously lascivious and letcherous . . . That night few or none went to Bed, but sate up revelling, robbing, and Tyranising over the poore affrighted Women and Prisoners, drinking drunke, healthing upon their knees, yea, drinking drunk Healths to Prince Rupert's Dog.

Nor did their Rage here cease, but when on the next day they were to march forth of the Towne, they used all possible diligence in every Streete to kindle fire in the Towne with Gunpowder, Match, Wispes of Straw, and Besomes, burning coales of fire, etc., flung into Straw, Hay, Kid piles [bundles of faggots], Coffers, Thatch and any other places, where it was likely to catch hold . . .

A minister who was said to have declared that the King was a papist and that he would 'rather die than live under such a King' was cut down and killed in the street. The people of the town said he was a lunatic and had only recently come out of a madhouse. A number of 'idle and foolish papers' were found on him, including a memorandum with the words, '28 March. A comfortable kiss from Mrs E . . . with some moistness. A cynamon kiss from a noted woman. A kiss from a girl 14 years old.' The Roundheads said this memorandum proved him to be mad.

One particular more I cannot pass [Nehemiah Wallington added to this catalogue of horrors] there was in Birmingham an old bachelor of almost fourscore years of age, he had much gold lay by him, as it was generally spoken: He was a great man for the King, and spent most of his time in arguing against this unnatural war. But when Prince Rupert had taken the town, the first man he called for was this old man, and at the first salute, he told him he was a man most pernicious and adverse to the King's Majesty, and his party. The old man, kneeling upon his knees, answered he was the most forward in the town for the King, and had made it his work to plead his cause. At which words a Cavalier took him by the throat, giving him a small prick on the side, saying, 'You old dog, you have three thousand pound which we must have, or your throat shall be cut.' The old man they dragged along to his lodging, who, for fear of death, opened a place in the wall, and brought them out eight hundred pound; but they were not satisfied with this, nor was his throat ever the further from cutting, but held the knife there and gave another prick, which brought out of another place five hundred pound more; but this was not enough, he had still the knife at his throat. At last he fell down upon his knees, taking a deep protestation that he had not ten groats more in all the world, and then they let him go with his life.

Before the flames were extinguished about eighty houses in Birmingham had been burned to the ground. As though this were not punishment enough, a large fine was imposed upon the townspeople, part of which they paid in stockings and shoes, commodities always much in demand in both armies since the inadequate footwear commonly issued to the soldiers soon wore out after long marches on rough roads. The Royalists also took money from the prisoners they had taken, charging them for their freedom, obtaining no more than a few pence for the poorer captives but getting a pound for one or two of the better off.

Later the Royalists plundered the town again, having first surrounded it so that no one could escape. 'They fell to plunder very cruelly for the space of four hours,' wrote Nehemiah Wallington, 'insomuch that the poor women and children did make such a lamentable cry that they might have been heard half a mile off, crying, "Murther! Murther!", and yet could find no pity.' The Royalists 'carried away all that they could lay hands on that was worth the carrying away', plundering Thomas Gisborne's shop of cloth, and Francis Millard's of ironware, pillaging also Widow Weyman, 'a godly poor woman that was gone that night to Coventry, and Widow Greaves, another godly poor woman. They took all she had from her and turned her out into the street in her bare smock and bare-legged. They also plundered William Allen, a shoemaker, and Widow Simmons, whose children were pulled out of their beds, and their bedding and clothes taken from under them, and many more, too tedious to set down the particulars, these being the least of their cruelties.'

From Birmingham, Prince Rupert moved on to Lichfield. Here the Roundheads, having taken the place from the Royalists and having lost Lord Brooke in the process, had established themselves in the Cathedral Close where the houses, surrounded by a deep ditch, had been turned into small fortresses and the cathedral tower had become an artillery battery, the cathedral itself having been desecrated with exceptional vigour, even the records being destroyed, the gravestones stripped of their brasses, the tombs broken open and their contents scattered. So impressed was Rupert by the defences of Lichfield Close that he decided not to make an immediate assault. He sent to the coal-mines at Cannock Chase for a party of experienced colliers and, with their help, dug beneath the works. On 21 March a tremendous explosion rocked the whole of Lichfield. The Cavaliers charged into the Close and, after suffering heavy casualties, secured yet another town for the Royalist cause.

Nor was it only on land that the Royalists were successful. It was one of the King's principal disadvantages in the war that he had failed to keep control of his navy as well as his main dockyard and magazine at Chatham. But he did at least have at his disposal the ships of West Country Royalists, while several key ports were in his hands elsewhere, including Chichester and Newcastle. He could also rely on the support of the governors of the Channel Islands, the Scilly Isles and Lundy Island; and the Isle of Man was firmly in the hands of the Earl of Derby.

Yet, despite the catalogue of successes which Royalists could cheerfully recite, the fortunes of the Parliamentarians in these early stages of the conflict were by no means all disastrous. Soon after the Cavaliers had taken Marlborough, a force of Roundhead cavalry occupied Winchester where they ransacked the cathedral, cutting up tapestries, burning books and manuscripts and smashing the organ. Then the Roundheads occupied Nantwich in Cheshire; and in Yorkshire, helped by country folk with scythes and pitchforks, they seized Bradford and, with the help of men from the rival town of Halifax, took Leeds, together with nearly five hundred prisoners who were released on swearing never to fight for the King again. The captives were ready enough to take such an oath. The fighting in Yorkshire had disrupted their lives: roads were unsafe; pack-horses could no longer carry their burdens of wool and cloth from fulling mill to market without the danger of being robbed by one side or the other. The poor were hungry; merchants and well-to-do farmers were worried by the consequences of putting arms into the hands of people who might well rise up against them when the troubles were over.

Worried Yorkshiremen asked for news of the peace proposals rumoured to be under discussion.

Negotiations were certainly being carried on, as they were with foreign countries where support was eagerly sought by Parliamentarians and Royalists alike. But neither Pym nor the King was seriously in search of a compromise, both being convinced that the issues must now be settled by force and equally intent upon making use of any temporary cessation of hostilities to enlarge and improve their armies as well as to throw the blame for the failure of peace talks on each other. 'The truth is Parliament is not willing to treat,' the King's Secretary of State, Edward Nicholas, told Prince Rupert, 'but would gladly have the people believe they could not obtain a peace.' The same could be said of the King who – still refusing to consider Parliament's requests that he reform the Church as they wanted and that he give up his control of the army – said as much in an intercepted letter to the Queen whose persistent urging of her husband not to give way to his enemies was, so Edward Hyde thought, largely responsible for his intransigence. Both the King and Pym were obviously hoping that a resounding victory in the field would settle the matter once and for all.

Parliament's forces did not seem at all likely to achieve this victory under the command of their Lord General, the Earl of Essex, who, exasperated by Prince Rupert's cavalry raids, had tried and failed to bring him to formal battle and had then withdrawn first to Reading and then into Bedfordshire, suggesting that either Parliament should sue for peace or that selected units from both armies should be drawn up to oppose each other in a kind of medieval trial by combat.

There was, however, another far more active general coming to Parliament's notice, a general who had already captured Portsmouth, with the help of the Scottish mercenary Sir John Meldrum, who had stormed Farnham Castle in Surrey, retaken Winchester, which his men had thoroughly plundered, and, occupying Arundel Castle on the way, had laid siege to Chichester and forced it to surrender.

This was Sir William Waller, a brave and shrewd officer, though erratic and, on occasions, impetuous. Less confident when directing infantry than when leading a cavalry charge, he was nevertheless an acknowledged master of defensive tactics, respected by his opponents as a brilliant 'shifter and chooser of ground', though never so popular with his men as the Earl of Essex was. The son of Sir

Thomas Waller, from whom he inherited the profitable sinecure of Chief Butler of England, and grandson of Lord Dacre, he had chosen to lead a military life on coming down from Oxford and had entered the Venetian army and seen service in Bohemia and the Palatinate. On returning home he had been admitted to Gray's Inn and had married the first of his three wives, an heiress who brought him a considerable fortune. It was said that he had been prosecuted and heavily fined for striking a member of her family, one of the King's attendants, and that this had produced in him 'so eager a spirit against the Court that he was very open to any temptation that might engage him against it'. Yet he himself declared that his only motives in joining the conflict were prompted by his desire 'to bring things to a fair and peaceable issue, so that there might be a general payment of all duties. That God might have had his fear: the King his honour; the Houses of Parliament their privileges; the people of the Kingdom their liberties and properties; and nothing might have remained upon the score between us, but that debt which must be for ever paying, and ever owing, love.' He later quarrelled with those who had been his companions in arms and worked for the restoration of the monarchy; but, for the moment at least, he was an undoubted Puritan, zealous in that faith as Member of Parliament for Wendover.

After his first brilliant campaign, which earned him the nickname William the Conqueror, Parliament appointed him Sergeant-Major-General of the Western Association, a military formation comprising Roundhead forces in the counties of Gloucestershire, Wiltshire, Somerset, Shropshire and the city of Bristol where he established his headquarters. In March 1643 Waller left Bristol and advanced upon Malmesbury which he took on 21 March. Three days later, having crossed the Severn by a hastily made bridge of boats and marched through the Forest of Dean, he surprised a Royalist force under Lord Herbert of Raglan on its way from Wales to Gloucester at High Ham in Gloucestershire in the early hours of the morning. He captured 1,500 men as well as wagonloads of arms and ammunition, and went on to take Monmouth, Chepstow and Ross-on-Wye, thus for the moment preventing any further Royalist troops reaching the King from south Wales.

The next month Prince Rupert's brother, Prince Maurice, sent from Oxford in the vain hope that he might reach Lord Herbert in time, came upon Waller at Ripple Field, north of Tewkesbury, surprised him and defeated him. Yet when Prince Maurice was recalled, Waller's triumphant march was soon resumed; and on 25 April he took Hereford and marched on to seize Wardour Castle.

The month before Sir William Waller rode out of his headquarters at Bristol, the Queen had landed on the Yorkshire coast. She had set sail from Holland on 2 February 1643; but after nine tempestuously stormy days at sea her ship had been driven back into Scheveningen and she was taken ashore in a fishing smack. It had been a fearful ordeal, bravely borne: she had never expected to see land again. For days on end she had been unable to leave her little cabin; apart from the crew, the only person aboard able even to stand up had been one of her priests who had once served as a Knight of Malta. Her ladies, who had been strapped to their bunks, had been carried ashore too battered, bruised, ill and dizzy to walk, and on landing all their clothing had to be burned. Their only comfort on the way had been their mistress's confident assertion that queens of England were never drowned.

Ten days later they had had to brace themselves for another attempt. On this occasion, although there had been grim warnings from the Queen's astrologers, they had had a perfect crossing and arrived unscathed on the Yorkshire coast at Bridlington, where they had seen the Queen to bed in a thatched cottage on the quayside. But their troubles had not ended; for Bridlington had come under bombardment from Parliamentary ships in the bay and they had had to fly from the village into the open, snow-covered fields inland, abandoning the Queen's little dog whose intrepid mistress had run back to save it, then plunged into a ditch as the bullets flew over her head. 'Tell me now by what road I may come to join you,' the Queen had written to her husband as soon as she was safe. 'I will not repeat that I am in the greatest impatience in the world to join you.'

It could not be doubted that she was. Her letters from Holland had been full of her desire to come back to him. 'I do not wish to remain in this country,' she had complained. 'I need the air of England, or at least the air where you are.' Her eyes had been giving her pain ever since she had landed on the Continent, and she could not decide whether this was the Dutch atmosphere, all the writing she had to do, or the tears that were 'weighing them down sometimes'.

She had sold or pawned what jewels she could, the Dutch merchants showing themselves wary of negotiating for the big pieces but giving her something – though but half what they were worth – for the smaller ones; and she had raised almost £100,000, and obtained two thousand cases of pistols as well as the services of several professional soldiers. This duty done, she had longed desperately to return.

It was not just that she had wanted to be with her husband again; she did not trust him to stand firm when she was away from him. She had dared not think what advice was swaying that moody, impressionable nature, and had felt it necessary to remind him constantly of his duty to their family and his promises to herself: 'I hope that you are constant in your resolutions; you have already learnt to your cost that want of perseverance in your designs has ruined you . . . My whole hope lies in your firmness and constancy, and when I hear anything to the contrary, I am mad . . . Delays have always ruined you. Take a good resolution and pursue it . . . It is not enough to declare yourself in writing; actions must afterwards be seen.'

Although she understood her husband's weaknesses well enough, her counsel to him in his adversity was rarely as realistic as she fancied; and, now that she had returned to England, Charles's more responsible advisers had cause to be apprehensive.

For the first few months, however, she had remained in the north, first at York in Sir Arthur Ingram's grand house near the Minster, then riding with Newcastle's army, priding herself on her hardihood, styling herself 'Generalissima', as, with her intimate friend, the indispensable though rather disreputable and none too scrupulous Henry Jermyn as colonel of her guards, she led 'three thousand foot, thirty companies of horses and dragoons . . . with a hundred and fifty waggons of baggage to govern in case of battle'. It was not until July, after inducing Parliament's Governor of Scarborough to change sides, that, slipping past the cavalry that Essex had sent to intercept her, she came south with an escort of 4,500 men under the command of another of her admirers, the Hon. Charles Cavendish, the King's godson, son of the Earl of Devonshire. She came through Ashby de la Zouch and King's Norton, to Stratford-upon-Avon where she stayed the night at New Place, the handsome house of William Shakespeare's granddaughter.

The King, accompanied by their two elder children, greeted her at Edgehill, a meeting place which many understandably considered

John Pym, one of the King's leading opponents in Parliament. Miniature by Samuel Cooper

Prince Rupert, the King's cavalry commander, aged twenty-two at the outbreak of war. Painting attributed to Gerard Honthorst

THE
Exercise of the English, in the Militia of the Kingdome of
ENGLAND.

ABOVE: Pikemen marching to battle led by a fifer and a drummer

LEFT: The title page of a tract depicting militiamen of the 1640s

The Earl of Essex, the son of Queen Elizabeth's courtier, was appointed to the command of Parliament's army in July 1642

ABOVE: The plunder of a
Royalist's house and the felling
of trees in his park, by George
Cattermole (1800–1868)

RIGHT: Sir William Waller,
the Roundhead General.
From a portrait attributed to
Edward Bower

OPPOSITE ABOVE: An early-nineteenth-century plan showing Parliament's defences encircling London in 1642–43 and comprising twenty-four forts and eighteen miles of linked trenches

OPPOSITE BELOW: The King raised his standard in a high wind in Nottingham on 27 August 1642

ABOVE: George, Lord Goring, the unpredictable and often drunk Royalist General. Engraving from a portrait by Van Dyck

George, Lord Digby, the Royalist general and close friend of the King and Queen. From a portrait by Justus van Egmont

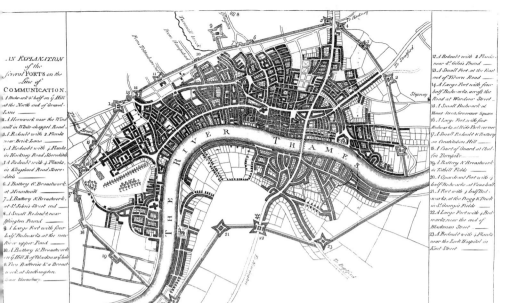

A PLAN of the City and Environs of LONDON as fortified by Order of PARLIAMENT in the Years 1642 & 1643.

Nottingham

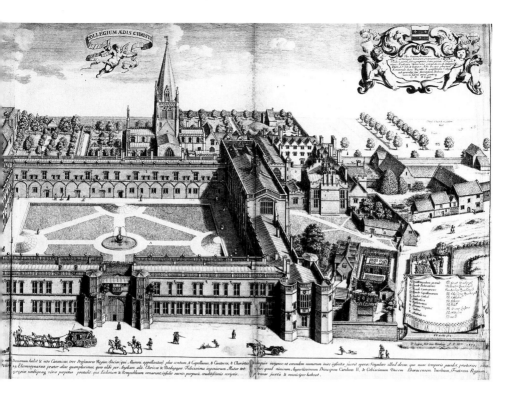

ABOVE: Christ Church, Oxford, where the King lived in the deanery, his parliament assembled in the hall, his privy council in the canonical lodgings, and the weddings and funerals of members of his court took place in the cathedral

RIGHT: A broadsheet of 1642 attacking 'The English Irish soldier' who would rather Bate [plunder] than Fight'

LEFT: Officers directing the fighting at the Battle of Edgehill on 23 October 1642. From a stylized representation by Van der Gucht

THE ENGLISH IRISH SOVLDIER:
With his new Discipline, new Armes, Old Stomacks, and new taken pillage : who had rather Bate then Fight.

IF any Souldate
think I do appeare,
In this strange Armes
and posture,as a jeere,
Let him advance up to me
he shall see,
Ile stop his mouth,
and we wil both agree.

Our Skirmish ended,
our Enemies fled or slain
Pillage wee cry then,
for the Souldiers gaine,
And this compleat Artillery
I have got,
The best of Souldiers,
I think, hateth not.

My Martiall Armes
dealt I amongst my foes,
With this I charged stand
'gainst hungers blowes ;
This is Munition
if a Souldier lacke,
He fights like Iohn a dreams,
or Lents thin Iacke.

All safe and cleare,
my true Arms rest a while,
And welcome pillage,
you have foes to foile ;
This Pot, my Helmet,
must not be forsaken,
For loe I seiz'd it
full of Hens and Bacon.

Rebels for Rebels drest it,
but our hot rost,
Made them to flye,
and now they kisse the post
And better that to kisse,
then stay for Pullits,
And have their bellies
cram'd with leaden bullets.

This fowle my Feather is,
who wins most fame,
To weare a pretty Duck,
he need not shame ;
This Spit my well charg'd
Musket, with a Goose,
Now cryes come eate me,
let your stomacks loose.

This Dripping pan's my
target,and this Hartichoke
My Basket-hilted blade,
can make 'em smoake,
And make them flash & cut,
who most Home puts,
Ile most my fury
sheath into his guns.

This Forke my Rest is,
and my Bandaleers
Canary Bottles,
that can quell bafe feares,
And make us quaffe downe
danger, if this not doe,
What is it then can raise
a spirit into fearfull men.

This Match are linkes
to light down to my belly
Wherin are darksom chinks
as I may tell yee,
Or Saffages, or Puddings,
choose you which,
An excellent Needle ,
Hungers wounds to stitch.

These my Supporters,
garter'd with black pots,
Can steele the nose,
& purg the brain of plots;
These tofts my shooestrings,
sleept in this strong fog,
Is abl' of themselves
to foxe a Dog.

These Armes being vanisht,
once againe appeare
A true and faithful Souldier
As you were ;
But if this wants,
and that we have no biting
In our best Armours
we make sorry fighting.

FINIS.

Printed at *London* for *R. Wood*,
and *A. Coe*. 1642.

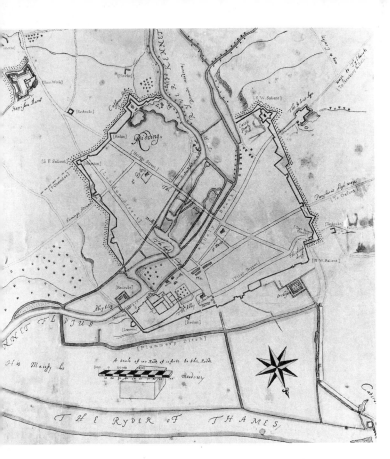

A plan of the fortifications
of Reading in 1643

'The exact Order in which
several Bodies of Infantry &
Cavalry were drawn up
Preparatory to the Battle of
Naseby fought the 14th of
June 1643'

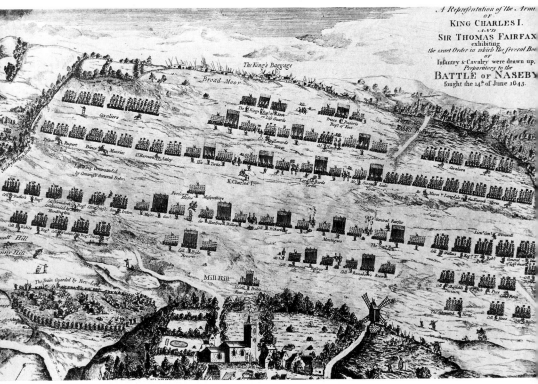

might have been more sensitively chosen, cheerfully granting her first request that Henry Jermyn should be given a peerage. Delighted to be with her again, and to be presented with the troops and supplies she had brought with her, Charles rode back with her to Oxford where the Warden's lodgings at Merton College had been set aside for her.

They arrived in Oxford on 14 July to be greeted with the news of a brilliant Royalist victory, the latest in a series of encouraging successes. Two months before, in the West Country, Sir Ralph Hopton's Cornishmen had charged against the Earl of Stamford's Roundheads near Stratton, three miles inland from Bude. They had been on short rations for several days; but they were, in Hopton's words, 'the handsomest body of men that had been gotten together in those parts all that warr', and were 'verie well contented with a drie biscuit apiece for want of other provisions' when, after prayers had been read at the head of every division, they marched up the hill towards the enemy. Time and again they were driven back by the Roundheads' superior numbers; and by three o'clock in the afternoon their powder was all but exhausted. Concealing this from the men, Hopton ordered one last charge with sword and pike; and this time, making their way forward in four columns, they reached the top of the hill, driving the enemy off after the fiercest of struggles, embracing each other 'with unspeakable joy, each congratulating the other's success'.

'Dearest Soule,' one of the victorious Cavaliers wrote to his wife, 'Oh Deare Soule, prayse God everlastingly. Reede ye enclosed. Ring out yr Bells. Rayse Bonefyers, publish these Joyfull Tydings . . . Excuse my writing larger. I have not tyme. We march on . . . to sease all ye Rebells left if we can ffinde such Lyvinge . . .'

They had taken 1,700 prisoners – including one of Stamford's best officers, James Chudleigh, the young son of a Devon landowner who was persuaded to change sides – as well as all the enemy's baggage, thirteen barrels of sorely needed powder and thirteen cannon. Three hundred enemy lay dead upon the field and so much blood had been spilled that the local people used to declare that the battlefield, afterwards sown with barley, produced sixty bushels of corn in every acre, 'the fertility whereof being ascribed to the virtue the land received from the blood of the slain men and horses and the trampling of their feet in this battle'.

Stamford had withdrawn as far as Exeter; and Hopton, in close pursuit, had galloped into Totnes and, finding it a market day, had made the most of his opportunity to help himself to a large number of horses. He had gone triumphantly on towards Taunton, while another Royalist force, commanded by Prince Maurice and the Marquess of Hertford, had been sent out from Oxford to join forces with him, obliging Sir William Waller to abandon the siege of Worcester, which had once again been occupied by the Royalists, and to retreat to Wells as fast as his men could march.

The two Royalist armies met at Chard in Somerset on 4 June. Hopton had his three thousand sturdy Cornish infantry under his command as well as about five hundred cavalry and three hundred dragoons, Prince Maurice some fifteen hundred cavalry and a thousand foot. Waller's Roundhead army was of roughly the same strength as these two Cavalier forces combined. For days on end the two sides manoeuvred around each other in the country outside Bath, each endeavouring to place the other at a disadvantage and neither succeeding. On 16 June, Hopton wrote to Waller to suggest that they meet under a flag of truce to discuss, amongst other things, a possible exchange of captured prisoners. The two men knew each other well. They were much of an age; they were both the sons of country gentlemen; they had served together on the Continent. Waller thought it as well to refuse the interview, giving his reasons in a moving letter which well expresses a common regret:

> The experience I have had of your worth, and the happiness I have enjoyed in your friendship, are wounding considerations when I look upon this present distance between us. Certainly my affections to you are so unchangeable that hostility itself cannot violate my friendship to your person, but I must be true to the cause wherein I serve . . . That great God, which is the searcher of my heart, knows with what sad sense I go upon this service, and with what a perfect hatred I detest this war without an enemy . . . The God of Peace in his good time send us peace and in the meantime fit us to receive it; we are both upon the stage, and must act the parts assigned to us in this tragedy. Let us do it in a way of honour and without personal animosities. Whatever the issue be, I shall never willingly relinquish the dear title of, Your most affectionate friend.

A few days later the two men were in battle. Waller had drawn his Roundheads up in a commanding position just north of Bath, on a wooded, steep-sided ridge about three miles long known as Landsdown Hill. On the lower ground, covered by the enemy's field guns, their barrels sharply depressed to enable them to fire down the steep slope, the Royalists waited, hoping to entice Waller to come down and fight. For much of the morning and throughout the early hours of the afternoon the two armies held their ground, the Round-heads behind breastworks of earth and the branches of trees which they had cut down the night before, the Cavaliers in a large field beneath them. As though he had decided not to risk an encounter, Hopton began to withdraw his troops towards Marshfield at about three o'clock in the afternoon. Observing this manoeuvre, Waller sent several troops of horse charging down the hill, while dragoons quickly occupied the hedges on either side of their advance. The Royalist cavalry were thrown back by this sudden assault; but the Cornish infantry behind them held their ground, and soon the whole Cavalier army rallied and moved forward again, driving back the Roundheads, only a few of whom succeeded in regaining the top of the hill.

Encouraged by this success and racked by the enemy's artillery fire, the Cornish infantry, so a Royalist captain said, cried out, 'Let us fetch those cannon!' Soon they were charging up the slope, dodging between the hedges and seeking what shelter they could find behind low stone walls. Many fell to the heavy musket fire, but the breath-less survivors struggled on.

> As I went up the hill which was very steep [wrote Richard Atkyns who was coming up behind them], I met several dead and wounded officers brought off, besides several running away that I had much ado to get by them. When I came to the top of the hill I saw Sir Bevill Grinvill's stand of pikes . . . They stood as upon the Eaves of an House for steepness, but as unmoveable as a Rock. I could not discover on which side of the Pikes our Horse were, for the air was so darkened by the smoke of the powder that for a quarter of an hour together (I dare say) there was no light seen but what the fire of the volleys of shot gave; and 'twas the greatest storm that ever I saw, in which I knew not whither to go nor what to do. My horse had two or three bullet holes in him which made him tremble

under me and I could hardly with spurs keep him from lying down.

Three times the Roundhead horse charged the Cornish pikemen and three times were driven off, 'cannon on both sides playing without ceasing, Legs and Armes flying apace'; and in the third charge Sir Bevil Grenville was mortally wounded by a blow on the head from a pole-axe. But by then victory had been assured. Waller's exhausted men withdrew behind a long stone wall, and slowly darkness fell.

Behind the wall fires could be seen flickering in the night. But there were no accompanying sounds; and Hopton's patrols came back to report that the Roundhead position had been abandoned: the lights came from matchcords left burning on the ends of pikes stuck through the branches of hedges. Waller had taken Parliament's army back into Bath, leaving the Royalists 'seated like a heavy stone upon the very brow of the hill which with one lustye charge might well have been rowl'd to the bottome'.

Left in possession of the field, the Royalists could claim the victory; yet it was a victory expensively bought. Most of their cavalry had disappeared; the Cornishmen, mourning the death of Sir Bevil Grenville, let it be known that they were anxious to go home; food was in short supply; so was ammunition. Grenville's friend, Sir John Trelawny, wrote a letter to his widow:

> Seeing it hath pleased God to take him from your Ladyship, yet this may something appease yr great fluxe of tears, that he died an Honourable Death, wch all Enemies will Envy, fighting with Invincible Valour, and Loyalty ye Battle of his God, his King, and his Country. A greater Honour than this, no man living can enjoy. But God hath called him unto himselfe, to Crowne him with Immortall Glory for his noble Constancye in this Blessed Cause.

The day after the battle a powder wagon exploded, killing a number of senior officers and bystanders and badly wounding many others.

> It made a very great noise [Richard Atkyns recorded], and darkened the air for a time, and the hurt men made lamentable screeches. As soon as the air was clear, I went to see what the matter was; there

I found his Lordship [Hopton] miserably burnt, his horse singed like parched leather, and [Major] Thomas Sheldon (that was a horse lengths further from the blast) complaining that the fire was got within his breeches, which I tore off as soon as I could. And from as long a flaxen head of hair as ever I saw, in the twinkling of an eye, his head was like a blackamoor. His horse was hurt, and run away like mad, so that I put him upon my horse, and got two troopers to hold him up on both sides, and bring him to the head-quarters [where] there was nothing but a cart provided for him and as soon as he was put in there he immediately died.

Hopton, who had already been shot through the arm, was temporarily blinded by the blast as well as badly burned. His face covered with bandages, 'having hardly so much life as not to be numbered with the dead', he was taken to Devizes which his dispirited army occupied, while Waller, his own men reinforced from the Parliamentary garrison at Bristol, marched out of Bath and took up position with his cannon on an eminence known as Roundway Down just north of the small market town of Devizes.

His bandaged head propped up on a pillow, Hopton gave his orders from his sickbed: he would attempt to hold Devizes until help came, but help must come quickly; Prince Maurice, the Marquess of Hertford and the Earl of Carnarvon were to take the remains of the cavalry and to ride for all their worth to Oxford for reinforcements.

They galloped off that night, making at first as though for Andover to confuse Parliament's spies, then swinging north-east, covering over fifty miles before morning. Richard Atkyns was with them at first; but, as he wrote:

My horse had cast two shoes, and I was forced to stay behind to set them at Lambourne, where leaning against a post, I was so sleepy that I fell down like a log of wood, and could not be awakened for half an hour: 'twas impossible then to overtake them; so I went to Farringdon, being not able to reach Oxford that Night; I fell off my horse back twice upon the downs, before I came to Farringdon, where I reeled upon my horse so extremely that the people of the town took me to be dead drunk: when I came to my house (for there I sometimes lived) I desired my wife's aunt to provide a·bed for me; the good woman took me to be drunk too, and provided a bed for me presently, where I slept at least fourteen hours together without waking.

The others reached Oxford early on the morning of 11 July to find that Prince Rupert had left not long before to escort the Queen through the Midlands. The King, who had already sent Lord Wilmot with one brigade to Hopton's help, could therefore spare only one other which he sent after Wilmot under the command of Sir John Byron. In all, when Wilmot and Byron met at Marlborough and were joined there by Prince Maurice, they had fewer than two thousand horse between them, a markedly smaller force than that commanded by Waller, whose infantry also far outnumbered the Royalists.

The Royalists' plight in Devizes was lamentable. Their provisions and powder were running out; they were so short of ammunition that they were reduced to tearing off roofs and guttering to melt down for bullets and to boiling in resin the ropes that supported the beds of the inhabitants to make into match for the cannon. In the warm summer weather the rain poured drearily down; Sir Ralph Hopton was still suffering from his wounds. Another day or two and all would have been over with them.

But the quickness of the Royalist cavalry's response took Waller by surprise. Wilmot attacked his hastily reassumed positions on Roundway Down without hesitation, even though most of his men had just ridden well over fifty miles from Oxford. They charged headlong through the Roundhead ranks and, supported by Byron, drove the Parliamentary cavalry before them, unhorsing several of Haselrig's 'Lobsters', including Sir Arthur himself, whose strong shell of armour saved him from pistol shots and swinging sword blades alike. Leaving Haselrig for dead inside his carapace, the Royalist cavalry sped on, the enemy horse flying before them, many of them tumbling over a hidden escarpment to perish in what became known as 'Bloody Ditch'. The Roundhead infantry also fled, chased off the field by Hopton's Cornishmen who had run up from Devizes to attack them in the rear. Over thirty Parliamentary standards fell into Royalist hands, as well as all Waller's field guns and baggage and most of his ammunition. Hundreds of prisoners were taken. Hundreds more men lay dead and wounded.

Waller took the dispirited remnants of his army back to Bristol, then on to Gloucester and Evesham, chased and harried all the way by Prince Rupert who had returned from his escort in the Midlands to play his part in the humiliation of Parliament's Western Association. Blaming the Earl of Essex for having let the Royalist cavalry get through to him from Oxford, Waller now rode to London to explain his defeat to Parliament.

Essex refused to take the blame. He had troubles enough of his own at Reading. He had been forced into inactivity for weeks by a fever raging amongst his troops, most of whom were also unpaid. In the second week in June, hoping to take advantage of the weakened state of the Oxford garrison, he had moved north. But warned of his belated movements by a deserter from the Parliamentary army, Prince Rupert had forestalled them. He had surprised one of Waller's outposts at Postcombe in the early hours of 18 June, and at dawn he had attacked a party of Parliamentary recruits in the nearby village of Chinnor, shooting or cutting down fifty of them as they tried to escape and taking over a hundred prisoners. That same day, during a short and savage engagement at Chalgrove Field between Thame and Abingdon, his troopers had mortally wounded John Hampden, one of Parliament's shrewdest, most energetic and attractive leaders, a man respected even by his enemies. Hampden was observed to 'ride off the field before the action was done, which he never used to do, with his head hanging down, and resting his hands upon the neck of his horse'.

'Poor Hampden is dead,' wrote one of his friends after the wounded man had endured six days of agony at Thame. 'I have scarce strength to write the word. Never kingdom received greater loss in one subject. Never man a truer and faithfuller friend.'

As though paralysed by this loss, Essex remained inactive while Cavalier raiding parties plundered the villages and small towns of the Chilterns almost at will, riding off with cattle and sheep and such provisions as the inhabitants had had no opportunity to conceal, and approaching as close to London as West Wycombe which was looted by the troopers of Sir John Urry, a Scottish mercenary who, ever ready to change his allegiance, had fought in Parliament's army at Edgehill and was later to serve them again.

The House of Commons, alarmed by the Cavaliers' close approach, exasperated by the Earl of Essex's apparent inability to stop the plundering, and urged on by nervous citizens, demanded that their military commander do something positive. Essex grumpily replied that if they would pay his soldiers, cure their sickness, and stop them deserting, he might be able to do so. As it was he could not. He threatened to resign.

In the meantime there came depressing news from the north where Sir Thomas Fairfax and his father had been defeated outside Bradford on Adwalton Moor on 30 June 1643. Here the Fairfaxes' horse had at first been successful against the cavalry of the far larger Royalist force under the Earl of Newcastle, the rich and generous dilettante, skilled horseman, graceful dancer, indifferent playwright and execrable poet. The Royalists had been on the verge of withdrawal when one of Newcastle's infantry commanders, Posthumous Kirton, 'a wild and desperate man' who had had long experience of Continental warfare, brought his pikemen against the Roundhead musketeers and sent them scattering in all directions, while Newcastle's artillery devastated the Fairfaxes' cavalry. Sir Thomas Fairfax managed to rally some of the cavalry and retreated to Bradford where the townspeople tried to protect the steeple of their church by placing wool-packs against its sides. But the Royalists 'cut the cords with their spiteful shot and shouted full loudly when the packs fell down'.

Unable to hold Bradford, Fairfax gave orders for a general withdrawal of his troops from the town where John Lister, a sixteen-year-old apprentice, on entering it to look for his master's wife who had disappeared during fighting near Colne, found 'few people left in the place and most of them scattered and fled away'.

> I lodged in a cellar that night [Lister recalled], but oh! what a change was made in the town in three days time! Nothing was left to eat or drink, or lodge upon, the streets being full of chaff and feathers and meal, the enemies having emptied all the town of what was worth carrying away, and were now sat down and encamped near Bowling-Hall, and there kept a fair and sold the things that would sell.
>
> In the morning I crept out of the poor cellar where I lay and walked in the street to enquire after my dame. At last I heard that she and my mother were both well and gone the day before to Halifax. The women were gathering meal in the streets. For when the soldiers found anything that was better than meal they emptied

the sacks and put that which was better into them. So that there was good store of meal thrown out both in the houses and streets.

Fairfax made for Leeds, followed by his intrepid wife who insisted upon accompanying him on his campaigns and was now captured in her carriage on the highway but was sent back to her husband by the compassionate Lord Newcastle.

When Fairfax joined his father in Leeds the garrison there was attacked and overwhelmed by hundreds of Royalist prisoners who had escaped from the town's prison; and the Fairfaxes were forced to abandon the town as they had abandoned Bradford and to ride away for the safety of Hull.

The Royalists were now in undisputed control of the West Riding. A messenger bringing this gloomy news to Parliament arrived in London at the beginning of July.

The atmosphere in London was already gloomy enough. In May Parliament had uncovered an elaborate plot to seize the City for the King. Lady d'Aubigny, the handsome, spirited widow of the King's cousin who had been killed at Edgehill, came to London, letting it be known that she had family business to attend to. She had brought with her the King's Commission of Array which was to be read out by Royalist sympathizers as soon as the Cavaliers began their march on London. At the same time the Tower of London and various other buildings and magazines of arms and powder were to be captured, while several leading Parliamentarians were to be taken from their beds into custody, including Pym and the Lord Mayor. All this and more was discovered when a leading conspirator, Edmund Waller, the poet and Member of Parliament for St Ives, was arrested and closely questioned. He confessed immediately, incriminating others to save himself. Lady d'Aubigny was brought to the Tower where her indignant hauteur exasperated her examiners, who eventually allowed her to go. Edmund Waller was also released after a term of imprisonment, the payment of a large fine, and in consideration of his betrayal of his fellow conspirators, two of whom, Waller's brother-in-law and a well-known City linen draper named Tomkins, were hanged.

Although the success of the plot had never been remotely plausible, for a time Parliament had believed itself in danger. A new oath of loyalty was imposed upon its Members and upon all men whose positions of authority were deemed to require it. A day of public thanksgiving was decreed for the deliverance of London from its peril, while a close watch was kept upon suspected Royalists who had escaped implication in this conspiracy but who might become involved in others. Several were arrested and taken to prisons from which some were later removed for tighter security to ships on the river, demands being made by the more rabid republicans that they should be sold as slaves in the West Indies. Rumours of intended coups and uprisings, as well as of conspiracies, abounded; and they were not all idle. In the middle of July there were riots in Kent where armed men broke into the houses of well-to-do Parliamentarians and seized guns from Parliament's ships in the Thames. Sir Henry Vane, Treasurer of the Navy, who lived nearby, protested to the men who immediately carried him off a prisoner and continued with their looting. 'We must plunder none but Roundheads,' one of them warned; but then another shouted, 'We will make every man a Roundhead that hath anything to lose.'

These particular troubles were soon over and Vane was released; yet other problems facing Parliament seemed insuperable. Convoys of wagons bringing food into London were frequently waylaid; prices in the markets were impossible to control; a purchase tax on sugar, beer, wine, leather and various other commodities to help pay for the crippling cost of the army and navy raised widespread protests; the creation of a Council of War of twenty-five members to take decisions formerly taken by the more representative but unwieldly Committee of Safety provoked fears of a dictatorship more autocratic than that of the monarchy. The arguments between those like the Earl of Essex's cousin, the Earl of Holland, who were for coming to terms with the King and his friends straight away, and those such as Henry Marten, the fiery Member for Berkshire, who demanded the most forceful stand against them, grew ever more bitter and cantankerous. Henry Marten, in particular, was a thorn in Pym's side. The son of a rich lawyer, Marten was described by John Aubrey as 'a great lover of pretty girls to whom he was so liberal that he spent the greatest part of his estate' upon them, and by the King, more bluntly, as 'an ugly rascal and whore-master'. One of the most extreme members of the war party in the House of Commons, he performed with evident relish his duties as a member of a committee appointed to destroy superstitious and idolatrous monuments and images. This committee of which Marten was so zealous a member soon saw to it that stained glass was smashed and the heads of statues knocked off in Westminster Abbey, St Margaret's and elsewhere, that the images in the Queen's Chapel at Somerset House were defaced, and a fine Rubens over the high altar was torn down and thrown into the Thames. At the same time the Common Council ordered the demolition of Cheapside Cross which had been erected in 1290 by Edward I to mark one of the resting places of the coffin of his beloved wife, Eleanor, on its journey from Northamptonshire to Westminster. Henry Marten is said also to have seized the royal regalia in Westminster Abbey and to have cried out that there 'would be no further use for these toys and trifles'. Sir Simonds D'Ewes described him as a man 'that used to snarl at everybody'. When there fell into his hands a letter which the Earl of Northumberland had written to his wife while negotiating on Parliament's behalf in Oxford, Marten did not hesitate to tear it open and read it. Northumberland upbraided him for his conduct; Marten retorted that he was 'no whit sorry'; Northumberland hit him over the head with his cane.

Exasperated by such squabbles between Members of Parliament, Pym had also to contend with the quarrels of his military commanders. At first he felt inclined to censure Essex for the disasters in the West Country; but when Waller arrived in London to the cheers of the crowd and was greeted by the extremists as the man destined to lead Parliament undeviatingly to victory, he realized the danger of abandoning Essex who, also in London at this time, made clear that he had powerful friends in the House of Lords and good cause to resent the attacks made upon him by his rivals.

Angered by criticisms of his leadership and annoyed by crude caricatures of him holding a glass of wine and complacently puffing at his pipe which were scrawled on walls all over London, Essex again threatened to resign. Demanding an enquiry into the causes of the débâcle on Roundway Down, he insisted that he could not possibly have been expected to do more than he had done so long as his troops were sick and hungry and, what was more, unpaid.

Pym did his best to conciliate Essex, to dissuade him from lending his still considerable influence to the proponents of peace, to encourage him to stand firm against Marten's strident championship of

Waller as supreme commander. Essex was mollified; but he still did not get the reinforcements he really required. When he returned to Reading that July of 1643 he had no more than three thousand infantry and 2,500 horse fit for duty. Nor did it seem likely that he would get many more men, at least from London. The bellicose Lord Mayor organized a march from the City to Westminster of some five thousand demonstrators shouting, 'No peace! No peace!' But this was followed by a march of hundreds of demonstrators calling for an end to the war. They marched into Palace Yard, white ribbons in their hats, battering on the doors of the House and crying out for Pym and other leading Roundheads to be delivered up to them so that they could all be thrown into the Thames. The guards on duty outside Parliament fired powder at them; but this merely provoked the women who hurled back stones and brickbats. The guards then fired with loaded weapons, killing two men amongst the crowd. Still the women would not disperse. 'Give us that dog Pym,' they cried, undeterred by a party of horse-soldiers who came upon the scene to help the foot. The cavalry laid about them with their swords, at first ineffectively with the flat of the blades, then with the cutting edges until, a few women being wounded, the rest drew back at last, leaving Palace Yard clear except for the body of a maid-servant who 'had nothing to do with the tumult' but 'was shot as she passed over the churchyard. The trooper that did it was sent to the Gate House in order to [stand] trial for her death, but he alleged his pistol went off by mischance.'

The demonstrations were over for the time being; but even from amongst the most vociferous supporters of a war to the death few recruits came forward to swell the numbers of Parliament's army from which on 27 July came news of a further shaming defeat.

7

BRISTOL AND
GLOUCESTER

---

*'Sometimes upon the sallies many prisoners
were taken who were always drunk.'*

Edward Hyde

The Royalists had taken Bristol. Its garrison, less than two thousand strong, for the most part hastily raised volunteers, had been commanded by Lord Saye's third son, Colonel Nathaniel Fiennes, a dismal, complaining man whose religious feelings had been deepened by a lengthy residence in Switzerland. His numbers in Bristol had been much reduced by Sir William Waller, who had taken over a thousand men away as reinforcements for his own army. Under protest from Fiennes he had brought about half of them back; but even so there was little hope that Fiennes could hold out in Bristol against the Cavaliers with so small a garrison. Nevertheless, he had grumpily rejected Prince Rupert's summons to surrender. The Royalists' guns at Clifton had consequently opened fire and after a day's exhausting battering – during which the captains of eight ships in the river below, loaded with the treasure of Bristol merchants, were persuaded to come over to the King – Prince Rupert had prepared to storm the defences against the advice of some members of his Council of War who, concerned by reports of the strength of the city's fortifications, had proposed a more cautious approach by mining operations and a closer investment to starve the garrison into surrender.

At first it had seemed that Prince Rupert would have been wise to heed this advice: to the south of the city the Cornishmen of the Western Army, triumphant at Landsdown Down, were driven back with devastating losses as they tried to escalade the wall and storm across the ditch under fire from Bristol's forts, leaving their dead behind, so Richard Atkyns said, in piles 'like rotten sheep'. Sir Nicholas Slanning and John Trevanion, two of the county's gentry who had helped to bring them to fight so well under the King's standard, were both mortally wounded. On the other side of the city, however, a breach was made; Colonel Henry Washington's men rode through it; the Royalist cavalry clattered across the river Frome; Prince Maurice came up with five hundred infantry to support them; and Colonel Fiennes was again called upon to surrender. He felt he now had no alternative but to submit. His ammunition was almost exhausted, his soldiers dispirited. The inhabitants, who disliked him, refused to make any further sacrifices. He agreed to march out of Bristol, leaving his arms and cannon behind him. As he did so, some of the gloating Cavaliers called out to his men, speaking through their noses in what was taken to be the Puritan manner, looking up to heaven. 'Where is your King Jesus now? Where were Thou at Runway Hill, O Lord, and where art Thou now?' Others ran off to see what they could find in the way of plunder; and, 'when they had done plundering', the Puritan Nehemiah Wallington was told, soldiers were 'billeted upon free quarter', twenty or thirty of them being placed in a single house 'upon men of but reasonable estates'.

> This puts them to an intolerable charge, and the more, because divers of the Cavaliers will not be content to feed upon good beef, but must have mutton and veal, and chickens, with wine and tobacco each meal, and much ado to please them at all; causing, also, men, women, and children to lie upon boards, while these Cavaliers possess their beds, which they fill with vermin. Besides, they fill the ears of the inhabitants with their blasphemous, filthy, and wicked language, which no chaste ear, nor honest heart, can endure; yea, so desperately wicked are they, that those that billet them dare not perform any act of religion, neither to give thanks at meals, nor yet to pray, read, or sing Psalms; but, instead thereof, they fill their houses with swearing and cursings, insomuch that they corrupt men's servants and children, that those who were

formerly civil have now learned to curse and swear almost as bad as they. And on the Lord's day these beasts spend their time in dicing, drinking, and carding, and other such abominations. And, whereas the chaplains that go with them should teach them better, some of them swear as bad as any of the soldiers. As, namely, one of the prince's chaplains swore by the flesh of God . . . with many other horrible oaths. And in a tavern the *Friday* after they came into the city, a lord's chaplain wished the devil might roast his soul in hell, if he did not preach such a sermon next Sunday as was never preached at *Bristol*, some part of which sermon was railing at the doctrine of predestination, calling it damnable doctrine of the Roundheads, and in his very sermon in the pulpit burst out into a fearful oath.

We may add further some other blasphemies of the Cavaliers when they entered the town, for they had certain fiddlers who sang blasphemous songs not fit to be mentioned, calling them the 4th and 12th Psalms.

After the fall of Bristol, England's second greatest city, a whole succession of places in Dorset, from Poole to Dorchester and Weymouth to Portland Island, were occupied by Royalist troops. The King himself came down to congratulate his officers and show himself to his supporters. He entered Bristol to the cheers of citizens who, while apprehensive of the money they would surely now be expected to find as one of the richest Royalist towns, were eager to seize the opportunity of taking over at least part of London's trade under royal patronage.

At Bristol the King's thoughts turned to Gloucester. Some of his advisers urged him to follow up his recent triumphs by marching directly upon London. Others, more circumspect, suggested that he should first secure his position in the west by taking the city whose geographical position on the river Severn between the Forest of Dean and the Cotswolds, between Worcester and Bristol and on the high road to Wales, was of such strategic importance and whose trade in wool and iron had made it so prosperous.

The Governor of Gloucester, Edward Massey, was, however, a far more determined man than Colonel Fiennes, though suspected of Royalist sympathies and eventually, indeed, becoming a Royalist himself. The fifth son of a Cheshire gentleman and grandson of

Richard Grosvenor, whose descendants were to be Dukes of Westminster, Massey was a young officer of far stronger Presbyterian convictions than those generally held by soldiers of fortune. He warned Parliament that many of Gloucester's citizens were against them and if help did not come soon he could not answer for the safety of the town. 'Alderman Pury [one of Gloucester's Members of Parliament and a prominent radical zealot] and some few of the citizens are still cordial to me,' he reported, 'but I fear ten to one incline the other way.' However, he soon showed himself determined to resist the King and capable of rousing the people and garrison to stand firm with him. The watch was doubled; a committee of defence established to supervise work on the fortifications; civic plate was sold to pay for the storage of provisions; houses outside the city walls were demolished. When Charles formally called upon the city to capitulate, a soldier and a citizen, 'with lean, pale, sharp, and bald visages', came out to deliver Gloucester's reply. Gloucester, they said, would be at his Majesty's service as soon as they were informed of the fact by both Houses of Parliament. They then, without further ado, clapped their orange-beribboned hats on their heads and marched off, the courtiers laughing at their ignorance of the etiquette to be observed on such occasions. Upon their return to the city, the outer suburbs were burned to the ground and two hundred more houses were destroyed.

Encouraged and inspired by Massey's stand, and anxious that, having lost Bristol, they must on no account lose Gloucester as well, Parliament energetically set about raising a force to relieve it. Meanwhile, as they waited for help to reach them, the inhabitants of Gloucester suffered a hard time. Royalist batteries beyond the walls maintained a merciless fire; the pipes carrying water to the city were cut; the flour mills ground to a halt as the streams driving them were diverted; arrows flew over the walls with leaflets warning the garrison that the army marching slowly and unwillingly to their relief had been defeated, that Parliament had deserted them, that they would be well advised to submit to the King's mercy. Miners, brought in by the Royalists from the Forest of Dean, worked their way forward through trenches and tunnels to blow a breach in the walls. But Massey showed no sign of concern. He walked about the city, talking cheerfully to the people, encouraging the soldiers, urging all to have trust in God's protection, supervising the repair of damaged earthworks. Treadmills took the place of watermills; drinking water was pumped up from the Severn.

> The sadness of the times did not cloud the countenance of the people [Massey's chaplain, John Corbet, recorded]. No great complainings were heard in our streets; no discontent seized on the soldiers . . . The usual outcries of women were not then heard . . . The enemy still prepared for a general storm . . . shooting grenades, fire-balls and great stones out of their mortar pieces . . . In one night they shot above twenty fiery melting hot iron bullets; some eighteen pound weight, others two-and-twenty pound weight, which were seen to fly through the air like the shooting of a star. They passed through stables and ricks of hay, where the fire by the swiftness of the motion did not catch, and falling on the tops of houses, presently melted the leads and sunk through. But all the skill and industry of the enemy could not set one house on fire . . . Besides their manne and batteries, they framed great store of those troublesome engines to assault the lower part of the city. Those engines ran upon wheels, with planks musket-proof placed on the axle-tree, with holes for musketshot and a bridge before it, and the end whereof (the wheels falling into the ditch) was to rest upon our breast works.

'They in the town behaved themselves with great courage and resolution, and made many sharp and bold sallies upon the King's forces, and did more hurt commonly than they received,' Edward Hyde confirmed; 'and many officers of name, besides common soldiers, were slain in the trenches and approaches, the Governor leaving nothing unperformed that became a vigilant commander. Sometimes, upon the sallies, many prisoners were taken who were always drunk; and after they were recovered they confessed that the Governor always gave the party that made the sally as much wine and strong water as they desired to drink; so that it seems their mettle was not purely nature. Yet it is very observable that in all the time the King lay there with a very glorious army, and after the taking of a city of much greater name [Bristol], there was not one officer that ran from the town to him, nor above three common soldiers, which is a great argument the discipline within was very good.'

The miners brought to Gloucester by the Royalists drew slowly closer to the walls and as yet there was no sign of the relieving force. It could only be a matter of days, so it seemed, before the walls were blown up by such an explosion as had shattered the fortifications of Lichfield. Massey's chaplain lamented, 'Gloucester did stand alone without help or hope.' Then, on the night of 24 August, a beacon was seen burning on the crest of a hill to the north. It was the long-awaited sign that help was on its way. A few hours later a heavy rain began to fall; the mines were flooded; and there was no immediate danger of the fearful explosion which had for days so anxiously been awaited.

A strong relieving force was on its way from London where shops had been closed to encourage recruitment and preachers from their pulpits had exhorted congregations to respond to the calls to arms. Essex had reviewed eight thousand men on Hounslow Heath on 22 August and by 4 September, harried though never halted for long by troops of Royalist cavalry, his numbers had increased to fifteen thousand.

The rain continued to pour down, turning the roads into bogs in which the wheels of his wagons sank to their axles. The rate of progress slowed down; food grew scarce; yet Essex came plodding on, determined to retrieve his reputation; and his men followed him doggedly. 'Such straits and hardships our citizens formerly knew not,' wrote a sergeant in one of the London regiments, 'yet the Lord that called us to do the work enabled us to undergo such hardships as he brought us to.' Watching the army passing through Chipping Norton, so a Royalist source reported, 'a woman of that towne whose zeal for the King and the justice of his cause could not containe itselfe, though in the mid'st of mortal enemies, said in the hearing of the rebells, "God bless the Cavaliers". This expression of the poore womans . . . so highly incensed the rebells that to punish so hainous a crime they tied her to the taile of one of their carts and stripping her to the middle for two miles march whipped her . . . They left her a lamentable spectacle of their cruelty . . . [She has] since died of those wounds which she received from them.'

As the army came within sight of Gloucester, where the besieged defenders' store of powder had been reduced to three barrels, the King – who had failed to dig the trenches and throw up the earthworks which military textbooks expected of armies required to hold back a relieving force – made up his mind to withdraw to Painswick and thence to Sudeley Castle, hoping to block Essex's return to London on the road by which he had come.

The night before had been rough and stormy, wrote Samuel Gardiner, 'and the sound of the cannon fired by Essex from Prestbury Hill to give the joyful intelligences of his approach had not been heard by the beleaguered citizens. With the light of the morning Essex learned that he had not come in vain, as he looked over the green valley of the Severn, and descried the grey tower of the cathedral standing out amidst the drifting smoke from the burning camp, and the dark masses of the Royalist army in full retreat. There was no need for him to hasten now. Driving a small force of the enemy out of Cheltenham, at that time a pretty market town, he gave his troops the rest which they sorely needed. On the 8th he marched into Gloucester amidst the ringing cheers of the citizens.'

Essex had succeeded in saving Gloucester; but, having reinforced and supplied the garrison there, he now had to make his way back to London with a reduced force over mile upon mile of difficult country with the enemy ever on his heels, charging down upon his flanks, or blocking his path. By feints and counter-marches, by making first for Evesham and Banbury, then turning sharply back to Cheltenham and Cirencester, Swindon and Reading, he managed to escape his pursuers, marching unwontedly fast, capturing a Royalist supply train at Cirencester, and surviving a charge by Prince Rupert's cavalry at Aldbourne Chase between Faringdon and Hungerford. This halt at Aldbourne Chase, however, delayed his progress, already slowed down by the muddy roads and by trailing herds of plundered cattle; and, when he moved on towards Newbury in the hope of finding shelter from the rain and food for his cold and hungry troops, he found that the Royalist army had reached the town before him and he would have to fight the battle he had almost managed to avoid.

The King had left his headquarters at Matson House outside Gloucester in a gloomy mood which the rainy, blustery weather could not but exacerbate, seeming to take little heart from the surrender of Exeter to Prince Maurice and the subsequent fall of Barnstaple and Bideford, while sadly lamenting the desertion of the Cornish levies who, dismayed by the death of their leaders and of so many of their friends, now decided to go home. It was said that on the way to Newbury the King sat down on a milestone in evident despair and replied to the Duke of York who asked his father if they might not now go home: 'We have no home.'

The battle fought outside Newbury on 20 September 1643 provided the King with no comfort and cost him the lives of three more of his noble officers, the Earls of Sunderland and Carnarvon and Viscount Falkland, his Secretary of State, who had recently confessed that the continuance of the war would break his heart and upon whom, as Edward Hyde observed, 'a kind of sadness and dejection of spirit' had descended since the beginning of 'this unnatural war', clouding his usual cheerfulness and vivacity.

Byron was in command of the Royalist cavalry on the right of the line where the small tree-lined fields, divided by ditches and hedges beneath a slight ridge known as Round Hill, made formal cavalry tactics impossible. Prince Rupert, who had been against fighting at all until more ammunition came up, was on the left, facing the more open ground of Wash Common. But he too was at a disadvantage, since the enemy had seized the higher ground in his front where Essex's guns were now sited.

In Parliament's army there were rather less than fifteen thousand men. The Royalists had about as many. Both sides were suffering from the effects of irregular meals, long, wet, exhausting forced marches and nights spent in the open, constantly disturbed by false alarms and sudden raids. ''Twas the terriblest thing in the world,' one officer thought, 'to have an Enemy fall unto one's quarters by night.'

Even so, Parliament's infantry came on at a good pace towards the Royalist musketeers whose ammunition was soon running very low. Prince Rupert's men galloped forward, driving the enemy cavalry off the Common, outflanking their infantry and attacking them from the rear. But the Roundhead infantry held their ground, driving off one assault after another, holding their pikes steadily, discharging their muskets in volleys which took a cruel toll, despite the relentless fire of the Royalist artillery. This was 'somewhat dreadful', Sergeant Henry Foster commented, 'when bowels and brains flew in our faces'. Captain John Gwyn saw 'a whole file of men, six deep, with their heads struck off with one cannon shot'.

On the right also Byron's cavalry were suffering grievously at the hands of Parliament's infantry and from dragoons firing from behind the thick hedges, receiving little support from the Royalist infantry whose ammunition was by now almost exhausted.

As the afternoon wore on the firing died down and by night had ceased altogether. 'The next day I view the bodies,' wrote Sergeant Henry Foster. 'There lay about one hundred stripped naked . . . The enemy conveyed away about thirty cartloads of maimed and dead men, as the town-people credibly reported to us . . . They buried thirty in one pit. Fourteen lay dead in one ditch . . . We were in great distress for water . . . and were right glad to drink in the same water where our horses did drink, wandering up and down to seek for it.'

The two armies withdrew from each other. The King marched back to Oxford, mourning his losses, most painfully the death of Lord Falkland who, 'dressed in clean linen as one going to a banquet', rode suicidally to his death as a volunteer in Sir John Byron's regiment, trotting slowly past a gap in a hedge through which the enemy's bullets were pouring, and falling from his horse with a musket ball in 'the lower part of the belly'. He had 'grown weary of the times', he had said, 'and foresaw much misery to his own country and foresaw he should be out of it by night'. Moreover, according to John Aubrey, he was overwhelmed with remorse for having advised the King to besiege Gloucester, thus fatally weakening the army, and deeply distressed by the 'death of Mrs Moray, who was his mistress, and whom he loved above all creation'. His dead body was stripped and so badly mangled that it could be identified only by a mole on the neck.

Essex withdrew to London, harried as before by Prince Rupert who narrowly escaped death when the ardent Presbyterian from Yorkshire, Sir Philip Stapleton, a man of 'thin body and weak constitution', brandished a pistol in his face and pulled the trigger, riding off again when the weapon failed to fire.

Leaving some of his troops in Reading, Essex rode into London to the welcome he had begun to believe could never be his, 'with all imaginable demonstrations of affection and reverence'.

For all the rejoicing in London, Parliament's outlook was far from auspicious. The ancient trading company, the Merchant Adventurers, contributed £30,000 to the depleted war chest, and a forced loan of over £60,000 was imposed. But the war chest remained chronically short of the funds which the conflict demanded. Reading had to be abandoned; to the north, Newport Pagnell, where Essex had hoped to find winter quarters, was taken by the Royalists who could now block the transport of supplies from that quarter. In the west Massey reported from Gloucester that his unpaid men were deserting to the enemy; in Shropshire, Sir William Brereton complained that the entire county was 'rotten' with Royalism; in the east, the Royalists led by Sir Hamon L'Estrange and his sons took over control of King's Lynn where the citizens had declined to pay the assessment Parliament had imposed upon them.

In the east, however, there was a Parliamentary commander who was becoming recognized as a cavalry leader to equal Prince Rupert, an officer of remarkable organizational ability, a man whose reputation was soon to be such that, confident of victory in a battle about to be fought in Yorkshire, Prince Rupert had shown a sudden apprehension when, interrogating a Parliamentary trooper who had been taken prisoner, he asked the single question, 'Is Cromwell there?'

8

COLONEL CROMWELL'S MEN

'I have a lovely company. They are honest sober Christians. You would respect them, did you know them. They expect to be used as men.'

Oliver Cromwell

One November day in 1640 that genial Member of Parliament, Philip Warwick, had entered the House of Commons during one of the Long Parliament's early debates. 'I came into the house well-clad,' he recollected in his memoirs, '(we courtiers valued ourselves much upon our good cloaths) . . . and perceived a Gentleman speaking (whom I knew not), very ordinarily apparelled; for it was a plain cloth sute, which seemed to have been made by an ill country-taylor. His linen was plain and not very clean; and I remember a speck or two of blood upon his little band, which was not much larger than his collar. His hatt was without a hatt band. His stature was of a good size, his sword stuck close to his side; his countenance swoln and reddish; his voice sharp and untunable, and his eloquence full of fervour [though] the subject matter would not bear much of reason, it being in behalfe of a servant of Mr Prynn's [the Puritan lawyer William Prynne] who had disperst libells against the Queen for her dancing and such like innocent and courtly sports, and he aggravated the imprisonment of this man unto that height that one would have believed the very Government itself had been in great danger by it . . . He was very much hearkened unto.'

This was Oliver Cromwell, Member of Parliament for the city of Cambridge, forty-one years old.

He had been born in Huntingdon, the son of Robert Cromwell, former Member of Parliament for Huntingdon, and the nephew of Sir Oliver Cromwell, the head of the family, a family of partly Welsh descent that owned a large part of the county and had been long in the King's service as Sheriffs and Justices of the Peace. 'I was born a gentleman,' he was later to say, 'living neither in any considerable height, nor yet in obscurity.' As a boy, the only brother of seven sisters, he had been sent to the local free school where under the strict guidance of a sternly Puritan schoolmaster he had shown more aptitude for games than for study, more interest in 'tennis, wrestling, running, swimming, handling weapons, riding, hunting, dancing and shooting with the long bow' than in the religious instruction which formed so large a part of the curriculum. At Cambridge these preferences seem to have remained marked. The tall strong young undergraduate became 'one of the chief match-makers and players at Foot-ball, cudgels or any other boisterous game or sport'. On his father's death, he left university without taking a degree to manage the small family estate in Huntingdon which had been left to his charge; and at the age of twenty-one, after a period of study at one of the Inns of Court in London, he married the daughter of a well-to-do London merchant, a woman older than himself, who within the next eight years bore him several children. Five of these, four sons and a daughter, survived – he was later to have three more daughters – and they all lived together in the stone house at the end of Huntingdon High Street. Also living with them there were Oliver's unmarried sisters as well as their mother, to whom he was devoted and from whom he was never to be parted until she died in her ninetieth year, giving her son, the great all-powerful Protector of England, her last, loving blessing: 'My dear son, I leave my heart with thee.'

Oliver was not happy at Huntingdon. Perhaps it was the constricting, crowded house that was to blame, the oppressively constraining, almost claustrophobic domesticity that made him long to escape from it to the society of male companions in the tavern, to the dicing table, to company more exciting and less genteel than that of Elizabeth his wife. A placid, affectionate and submissive woman, she was to play so little part in the years ahead that long after her husband's death a petition to Charles II was succinctly

labelled by a secretary as having come from 'old Mrs Cromwell.
Noll's wife.' It was virtually all that was known of her.

Stories of Cromwell's dissipations were, of course, afterwards
exaggerated if not invented by his enemies. The sins of which he
himself felt conscious seem to have been sins of the spirit, the
memory of which was always painful: 'O, I lived in darkness and
hated light. I was a chief – the chief – of sinners. This is true. I
hated godliness.' He admitted also that he had as little ambition as
godliness. Through the influence, so it was supposed, of the friendly
Montagu family, Earls of Manchester, he entered Parliament as
Member for Huntingdon in 1628; but this, after all, was the sort of
thing his family did: soon he was to have nine relatives in the House,
including John Hampden, his first cousin. When he returned to the
country after the dissolution of 1629 he disappeared once more into
the Fenland mists. For a time he rented a farm at St Ives in Huntingdonshire but 'scarce half a crop ever reared itself upon his grounds';
then he inherited property from an uncle and moved to Ely but, so
a friend wrote of him, he was restlessly discontented, in 'very great
troubles of soul, lying a long time under sore terrors and tempta-
tions, and at the same time in a very low condition'. A doctor whom
he had consulted in London had noted in his casebook that the patient
was 'excessively melancholic'. This condition was alleged to have
been noted also by a local doctor who added that he was 'a most
splenetic man and had fancies about the Cross in the town', and that
he called for treatment at midnight 'and such unreasonable hours,
very many times, upon a strong fancy that made him believe he was
then dying'. He appeared in church at St Ives – with a red flannel
round his neck as a comfort for his chronically inflamed throat –
brooding and miserable; his farm workers were summoned to long
prayers with his family before starting work in the morning and
again after their midday meal, but he himself appeared to derive little
comfort from these devotions. And then at last 'his will was broken
into submission to the Will of God'.

It was as though at last Cromwell had found both peace of mind
and a purpose in life in overcoming all his objections to the Puritan
faith. As a boy, he had been taught that God was intimately involved
in every detail and every seemingly insignificant action in life, that
He watched the daily deeds and punished the daily sins of all men,
and above all that the Elect, those who obeyed God's laws and

'consequently the laws of man and nature', would be saved. By prayer and torment, through misery and distrust, Cromwell had come to believe – as so many of his contemporaries believed – not merely that everything that happened in the world was due to the anger or favour of God, that the Bible was His direct word, that those who 'are instructed in the science of truth by the Holy Scriptures know the beginning of the world and its end', but that he himself was so instructed, that he was one of the Elect. It was his duty, he saw now, to devote himself to God's fight and to the establishment of His Kingdom on earth. He did so from then on with an ever-burning zeal, an unswerving fixity of purpose, a ruthless, powerful dedication and self-confident patriotism that forced men to recognize that there had risen amongst them in the shape of this middle-aged, clumsy, East Anglian farmer, his rough-skinned reddish face marked by conspicious warts, a man of destiny.

'Pray, Mr Hampden,' the Member for Wendover was once asked by a colleague, 'who is that sloven?'

'That sloven, that sloven whom you see before you hath no ornament in his speech; but that sloven, I say, if we should ever come to a breach with the King (which God forbid!), in such a case, I say, that sloven will be the greatest man in England.'

When the breach with the King did come, Cromwell reacted with that forceful determined spirit which was, indeed, to make him the greatest man in England. He rushed from Westminster to Cambridge, collecting recruits on the way; placed pickets on the roads leading out of the town to prevent further supplies of college plate being sent to the King; captured the castle and its ammunition; arrested the Royalists who had come to the town to read the King's Commission of Array. He then enlisted and – out of his own slender resources equipped and paid – a troop of horsemen to fight for the 'preservation of the true religion, the laws, liberty and peace of the Kingdom', explaining to his recruits that he would have nothing to do with Parliament's refusal to admit that they were fighting the King, their special protests that they were taking arms for the 'safety of the King's person' and the 'defence of both Houses of Parliament' against his Majesty's 'evil counsellors'. He would not deceive or cozen them by such expressions, he bluntly told his troopers. If the King happened to be in the body of the enemy that he was to charge, he would fire his 'pistol upon him as at any other private person', and if their conscience did not allow them to do the same, he advised them 'not to enlist themselves in his troop or under his command'.

Welcoming Parliament's decision to unite the counties under its control in various associations, Cromwell, so little known in the early months of the war, had become one of the leading spirits of the Eastern Association of Norfolk, Suffolk, Essex, Cambridgeshire and Hertfordshire, and later of Huntingdonshire and Lincolnshire, an Association which was to become of essential importance to the Parliamentary cause in its control of a great farming and fishing area, of the East Anglian cloth industry and of trade with the Continent from East Anglian ports. He organized the Association's resources, training its men, issuing orders which brooked no opposition: 'Let me assure you it's necessary, and therefore to be done . . . Get what volunteers you can . . . Hasten your horses . . . You must act lively . . . Do it without distraction . . . Neglect no means . . . Send at once . . . Remember who tells you . . .' He had enlisted men and commissioned officers eager to fight not for adventure or for pay – though they were paid more regularly than any other large body of troops on either side – but for their faith: 'Such men,' as he described them himself, 'as had the fear of God before them and as made some conscience of what they did.' It was suggested by his critics that he purposely filled his ranks with artisans and labourers and with men of outlandish religious persuasions; yet, while it was true that he set little store by social rank, he would have enlisted more gentlemen had he been able to find them. 'It had been well that men of honour and worth had entered into these employments,' he wrote, 'but seeing it was necessary the work should be done, better plaine men than none.' 'I had rather have a plain russet-coated captain that knows what he fights for, and loves what he knows,' he said on another occasion, 'than that which you call a gentleman and nothing else.' But he added, 'I honour a gentleman that is so indeed.'

His men were freeholders for the most part, and freeholders' sons, 'who upon a matter of conscience engaged in this quarrel'. They were forbidden to plunder, to get drunk, to go whoring, even to swear, but such prohibitions were scarcely necessary. 'I have a lovely company,' he had written proudly to his cousin, Oliver St John. 'They are honest sober Christians. You would respect them, did you know them. They expect to be used as men.'

The Parliamentary newspaper, *Special Passages*, commended

Cromwell's men highly. They were 'brave men and well disciplined; no man swears but he pays his twelve pence; if he be drunk he is set in the stocks . . . The countries [counties] where they come leap for joy of them, and come in and join with them . . . How happy it were if all the forces were thus disciplined!'

They certainly proved to be good soldiers, well trained not merely to charge in a mass but to rally quickly after either victory or defeat. In May 1643, although greatly outnumbered and with some recruits, so Cromwell said, 'so poor and broken that you shall seldom see worse', they had charged some twenty troops of Cavaliers near Grantham in Lincolnshire 'at a pretty trot', had scattered them and captured five of their standards, losing only two men to almost a hundred enemy dead. Two months later Cromwell's men laid siege to Burghley House, the huge mansion in Lincolnshire built for Queen Elizabeth's Secretary of State and then occupied by the widow of the third Earl of Exeter and her son; and here also they showed what a disciplined body of men they were. At first the garrison refused to submit, but a few well-directed cannonballs and several volleys of musketry persuaded them to change their minds. Two hundred Royalist prisoners were taken, and Cromwell's men, threatened with death if they harmed the house's inhabitants, marched off to their next victory, Cromwell himself thankful to be away since he already recognized, as so many others then did not, the futility of tying men down in long, unprofitable sieges of fortresses of little strategic importance. His next fight was at Winceby on the edge of the Lincolnshire Wolds where, according to a contemporary report, Colonel Cromwell, again outnumbered, came down with 'brave resolution on the enemy. His horse was killed under him at the first charge and fell down upon him, and, as he rose, he was knocked down again. But afterwards he recovered a poor horse in a soldier's hands, and bravely mounted himself again. Truly, this first charge was performed with so much admirable courage and resolution by our troops that the enemy stood not another.'

Cromwell's troopers went thundering on into the fire of the Cavaliers, supported by Sir Thomas Fairfax who, after an unfortunate encounter with Royalist horse on Seacroft Moor, had made a night attack on Wakefield on 24 May, had routed there an enemy force of 2,500 men and had captured the Royalist commander, Lord Goring, and sent him a prisoner to London. At Winceby, Fairfax and Cromwell broke the Royalists' ranks and sent them scattering, taking eight hundred prisoners and capturing twenty-six colours in an action which sealed the already formidable reputation of the Eastern Association. 'Our men had little else to do,' the Earl of Manchester reported, 'but to pursue a flying enemy which they did for many miles.'

Edward Montagu, second Earl of Manchester, had been appointed commander of the Eastern Association the previous summer, in place of the inept young local magnate Lord Grey of Werke. As a young man Lord Manchester had represented the county of Huntingdon in Parliament; and, after being raised to the peerage, he had become an acknowledged leader of the Puritan party in the House of Lords. Cromwell, who had with characteristic forthrightness complained to Parliament of the incompetence of his former commander, welcomed the appointment of Lord Manchester, an attractive man, universally well liked. 'He was of a gentle and generous nature,' Edward Hyde wrote of him, 'civilly bred, had reverence and affection for the person of the King, loved his country . . . and was of so excellent a temper and disposition that the barbarous times, and the rough parts he was forced to act in them, did not wipe out or much deface those marks insomuch as he was never guilty of any rudeness towards those he was obliged to oppress, but performed always as good offices towards his old friends, and all other persons, as the iniquity of the time, and the nature of the employment he was in, would permit him to do, which kind of humanity could be imputed to very few.'

He and Cromwell were much the same age; they were both Huntingdonshire men and had both attended Sydney Sussex College, Cambridge; they shared the same political allegiances. Manchester had little military experience but he was a skilful and conscientious administrator, as Cromwell was. Their combined efforts to improve the discipline and training of the Eastern Association, of which Cromwell was appointed Lieutenant-General of Horse, were soon to be well rewarded.

Good news for Parliament came from Yorkshire as well as from Lincolnshire, where the victory at Winceby was followed on 20 October by the surrender of the county town together with large quantities of arms and ammunition. The important town of Hull, which was still being besieged by the Earl of Newcastle, had been saved by the Scottish professional soldier Sir John Meldrum after a high tide had flooded the Royalists' siege works. Meldrum had been joined at Hull by Sir Thomas Fairfax and Oliver Cromwell, who agreed to get twenty troops of cavalry away from Hull into Lincolnshire while Meldrum led a sally from the town. This sally had been completely successful. The garrison captured the Royalists' immense siege cannon which fired a thirty-six-pound shot and which, known as 'the Queen's Pocket Pistol', was renamed 'Sweet Lips' after Hull's most celebrated prostitute. After the loss of this huge cannon – which Prince Rupert was to recapture at Newark the following year – the Earl of Newcastle raised the siege of Hull. A week later the Earl of Manchester marched into Lincoln.

Parliament was also heartened by news from Bedfordshire, where it was reported that the Royalist Governor of Newport Pagnell, Sir Lewis Dyve, desperate for supplies of ammunition, had withdrawn from the town, opening up for Parliament a vital route between London and the Eastern Association.

From the south came encouraging despatches from Sir William Waller, who had been contending with Sir Ralph Hopton for the valuable iron foundries of the Sussex Weald whence most of Parliament's armaments came. Waller had earlier been thrown back from Basing House – the huge castle near Basingstoke close to the main road between London and the sheep pens of the Wiltshire Downs – which had been strongly fortified at great cost by the King's rich supporter the Marquess of Winchester. Waller's men had quailed before the guns of the great house's garrison; many had deserted; the London regiments had threatened mutiny after watching their cannon throw shot after useless shot across the Iron Age earthwork and into the thick Norman and sixteenth-century walls of the castle. Waller had thought it as well to give the men a short rest and shelter from the wind and the pouring rain by taking them away for two days to Basingstoke. But on their return they had been just as dispirited. An attempt had been made at storming the place: the first wave had fled as soon as the castle's guns opened up; the supporting troops had refused to advance across the park. The rain had continued to fall. Waller had endeavoured to encourage his men by abandoning his tent to sleep beside them in the open, yet in the morning the familiar cry had been raised once more, 'Home! Home!' This was so often the trouble with trained bands whether from London or from the counties. They could be relied upon to serve well within their own boundaries, but once taken outside them they were soon agitating to return, urged to do so by such letters as one addressed to 'my very loving husband Robert Rodway, a trained soldier in the Red regiment under the command of Captain Warrin, deliver this with speed, I pray you':

Most dear and loving husband, my kind love, remember unto you hoping that you are good health as I am at the writing hereof . . . I pray you to come home if you can come safely. I do marvel that I cannot hear from you as well other neighbours do. I do desire to hear from you as soon as you can. I pray you to send me word when you do think you shall return. You do not consider I am a lone woman. I thought you would never leave me this long together. So I rest ever praying for your safe return.

Your loving wife
Susan Rodway, ever
praying for you till
death I depart.

'We know they are men of trade and employment,' a Parliamentary committee wrote of the Essex bands, 'and cannot well be absent from their occasions . . . Besides, they are men of that quality and course of life as cannot well bear the difficulties of a soldier's life.' Although plagued by demands from his own trained bands to be taken back to their families and places of work, Waller, having abandoned the siege of Basing House, had succeeded in taking Alton. Here, after fierce fighting in the parish church – where the Royalists had fought to the last behind a barricade of dead horses and their commander Colonel Richard Bowles had been bludgeoned to death after killing seven Roundheads – over eight hundred prisoners had fallen into Waller's hands, those who declined to change sides being sent to London to be paraded through the streets after being required to listen to sermons 'containing better doctrine' than they were taught in the Royalist camp. From Alton, Waller had marched on into Sussex and, in a rainstorm that drenched his men, he had attacked the Royalists in Arundel, driven them out of the town and into the castle which soon afterwards surrendered, releasing more soldiers who agreed to change sides and fight for Parliament. In the harbour at Arundel a ship bound for Spain was stopped and searched. In the hold was discovered a painting of a scene from the life of the virgin martyr St Ursula, destined for a church in Seville. It was sent to London to be exhibited as a picture of King Charles and the Queen handing over England as a present to the Pope.

Left behind in Arundel, Sir William Springate succumbed to the 'bloody flux and spotted fever' then raging through the town. His pregnant wife came from London to be with him.

> When we came to Arundel we met with a most dismal sight, the town being depopulated, all the windows broken with the great guns, and the soldiers making stables of all the shops and lower rooms; and there being no light in the town but what came from the light in the stables . . . It was about twelve at night when we arrived [at her husband's quarters] and as soon as I put my foot into the hall I heard his voice, 'Why will you lie to me! If she be come, let me hear her voice,' which struck me so that I had hardly power to get up the stairs. But being borne up by two, he seeing me, the fever having took his head, in a manner sprang up as if he would come out of his bed, saying, 'Let me embrace you before I die.' The purple spots came out the day before and now were struck in. But such was his activeness of spirit and stoutness of his heart that he would not yield to this ill that was upon him, but covenanted with them that he would shoot birds with his cross-bow out of the windows, which he did till the fever took his head and the spots went in. And after that the fever was so violent and he so young and strong of body, and his blood so hot (being but about the age of 23) that they were forced to sit round the bed to keep him in, but he spake no evil or raving words at all, but spoke seriously about his dying . . . When he was dead, then I could weep.

In London, despite Waller's successes, there was little rejoicing. The theatres and bear gardens were closed; the Lord Mayor's Show was cancelled; in churches prayers were said for less troubled times; houses were searched for deserters from the army; in the House of Commons, reduced to less than half of its original strength of six hundred Members, and in the even more severely attenuated Lords, debates were held in an atmosphere of acrimony and foreboding. Rare diversions were a hanging or a parade of dejected prisoners of war, or a bonfire in Cheapside of popish books and rosaries.

There were reports of constant quarrels among the generals as well as the politicians. Essex and Waller made no secret of their mutual antipathy. An indignant Nathaniel Fiennes was put on trial for his conduct at Bristol and sentenced to death. Cromwell's lack of respect for some of his more highly born colleagues and the trust he reposed in devoted Puritans of humble origins aroused ever deeper suspicions. Pym, exhausted and wasted, was obviously dying; and on 8 December he did die, in 'great torment and agony', of cancer of the bowel, which 'rendered him an object very loathsome to those who had been most delighted with him'. Much of his work was taken over by Oliver St John and Sir Harry Vane.

Vane, eldest son of Sir Henry Vane, the former Secretary of State, was liked well enough. He was ugly and on occasions impatient; as a boy he had turned away from the cheerful frolics he had once enjoyed with his friends, and become the serious-minded, questioning Puritan he had ever since remained. But he had a certain charm of manner and a pleasant tolerant temperament, qualities singularly lacking in the severe and clever, remote and contentious lawyer, Cromwell's cousin, Oliver St John, the Solicitor General, who was widely disliked and particularly so by the Earl of Essex, mourning the loss of Pym.

Throughout the last stages of his illness, Pym had been negotiating for a treaty with Parliament's 'brethren of Scotland'. While the King was vainly intriguing for help from all over Europe and across the Irish Sea, Pym was actually coming to terms with the Scots, formulating with them a Solemn League and Covenant by which the English Parliament swore to maintain the existing structure of the Scottish Church and to reform the Anglican Church 'according to the word of God and the example of the best reformed churches', in exchange for military help against the King. The dour army of the Solemn League and Covenant with their 120 cannon lumbered down from Scotland through the snow in January 1644. The men, for the most part 'raw, untrained and undisciplined', warned against looting, drinking, swearing and whores, were supervised by a minister and a lay elder in each regiment. Their commander was Alexander Leslie, Earl of Leven and Lord Balgonie, an old, scarcely literate professional soldier, 'in person little and crooked'. The cavalry, some troops mounted on 'the veriest nags', were entrusted to David Leslie, later Baron Newark, who, like his namesake, had had experience of fighting in the service of Gustavus II Adolphus. The cold was so severe that the Tweed was frozen from bank to bank and the army, twenty-two thousand strong, was able to march across the ice.

Delayed by heavy snowfalls, then by floods, through which the soldiers marched sometimes up to their armpits in water, they reached Newcastle at last, only to be held there by the garrison and obliged to settle down to a long siege, unable to obtain supplies in that inhospitable countryside and having to rely on the cargoes that came to them from time to time from Scotland, losing prisoners to the tough cavalry of Sir Marmaduke Langdale, a Roman Catholic Yorkshireman known as 'the Ghost' because of his thin, pale, lugubrious appearance.

PART TWO

9

SWINGS OF FORTUNE

'I put them all to the sword, which I find to be the best way to deal with these kind of people.'

Lord Byron

The King at Oxford was in despondent mood, even playing tennis, it was noticed, in a mournful way, while his court, no longer confident of victory, was more *intrigant* and quarrelsome than ever. The lack of a decisive victory was far more of a catastrophe for him than it was for the Parliamentarians, who became relatively stronger with each passing month, whose control of the navy allowed them to supply the coastal towns in their hands, and the morale of whose soldiers was gradually improving.

The arrival of the Queen had added to the dissidence of the court, exacerbating all the old quarrels between the 'Queen's party' and their opponents, between George Digby of whom she was fond and Prince Rupert whom she disliked, between Protestants and Catholics, between those whom the King chose to honour with baronies and knighthoods, and those whom he neglected. Lord Byron grew sulky when he was not appointed Governor to the Prince of Wales. Prince Maurice was annoyed when one of his officers, whom he had suggested as a suitable candidate for the governorship of Weymouth, was passed over in favour of a protégé of the Marquess of Hertford, Anthony Ashley Cooper, later created first Earl of Shaftesbury, who soon afterwards went over to the other side. The King gloomily complained that the quarrels of his friends caused him as much pain as the attacks of his enemies.

Prince Rupert was at odds not only with the devious George Digby but also with Henry Wilmot, whom he blamed for allowing Parliament's army to get through to Gloucester, and with another of the Queen's friends, Henry Percy, younger son of the ninth Earl of Northumberland, recently created Baron Percy of Alnwick, a 'proud and supercilious person' who had for no very good reason, other than the Queen's approval, been appointed General of the Ordance. In this capacity he was harshly condemned by Prince Rupert for having failed to supply Newport Pagnell in time to prevent Sir Lewis Dyve's withdrawal.

Prince Rupert also made enemies among his subordinate cavalry commanders, men for the most part much older than himself, who were resentful of the manner in which he took them to task for the ill-disciplined behaviour of their troops, their repeated squabbles over quarters and supplies, their frequently riding off on plundering expeditions into the Oxfordshire countryside.

The city was more crowded than ever, and even more unruly despite the gallows set up at Carfax by the Governor, Sir Arthur Aston, formerly Governor of Reading, one of the Queen's highly undesirable nominees, the detested martinet who, so Nehemiah Wallington was told, 'doth tyrannize over all the inhabitants'.

> There was a gentleman that was in Oxford at a Tavern and called for a pint of sack [Wallington wrote, recording some characteristic stories of this 'grand papist']. The vintner asked him from whence he came; he answered from *London*. The said vintner gave notice thereof to Sir *Arthur Aston*, who caused him to be apprehended, and the next day to be racked, and examined upon the rack; he made it appear that his business was about monies due to him, and produced a note, and nothing could be suspected . . . Yet, nevertheless, such was the Governor's cruelty, that after he had racked him, he caused him the next day to be hanged upon the gallows. But he died cheerfully, only he said it grieved him to part with his wife and two children, whom he left at *London*. And after they had hanged him, they stripped him of his very shirt, and buried him naked.
>
> There was also another hanged because he came from *London*,

though nothing proved against him; and Prince *Charles* had got a pardon for the prisoner that was going to execution, and brought the pardon himself for him; and when he heard that the Prince was coming with a pardon, Sir *Arthur* with his foot turned the ladder himself, the prisoner being then upon it; and when the pardon came, he was so far gone that he could not be recovered . . .

One *Mary Brook*, servant to Mr. *Church*, an Inn Keeper in *Oxford*, sweeping of the door, said that was the dirt of the papist horses' feet, and wished they were all hanged; at which time Sir *Arthur* himself riding by heard her, and called for her, and caused her to be fettered and manacled with irons, and sent to prison, and from thence to the gallows and hanged. But she having a brother that is page of his Majesty's Buttery, he did petition for her to his Majesty, who called for her, and discharged her; since which she hath made an escape, and is now in *London*, and affirms the same.

Aston walked the streets of the city at his peril and one night was 'wounded in the side in the dark by a scuffle in the street'. Anthony Wood described him as a 'testy, forward, imperious and tirannical person, hated in Oxon and elsewhere by God and man. Who kervetting on horseback in Bullingdon Green before certaine ladies, his horse flung him and broke his legge: so that it being cut off and he thereupon rendered useless for employment, one Col. [William] Legge succeeded him. Soone after the country people comming to the market would be ever and anon asking the sentinell "Who was Governor of Oxon?" they answered "one Legge". Then replied they, "A pox upon him. Is *he* Governor still?"'

In the recent warmer weather, soldiers had been sleeping out in the streets; and officers had been forced to share small and airless rooms. With lodgings crowded and drains blocked, the atmosphere had been foetid; fever had spread amongst troops and servants, courtiers and ladies alike. In one epidemic in 1643 there had been no fewer than 875 burials in seven parishes. The authorities had done what they could to keep the crowded city clean and the rivers unpolluted. John Taylor, the former London waterman who had been pressed into the navy and, because of his knack of easy rhyming, had become known as 'the water poet', had come to Oxford, where he kept a tavern for a time, and helped in this work:

I was commanded by the Water Bailey
To see the rivers cleansed both nights and daily.
Dead hogs, dogs, cats and well-flayed carrion horses
Their noisome corpses soiled the water's courses;
Both swines' and stable dung, beasts' guts and garbage,
Street dirt with gardeners' weeds and rotten herbage.
And from those waters' filthy putrifaction,
Our meat and drink were made, which bred infection.
Myself and partner, with cost, pains and travail
Saw all made clean, from carrion, mud and gravel.

To protect themselves from infection, so Taylor said, people walked through the streets with their nostrils plugged with wormwood, or holding to their noses pieces of well-tarred rope or nosegays or even 'socks from sweating feet'.

As well as plague, fires were a constant hazard, as often as not caused by people cooking in rooms without chimneys. One of the worst of these fires broke out 'about two of the clock in the afternoon in a little poor house on the south side of Thames Street'. According to Anthony Wood it was 'occasioned by a foot-soldier's roasting a pig which he had stolen. The wind being very high and in the north, blew the flames southward very quick and strongly, and burnt all houses and stables that extend from the North gate.' For over ten hours the fire raged, destroying ten bakehouses, eight brewhouses and nearly three hundred houses, mostly of wood. Overcrowding in Oxford had become even worse in December when the King, prompted by Parliament's alliance with the Scots, which he believed to be widely resented, issued a call to all Members of Parliament to turn their backs on the men responsible for the 'lasting miseries which this foreign invasion must bring upon the Kingdom' and to assemble in a free Parliament at Oxford.

Rather more than a hundred Members of the Commons had responded to the King's call when he formally opened his Parliament in Christ Church Hall on 22 January 1644. They were joined by about thirty peers, several of them army officers recently ennobled, including Prince Rupert, who was created Duke of Cumberland.

In his speech of welcome the King condemned the actions of the Westminster Parliament, accusing it of bringing in a foreign power to invade the realm. He urged the Oxford Parliament to restore his own rights and honour, and to struggle to preserve its privileges, as well as its religion.

The Oxford Members listened with respect and acted complaisantly, proclaiming the Scots to be unwelcome invaders, denouncing the Members of Parliament at Westminster as traitors for having called 'these foreigners' into the country, and commanding the Earl of Essex to lay down his arms and to appear before them to answer for his conduct. Their command was, of course, ignored; and it was not long before most of them accepted that their presence in Oxford was an irrelevance. Uncomfortable in their lodgings, unhappy in the town, and expelled from the Parliament in Westminster by its other Members, many of them made up their minds to leave Oxford as soon as they conveniently could.

They felt all the more inclined to do so when news reached Oxford of Roundhead successes in the north. Two days after they had met in Christ Church Hall, Sir Thomas Fairfax had appeared before the Cheshire town of Nantwich to which Lord Byron was laying siege. The Parliamentary commander in Cheshire was Sir William Brereton, the convinced Puritan who had declined to hand over the Earl of Northampton's body after the battle on Hopton Heath. The year before he had taken care to seize Beeston Castle, a fortress on a massive outcrop of rock which commanded the surrounding countryside between his garrison at Nantwich and the Royalist troops in Chester. Beeston Castle had been lost when a daring officer from Ireland clambered by night up the precipitous crag on which its ruins still stand and with eight men gained entry into the upper ward. The castle's governor, a cheesemonger by trade, was so shaken by this sudden incursion into a stronghold deemed impregnable that he not only surrendered with his sixty men, but invited the intruder to dinner and had his fellow rock climbers regaled with beer. Learning that a party of Royalist troops from Chester had by then appeared before the gatehouse of the lower ward, the governor agreed to march out of the castle, provided his men could do so with all 'the honours of war', that was to say with arms shouldered, colours flying, drums beating, the musketeers carrying match lit at both ends and with bullets clenched between their teeth. Upon his arrival at Nantwich he was imprisoned to protect him from the anger of the people, who threatened to kill him, and later he was shot.

Having lost Beeston Castle through the incompetence of the unfor-

tunate cheesemonger, Sir William Brereton was determined that
Nantwich should not be lost as well. Already it was under threat
from Lord Byron's troops, who had occupied most of the surrounding villages, including Barthomley, where several people led by a
Puritan schoolmaster had been smoked out of the parish church and
wantonly killed. 'I put them all to the sword,' Byron reported to the
Earl of Newcastle, 'which I find to be the best way to deal with these
kind of people, for mercy to them is cruelty.'

Shortly after this massacre, Byron launched an attack upon Brereton who, having assembled troops around Kinderton Hall, was
marching through Middlewich in an attempt to relieve the beleaguered garrison at Nantwich. Caught outside Middlewich by Lord
Byron's vanguard under his brother Robert Byron, Brereton endeavoured to escape through the narrow streets of the little town and lost
more than five hundred men in the ensuing struggle.

Taking advantage of this success, Lord Byron marched upon
Nantwich, whose 'officers, soldiers and gentlemen' were called upon
to surrender in a curiously worded summons:

> Let not your zeal in a bad cause dazzle your eyes any longer; but
> wipe away your vain conceits that have too long led you into blind
> errors . . . If you love your town accept of quarter; and, if you
> regard your lives, work your safety by yielding your town to Lord
> Byron for his Majesty's use. You see how my battery is fixed,
> from whence fire shall eternally visit you, to the terror of the old
> and females, and corruption of your thatched houses. Believe me,
> gentlemen, I . . . am now resolved to batter, burn, stone and
> destroy you.

This summons being rejected, the Royalists assaulted Nantwich
in the cold dawn of 18 January 1644. Byron's infantry rushed forward
with scaling ladders, clambered over the mud walls and poured into
the town where there was savage hand-to-hand fighting until at
length the Cavaliers were driven back by the garrison, leaving scores
of dead and dying in the streets. By now Sir Thomas Fairfax was on
his way from Lincolnshire. With him was his cousin, Sir William
Fairfax, a brave cavalry commander who was to die later that year
suffering from fifteen wounds at the relief of Montgomery Castle.
Also with Fairfax was Colonel Lambert, 'honest John Lambert',

another Yorkshireman, who was to become one of the Roundheads' most successful commanders. At Nantwich on 25 January 1644, these men achieved one of Parliament's most significant successes.

Forcing a fight upon Byron in enclosed ground much to his advantage, Sir Thomas Fairfax won a quick victory with little loss. He took over 1,500 prisoners, including more than a hundred Irish women camp followers – 'who had with them long knives with which they were said to have done mischief' – and all the senior Royalist commanders with the exception of Lord Byron and his brother who escaped with what remained of their cavalry to Chester. Sir William Brereton rode south with these captives to London where Parliament, deeply gratified that most of Cheshire and much of Lancashire was now safely in their hands, thanked him for his 'great and faithful services'. In commemoration of the raising of the siege the inhabitants of Nantwich wore sprigs of holly in their hats on every anniversary of it until well into the nineteenth century.

Ordered further north to help the Scots in their so-far uninspired struggle with the Earl of Newcastle, Fairfax now passed through Lancashire where, in the absence of her husband the Earl of Derby, the redoubtable Countess, mother of his nine children, was making life miserable for all supporters of Parliament, real or imagined, within miles of the family home, Lathom House near Ormskirk, which had been turned into a fortress with its twenty-five-feet-wide moat protected by a high palisade. From one of the fortress's nine massive towers, which rose above walls six feet thick, flew a standard upon which was emblazoned the defiant motto of the Stanley family, 'Sans changer'.

Fairfax's summons to surrender was scorned by the Countess, a stout French lady, the daughter of the duc de Thouars and granddaughter on her mother's side of William the Silent, Prince of Orange. At first she asked for time to consider the summons, declining to leave her fortress to discuss terms, and reminding Fairfax of her high social rank, observing that 'notwithstanding her present condition, she remembered both her Lord's honour and her own birth, conceiving it more knightly that Sir Thomas Fairfax should wait upon her, than she upon him'. Later she maintained that she would rather set fire to her castle and perish with her children in the flames than submit to the besiegers. 'Although a woman and a stranger,' she declared, 'divorced from my friends and robbed of my estate, I am ready to receive your utmost violence, trusting in God for protection and deliverance.' Her house was of no great strategic importance, but it was a symbol of resistance which Alexander Rigby, Member of Parliament for Wigan, strongly urged Fairfax to reduce. Rigby, a dedicated Parliamentarian – or, as Lady Derby described him, an 'insolent rebel', who was credited with the proposal of selling the recalcitrant heads of Cambridge colleges into foreign slavery – had himself reduced Sir John Girlington's castle at Thurland and was determined that Lathom House should go the same way. Fairfax, having satisfied himself that the place could not be stormed, left Rigby to do what he could with it and went on his way.

Rigby's efforts were entirely unavailing. Lathom House lay in a hollow, so that when his gunners depressed their guns far enough to hit their target the shot rolled out of the barrels, and when they took their guns closer to the building its occupants drove them back with musket fire. Rigby then ordered siege trenches to be dug; but, even when protected by these and firing at close range, his guns were quite ineffective against the immensely thick walls of the medieval keep, denting them in many places but leaving them otherwise unharmed. An enormous mortar firing a stone ball almost a hundred pounds in weight was then brought into action and also proved useless. After a day's intermittent bombardment by this mortar, Lady Derby's men crept out at night, pushed it over and stuffed rubbish down its barrel. A fortnight after this they stole out of the castle again and dragged the mortar back with them into the keep. A month later Rigby was still as far from taking the place as ever.

While Fairfax was enjoying minor successes in the north, elsewhere the fortunes of war were turning once more in the Royalists' favour. In the Midlands, Prince Rupert had scored another resounding victory. Riding through Cheshire in search of reinforcements he had passed by Nantwich, where the Parliamentary Governor provocatively hanged thirteen Royalist prisoners, supposed to be Irishmen, from the walls of the town. The Prince had hanged thirteen of his own prisoners in retaliation, and had sent a fourteenth to the Earl of Essex's headquarters with a threat that he would in future hang two Parliamentary prisoners for every Royalist thus treated. He then rode on to Newark which the wily Scotsman Sir John Meldrum, with an army of about seven thousand men, had endeavoured to take from its Governor, Sir Richard Byron, another of Lord Byron's eight brothers, and thus secure an important position on the road to the north. Meldrum had assembled his infantry and guns in the shell of a large burned house known as the Spittle to the north of the town, with his cavalry drawn up in front of it. On coming upon the enemy here, Prince Rupert charged without hesitation; and, although Meldrum counter-charged, the force of the Cavaliers' assault was decisive. The Roundheads retreated hastily over a bridge of boats across the river Trent. The Newark garrison poured out of the town, and Meldrum was soon surrounded. Since Rupert's men were needed elsewhere, he allowed the Roundheads to march off towards Hull; but he accepted those who wished to change sides into his own ranks, taking possession of all their arms and ammunition, including two thousand muskets, as many pistols and over thirty cannon. There was good cause for celebration.

Within a matter of days, however, Parliament also had reason to celebrate what Sir William Balfour called 'a great victory over our enemies beyond all expectation'. This victory had been won near Alresford in Hampshire where, on 29 March, several companies of Roundheads from London had attacked a Royalist encampment in Cheriton Wood and had been halted by heavy musket fire, then chased away by a cavalry charge. Sir Arthur Haselrig's 'Lobsters' had come to the help of the Londoners and had soon been joined by Waller's infantry coming up the hill from the direction of Hinton Ampner and by Balfour's cavalry who, between them, drove the Royalists off in every direction.

Parliament made the most of their unexpected and overdue victory, organizing celebrations and thanksgiving services, issuing appeals for more recruits and for contributions to the cause in money and in kind, lavishing praise upon Waller and Balfour and, much to the annoyance of Essex, issuing orders for the enlistment of hundreds more men to be placed under Waller's command.

'Newark is not taken,' Essex pointed out in his pique at the praise bestowed upon and the reinforcements promised to his rival. 'Lincolnshire is lost; Gloucester is unsupplied and the last week there was but a step between us and death and – what is worse – slavery.' It was all very well to celebrate the victory in Cheriton Wood, he argued disgruntledly; but such an isolated triumph was of little consequence were it not to be followed up by a march against the King's main army around Oxford. 'For my part,' Essex continued with pathetic petulance, 'as I first engaged myself in this cause and undertook this service with an honest and single heart, without any particular end of my own, but merely to serve my country and defend religion and liberty . . . so I shall be ready still to prosecute it with the utmost of my endeavours . . . and though you have been pleased to reduce my army to 7,000 foot and 3,000 horse, when my Lord of Manchester is allowed an army of 14,000 and receives 34,000 l. a month for the pay of it – since it is done by you I submit, and with them or a lesser number, if it be your pleasure, I will, as I have several times already, adventure my life for the service of this cause.' There was much to undergo, Essex added with glum forboding, before that cause could triumph, and the Royalists were defeated. 'The seas, it must be remembered, have been and still are open to them out of Ireland.'

For months, indeed, the King had been negotiating for aid from Ireland with the help of the Marquess of Ormonde, and once agreement had been reached for an armistice with the rebels, soldiers from the Irish army had been coming across the Irish Sea to be sent from their ports of disembarkation to serve with units of the King's army as occasion demanded. Reviled as Irish papists by Parliamentary propagandists, they were, in fact, for the most part English Protestants. Many of them mutinied when they discovered they had been brought over to fight in the King's name against others of their kind. Many others, however, fought with spirit in the Royalist units to which they were assigned, as did the Irishmen. Indeed, Lord Byron said he preferred Irish soldiers to Englishmen. 'My Lord,' Byron wrote to the Marquess of Ormonde as the King's recruiting officer in Ireland, 'the enemy is grown so strong upon their late success that without a larger supply we shall be able to do little good; and I wish they were rather Irish than English, for the English we have already are very mutinous, and . . . so poisoned by the ill-affected people here, that they grow very cold in this service. And since the rebels here call in the Scots, I know no reason why the King should make any scruple of calling in the Irish, or the Turks if they would save him.'

In fact, the well-founded rumours that the King was bringing over native Irish Catholics as well as English soldiers from Ireland did his cause great harm. 'This victory so successfully obtained,' one

London newspaper, *The True Informer*, suggested, after the fighting at Nantwich, 'doth eminently confirm that general observation concerning the unsuccessfulness of his Majesty's forces since the coming over of the Irish, since which time his Majesty hath lost the affections and assistance of most of his English subjects which were formerly addicted to neutrality.' For many years the popular fear of Roman Catholics in England had led to periodical panics. Reports that Catholic families were buying large quantities of food would lead to fears that an uprising was imminent. 'As much meat is dressed in Sir Basil Brookes' daily as three cooks can make ready,' runs one characteristic warning, 'and it is not seen or known who eats it.' 'It is generally observed,' runs another, 'that the Papists in these parts [Carlisle] never kept greater families than they do at present, which is much to be feared.' Earlier in the 1640s there had been warnings in several areas that Papists were hoarding not only food but guns and ammunition, swords and axes as well. The reports of the King's importing thousands of Catholic Irish into the country now led to similar scares.

The people's disillusionment with the King was deepened when newspapers reported that over a hundred Irish women were captured after the fighting at Nantwich and that they were found to be armed with knives over three feet long. These knives, by no means a superfluous weapon for camp followers, were said to have a hook at the end and were thus capable not merely of stabbing but also of tearing 'the flesh from the very bones' of their enemies. The women, *The True Informer* said, were either to be put to the sword or tied back to back and thrown into the sea. In fact, Fairfax, who enrolled eight hundred of their men into his army after their capture in Cheshire, allowed them all to go home.

Despite the anger aroused in England by his bringing over soldiers from Ireland, the King continued to press for them. By the time of the fighting in Cheriton Wood over seventeen thousand troops had crossed the Irish Sea and more were expected, despite the efforts of Rowland Laugharne and Richard Swanley to prevent them.

Laugharne, a Welshman who had once been a page in the Earl of Essex's household, had been appointed by Parliament Governor of Pembroke and commander of Parliamentary forces in the area. An energetic and resourceful man, he had soon captured Carew Castle, Roach Castle and various other Royalist garrisons as well as Tenby and Haverfordwest, thus providing harbours for the ships of Captain

Swanley, an experienced naval commander formerly in the service of the East India Company. Swanley diligently patrolled the Irish Sea, stopping vessels suspected of carrying troops from Ireland and, on one occasion at least, persuading the English and Welshmen on board a ship out of Dublin to swear allegiance to Parliament, and tying the Irishmen aboard back to back with two women before throwing them all overboard 'like water rats'.

Gloomy as Essex insisted were Parliament's prospects, with Royalist reinforcements coming over from Ireland and with decisive Roundhead victories as remote as ever, encouraging reports were now reaching London from the north. The bitter winter over, the Scots had moved south across the Wear and were approaching Durham, while Sir Thomas Fairfax and his father had stormed the strategically important town of Selby where they had captured large stores of ammunition and almost the entire garrison of over 1,500 men and nearly seventy officers. The Fairfaxes had advanced north from Selby, while the Scots, having obliged the Royalist commander, the Marquess of Newcastle, to abandon Durham, had moved south to meet them. The two forces, English and Scots, joined forces at Wetherby on 20 April. The Marquess of Newcastle immediately scurried off to the safety of York with his infantry and artillery, considering himself fortunate in getting behind the city's strong walls without molestation. Sir Charles Lucas thought himself equally lucky in escaping to Newark with his cavalry.

From York, Newcastle despatched an urgent message to Prince Rupert, warning him that if his Highness did not 'please to come hither and that very soon too', the 'great game of his Uncle's would be endangered, if not lost'. Doubting not 'that his Highness would come and that very soon', he subscribed his letter 'Your Highness's most passionate creature, W. Newcastle'.

The Marquess's urgent plea was not the only one Prince Rupert received at this time. Since the war was being fought on so many scattered fronts, he was wanted in the south and the west as well as in the north. The army facing Manchester's Eastern Association wanted him. So did the Queen who was in need of an escort to take her to Bath. So did the King who required his advice at Oxford, now threatened again by Sir William Waller. His presence was universally acknowledged to be virtually indispensable; his name was worth 'half a conquest'.

Ignoring the other demands upon him, Prince Rupert obeyed the summons of the King and rode to Oxford for one of those councils of war which so often ended in shouted argument, with Wilmot blaring at the Prince, the Prince blaring back when not reprimanding Lord Percy or casting aspersions upon George Digby as well as Sir John Culpeper, the Master of the Rolls, who had once been a soldier and fancied himself an expert in military matters. During these rowdy and fatiguing discussions Lord Forth pretended to be more deaf than he was so as to escape taking sides; Sir Jacob Astley, who had once been Prince Rupert's tutor and was now evidently in awe of him, endeavoured not to let it be seen that he was no great strategist; while the King was as ready as ever to be swayed first by one argument, then by the next.

On this occasion a majority of the councillors appeared to favour an immediate attack upon the enemy around Oxford; but Rupert advised against any move in this part of England while the north was under so serious a threat. Far better, he argued, to remain on the defensive at Oxford and to reinforce Prince Maurice in the west, while he himself marched north to the relief of York which was now invested by some twenty thousand Parliamentary troops well supplied with heavy artillery.

Supported as it was by the King, Prince Rupert's plan was approved; and on 16 May he moved north for York, being joined on the way by John Byron's troops from Chester. When their march was resumed the Prince and Byron had rather more than fourteen thousand men between them. They would undoubtedly need them all. For, since the investment of York by the Scots and the Fairfaxes, the Earl of Manchester's Eastern Association had attacked and captured Lincoln and, with the surrounding countryside now firmly in Parliament's hands, the Association's troops had marched towards York to swell the numbers of Roundheads already encamped beneath the walls of the 'pleasant, spacious and beautiful capital of the north'.

Yet, if he had doubts as to the successful outcome of his campaign, Prince Rupert let no one know of them. Marching smartly north, he took Stockport in Cheshire and stormed into Bolton in Lancashire, a largely Puritan, cotton manufacturing town whose garrison was massacred and whose poor inhabitants the Cavaliers plundered indiscriminately, killing well over a thousand of them in revenge for the Governor's having hanged a Royalist prisoner from the walls of the town at Prince Rupert's approach. Joined by a further five thousand men under George Goring, and by the Earl of Derby who had come over from the Isle of Man, the Prince marched on to Wigan where the people came out to welcome him, throwing spring flowers and wreaths of foliage at his feet. Calling at Lathom House, from which the besiegers had fled at his approach, he was hugged by the brave and corpulent Lady Derby before marching west to Liverpool, 'the Bristol of this part of England', a thriving port on the Mersey, 'a noble harbour able to ride a thousand sail of ships at once'.

He was held up for a time in Liverpool by the men of the garrison, determined to get their stores loaded aboard the ships in the docks and carried out to sea before they were forced to succumb to the Royalist shot thundering against their defences, at a heavy cost in gun powder which Prince Rupert could ill afford. After five days the Parliamentary commander submitted; Prince Rupert rode into the town which, like Bolton, was thoroughly plundered after most of the garrison of four hundred men had been butchered; and a fine port was secured for the reception of soldiers sailing over from Dublin.

With most of Lancashire now under Royalist control, Prince Rupert was preparing for his assault upon the rest of the county when a letter reached him from London urging him to make haste in completing his work in the north and to come south again to help the King as soon as he possibly could.

The King's letter was couched in apologetic terms, for the decision taken to remain on the defensive in the south and west for the time being had been reversed in Rupert's absence, with disastrous results. 'I confess,' the King wrote, 'the best had been to have followed your advice . . . We doubt not but to defend ourselves until you have time to beat the Scots, but if you be too long in doing of it, I apprehend some great inconvenience.'

The King admitted that, after his nephew had left Oxford, it had been decided at a council of war that the Royalists in and around Oxford should go on the offensive, that the garrisons to the south of the city, at Reading, Abingdon and elsewhere, should be withdrawn and that the King's army should move purposefully west. The outcome of these manoeuvres had been lamentable: Waller's army occupied the towns which the Cavaliers had abandoned, including Abingdon where the ancient market cross which was decorated with images of saints and kings was torn down. Waller had then advanced within a mile of two of Oxford, threatening to capture the King who was then at Woodstock. Rejecting a suggestion that he would be well advised to surrender to Parliament with the words, 'I may be found in the hands of the Earl of Essex but I shall be dead first,' the King hurried back to Oxford. But warned that with both Waller and Essex so close to the town and with provisions there running so low, he would be starved out within a fortnight, he left as though intent upon attacking Abingdon and then, with three thousand horse and 2,500 infantry, he marched through the Cotswolds to Evesham and Worcester, learning on the way that Parliamentary forces had taken Tewkesbury and that Waller and Essex were both on his heels.

'When I have told you that Essex comes upon us one way,' Lord Digby wrote to Prince Rupert, 'and that Waller [is] likely to go about us on the Welsh side by Gloucester, that Massey and the Lord Denbigh [are] towards Kidderminster, both with considerable forces; and when to all this I shall add . . . that Oxford is scarcely victualled for a month, and for aught we know blocked up in a manner by the enemy's horse, your Highness will easily frame to yourself an image of our condition.'

On 9 June the King learned that Lord Chandos's fifteenth-century castle at Sudeley, north-east of Cheltenham, had surrendered after a long siege, and that the Roundheads were now threatening to capture the Queen at Exeter.

Escorted by her friend Lord Jermyn, the Queen had left for Exeter to await the birth of her ninth child on 17 April. She had begun to lose heart in Oxford where she suffered from a perpetual racking cough for which she blamed the damp Thames Valley air. She was suffering, too, from spasmodic and violent pains which she felt could not be attributed to her pregnancy. Charles had accompanied her as far as Abingdon and had said goodbye to her there. She was convinced she was going to die, that she would never see her husband again. Her doctor said that she was hysterical.

She did not die; her baby, a healthy daughter, was born at Exeter on 16 June and was given her mother's name. But the Queen was right in one respect: she never did see her husband again. By the time of her confinement Parliamentary troops were closing in upon

Exeter; and, as soon as she could travel, dangerously ill now with puerperal sepsis, she crept out of the town accompanied only by a priest, one of her ladies and a doctor who, so he complained, had to walk 'most of the way into Cornwall'. The night before she sailed for France from Falmouth she wrote to her husband, 'Adieu, my dear heart. If I die, believe that you will lose a person who has never been other than entirely yours, and who by her affection has deserved that you shall not forget her.'

Charles, campaigning with his army in the west, moved down into Devonshire and arrived in Exeter a fortnight after his wife had gone.

He could take some comfort in his grief at having to say goodbye to her that his enemies were not enjoying the successes in the West Country by which they had set such store. The Earl of Essex, as well as hoping to capture the Queen, had also intended to relieve Lyme, the small but extremely useful port on the Dorset coast between Weymouth and Exeter. He had received orders to return from the West Country to lay siege to Oxford while Waller was to receive reinforcements to advance against the King. This predictably made Essex extremely grumpy. Taking umbrage once again, he replied, 'If you think fit to set [Waller] at liberty and confine me, be pleased to make him general, and me the major-general of some brigade . . . That army which hath the greatest strength of foot will be most able, by God's blessing, to reduce the West and I believe that I have the most resolute foot in Christendom.' He would stay where he was and not return to the Thames Valley. From his ship lying off the shore here, Essex's friend the Earl of Warwick, commander of Parliament's navy, had asked for the cooperation of land forces in bringing relief to Lyme. For weeks on end this town had withstood a besieging army commanded by Prince Maurice who had stormed it three times, only to be driven back by the determined resistance of the garrison, by seamen landed from the Earl of Warwick's ships, and by the local inhabitants who vigorously supported them under the direction of Robert Blake, the eldest of the twelve sons of a Somerset merchant, a merchant himself and Member for Bridgwater since 1640. Blake had once had thoughts of an academic career and had spent almost ten years at Wadham College, Oxford, before standing unsuccessfully for a fellowship at Merton, his failure being due, so it was said, to his 'short, squat, ungainly figure' which offended the aesthetic sensibilities of the Warden. A resolute, blunt and fearless man, he was eventually to become one of England's greatest admirals. At Lyme in this early summer of 1644 Blake was tireless in his efforts to encourage the defenders to stand firm behind their earthen defences, to be sparing of the supplies which the Earl of Warwick's ships brought them, to endure the bombardment of the harbour, and to foil attempts to set fire to the town by the discharge of red-hot shot.

Their courage was repaid. On the night of 14 June, Prince Maurice, warned of the Earl of Essex's approach, at last accepted the impossibility of taking Lyme and early the next morning withdrew towards Exeter 'with some loss of reputation for having lain so long, with such a strength, before so vile and untenable a place, without reducing it'. An Irish woman left behind by a regiment from Munster 'was slain and pulled almost to pieces by the women of Lyme'.

By now a Committee for Both Kingdoms had been formed in London, a council of five peers, ten Members of Parliament and three Scottish representatives, which met every day at three o'clock. They ordered Essex to return towards London after relieving Lyme; but he, disregarding these instructions, marched west into Cornwall, offering the Royalist command an opportunity to take advantage of the widening separation of the Roundhead armies, which the Committee had been anxious to avoid, to deal a crippling blow to Sir William Waller.

The Cavaliers came up with Waller near Banbury on 28 June. In an attempt to lure him into open ground where his London regiments would have to fight the Cavaliers at a disadvantage, they marched north by the banks of the Cherwell, in sight of the Roundheads who were also marching north on the far bank of the river. By the time they reached Cropredy Bridge five miles north of Banbury, a gap had opened up in the Royalist line of march, over a mile separating rearguard and vanguard; and Waller, looking down upon the scene from a nearby hill, saw his chance of becoming the hunter rather than the hunted. He sent one strong detachment across Cropredy Bridge and raced back with another to a ford, hoping to surround and destroy the Royalist rearguard. He failed to do so. His own detachment was repulsed at the ford, while at Cropredy Bridge fierce fighting resulted in heavy casualties and the loss of most of Waller's guns.

For the whole of the next warm summer day the two armies remained on opposite banks of the river watching each other warily, while the King sent messages to Waller vainly pressing him to come to terms. The Royalists then moved off south on the road to Bicester and thence to Evesham, while the Parliamentarians marched towards Towcester. Waller assured the Committee of Both Kingdoms that the Royalists' army had been severely weakened.

His own army, it would have been more accurate to report, was on the verge of dissolution. The London regiments, never happy to serve far away from home and having marched over two hundred miles in the past four weeks, began to raise the common cry of 'Home! Home!' Hundreds of Waller's unpaid men succumbed to this call and wandered off through a countryside offering little shelter or comfort; while he himself, well aware that he was losing both popularity and respect, dispiritedly reported to London that it was for the time being impossible to undertake any worthwhile enterprise so long as the soldiers were more concerned about their homes and shops, their farms, jobs and businesses than they were about soldiering and so long as the local committees continued to lose interest in winning the war once the danger to their own districts was passed. 'In these two days' march,' Waller reported to London, 'I was extreme plagued with the mutinies of the City brigade who are grown to that height of disorder that I have no hope to retain them, being come to their old song of "Home! Home!"' . . . I am confident that above 2,000 Londoners ran away from their colour.' The soldiers from Hertfordshire were just as bad, he went on, grumbling 'at a night or two's ill quartering'. 'My Lords,' he concluded, 'I write these particulars to let you know that an army compounded of these men will never go through with your service, and till you have an army merely your own, that you may command, it is in a manner impossible to do anything of importance.'

Major-General Richard Browne, the London timber merchant and commander of a Parliamentary force raised in the counties of Berkshire, Buckinghamshire and Oxfordshire, who had been ordered by the London Committee to cooperate with Waller, was equally disheartened and just as troubled by ill discipline among his men, some of whom refused to carry out his orders, going so far as to set upon him when he insisted that they obey him. 'Major-General Browne's men,' Waller reported, 'being most of them trained band men of Essex and Hertfordshire, are so mutinous and uncommandable that there is no hope of their stay. They are likewise upon their march home again. Yesterday they were like to have killed their Major-General, and they have hurt him in the face. Such men are only fit for a gallows here and a hell hereafter.'

Browne had a different solution: deciding that he could keep his troops together only by allowing them to plunder, he took them off, without Waller's permission, to Greenland House, the Royalist post on the river between Henley and Marlow, where they were permitted to loot to their hearts' content; and having pillaged the house, they destroyed what was left of it.

Yet, desperate as seemed the condition of the Parliamentary armies, the King considered his own position scarcely more favourable. He had recently written to Prince Rupert in reply to a letter now lost:

> If York be lost, I shall esteem my crown little less . . . Wherefore I command and conjure you, by the duty and affection which I know you bear me, that, all new enterprises laid outside, you immediately march according to your first intention, with all your force to the relief of York. But if that be either lost . . . or that for want of powder you cannot undertake that work, that you immediately march with your whole strength immediately to Worcester to assist me and my army, without which, or your having relieved York by beating the Scots, all the successes you can afterwards have most infallibly will be useless to me.

This letter reached Rupert soon after he had captured Liverpool. Taking it as a command to proceed immediately to York, he set off without delay, crossing the Pennines at Clitheroe, reaching Skipton on 26 June and Knaresborough on the thirtieth. Learning of his approach from the east, the Parliamentary commanders withdrew their forces from the north side of York, crossed the river Ouse by a bridge of boats and formed up near the village of Long Marston to block Prince Rupert's approach from Knaresborough. But the wily Prince suddenly changed direction. He turned north to Boroughbridge near Ripon, crossed the Ure there and came down upon York's now undefended northern side.

IO

ROADS TO
MARSTON MOOR

'The runaways on both sides were so many,
so breathless, so speechless, so full of fears that
I should not have taken them for men, but by
their motion.'

Sir Arthur Trevor

For two months now the city of York had been isolated, and its inhabitants reduced to existing on a diet composed largely of bread and beans. At the beginning of the siege the garrison had occupied outlying suburbs and the fields where the city's cattle were grazed and had defended this large perimeter by recently erected fortifications. But after the arrival of the Eastern Association under the Earl of Manchester, with supplies for the besiegers, they were no longer able to defend so extended a front and had withdrawn behind the ancient yet still well-preserved walls of the medieval city, setting fire to the suburbs to deprive the enemy of cover. Behind these walls, which stretched for rather more than two and a half miles, enclosing an area divided by the rivers Ouse and Foss, the defenders, commanded by the Marquess of Newcastle, had stood their ground, diligently watching the Parliamentary armies that surrounded them upon every side, constantly improving the fortifications of the gates known as bars which pierced the walls at irregular intervals.

Should the defenders be forced back from the walls, preparations had been made to hold a smaller area between the rivers over which the bridges were to be blown up. This area was to extend from the castle in the south to the gate in the north known as Bootham Bar, close by the Minster, the largest of England's medieval cathedrals.

But Newcastle did not expect to be pushed back so far. He had firmly rejected a summons to surrender the city on 14 June 1644 and soon afterwards the garrison had withstood an attack upon Bootham Bar which the besiegers had mined.

Even so, Newcastle could not be expected to hold York much longer. His supplies were almost exhausted; his men were tired out; the besieging force was almost twenty-five thousand strong. News of Prince Rupert's approach towards the city's northern gate was, therefore, greeted with profound relief. 'You are welcome, Sir, so many several ways, as it is beyond my arithmetic to number,' Newcastle wrote with characteristic fulsomeness to the Prince who, crossing the Ouse near Boroughbridge and the Swale at Thornton Bridge, and marching his infantry over twenty miles in a day, had approached within four miles of the city. 'You are the Redeemer of the North and the Saviour of the Crown,' Newcastle continued in his most blandiloquent vein. 'Your name, Sir, hath terrified three great generals and they fly before it.'

Certainly the three besieging generals, the Earl of Leven, commanding the Scots, Fairfax's army from northern England, and Manchester's Eastern Association, had withdrawn from their lines at Prince Rupert's approach, leaving their camps to be plundered by the garrison and citizens of York who rushed out through the gates to find that in their haste to get away the Roundheads had left, in addition to siege guns and piles of ammunition, no fewer than four thousand extremely welcome pairs of new boots and shoes. The generals had marched their troops south-west of York to Marston Moor, intending to block the road to Tadcaster in the expectation that, now Prince Rupert had relieved York and brought supplies and reinforcements to the garrison, he would turn that way to join forces with the King.

But Rupert had as yet heard nothing of his uncle's victory at Cropredy Bridge and, believing him to be still in the parlous state his last letter had described, had determined to make an immediate attack upon the Parliamentary armies as soon as the Marquess of Newcastle's troops joined him.

In his complimentary letter of greeting, Newcastle had added, 'It seems [the three enemy generals'] design is not to meet Your Highness for I believe they have got a river [the Ouse] between you and them, but they are so newly gone as there is no certainty at all of them or their intentions. Neither can I resolve anything since I am made of nothing but thankfulness and obedience to Your Highness's commands.'

Taking this as an offer by Newcastle to serve under him, Prince Rupert ordered George Goring to go into the city and to tell Newcastle that he would expect him at four o'clock the following morning when they would march out together against Parliament's forces. The Marquess of Newcastle did not take kindly to what he took to be a peremptory, not to say impertinent summons from a young man who seemed not only to disregard his own seniority and experience but who also apparently failed to appreciate the exhausting and meritorious service upon which he and his army had for so long been engaged. Provoked to the quick, Newcastle, who had, after all, raised a large part of his army at his own immense expense, threatened to resign. He had done so before, and had been dissuaded by the King who implored him to consider, 'If you leave my service, I am sure all the north is lost. Remember all courage is not in fighting, constancy in a good cause being the chief, and the despising of slanderous tongues and pens being not the least ingredient.' On this occasion, too, Newcastle allowed himself to be persuaded that duty and honour impelled him to remain with the army until at least the conclusion of the imminent battle and to go out to Prince Rupert to offer him his advice. Soon after midnight, in the company of several of York's leading citizens, he left the city for Prince Rupert's headquarters on Marston Moor, leaving his men under the command of his deputy, a Scottish mercenary from the Swedish army, James King, recently created Lord Eythin and Kerrey, whom the Queen had brought over with her from the Continent.

'My Lord,' said Rupert in greeting Newcastle, 'I wish you had come sooner with your forces. But I hope we shall have a glorious day.' He had wanted, he said, to attack without delay, while Parliament's armies were still unprepared and had not yet come onto the moor in full strength. Even now he proposed attacking without waiting for Lord Eythin to bring up the men from York. There were already some fourteen thousand Royalist troops on Marston Moor, half of them excellent cavalry. Admittedly the Roundheads outnumbered them, but they were a far less cohesive force with three different commanders. Newcastle demurred: Eythin would not be long; it would be wiser to wait for him. Prince Rupert gave way.

Lord Eythin was long in coming, however. He did not like Prince Rupert. They had served together in 1638 in Münster where the Prince had been taken prisoner and Eythin had been accused of an error which he strongly contested was not his; and the incident had rankled with him ever since. Before Newcastle had left York, Eythin had fuelled his resentment against the Prince; and after Newcastle had gone, he had shown how reluctant he was to get his men on the march to fight against his fellow-Scots. The men themselves were in no hurry to move, demanding that they were paid before they did so. It was not until after four o'clock in the afternoon of 1 July that four thousand of his five thousand troops appeared on the moor, marching through the summer rain, hearing the Roundheads singing hymns amidst the rye on the summit of the ridge. Lord Eythin was as surly as any of his men. 'By God, sir!' he exclaimed when shown a draft of Prince Rupert's battle plan, 'It is very fine on paper but there is no such thing in the field.' The men were drawn up far too close to the enemy. They could be pulled back, Rupert suggested, uncharacteristically accommodating. 'No, Sir, it is too late.' As for Prince Rupert's suggestion that they should attack immediately while the daylight lasted, this was utterly perverse: 'Sir,' Eythin said rudely, 'your forwardness lost us the day in Germany where you yourself were taken prisoner.'

'We will charge them tomorrow morning,' Prince Rupert suddenly announced, giving way again. It was then about half past six. He dismounted and called for his supper. The Marquess of Newcastle strolled off to his coach to smoke his pipe. 'Happen what will,' he said to friends who had told him it would be unworthy of his honour to serve under Prince Rupert, 'I will not shun to fight, for I have no other ambition but to live and die a loyal subject of his Majesty.'

Prince Rupert's cavalry were on the right of his two-mile line behind a screen of musketeers who were sitting down along a hedge-lined ditch, deep in places, which separated the rye enclosures of Marston Field from the heathland of Marston Moor. The horse had been drawn up here in the Swedish manner, the squadrons interspersed with musketeers, by the Major-General of the Horse, Sir John Urry, the veteran Scottish mercenary who had formerly served Parliament and was to serve it again. In command of the first line, although he had proved himself a reckless leader at Edgehill, was Lord Byron,

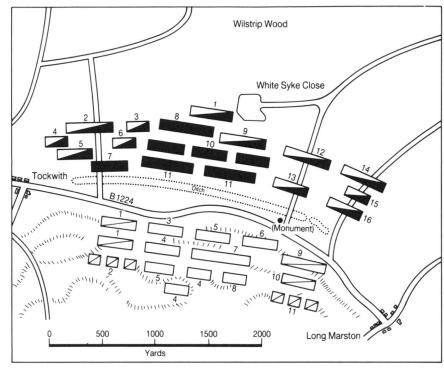

White Syke Close

Wilstrip Wood

Tockwith

Ditch

B 1224

(Monument)

Long Marston

0   500   1000   1500   2000

Yards

ROYALISTS

▨ Cavalry   ■ Foot

1   Prince Rupert (Reserve)
2   Lord Molyneux
3   Prince Rupert
4   Lord Byron
5   Sir Samuel Tuke
6   Marcus Trevor
7   Colonel Napier
8   Sir Francis Mackworth
9   Sir William Blakiston
10 Newcastle's Whitecoats
11 Henry Tillier
12 Sir Charles Lucas
13 Lord Goring
14 Colonel Dacre
15 Colonel Carnaby
16 Colonel Langdale

PARLIAMENTARIANS

▨ Cavalry   ☐ Foot

1   Oliver Cromwell
2   Sir David Leslie
3   Lawrence Crawford
4   Scots
5   Lord Fairfax
6   Sir William Baillie (Scots)
7   Major-General Lumsden (Scots)
8   Lord Manchester
9   Sir Thomas Fairfax
10 John Lambert
11 Lord Eglinton (Scots)

The Battle of Marston Moor

recently Governor of Chester where his soldiers, already notorious as pillagers, had enraged the citizens by plundering their houses when they were at church and pawning the contents. Behind Byron, commanding the reserve was Lord Molyneux. On their left the infantry – including the Marquess of Newcastle's regiments, known as 'Lambs' or 'Whitecoats' because of the uniforms of undyed woollen cloth worn by two of the four regiments – were arranged in three lines. Behind the infantry, south of Wilstrop Wood, were Prince Rupert's life guard; and on their left were over two thousand more cavalry under Lord Goring, with Sir Charles Lucas, a brave soldier who served the King throughout the war, in command of the second line.

Facing Goring, across the ditch on the outskirts of the village of Long Marston, were the right wing of the Roundhead cavalry under Sir Thomas Fairfax, drawn up below a slight, wooded eminence, Marston Hill, which was crowded with excited spectators milling about in front of the baggage train. Behind them, facing the Royalist foot, were the Parliamentary infantry, commanded by Lord Leven, men from the Earl of Manchester's Eastern Association, levies from Yorkshire and Lancashire, and the Scots, their officers wearing white bands of paper in their hats as field signs. On Parliament's left wing facing Prince Rupert's cavalry was Oliver Cromwell, commanding the horse of the Eastern Association, supported by three Scottish regiments under David Leslie, riding their 'little light Scotch nags'. In all Parliament's forces numbered some twenty-seven thousand men, the Royalists' about eighteen thousand. The two armies, less than a quarter of a mile apart on the wings, could see each other quite clearly, observe every movement in the opposite lines, every musketeer and pikeman in the leading ranks, every colour flapping in the intermittent showers of rain.

There had been a brief exchange of cannon fire in the early afternoon, but for two hours now there had been no sounds of war. Only the neighing of horses, the murmur of voices, the chink and rattle of harness, and the occasional singing of hymns and psalms in the Roundhead ranks broke the afternoon's quiet. Then, sometime after six o'clock, when many of the spectators on Marston Hill had gone home in the belief that there would be no battle to enjoy that day, a roll of thunder gave warning of a storm in the darkening sky; and as hailstones began to fall, the Roundhead infantry under the Earl of

Leven advanced down the slight incline that led towards the ditch separating the two armies, trampling the wet rye underfoot. They went forward through the smoke from the cannon, so one of their chaplains said, 'like unto so many thick clouds', Cromwell's cavalry on the left moving forward at a steady trot against Byron's first line whose troopers, riding forward to meet them, passed through the musketeers in their front, masking their fire, and were soon being forced back in such confusion that Prince Rupert galloping up, shouting, 'Swounds, do you run? Follow me!' had difficulty in rallying them for the counter-charge.

Cromwell was slightly wounded in the neck and seems to have briefly left the field to have the cut bandaged in a cottage on the outskirts of Tockwith; but David Leslie came up with his Scotsmen to fall on the flank of Prince Rupert's horse who were then charged again by the well-trained cavalry of the Eastern Association. Within minutes scores of Royalist troops were 'flying along by Wilstrop Wood as fast and as thick as could be'. It was then that Cromwell's men reaped the reward of their stern and assiduous training. Instead of giving way to the temptation to pursue the flying horsemen, they rallied, and obedient to voices of command, wheeled to gallop back to support the Scotsmen still holding their ground.

On the right of their line the charge of the Roundhead cavalry under Sir Thomas Fairfax had been far from successful. The ground here, crossed by ditches and covered with bushes and furze, was much more difficult for cavalry operations, while the ditch and hedge in their front were major obstacles. After savage fighting, during which several Royalist companies were put to flight, Fairfax had suffered many casualties; his brother Charles was dying; he himself was wounded in the cheek and, surrounded by enemies, would have been captured had he not removed the white band which he was wearing as a field sign in his hat. The infantry who had managed to clamber across the ditch were pushed back into it and over it by Newcastle's 'Whitecoats', only two regiments, both Scottish, standing their ground, firmly grasping the shafts of their pikes, refusing to give way. Lord Goring's Cavaliers rode through Fairfax's second line, then through his rearguard, scattering the remaining spectators on Marston Hill, plundering the baggage, and cutting down the Scots reserves who tried to run away towards Selby. 'The runaways on both sides were so many, so breathless, so speechless, so full of fears,' recalled Sir Arthur Trevor who came onto the field to deliver a message to Prince Rupert, 'that I should not have taken them for men, but by their motion. Both armies [were] mingled, both horse and foot, no side keeping their own posts.' He saw a party of Scotsmen running helter-skelter down the hill, crying, 'Woe's us! We are all undone!'; and one 'little foot officer without hat, band, sword or indeed anything but feet and so much tongue as would serve him to enquire the way to the next garrison'. 'In the fire, smoke and confusion of that day,' he added, 'I knew not for my soul whither to incline.'

Carried away by the rout of his troops, Lord Fairfax fled as far as Cawood; while Lord Leven – also believing in the confusion and the smoke now covering both field and Moor that the battle was lost – galloped away almost as far to Wetherby.

The battle, though, was far from lost. Informed of the rout of most of their right wing, Cromwell, his wound bandaged, and Leslie, also wounded, galloped off behind their own lines to attack Goring's troopers in their rear. They dispersed them at once, then turned back towards Wilstrop Wood to fall upon Newcastle's 'Whitecoats' who stood firm with their pikes long after the sun had set, choosing to die rather than surrender. Scattered survivors of these Yorkshiremen fought on under the light of a bright harvest moon, while the Roundheads hacked at them mercilessly, and Sir Thomas Fairfax, bleeding copiously from the deep cut in his cheek, did his best to save the lives of the wounded, knocking up his men's weapons with his sword, appealing to them, 'Spare your countrymen!'

The 'Whitecoats' 'would have no quarter', it was said of them, 'but fought it out till there were not thirty of them living whose hap it was to be beaten down upon the ground. As the Roundhead troopers came near them, though they could not rise from their wounds, yet [they] were so desperate as to get a sword or pike or piece of them, and to gore the troopers' horses as they came over them or passed them by.'

About four thousand Royalists were killed that day and some 1,500 taken prisoner; fugitives attempting to escape the Roundheads' swords fled for York's western gate, but few managed to gain entrance for, as Sir Henry Slingsby said, 'at the bar none was suffered to come in but such as were of the town, so that the whole street was thronged up to the bar with wounded and lame people, which made a pitiful cry among them'.

The Roundheads' losses were less severe than those of the Cavaliers; but it was the fiercest and bloodiest battle they had yet fought. Ensign Gabriel Ludlow, a cousin of Edmund Ludlow, a major in Sir Arthur Haselrig's regiment, was one of the many young officers killed, dying in agony 'with his belly broken and bowels torn, his hip-bone broken, all the shivers and the bullet lodged in it'. Prince Rupert's white poodle, 'Boy', also lay dead upon the field; whilst his black dog was captured, so a Parliamentary tract reported, 'and, our officers have cut his ears and made him a round head'. The Prince's splendid standard of black and gold, blue and silver had also been captured and sent to London for display, together with nearly fifty other standards or the remnants of standards torn apart by soldiers eager to return home with mementoes of their victory. Indeed, it was said that enough colours had been taken 'to furnish all the cathedrals in England'. Prince Rupert, forced to hide for a time in a beanfield, rode back to York along a road strewn with the dead and dying bodies of Royalist soldiers cut down in retreat. He found the city crowded with wounded, men lying in the streets as well as in the houses, as their officers 'came dropping in one by one, not knowing, but marvelling and doubting, what fortune might befall one another'.

Their enemies returned to the field of their victory to offer thanks to God for their triumph and, having prayed, to strip naked the corpses of the enemy dead, searching for food as well as for valuables since their wagons had been plundered not only by Royalists but also by deserters from their own army and by the hangers-on of both. Water, too, was short and men could be seen on their knees sucking at puddles and in the ditches which cut across the eastern end of the moor. The Earl of Manchester rode from regiment to regiment, thanking them for their services, urging them to thank God for the victory He had granted them. Next day a captured Cavalier officer, Sir Charles Lucas, was taken round to inspect the thousands of partly clothed and unclothed bodies to decide which deserved a burial more decent than being tipped into the huge common pits. He could not hold back his tears. 'Alas for King Charles!' he murmured. 'Unhappy King Charles!'

Charles, to be sure, had cause for grief. He not only had to face the imminent surrender of York and the loss of the north, apart from a few isolated strongholds, but the Marquess of Newcastle, unwilling to be any longer associated with so forlorn a cause and so uncongenial a commander as Prince Rupert, had ridden off to Scarborough with Lord Eythin and other disillusioned and disgruntled officers. Rupert had tried to dissuade him, but Newcastle had been adamant. He had always, as Edward Hyde said, 'liked the pomp and absolute authority of a general well, and preserved the dignity of it to the full; and for the discharge of the outward state and circumstances of it, in acts of courtesy, affability, bounty, and generosity, he abounded . . . But the substantial part, and fatigue of a general, he did not in any degree understand nor could submit to.' He had now, he decided, had quite enough of it.

No, he announced, he certainly would not stay in England where he had spent a fortune in the King's cause and where his estates were now occupied by the enemy. 'I will not,' he said, 'endure the laughter of the court.' He sailed for Hamburg and went from there to Paris where he remained for three years.

Hopeless as Newcastle now thought it, the King's cause was, however, not yet lost. Prince Rupert managed to escape from York-shire by way of the western dales with six thousand men; and the three armies which had combined to defeat him, following a prece-dent which the Civil War had long since made familiar, went their separate ways on isolated and local operations: the Scots went north to besiege Newcastle; Sir Thomas Fairfax remained in Yorkshire to attack those strongholds which still held out against him, Pontefract, defended by the uncompromising Richard Lowther, and Scar-borough, held by Sir Hugh Cholmley who had spurned Newcastle's pleas to escape with him to the Continent. The Earl of Manchester took the Eastern Association back to Lincolnshire where he showed himself unwilling to pursue the war with vigour anymore, being in Cromwell's later accusation 'always indisposed and backward to engagements' now the complete victory for Parliament presaged what Manchester called 'an occasion of rising again or of a future quarrel.'

Fearing a Parliamentary victory which would now certainly bring dangerous men like Cromwell to the fore, Manchester declined to move on Newark, accepted the surrender of Welbeck with grumpy reluctance, and quarrelled fiercely with John Lilburne who, like

Cromwell, was endeavouring to bring some vigour into the Eastern Association's operations.

There were bitter quarrels, too, in London where religious differences were becoming ever more deep and unbridgeable. Independents – men who held views which may be compared to those of the later Congregationalists – claiming to have been largely responsible for the victory at Marston Moor, argued endlessly with Presbyterians.* Episcopalians differed from them both. Two Roman Catholic priests were hanged. Detractors of Cromwell railed against him for filling his ranks with sectaries and Anabaptists and raising such ill-disposed troublemakers to positions of command. Men of property feared a general uprising of the lower orders encouraged by agitators of wild doctrinal views. Books and pamphlets streamed from the printers' presses proposing all manner of strange and subversive tenets, questioning the most fundamental Anglican doctrines. From their pulpits preachers raged against the evils and fallacies of the times. 'Since Pym died,' wrote Robert Baillie, one of Scotland's envoys in London, there was 'not so wise a head amongst them': many were 'good and able spirits, but not any of so great and comprehensive a brain . . . If God did not sit at their helm, long ere this they had been gone.'

While not so deeply divided by political and religious differences as the Parliamentary leaders, the commanders in the King's camp could certainly not be described as living in agreeable harmony. Henry Wilmot's recent elevation to the peerage as Baron Wilmot of Adderbury and his marriage to the rich widow of Sir Francis Henry

---

* 'Presbyterian,' as John Kenyon has observed, is 'almost as difficult a word to construe as "Puritan".' In its original sense it was applied to a member of a Church which was governed by elders or presbyters (Greek *presbuteros*, elder) and in which no higher order, such as bishop, was recognized. Presbyterianism was adopted in Scotland after the Reformation in 1560; and although it had never found many converts in England, by the Solemn League and Covenant of 1643 Parliament pledged itself rather ambiguously to introduce Presbyterianism into the English Church. Opposed to the Presbyterians were the Independents, who rejected both elders and bishops and who advocated the autonomy of local church congregations.

As the Independents gained influence in the army, the term 'Presbyterian' was increasingly used to describe laymen of conservative or moderate views like Sir William Waller and the Earl of Manchester, the old guard of Parliamentarianism. At the same time, the term 'Independent' was applied to all degrees of radicalism both religious and political. Cromwell was described as an Independent, as he was in his religious beliefs; but his respect for the social order was in line with Presbyterian thinking.

Lee had not improved his sullen temper. Repeatedly he spoke ill of Prince Rupert and hinted darkly that the Royalist cause might prosper better were the King not to lead it. Wilmot also spoke out against Lord Digby who, since the Queen's departure for the Continent, had become, with the Duke of Richmond, one of Prince Rupert's warmest supporters, much to the annoyance of Lord Percy, who disliked the Prince as much as ever.

Urged by Prince Rupert to get rid of the devious and argumentative Lord Wilmot who, like Manchester, doubted the wisdom of continuing the war, the King had him arrested and sent under guard to Exeter. At the same time the elegant person of George Goring arrived from Lancashire in answer to the Prince's summons and was appointed Lieutenant-General of the Horse in his old rival's place. Angered by this treatment of Wilmot, who had led them to victory more than once, his officers expressed their 'great amazement almost to distraction', while their men became so unruly that the King felt obliged to ride up and down their ranks in an effort to placate them. This really was, Lord Digby expostulated, the 'most mutinous' army he had ever come across, horse and foot alike.

As angered as his officers by Wilmot's arrest, Lord Percy, to Prince Rupert's ill-concealed delight, promptly resigned and was succeeded by Lord Hopton as General of the Ordnance. Prince Rupert himself, who was still in the north, hoped to succeed Lord Forth, now Earl of Brentford, as Commander-in-Chief; and was, indeed, assured by Lord Digby that this was now merely a matter of time: all that stood in the way was finding some suitable alternative office for the old Scotsman. But before this could be arranged, the Prince's elder brother, the Elector Palatine, arrived in London with the declared intention of acting as peace negotiator between King and Parliament and with the secret hope of replacing his uncle as King of England. Although the Parliamentary leaders had no mind to consider so bizarre a scheme, the King thought it as well not to make Prince Rupert Commander-in-Chief so long as his brother remained an honoured guest of Parliament at Whitehall Palace.

Prince Rupert was in Bristol at this time. He had spent the earlier part of August at Chester where his officers had been busily recruiting men and sending them down to Shrewsbury for training; and he was now endeavouring to placate the people beyond the Welsh border – whose fragile loyalty to the King depended upon the

uninterrupted enjoyment of their trade – and to capture the stronghold of Montgomery Castle which its owner, the unpredictable Lord
Herbert, had allowed the Roundheads to occupy on condition that
they did not go into the library.

The King, having spent most of July in Devonshire, was now in
Cornwall, pursuing the Earl of Essex down the peninsula towards
Fowey. Predictably blaming Sir William Waller for not having intercepted the King on his way south, Essex was disappointed in his
hopes of raising support for Parliament in these parts. He entered
Fowey, expecting that the Earl of Warwick's ships would come there
to rescue him. Contrary winds delayed Warwick's arrival, however;
and by the time the ships did come the Royalists had occupied so
many strategic positions around Fowey harbour that Essex decided
he would have to escape while he still could. Ordering the Dutch
mercenary Hans Behre to creep away with the cavalry by night
through the Cavaliers' lines, and leaving his infantry and gunners to
defend themselves as best they could under the command of Philip
Skippon, Essex took a fishing boat to one of Warwick's ships and
sailed in her for the Hampshire coast. 'I thought it fit to look to
myself,' he explained, 'it being a greater terror to me to be a slave
to their contempts than a thousand deaths.'

Behre succeeded in leading his stealthy cavalry past the Royalist
outposts; but Skippon could not persuade the infantry to fight their
way out after them. At a council of war several officers protested
that their men were in no spirits for such an enterprise and some
grumbled about being asked to fight when their commander had
deserted them. Skippon was accordingly forced to surrender, handing over all his guns and ammunition and almost ten thousand muskets to the King's troops. A few of his men, drenched to the skin
and on the verge of starvation, were prevailed upon to join the
Cavalier army, the rest being told to march off on the understanding
that they would not fight for Parliament again. One of the King's
officers watched them depart to Portsmouth:

> It rayned extremely as the varlets marched away . . . They all
> except here and there an officer (and seriously I saw not above three
> that looked like a gentleman) were strucken with such a dismal
> feare that as soon as the colour of their regiment was passt (for
> every ensigne had a horse and rid on him and was so suffered) the

rout of soldjers of that regiment presst all of a heap like sheep, though not so innocent. So durty and so dejected as was rare to see. None of them, except some few of their officers, did looke any of us in the face.

They were thankful at least not to have been treated as prisoners of war had been at Holt Castle where they had been murdered and tossed into the moat, or at Bolton where all the enemy and as many civilians as could be found were slaughtered, at Barthomley where they had been killed 'most barbarouslie' in cold blood, or on the road to Oxford in 1643 when they 'had in all their passage, not so much as water; for some being drie, would faine have dranke of the water in the high-way, but they would not suffer them; nay, they strook many of them over the heads with their canes, for stooping to take a piece of ice, to hold in their mouths, to quench their violent thirst'. Most of these captives, so one of them complained, were tied together with cord and were 'without stockings on our legs, or shoes on our feet, or hats on our heads, many of us having no doublets, and some gentlemen of good quality without breeches; the wind blowing very cold and we standing barefoot and bareleg'd in the snow'.

In London the Committee for Both Kingdoms learned the news of the disasters in Cornwall with a dejection as deep as their soldiers'. From all over the south, indeed, there came news of failures and disorder: Essex, continuing to castigate Waller, complained that he could not possibly reorganize his disintegrating army without more positive support, his letter explaining his recent conduct being greeted by derisive laughter from Sir Arthur Haselrig when read out in the House of Commons. Waller, at odds with General Browne as well as with Essex, was equally downhearted; his men at Farnham, unpaid and ill-fed, were on the verge of mutiny. Parliament had sent him 1,400 reinforcements, but these were not much use, he grumbled, because they had 'brought their mouths with them'. Browne at Abingdon gloomily reported that his troops were being driven by want to plunder; Hans Behre resigned his command as soon as he got back from the west and returned sulkily to Holland. Richard Norton, a close friend of Oliver Cromwell, remained impatiently week after week before the massive walls of Basing

House, while his men sickened in the changeable late summer weather. The Earl of Manchester, moving very slowly south and as garrulous as ever, ignored Parliament's instructions to join forces with Waller in Dorset and to intercept the Royalists coming up from the West Country, arguing that it would be folly to risk a confrontation with them until Essex's army had been reorganized. Cromwell considered this to be a defeatist attitude only too typical of Manchester. In Scotland the Marquess of Montrose was winning a series of victories for the King over the Scottish Presbyterians.

Only to Cromwell, one of his supporters said, could Parliament look with hope, although Cromwell, in the opinion of the Scottish professional soldier Lawrence Crawford, was not to be trusted. Cromwell in turn spoke slightingly of Crawford, as he did of most Scottish soldiers, and was appalled when he learned that this dedicated Presbyterian and protégé of the Earl of Manchester, twelve years younger than himself, had been appointed second-in-command of the Eastern Association. The Committee for Both Kingdoms pleaded with Cromwell and all the other squabbling commanders to 'lay aside all disputes of their rights and privileges, and to join heartily in the present service'. Eventually the Committee concluded that the only solution was to appoint a war council from among their senior officers with authority to take decisions by majority vote.

II

FIGHTING LIKE
BEASTS

---

*'If we beat the King ninety and nine times, yet
he is King still, and so will his posterity be
after him: but if the King beat us once we shall
all be hanged and our posterity made slaves.'*

The Earl of Manchester

After the battle of Marston Moor, Prince Rupert, in reluctant admiration of Cromwell's hard tenacity, had called him 'Ironsides', and the nickname was soon applied to all the fine troops he commanded. Yet Cromwell realized that, reliable as his own men were, victory could not be won until far more of Parliament's forces were as well organized and trained as the Ironsides were. Pursuing with relentless determination Sir William Waller's idea that Parliament should have a standing army 'merely of their own', Cromwell urged the creation of a truly professional, regularly paid force under the firm control of a single commander. Until the 'whole army were new modelled and governed under a stricter discipline,' he told the House of Commons, 'they must not expect any notable success in anything they were about.' No good soldier should be excluded from this new army, Cromwell insisted, merely because his own way to God differed from the orthodox way of the Presbyterians. He had been exasperated in the past when men and officers had been criticized, punished or even dismissed from their regiments not because of any military lapse or incapacity, but because they happened to hold some sectarian view. The new army must not on any account deny itself the services of Independents, nor must it deny promotion to them; certainly it must not be placed under the command of officers of the old school, like Essex and Manchester, who had proved not only their incapacity but also their unwillingness to bring the King to final and total military defeat 'through the ending of the war by the sword'.

Well aware of this growing fear in the Parliamentary army of the consequences of outright and decisive victory over the Royalists, Charles returned to Oxford in the brief hope of arranging a negotiated peace on favourable terms. He knew that the Scots were dismayed by the dismissal of the Presbyterian Manchester in favour of that 'darling of the sectaries', Oliver Cromwell, a man who should, in the opinion of the Scots, himself have been dismissed for his religious beliefs as a known sympathizer with the Independents; and he had been much cheered by his victory over Essex in Cornwall. He had returned north with a sense of pride in his military skill, though Essex's defeat had been achieved more by the Earl's incompetence than by the King's own dexterity. The more realistic members of his staff could not share his Majesty's optimism. They knew well enough that their army was poorly supplied, disconcertingly short of cavalry, and severely weakened by the need to leave garrisons and siege detachments in the West Country. Moreover, the Royalists' control over the kingdom was now largely limited to the south and west of the country; while the King's continuing negotiations for help from Ireland were losing him much sympathy and costing him much support. Yet his confidence appeared to be undimmed; and whenever he seemed momentarily downcast in the autumnal rain, there was the genial Lord Digby, possessed 'of great gaiety', to cheer him up as they marched off together, 'victorious and strong'.

They entered Salisbury 'in excellent spirits' on 15 October 1644; they sent Waller scuttling from Andover; they obliged Parliament's investing force to abandon the siege of Donnington Castle, the fourteenth-century Royalist stronghold north of Newbury which, held for the King by Colonel John Boys, commanded the Great Bath Road from London to the west as well as the road from Oxford to Portsmouth. They heard with delight that yet another assault on Basing House had been driven off; and, while they were obliged to face a serious setback by the fall of Newcastle to the Scots, they were cheered by continuing good news from Scotland.

The Parliamentary leaders were, by contrast, in utter disarray. The

Earl of Manchester, on bad terms with both Cromwell and Waller and increasingly convinced that the war was becoming futile, protested repeatedly about his men's arrears of pay, his losses through sickness and desertion, and about the orders that Parliament gave him. 'They would have me march westward,' he wrote discontentedly, 'Westward Ho! But they specify no place . . . It may be the West Indies or St Michael's Mount.' Essex, marching through the pouring rain with the infantry who had not forgiven him for deserting them at Fowey, declared that he was really too ill to carry on. Balfour's cavalry was in a sorry state.

Reluctant colleagues, the Roundhead commanders moved disconsolately towards Newbury with the intention of blocking the King's road to Oxford before Prince Rupert rejoined him and before 1,500 horse returned from Banbury whence they had been sent to relieve the besieged garrison commanded by Sir William Compton, the eighteen-year-old son of the Earl of Northampton, who had replied to demands that he surrender with the declaration that 'he kept the castle for his Majesty, and, as long as one man was left alive in it, witted them not to expect to have it delivered'.

Despite their mutual antipathy and lack of trust, the Roundhead generals were eventually persuaded to agree upon a plan to force the King to fight them while he was still outnumbered. The larger part of their force, comprising Essex's regiments, the London Trained Bands and both Cromwell's and Waller's cavalry, were to make a circuitous march and then to fall from the west upon Speen Heath, the rising ground to the north-east of Newbury where the Royalist main body was drawn up. At the same time the rest of the Parliamentary infantry, commanded by the Earl of Manchester, were to make an assault upon Shaw House, a fortified manor house protected by earthworks, on the other side of the Royalist position.

Although the Cavaliers' position was a strong one, protected by the guns of Donnington Castle and by Prince Maurice's artillery on Speen Hill, the Roundheads had reason to feel confident of victory: they had over seventeen thousand men under command, facing less than half that number. At first all went well with them. The attack on Speen Heath was delayed following a slow and laborious march; but, after heavy fighting, the Royalists were driven off the high ground towards Speen village, losing several guns on which a party of Roundhead troops, recognizing them as those captured from them in Cornwall, 'clapped their hats on the touchholes to claim them as their own'. To the east, however, the Earl of Manchester had delayed his attack with disastrous consequences. It was not until the late afternoon of that October day, an hour after the assault on Speen Heath, that he began his own attack. Ill deployed and ill led, his men were thrown back with losses so heavy that the Royalists, leaving their guns in Donnington Castle, were able to escape unscathed, Sir Charles Lucas having taken off his buff coat so that his men could see his white shirt in the gathering darkness. The King got away with a small escort to Bath where Prince Rupert was awaiting him; the rest of his army escaped to the safety of Oxford, ineffectually pursued by the Roundhead horse and, for a short distance only, by Manchester's infantry whose commander, refusing to respond to the pleas despatched to him, was more than ever convinced that peace was the only answer to the country's ills. 'Thou art a bloody fellow,' he exclaimed furiously at a council of war when Haselrig proposed an attack upon the King and Prince Rupert at Bath. 'God send us peace, for God doth never prosper us in our victories to make them clear victories.'

The Royalists were now in no mood for peace. Having joined forces at Bath with Prince Rupert, recently appointed *de facto* Commander-in-Chief in place of Lord Brentford who had been wounded in the recent battle – and whose carriage containing his elderly German wife was captured in the retreat – the King made for Burford, on the edge of the Cotswolds north of Oxford; then, returning to Donnington Castle to fetch his heavy guns, he threatened the Roundheads with them in the open field before marching off again with drums beating and banners flying triumphantly as though in celebration of another victory.

Manchester was not the only senior Roundhead officer reluctant to respond to the King's provocation. At a council of war Cromwell was alone in advocating another battle. Voices previously raised in support of him were silent. Waller had said some time before, 'Break the [Royalist] army never so often, his person will raise another.' Manchester now declared: 'If we beat the King ninety and nine times, yet he is King still, and so will his posterity be after him; but if the King beat us once we shall all be hanged and our posterity made slaves.'

'My Lord, if this be so,' Cromwell objected, 'why did we take up arms at first? This is against fighting ever hereafter.'

But many now, even Haselrig, were coming to think that Manchester was right, and when the Committee for Both Kingdoms ordered the generals not to go into winter quarters while the enemy was 'still in the field and to have a care to prevent the relief of Basing', they protested their utter inability to obey. With men deserting every day, with sickness ever increasing, with mutiny threatened at Windsor, with wholesale desertions at Gloucester, with horses in short supply, with adequate supplies unobtainable and spirits so low, further action against the enemy was for the moment impossible. Even Cromwell was forced to concur that the army was in no condition to fight, 'very unable for marching or watching, having now for so long time been tired out with hard duty in such extremity of weather as hath been seldom seen'. The King, marching into Oxford, was seen for once to smile.

Twice every week the King walked round the Oxford fortifications, talking in his distantly gracious way to the citizens still hard at work on them, encouraging them with news of recent victories in the field, assuring them that the war would soon be over. He seemed, indeed, to believe himself that this would be so. When a Parliamentary delegation arrived in Oxford to propose a treaty, he saw to it that they were kept waiting before being admitted through the walls into Christ Church garden, then treated them with cold dismissiveness, handing them his answer in a sealed letter which he disdained to discuss with them, Prince Rupert and Prince Maurice looking down upon the Roundhead delegates with amused contempt. Soon afterwards the King sent the Duke of Richmond and the Earl of Southampton to London with a fuller response, but making it clear to them that, although he agreed that the two sides must stop 'fighting like beasts', his views on episcopacy and the command of the army were unalterable. He did not expect the negotiations, which were desultorily discussed for most of the rest of that winter at Uxbridge, to come to anything; but his two envoys would at least have an opportunity of discovering the mood of the Parliamentary leaders and of the people of London and might be able to exacerbate his enemies' religious differences.

The reports which came back to the King from London were most encouraging – coal was still in short supply and many households were reduced to burning turf, since the Scots who had taken New-castle were refusing to allow coal to be shipped south until their army had been paid. Equally encouraging was the news that the Parliamentary generals were still at loggerheads: Cromwell had con-demned the Earl of Manchester's 'backwardness' in a report submit-ted to the House of Commons in which he had written of the Earl's 'averseness to engagements' and 'neglecting of opportunities'. Man-chester and his friends had retaliated by attacking Cromwell as an unreliable and unfaithful subordinate commander whose officers were unsuitable men of 'mean parentage', some of them vagabonds who had come back from America where they had failed to settle happily, and many of them religious fanatics who interpreted the Bible in their own peculiar ways for the benefit of their illiterate troopers. Some of these troopers, making wild claims to supernatural experiences, actually presumed to preach in church. Cromwell's friends, supported by St John and Vane, responded to these attacks, while pamphlets and broadsheets appeared from London's presses, condemning one side or the other, sometimes both.

At the same time, in a vain effort to enforce obedience to Parlia-mentary injunctions and accepted doctrine, the executioner was kept busily occupied. Sir Alexander Carew, second-in-command of the garrison at Plymouth, was executed for having attempted to surren-der the place to Prince Maurice. Sir John Hotham and his son were also beheaded for their similar offence at Hull. Henry Morse, a Roman Catholic priest who, in the past, had worked unsparingly among the plague-ridden poor of London, many of whom he had converted to his faith, had also been taken to the scaffold and there made to suffer a traitor's death. His clothes were stripped off and he was left to hang naked from the noose before being cut down. 'His heart was then torn out,' recorded the Marquis de Sabran, the French Ambassador, 'his entrails burnt and his body quartered.' 'My Lords,' said the Sheriff, apologizing both to de Sabran and the Spanish Ambassador, 'I regret that you should have witnessed such a spec-tacle, but such are our miseries that it must be done.' The large crowd looked on in silence.

A few days before it had been Archbishop Laud's turn to die, and he, too, suffered his fate in dignity, even when his vicious enemy, the blustering Irish Presbyterian Sir John Clotworthy, thrust his way onto the scaffold to ply the Archbishop with questions and to trick him into some damning statement. But Laud would have none of it. 'I have always lived in the Protestant religion as established in England,' he declared to the surrounding multitude and to the people standing beneath the scaffold and staring up at him through the gaps in the boards on which he stood, 'and in that I come here now to die.' The King also, he said, was 'as sound a Protestant as any man in the Kingdom'. Then, turning away from the petulant harassment of Clotworthy and giving himself up to the attentions of the executioner, the 'gentler of the two', he laid his head on the block. It was severed at a single blow and held up to the crowd, the once red face now white. His body was buried in the church of All Hallows, Barking, the officiating clergyman bravely repeating the words of the Prayer Book whose use had been forbidden on the same day as the Bill of Laud's Attainder had been passed. When told of his Archbishop's death, the King expressed the characteristically self-centred belief that this murder by Parliament would be regarded by God as atoning for his own guilt in signing the death warrant of his other faithful servant, the Earl of Strafford. He then returned to considerations of war.

There were still successes to encourage him: a garrison had been well established at Chipping Campden; Sir Lewis Dyve had captured Weymouth on the Dorset coast; and, at Bristol, Spanish ships containing cargoes worth more than £200,000 had been seized when they sought shelter there from pirates. Edward Massey's hold on Gloucester seemed to be loosening week by week. Early in the New Year Sir Marmaduke Langdale led the Northern Horse, an élite corps comprised in its commander's words of 'officers, gentlemen of quality and their attendants', back to their home land. Having defeated one Parliamentary force at Market Harborough, they routed another at Ferrybridge, killing three hundred Roundheads and taking another eight hundred prisoner before demolishing the siege works at Pontefract.

From elsewhere there came comforting reports of growing trouble in the Roundhead ranks: their troops mutinied at Henley; there was a mutiny, too, at Leatherhead, when some of Essex's cavalry regiments were threatened with transfer to William Waller. 'We would rather go under any the Lord General should appoint,' they protested, 'than Sir William Waller with all the money in England.'

Even Cromwell's unpaid men, sent to Weymouth, had mutinied.

Yet there was more to lament than to celebrate. The King was chronically short of infantry and was constantly losing men who deserted either to go home or to join the other side where pay, although difficult enough to come by at times, was rather more regularly issued than it was to the Royalist ranks in which the six shillings a week offered them – two shillings of that reportedly placed to their credit – was rarely forthcoming and often held back to meet the cost of their food and clothing. The King raised money by so-called contributions in the areas where his forces held sway; but the funds thus realized rarely reached the soldiers' pockets, the other expenses of war – not least the cost of ammunition and powder imported in huge quantities from France – having to be considered first.

Day by day there came news of setbacks in the field: Prince Rupert failed in his attempt to capture Abingdon when the Parliamentary Governor, Richard Browne, led his men across a ford in the Thames, charged into the Cavaliers' flank and forced them to withdraw with losses they could ill afford, including Henry Gage, the skilled, recently knighted veteran of Continental wars who was mortally wounded. This was 'a wonderful loss' to the King, so Hyde said, 'Gage being a man of great wisdom and temper, and amongst the very few soldiers who made himself to be universally loved and esteemed'. Five other officers who had come over from Ireland were taken prisoner and hanged by General Browne in Abingdon market place in loose accordance with an ordinance issued by Parliament creating it a capital offence for any Irishman, or any Roman Catholic Englishman born in Ireland, to fight for the King.

Meanwhile, in the south-west, the rich, young Anthony Ashley Cooper who had gone over to Parliament's side after being appointed Governor of Weymouth, brought a much-needed convoy of supplies past Royalist outposts to the Parliamentary garrison at Taunton; in Hampshire, George Goring was repulsed when he made an ill-conducted attack upon Christchurch; while in Devon, Sir Richard Grenville suffered a similar and costly defeat when he made an assault upon Plymouth. In Wiltshire, Oliver Cromwell, having restored order in his mutinous regiments, led them into Devizes where he took three hundred prisoners, including the Sheriff of the County, before moving on into Dorset. In Dorset, a Royalist force admitted

by night into Melcombe was soon thrown out again by the Roundhead garrison and forced to retreat to Dorchester; in the Forest of
Dean a raiding party from Edward Massey's garrison at Gloucester
fell upon the troops of the King's ironmaster, Sir John Winter, and
routed them; and, most dispiriting of all, in Shropshire the Cavaliers
lost Shrewsbury, for long their training and recruiting centre, an
important stronghold on the line of communication between Chester
and Oxford, and one without which Hereford and Worcester were
at risk.

The Governor of Shrewsbury was Sir Michael Erule, a sickly man,
ill-suited even when in better health for the responsibilities of his
command. His men carried out their duties with surly reluctance
under the eyes of resentful inhabitants only too anxious to be rid of
them. Two of these disenchanted civilians undertook to help the
Parliamentary army to get into the town; and when Colonel Thomas
Mytton, in command of a force of over a thousand Roundheads,
slipped past the inattentive outposts and crossed the river with an
advance party in rowing boats by night, these two guided him to a
gap in the defences. Colonel Mytton's men crept through, sprang
upon the guards on the gate by the river, killed some, disarmed the
others, and opened the gate for the rest of Mytton's force to rush in
upon Shrewsbury at four o'clock in the morning.

Ill though he was, Erule rose from his bed, buckled on his sword
and hurried out of his house to die in the street. Most of his subordinate commanders fled with their men to the castle where they soon
surrendered. Permitted to withdraw to Ludlow, they agreed to abandon all their guns and stores as well as all the soldiers who had come
over to fight for the King from Ireland. Thirteen of these were
hanged, an atrocity which Prince Rupert – after protesting to the
Earl of Sussex that the Royalists had always allowed quarter to prisoners of 'all religions and opinions' – met with reprisals equally
savage:

> The next day the Prince caused [his own prisoners] to be brought
> before him [wrote Richard Gough, historian of the Shropshire vil-
> lage of Myddle, then a schoolboy], and he ordered thirteen of them
> to be hang'd. They cast the dice on a drum head to see who should
> die, and amongst them there was one Phillip Littleton, who had
> been servant and keeper of the park to my old master, Robert

Corbett of Stanwardine, Esq. This Phillip saw Sir Vincent Corbett, of Morton Corbett, ride by, and said to some that stood by, 'If Sir Vincent Corbett did know that I were here, he would save my life.' Upon this a charitable soldier rode after Sir Vincent and told him what one of the prisoners said. He came back immediately, and seeing Phillip, he alighted from his horse and fell on his knees before the Prince (who sat there on horseback to see the execution) and begg'd for the life of Phillip, which was readily granted .on condition he would never bear arms against the King. Phillip promised and escaped.

Much disheartened by the loss of Shrewsbury, the King had other misfortunes to face. In an attempt to bring new life into his cause in the West Country he sent the Prince of Wales, now aged fifteen, with Edward Hyde and John Culpeper to establish a separate court at Bristol. They left Oxford in the first week of March 1645; but when they arrived in Bristol they found the Royalist commanders in the West Country far more active in pursuing personal vendettas than in raising money and troops for the King. Sir Richard Grenville, indeed, was behaving as vindictively and outrageously as a thirteenth-century baron in the civil wars of Henry III's time, arresting citizens and demanding ransoms, forcibly extracting fines from men who exercised their right to fish in what he insisted were his rivers or who refused to grind their corn at his mill, throwing into gaol and even hanging enemies and rivals and those who disputed his manorial rights – 'so strong was his appetite to those executions he had been used to in Ireland' – taking over the estates of his estranged wife (whom he had treated with the 'greatest barbarity') and hanging the solicitor who had conducted her case against him. Frequently he proposed wild schemes; but when it came to executing the more sensible of these plans, few turned out as promised; once, for example, 'having with great importunity gotten from the Commissioners of Devon above 1,000 deal-boards to make huts for the soldiers, he employed them all in building a great riding-house at Buckland for his own pleasure'.

He refused to take orders from Lord Goring who, claiming to be his superior, was behaving almost as reprehensibly as Grenville, committing 'horrid outrages and barbarities' and ravaging the countryside 'in most scandalous manner, a great part of his horse living upon free quarter and plundering to the gates of Exeter'. His men were guilty of such 'continual butcheries, rapes and robberies' that over a hundred years later a local historian maintained that in those parts 'the name of Goring's Crew is even now remembered with abhorrence'.

So also was that of another Cavalier commander in the west, Sir Francis Dodington, a deeply unpleasant man who hanged several prisoners after the capture of Wardour Castle and, having captured Woodhouse, a small Roundhead garrison on the borders of Wiltshire and Somerset, hanged fourteen more, one of whom he assaulted before he was strung up, so another officer said, striking him 'so many blows upon the head and with such force that he broke his skull and caused him to fall into a swoon'.

'Who art thou for, priest?' Dodington had once called out to a clergyman he had come across on the road outside Taunton, giving a well-known challenge to which prudent men answered, 'For the King.' 'For God and his gospel,' the parson replied. Dodington then shot him dead.

Like Dodington, Lord Goring was frequently drunk and, while disregarding orders that came to him from the Prince of Wales's Council, he used that Council as an excuse to ignore the commands of Prince Rupert.

'I expect nothing but ill from the west,' Rupert lamented. How could the war be carried on with such generals as these? He might also have asked how could the army as a whole be reorganized when neither he nor the King was suited to the task? Certainly there could be little hope of success for them in the field against the new army which the Parliamentary leaders were at last bringing into being.

12

THE NEW
MODEL ARMY

'Never did hardly any army go forth to war
with less confidence of their own side.'

Thomas May

In December 1644 Oliver Cromwell had made an impassioned speech in the House of Commons in which he had expressed the hope that, having 'such true English hearts and zealous affections towards the general weal of [their] Mother Country . . . no Members of either House [would] scruple to deny themselves, and their own private interests, for the public good'.

Cromwell's friend Zouch Tate, Member for Northampton, probably acting under the influence of Sir Henry Vane, then rose to propose a measure which became known as the Self-Denying Ordinance and which obliged all Members of both Houses of Parliament to resign any military command they might be holding. The Ordinance applied to Cromwell himself, of course, as much as to Essex and Manchester and those officers of the old school it was designed to remove without undue ill feeling; but it did not preclude the possibility of an officer from the House of Commons being reappointed to his command, and there was never any doubt that the Self-Denying Ordinance was not intended to apply to Cromwell himself, who became General of the Horse.

Nor did it apply to Philip Skippon, who was appointed Sergeant-Major-General of the new army, nor to Sir Thomas Fairfax, who did not become a Member of Parliament until later, who had never sought political influence and had never pressed such religious views as he held upon others. Cromwell regarded him as highly as did anyone; and when he was called before the Commons in February 1645, not long after his thirty-third birthday, to accept the office of Commander-in-Chief, there was scarcely a Member present who did not welcome him, who did not endorse the Speaker's thanks for his past services, and who did not wish him well in undertaking 'the greatest trust that was ever put into the hands of a subject'. Declining to sit down, he replied briefly to the Speaker's address, his stammer rather more pronounced than usual, his arm in a sling, recovering from a musket wound in his shoulder suffered during the siege of Helmsley Castle. He then returned to his duties.

The New Model Army, the 'New Noddle' as the Royalists called it, the Army of Parliament under the Command of Sir Thomas Fairfax as it was officially known, was already taking shape. The money to pay for it was still to be raised locally but its disbursement was to be supervised by Parliament, which felt obliged to consider every means at its disposal for raising more. It was suggested, for example, that the valuable paintings at York House which had been collected by the Duke of Buckingham should be sold. There was a problem here, however, as one primly fastidious Member pointed out: 'Most of those pictures were either superstitious or lascivious and it was not fit to make benefit of the superstitious ones but to have them burnt.' Before the superstitious ones could be burned and the lascivious ones sold, the Earl of Northumberland intervened. As tenant of York House, he declared that the place would not be fit for habitation if the pictures, Titians and Rubenses amongst them, were to be removed from its walls, and that if he had to move to another house he would expect the House of Commons to pay his rent. No more was heard of the matter.

There was to be no question in the future of men enlisted into the army by one county leaving to serve in another for the sake of higher pay. Rates of pay were to be standardized; and since so many disorders and mutinies had been occasioned in the past by the men's pay not being forthcoming, recruits were to be assured that, while the cause for which they were to fight was a noble one, they would be rewarded in this world as well as the next for embracing it. They were to be 'well clothed' in scarlet woollen coats which the British Army was to wear until the advent of khaki in the nineteenth century;

foot soldiers were to paid 1s.6d. a day, and while this was scarcely more than a farm labourer could then expect, the money, they were assured, would be regularly forthcoming – as, in times of scarcity and distress, agricultural wages were not. The cavalryman was to receive two shillings a day for himself and his horse, a quarter of this being retained for future payment in accumulated arrears as security against desertion. They were also to be provided with buff coats of thick leather to be worn under their back and breast plates.

When endeavouring to persuade old soldiers of Essex's army to enrol in the new army, Philip Skippon took care, in an 'excellent, pious, and pithy hortatory speech', not only to assure them that he would 'by the help of God, be willing to live and die with them' but also to pledge his word that they would receive 'constant pay'. As an earnest of this, they could draw fourteen days' pay immediately.

Even so, recruiting into the infantry was not an easy process. From the old armies of Essex, Manchester and Waller, scarcely more than seven thousand foot came forward, less than a third of the establishment required. To make up the balance conscription had to be used – as it had been by the Royalists – and was stubbornly resisted. Eventually the death penalty was imposed as a punishment for conscripts who did not report for duty within six days and was later inflicted upon deserters, plunderers and mutineers, while a blasphemer had his tongue pierced with a red-hot iron. But as a deterrent to desertion, capital punishment proved useless. A party of conscripts in Kent ran off while being marched to join their unit and barricaded themselves in a country house near Wrotham. They were forced to come out; but, once escorted to their depot, they ran away again. The French Ambassador, the Marquis de Sabran, reported that young men were being stopped by recruiting parties on the streets of London and being hustled away to boats which took them up the Thames to Maidenhead.

Despite all endeavours Fairfax's army never achieved the strength Parliament intended for it; and few of its regiments were not weakened by desertions from time to time. As in the Royalist army, cavalry were raised more easily than foot, since the pay of cavalrymen, when they got it, was not only higher than that in the infantry, but there was also slightly less chance of being killed in battle and a better chance of escape after a defeat. Moreover, a horse soldier could cover far more ground than an infantryman in his search for food, plunder and lodgings. Cavalry recruits, however, were liable to be just as obstreperous as those levies from Suffolk who were 'so mutinous' that Cromwell feared they might well cut his throat.

Officers were more easily found than other ranks; and relatively few of them came from lower-class families, much as Cromwell's enemies would have it otherwise and much as was made in Royalist circles of the origins of such men as Colonel Thomas Pride, said to have been a brewer's drayman, Colonel John Hewson, 'sometime an honest shoemaker in Westminster', and Colonel Thomas Shelbourne, formerly John Hampden's shepherd. It has been calculated that of thirty-seven officers of colonel's rank and above in the New Model Army, only seven were of 'the lower or middling sort'; nine were related more or less closely to noble families; twenty-one were gentlemen by birth.

On the night of 24 April 1645, Oliver Cromwell summoned the garrison at Bletchingdon House near Islip in Oxfordshire to surrender. Ordered by the Committee for Both Kingdoms to march towards the Cotswolds, cutting across the King's communications between Oxford and his troops in the west, he had crossed the Cherwell at Islip, scattering a Royalist patrol and capturing a Royal Standard. At Bletchingdon House the young and recently married Cavalier commander, Francis Windebank, a son of a former Secretary of State, believing himself far from the war, had gone to bed after a dinner party given for his young wife's friends, several of whom were staying in the house. Concerned that they should be spared an assault on the house by Cromwell's troops, he agreed to surrender. He was allowed to leave the house for Oxford, but was arrested on his arrival there and court martialled. The King, 'often so merciful, was obdurate'. The young man was condemned to death and shot in the Castle garden.

Cromwell's troopers trotted on, past Kidlington and Witney to Bampton on the road to Faringdon. Here he had another encounter with the Cavaliers who retreated before him, as they had done in Islip. 'The enemy is in high fear,' he reported to the Committee in London. 'God does terrify them.'

The King, at least, was far from terrified. His opinion of Parliament's new army was no higher than that of Thomas May, the poet and playwright, who was called upon to write the *History of the Long Parliament* and who described the New Model Army as one 'seeming no way glorious either in the dignity of commanders or [experience] of soldiers . . . Never did hardly any army go forth to war with less confidence of their own side.'

The King's confidence, boosted by the cheerful presence of Lord Digby and news of further victories by Montrose against the Scots, appeared to be boundless. His army had admittedly suffered some setbacks in the west, but the Royalists remained strong in the area. They had not yet taken Gloucester, but they were successfully preventing much of the wool from the district reaching London. They still drew tin from the mines of Cornwall and iron from the Forest of Dean. Indeed, industries all over England were as busily producing arms and armaments, uniforms and shoes for his army as they were for the Parliamentarians. The Royalists had musket factories in Oxford and Bristol, armaments works in Worcestershire, clothing mills and shoe factories in Oxfordshire.

Most of the King's supplies, however, came, as gunpowder did, from the Continent, although the still continuing Thirty Years' War made supplies difficult to obtain and a large part of what was shipped over was of poor quality. Much Continental weaponry was declared to be wanting by the King's Pike-Maker, Robert Thatcher.

As well as for weapons and supplies the King vainly looked to the Continent for reinforcements. He approached the Vatican; he applied to the Doge in Venice; his wife was in touch with both the Duke of Courland and the Duke of Lorraine, not to mention the Prince of Orange whose daughter, the King suggested, would make an excellent bride for the Prince of Wales.

While the King remained confident, several of his officers could best be described as insouciant. Lord Goring, for example, obeying such orders as he pleased and ignoring the rest, went to take the waters at Bath. In Cornwall, Richard Grenville, claiming to be independent of Goring and declining to take orders from anyone else, remained a law unto himself, exasperating Sir John Berkeley, Governor of Exeter, who refused to allow him any share of the supplies which were collected in Devon, thus provoking Grenville to send foraging parties to collect them for himself.

13

LEICESTER AND
NASEBY

---

*'There was scarce a cottage left unplundered
and no quarter given to any in the heat.'*

Captain Richard Symonds

Leaving his commanders in the west to their own devices, the King
left Oxford on 7 May, encouraged by an astrologer who had predicted a great victory for his forces and misery for his enemies in
London. Riding at the head of his troops, he made for Stow-on-the-
Wold where, with the Princes Rupert and Maurice at his side, he
held a grand review. He also held a council of war at which Prince
Rupert disagreed with the views of the majority of the other
members. They proposed to march west to block Fairfax's route to
Taunton, 'the fairest, largest and richest town in Somersetshire'; he
argued that it would be far wiser to march towards Carlisle, picking
up Langdale's Northern Horse on the way, to engage the weakened
Scottish army and perhaps to regain the north once and for all. With
the generals still at loggerheads in the west, Prince Rupert did not
believe that much of consequence could be achieved there for the
time being. Indeed, on the very day that the King had arrived at
Stow-on-the-Wold, the Royalists had made an unfortunate assault
on Taunton's East Gate. Inside the town Colonel Robert Blake,
who had so distinguished himself at Lyme the year before, had been
tirelessly encouraging the ill-supplied garrison in their resistance,
going so far as to cut the thatch from Taunton's cottage roofs to
feed their hungry horses. His men could not prevent the Cavaliers

storming through the gate; but he saw to it that they had a hard time of it trying to force their way up the narrow East Street, the houses on both sides of which he filled with his musketeers. Eventually, Blake's troops were forced back from house to house, as the Cavaliers' heavy guns roared through the smoke from the burning buildings, and were obliged to take up new positions around the church and castle. Blake was called upon to surrender here; he replied that he would sooner eat three of his last four pairs of boots; relief, he said, was on the way. And so it was. The Cavaliers, persuaded to believe that this relieving force was far larger than it was, resolved upon immediate withdrawal. So, cutting down the fruit trees in the surrounding orchards, already in blossom, and dragging the trunks across the approach roads, they abandoned Taunton to Parliament, whose troops entered the town to find over half the houses destroyed, 'heaps of rubbish . . . here a forsaken chimney, there a little fragment of a wall'.

At Stow-on-the-Wold, Prince Rupert had his way. The other generals, reluctantly conceding the force of his arguments, agreed to march north. So the Royalist army set out for another rendezvous at Market Harborough in Leicestershire where it was hoped the unpredictable Lord Goring would consent to join them. As they set off they were given encouraging news. The Roundheads had withdrawn their besieging force from Chester; and in Wales, Charles Gerard, one of the Cavaliers' most effective cavalry commanders, had obliged Rowland Laugharne to abandon both Haverfordwest and Cardigan and was now on his way with most of his troopers to join the King's army. If he arrived before Cromwell joined Fairfax, Parliament's new army would surely be defeated almost as soon as it had been created. The irrepressible Lord Digby naturally believed so. 'On my conscience,' he declared, 'it will be the last blow in the business. We never had more cause to thank God since this war began.'

All did not go as smoothly as Digby hoped, however. Gerard could not bring his troopers to join the King as quickly as was expected; and Goring, though he did for once agree to obey his summons, was interrupted on his way to the Midlands when his left and right wings, falling simultaneously upon an illusory Parliamentary patrol, fought each other for an hour or two in what Goring described as 'the most fantastical accident since the war began'. But

Royalist hopes revived again when Langdale's Northern Horse arrived at Ashby, and Henry Hastings, the Earl of Huntingdon's son, now Lord Loughborough – and popularly known as 'Rob-carrier' because of his success in waylaying Parliamentary convoys on their way north – also joined the King's army with several troops of horse. Together they rode on to Leicester, a town made prosperous by its brewers and stocking manufacturers, scattering a Parliamentary patrol so unprepared for battle that they had brought out their greyhounds with them, hoping to encounter a hare rather than the enemy.

The Royalist army halted outside Leicester's ancient walls while Prince Rupert's herald sought entrance to the town, demanding the gates be opened to the King. The town's corporation responded by sending out a trumpeter to ask for time to consider their reply and to protest at the Royalists' continuing to work on improving their batteries while negotiations were in progress. Much irritated by this, Prince Rupert angrily told the trumpeter that the garrison had precisely fifteen minutes to choose between surrender and assault.

Leicester was scarcely in a position to resist attack. The garrison numbered no more than 1,500 men; the fortifications were in poor condition; the suburbs, which had not been burned down as they had been at York and in other towns determined upon resistance, offered cover for the besieging force. Even so, the acting Governor, after conferring with two officers of the New Model Army who had ridden into the town with two hundred dragoons, refused to hand it over and prepared to withstand an assault. They did not have long to wait.

That afternoon the Royalist guns opened fire on the walls, and, after three hours of steady battering, opened up breaches 'which by the industry of the men and women of the town were some of them made up again with wool-packs and other materials'. When night had fallen, however, the expected assault was launched, one storming party attacking the breach by Newarke (the 'new work' added to the Norman castle in 1332), hurling grenades as they clambered up the scaling ladders and over the rubble. Here, according to one of the town's defenders, 'was the fiercest assault, the enemy coming up to push of Pike. Four times they attempted and were as often repulsed, our men taking two of their Colors from them. Captain Hacker and Captain Babington, with their horse and a cannon from a corner of the wall, made a miserable slaughter of them. Amongst the rest their Colonel St George in a bravery came up to our cannon, and was by it shatter'd into small parcels and with him many more, for, after the manner of the Turks, the horse forced on the foot to fight, and they being beaten upon by our Musketeers, great slaughter was made of them.'

While this fierce fighting was in progress, however, the Royalists had forced entrances through breaches on the other side of the town at Eastgates and, 'careering in a body six hundred strong', had fallen upon the backs of the defenders by the Newarke breach. Within an hour the fighting was over; the gates had been opened; the cavalry had galloped in; and the town was thoroughly plundered, merchants' houses being pillaged from cellar to attic, 'churches and hospitals made a prey to the enraged and greedy soldier to the exceeding regret of the King'. Shop shutters were splintered, the cottages of the stocking-frame workers 'ransacked without mercy', the tools of their trade hurled into the street, their hard-earned coins pocketed. One of the looters, so it transpired when the Mayor came to attend the King to morning prayer, had even taken the mayoral mace. It was estimated that during the course of the day 140 carts packed high with loot, together with about a thousand muskets and five hundred barrels of powder, rattled out of the town for Newark and Lichfield, for the Royalist garrison at Belvoir, the Earl of Rutland's castle, and for Ashby Castle which Roundhead propaganda depicted as being occupied by 'wretches' as 'debased and wicked as if they had been raked out of hell, and three malignant priests such as will drink and roar and swear and domineer so it would make one's heart ache to hear the country people relate what they heard of them'.

It was afterwards alleged that hundreds of the inhabitants of Leicester had been massacred by command of Prince Rupert, that, as Bulstrode Whitelocke said, the Cavaliers 'hanged some and cut others to pieces. Some letters say the kennels ran down with blood.' But a Puritan pamphleteer, reluctantly giving 'the Divell his due', conceded that he could 'not learne of any order to destroy all, as is said by some', though it was certainly true that 'there was indeed many slaine at the first entrance and some that made little resistance and some women and children amongst the multitude, by the rabble of common souldier'. Captain Richard Symonds, a Royalist officer, admitted that 'there was scarce a cottage left unplundered and no quarter given to any in the heat'. Some men were hanged; 'diverse women inhumanly put to the sword'; one woman who survived but who lost all she and her husband possessed went mad from shock and grief.

Although most of the King's senior officers now proposed with-drawing to Oxford which, alarmed by worried messages from Sir Edward Nicholas, they believed might fall to Fairfax any day, Prince Rupert strongly advocated leaving a garrison under Lord Lough-borough at Leicester and marching deeper into the Midlands to draw Fairfax off from their headquarters. The Prince, however, was unable to get his own way, for Langdale's Northern Horse, fearing that they were to be taken south, threatened to march off and 'could hardly be kept from disbanding or returning home in disorder'. Besides, Lord Goring had still not joined the King's army. The Royalist war council, therefore, concluded that their forces were not yet strong enough to undertake any such campaigning in the Mid-lands as Prince Rupert proposed.

Even so, the King remained in good heart, still evidently confident of ultimate victory. He was further encouraged when told that Fair-fax had withdrawn from Oxford and that the city was no longer in danger of assault. 'My affairs,' he wrote to the Queen, 'were never in so fair and hopeful way.' A day or two later he was said to be 'a-hunting' at Fawsley Park near Daventry, 'the soldiers in no order, and their horses all at grass' while Fairfax's army was less than two miles away.

Fairfax had been on his way to the relief of Taunton when recalled to besiege Oxford. 'I am very sorry,' he told his father, 'that we should spend our time unprofitably before a town, whilst the King hath time to strengthen himself.' He was deeply thankful when orders came to raise the siege; and he marched north-east as fast as he could in search of the King's army, hoping that he could engage it in battle before Lord Goring's cavalry joined it, and hoping, too, that Cromwell, on his way from Huntingdon, would reach him in time to add decisive strength to his own army. Even without Cromwell's men his army was stronger than the King's. He seems to have had rather more than six thousand cavalry and nearly seven thousand infantry as against some 3,500 Royalist horse and rather more than four thousand Royalist foot.

As soon as they learned of Fairfax's approach the Cavaliers withdrew from Daventry to Market Harborough, scouring the countryside for plunder and cattle with exceptional rapacity: it was later said of those taken prisoner that they rarely had less than 50 shillings in their pockets. Digby, optimistic as ever, was eager to find suitable ground on which to stand and fight, and was supported by Jack Ashburnham, a Groom of the Bedchamber, upon whose opinions the King set great store. But Prince Rupert, increasingly wary as the weeks went by and more and more inclined to the cautious views of the Marquess of Hertford and the Earl of Southampton, argued that it would be better to deny Fairfax the battle he was evidently seeking until Goring and Gerard joined them.

There was no such disagreement in the Parliamentary army. When Cromwell's troopers joined it to be greeted by loud cheers on 13 June, their commander consented to Fairfax's proposals without demur; so did Philip Skippon, commander of the infantry; so, too, did Henry Ireton, the tall, dark, clever young Nottinghamshire lawyer, Colonel Hutchinson's cousin, soon to become Cromwell's son-in-law, who was to command the cavalry on the New Model Army's left wing, and who, at Cromwell's insistence, was appointed Commissary General over the heads of more experienced officers.

The Parliamentary commanders moved off together towards Market Harborough where the King was now reported to be, encouraged by an intercepted letter addressed to Prince Rupert by Lord Goring who, while urging him not to engage the Roundheads in battle until he joined him, warned him that he could not possibly leave the West Country for the moment. They came across the King's outposts south of the town, just across the Northamptonshire boundary not far from the village of Naseby.

Digby and Ashburnham, carrying the more excitable and vociferous of the courtiers with them, had persuaded the King to fight, and Prince Rupert had consequently chosen to occupy a ridge of dry ground facing almost due south over a shallow marshy valley of heath and large open fields. This position gave them the advantage of a strong north-west wind which would otherwise have blown back the smoke from the musket and cannon into their eyes, almost blinding them, as it so often did. The King himself chose the password for the day: 'Queen Mary'.

On the far side of the ground known as Broad Moor which

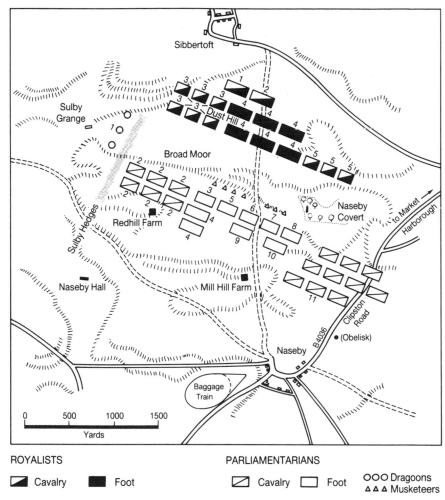

ROYALISTS

▨ Cavalry   ■ Foot

1. Kings Life Guard
2. Prince Rupert's Bluecoats
3. Prince Rupert
4. Lord Astley
5. Sir Marmaduke Langdale

PARLIAMENTARIANS

▨ Cavalry   ☐ Foot   ○○○ Dragoons
                                           △ △ △ Musketeers

1   John Okey's Dragoons
2   Henry Ireton
3   Philip Skippon
4   Thomas Pride
5   Sir Hardress Waller
6   Colonel Pickering
7   Colonel Montague
8   Lord Fairfax
9   Colonel Hammond
10   Thomas Rainsborough
11   Oliver Cromwell and Sir Thomas Fairfax

The Battle of Naseby

separated the two armies, Thomas Fairfax drew up his forces on a
grassy shoulder of land which rose gently above the marshy ground
between himself and the more northerly ridge where the Royalists
had chosen to make their stand. The Parliamentary army still outnumbered the Cavaliers by about five thousand; but their infantry,
as Fairfax recognized, were less reliable and less experienced than the
enemy's and he took what measures he could to spare them the sight
of the glittering array of the King's army manoeuvring into position
in the summer morning sunlight.

The Royalist troops were certainly an impressive and alarming
sight as they marched across the New Model Army's front, their
colours flying in the wind, their arms and armour gleaming in the
sun, the infantry wearing beanstalks in their hats as a field sign, the
King himself in full and shining gilt armour riding a Flemish horse.
And it was probably to keep this unnerving muster out of sight of
his impressionable soldiers – 'poor ignorant men' as Cromwell called
them – that Fairfax ordered the whole of his line a hundred yards
back behind the brow of the ridge. Cromwell had no doubt as to
the outcome of the battle. Convinced that God would give his army
another victory, he seemed exalted. Richard Baxter described the
'vivacity, hilarity and alacrity' which came over him in battle; he
behaved 'as another man is when he hath drunken a cup of wine too
much'. On this occasion, before the battle began, he was heard to
laugh in his exhilaration. There was, said Baxter, 'a most triumphant
faith and joy in him.' And Cromwell himself recorded, 'I could not,
riding alone about my business, but smile out to God in praise, in
assurance of victory, because God would, by things that are not,
bring to naught things that are.'

His men did not have to wait long behind the brow of the ridge
where Fairfax had withdrawn them, for Rupert, no doubt remembering the delay that had lost him the advantage at Marston Moor,
determined to attack as soon as his men were ready. Shortly after
ten o'clock, after a few token shots from his forward guns, the first
charge of his cavalry was made. Led in person by himself and his
brother, Prince Maurice, the Cavaliers came thundering down the
slopes, 'very stately' at first, then gathering speed, keeping well
together under heavy fire from John Okey's dragoons concealed
behind a hedge on their right, making straight for the New Model
Army's left wing. Ireton in command here led his men forward to

meet the Cavaliers as they came up the rise towards them, pausing once to dress his lines, then charging forward so impetuously that he rode right through the enemy ranks and, wounded in the thigh and face, lost control of them. He saw the Cavaliers break triumphantly through the left wing, scattering parts of it and sending two regiments 'clear away to Northampton'. Shouting and whirling his horse about, he did his utmost to rally his men. He could not do so, but nor could Prince Rupert whose Cavaliers went galloping away until they came up with Fairfax's baggage train a mile behind the lines. Here Rupert, wearing a red montero like the one Fairfax sometimes wore, was mistaken by the baggage commander for his own general. The baggage commander went up to him, cap in hand, to ask how the battle went. Rupert answered him by abruptly demanding that he and his men should surrender. Soon recovering from their surprise, they shouted 'No!' and threatened him with their muskets; Rupert, taking advantage of the incident to rally his excited men, led them back to the field. He was appalled by the situation he found there.

Soon after his cavalry had charged into Ireton's men, the Royalist infantry had lunged into the centre of the New Model Army's line, firing but one volley from their muskets, before gripping them by the barrels and wielding them as clubs. Although these Royalist musketeers had had to advance uphill, and had marched hard both that morning and the day before with little sleep or food, they and their supporting pikemen had soon gained the upper hand and had begun to drive the enemy back. Philip Skippon, in command of the wavering Roundhead infantry, had been wounded by a musketball which pierced his breast plate; and, while he had managed to stay in the saddle, he had not been able to prevent his first line breaking and his men falling back onto the second line. Lord Astley, commander of the Royalist infantry, had begun to hope that victory would soon be theirs – as well it might have been had it not been for the Ironsides on their left.

Cromwell had led his Ironsides in a charge on the Royalist left wing which had proved as successful as Prince Rupert's. The troopers of Colonel Whalley's regiment had been the first engaged. Exchanging pistol shots with Langdale's Northern Horse, they had then set about them with their swords and were driving them back in confusion when Cromwell and Colonel Rossiter, impeded by the furze bushes and rabbit warrens in this part of Broad Moor, came up to complete the rout. Cromwell broke right through the ranks of struggling men and suddenly appeared, like a *deus ex machina*, before the King's reserve which stood on Dust Hill behind Lord Astley's shouting, brawling ranks on the moor below. The King, nominally Commander-in-Chief, now had his first opportunity to take an active part in the battle. He lined up his Life Guards and would have led them against the Ironsides had not the Earl of Carnwarth, one of his Scottish friends, grabbed hold of his bridle, 'swearing two or three full-mouthed Scots' oaths' and shouting above the din, 'Will you go upon your death!' Carnwarth's sudden action so startled the King's horse that he wheeled suddenly round to the right followed by part of the reserve which – in response to an order, 'March to the right hand!' – rode away carrying the King with them.

Cromwell, declining the opportunity to chase the Life Guards off the field, had reformed his well-disciplined regiments and had taken them down the slope again to charge into Lord Astley's now unprotected infantry. Fairfax, clearly exhilarated, his helmet lost, black hair loose about his shoulders, had joined Cromwell in the charge, while Colonel Okey remounted his dragoons and brought them galloping over from Sulby Hedges in the west to help the Ironsides. By the time Prince Rupert returned to the field many if not most of the Welsh infantry had surrendered, hoping to save both their lives and their plunder; and there was little he could do but cover the retreat of the King who, riding through Leicester to see his wounded soldiers, went on to Ashby de la Zouch and then made for the Welsh border calling, so tradition relates, at Sir Richard Halford's house where he changed his highly decorated saddle for one less conspicuous, leaving his own as a treasured memento of his visit.

Between four and five thousand Royalist troops were captured on the field, where several hundred of their companions lay dead, strewn naked across the landscape, so one observer said, 'about four miles in length but most thick upon the hill'. Among them were many wounded, also naked. The 'crying there was for surgeons as never was the like heard'.

Most of the prisoners not seriously wounded were herded into Market Harborough church and afterwards marched to London to be paraded through the streets as proof of Parliament's great victory. Their companions, endeavouring frantically to escape along the road to Leicester, were cut down mercilessly in a vigorous pursuit as they tried to run away, weighed down by plunder, or paused to scoop up the coins which had tumbled onto the road from the upturned wagons of the baggage train. Some escaped from their pursuers only to be killed in outlying villages. A troop of galloping horse missed their turning and were cornered in Marston Trussell churchyard where they were all killed and thrown into a clay pit. One straggler, caught trying to steal a loaf of bread from a farmhouse in the village of Ravenstone, was attacked by a sturdy maidservant who knocked him onto a dunghill and killed him with the 'puddle' she was using to stir washing in a tub.

Before Leicester was reached the pursuers caught up with the royal coaches, the sumpter-wagons and hundreds of women, mistresses and wives, camp followers, whores, 'leaguer-bitches' and 'the camp-sluts that followed this wicked army'. Those with money or jewels paid the soldiers not to kill them, but many of the poor slatterns who could not afford to buy mercy were murdered or had their cheeks and noses slashed to the bone. According to one observer, 'a number of souldiers' wives and some of them of quality' were also murdered or disfigured.

The King's enemies felt no need to apologize for this gross violence. It was, they said, well known that hundreds of Irishwomen followed the royal armies – though in fact most of the victims were more likely to have been wives of the Welsh recruits – and that Irishwomen would murder good Protestants as soon as look at them. The outrage, in any event, was soon forgotten. For captured in the retreat, as well as numerous colours and stores, was the King's secret correspondence, all the letters he had received from the Queen, copies of all the letters he had written to her, all the evidence necessary to show how anxious they had both been to bring over foreigners and papists from the Continent and Ireland to help him in the struggle. After the publication of this correspondence, many Englishmen who had formerly felt some sympathy for the King's cause now turned their backs on him.

Excited by the news from Naseby, the City gave a splendid banquet for the two Houses of Parliament on 19 June, a day of thanksgiving. It was held in Grocers' Hall in Princes Street and afterwards guests and hosts joined in singing the 46th Psalm: 'God is our refuge and strength, a very present help in trouble . . . The Lord of hosts is with us; the God of Jacob is our refuge.' Two days later some three thousand Royalist prisoners, many if not most of them Welsh, were paraded through the city in what appeared to one onlooker 'a never-ending stream'. After spending two nights in the open in Tothill Fields, they were required to listen to a sermon by a Welsh clergyman, Dr Walter Cradock, who – described by the Bishop of Llandaff as a 'bold, ignorant young fellow' – had been deprived of his curacy in Cardiff because of his extreme Puritanical views. They were then offered the opportunity of serving in Parliament's army in Ireland. A few did so; a few others, approached by agents of the Spanish Ambassador, agreed to serve the Spanish King in the Netherlands; most remained in uncomfortable captivity until the war was over.

14

DEATH THROES

'I am nowise disheartened by our late misfortune,' the King wrote
unconcernedly to Lord Herbert of Raglan, now Earl of Glamorgan,
after the battle of Naseby, and the subsequent surrender of all his
remaining guns and over five hundred horses. 'I hope shortly to
recover my late loss with advantage.' Once the large numbers of
troops he expected from Ireland had arrived in England the position
would be transformed. He was confident, he told the Marquess of
Ormonde, that Naseby would quickly be forgotten and with Irish
help he would soon be 'in a far better condition' than he had been
'at any time since the rebellion began'. Besides, Montrose was still
doing well in Scotland; in the West Country the Royalists were still
a force to be reckoned with; and recruitment in Wales would soon
bring his numbers up to strength again. Lord Digby, as sanguine as
ever, shared the King's sublime confidence and appeared in no way
abashed by his having advised him to ignore Prince Rupert's prudent
warnings before Naseby. There had admittedly been 'the unfortunate
loss of a most hopeful battle' but its consequences would be 'of no
great extent'. Hosts of men – in fact about four thousand – had
deserted from the New Model Army after the battle of Naseby, as
soldiers so often did in the wake of a victory.

'We have had many little successes,' Digby later told the Queen.

'Every day may beget alterations for the better.' He and the King rode west together with other favoured courtiers through Lichfield and Wolverhampton to Hereford, then on to Raglan Castle, a vast fortress extending over four and a half acres of ground, where their every need was catered for by an immense staff including a steward, a comptroller, a chaplain, a librarian, a master of the horse, a master of the fishponds, masters of the wardrobe, of the armoury, the hounds and the hawks, a sewer, a clerk of the kitchen, a groom of the chambers, a purveyor, a closet-keeper, a gentleman of the chapel, an auditor, a clerk of accounts, and a keeper of the records, twelve master grooms, twenty-four gentlemen waiters and pages and 150 assorted domestic servants.

At Raglan his Majesty played bowls every day, went to the village church every week, talked amicably to his friends and read poetry as though oblivious to the peril that threatened him. 'We were all lulled asleep with sport and entertainments,' wrote one of his companions, 'as if no crown had been at stake or in danger to be lost.'

It was left to Prince Rupert, worried and irritable, annoyed that he seemed to be held responsible for a defeat he had endeavoured to avoid, to go into the West Country to discuss with the Prince of Wales the measures to be taken for the defence of the diminishing areas under Royalist control. He rode down to Cardiff, and sailed from there to Barnstaple where he met Prince Charles, who could not but paint a gloomy picture of affairs in that part of England. Grenville and Berkeley were pursuing their seemingly endless quarrel; Goring, as often drunk as not, had let several wagonloads of stores for the Parliamentary garrison at Taunton slip through his lines; troops were deserting day by day. Frequent attacks were being made upon outposts and convoys by 'Clubmen', those bands of cudgel-carrying country people which had been formed by yeomen, lesser gentry and clergymen to resist the depredations of Roundheads and Cavaliers alike but which in most areas increasingly came to be dominated by conservative-minded men who favoured government by 'gentlemen of worth, birth and integrity and known among us'.

By this stage of the war the Clubmen had good cause to feel aggrieved. 'We, our wives and children have been exposed to utter ruin by the outrages and violence of the soldiers,' runs one typical complaint. 'And we are now enforced to associate ourselves in a mutual league for each other's defence against murders, rapines, plunders, robberies or violence which shall be offered by the soldier or any oppressor whatsoever.'

The experiences of the villagers around Burnham-on-Sea in Somerset were characteristic. Coming down from Bristol, a party of Cavaliers rode into the village of Brent Knoll intent upon plunder. Having seized a bullock from a farmer on his way back from Axbridge fair, they attacked the farmer's servant and threatened to hang him unless he handed over his money. They also robbed the village constable, then searched his house and told him that they would 'tie him neck and heels together' unless he produced more money than they had found. At the nearby village of Berrow they pushed their way into the house of a William Lush, ransacked it, took away clothing and bedding, and responded to Lush's protests by threatening to burn the place down with his wife inside it if he did not shut up. 'Others with execrable oaths swore that they would burn the whole village if the inhabitants did not cooperate.' At Lympsham the villagers were told to 'lie upon straw . . . the soldiers would lie in their beds'. On their way from Axbridge, where one of the soldiers struck at a man who tried to defend himself with a staff and beat him over the head 'very dangerously', a butcher was robbed and a labourer killed on the highway. It was not until a local gentleman from South Brent – not himself a Roundhead but a man who had served as a Cavalier officer – organized the villagers into a home guard with staves and pikes and a few muskets that some sort of order was restored.

The misfortunes of these villagers in Somerset were far from uncommon. In his small Shropshire village of Myddle, Richard Gough recorded the deaths of thirteen men who had gone off to fight for the King: one was burned to death in Bridgnorth Castle; two others were killed in the storming of Hopton Castle; of a fourth nothing was heard after Edgehill; a fifth was hanged for stealing horses; three were known to have been killed in battle; of the fate of the last five nothing was known for sure but it 'was supposed they all died in the wars'. 'There were but few that went out of this parish to serve the Parliament,' Gough added, 'and of them there was none killed (as I know of) nor wounded, except John Mould . . . a very pretty little fellow, and a stout adventurous soldier. He was shot through the leg with a musket ball, which broke the master bone of his leg and slew his horse under him. His leg was healed but was very crooked as long as he lived.'

While these men were away from home the village was plundered by Royalists, one of whom in particular, a Cornet Collins, was particularly troublesome:

This Collins made his excursion very often into this parish, and took away cattle, provision, and bedding, and what he pleased. On the day he had been at Myddle taking away bedding, and when Margaret, the wife of Allen Chaloner, the smith, had brought out and showed him her best bed, he thinking it too coarse, cast it into the lake, before the door, and trod it under his horse feet. This Cornet [later] came to Myddle and seven soldiers with him, and his horse having cast a shoe, he alighted at Allen Chaloner's shop to have a new one put on.

There was one Richard Maning, a garrison soldier at Morton Corbett, for the Parliament. This Maning and his companions . . . came into Myddle at the gate by Mr Gittin's house at what time the Cornet's horse was a shoeing. The Cornet hearing the gate clap, looked by the end of the shop and saw the soldiers coming, and thereupon he and his men mounted their horses; and as the Cornet came at the end of the shop, a brisk young fellow shot him through the body with a carbine shot, and he fell down in the lake at Allen Chaloner's door. His men fled [and] the Cornet was carried into Allen Chaloner's house, and laid on the floor; he desired to have a bed laid under him, but Margaret told him she had none but that which he saw yesterday. He prayed her to forgive him, which she did.

Mr Rodericke [the village schoolmaster] was sent for to pray with him. I went with him, and saw the Cornet lying on the bed, and much blood running along the floor. In the night following, a troop of horse came from Shrawardine . . . and so took the Cornet to Shrawardine, where he died the next day.

From all over the country came reports of houses being broken into and plundered. A Yorkshire gentleman wrote to Lord Fairfax with a typical complaint that Roundhead soldiers had burst into his house and sorely wounded two of his servants in his wife's presence.

She was forced to flee to her chamber [this man submitted] and there a naked sword was tendered her by a young ruffian who told her he came for money and with fearful oaths that money he would have; and calling all Romish Whores, wherein I thank God none with me are guilty. He had his desire in part, for he snatched a purse with a gold ring in it from a servant that was giving some to quiet him.

Nor were the poor spared. An aged Oxfordshire labourer made a pathetic inventory of his household goods, all of which had been stolen by Parliamentary soldiers: '7 pair of sheets, 3 brass kettles, 2 brass pots, 5 pewter dishes, 4 shirts, 4 smocks, 2 coats, 1 clock, 1 waistcoat, 7 dozen of candles, 1 frying pan, 1 spit, 2 pairs of pot hooks, 1 peck of wheat, 4 bags, some oatmeal, some salt, a basketful of eggs, bowls, dishes, spoons, ladles, drinking pots and whatsoever else they could lay their hands on.'

Houses had been taken over as army quarters and their inhabitants ejected; crops had been trampled down by marching men or eaten by cavalry horses; taxes had been imposed and levies extracted first by one side then by the other, and often enough by both at the same time; women had been violated and the rapists haphazardly punished. At Marston a Royalist foot soldier had been 'tyed (with his sholders and breast naked) to a tree, and every carter of the trayne and carriages was to have a lash, for ravishing two women'. But severe punishment for rape was not common and such penalties as were imposed seem not to have diminished the incidence of the crime. Households quartering soldiers were meant to be paid for doing so, sixpence a day being the average rate for the board and lodging of an infantryman, eight pence a day for a trooper. But money was rarely available and the vouchers offered in exchange were frequently worthless, particularly so in the case of Royalist vouchers, less so with those issued by the Eastern Association, many of which were eventually redeemed. As for the behaviour of the opposing armies, there was little to choose between them.

A poignant Devonshire ballad makes this point:

Ich had six oxen tother day,
And them the Roundheads got away,
A mischief be their speed.

Ich had six horses in a hole,
And them the Cavalieres stole,
Ise think they be agreed . . .

They vet my corn, my bean and pease,
Ise dare no man to displease,
They do so swear and vaper;
And when Ise to the Government come,
Desiring him to ease one zome,
Chave nothing but a paper.

But dost thou think a paper will
My back cloath and my belly fill?
No no, goe take thy note.
If that another year my vield,
No better profit do me yeeld,
Ise may go cut my throate.

And if all this be not griefe enow,
They have a thing call'd Quarter too,
O! tis a vengeance waster.
A plague upon't; they call it vree.
Cham zure theyve made us slaves to be,
And every rogue our master.

On one of the Clubmen's banners was written a warning intended
for Royalist and Roundhead alike:

If you offer to plunder, or take our cattel
Be assured we will give you battel.

Here is a letter sent to the commander of the Western Association:

We have received very great complaints from the country of the
intolerable miscarriages of your troopers . . . whereby great dis-
service is done to the Parliament by the robbing, spoiling and
plundering of the people, they also giving extreme offence by their
swearing, drinking and all kinds of debaucheries. Inflict exemplary
punishment upon such notorious misdemeanours, and let a better
discipline be maintained, they being now looked upon as the greatest enemy in those places where they come.

Similar complaints were addressed to Royalist commanders, one such reproach maintaining that 'this country [Worcestershire] is fallen into such want and extremity through the number and oppression of the Horse lying upon free quarter that . . . children are ready to starve for want of Bread'. Troopers not only exacted free quarter but extorted sums of money from the local people, 'mingled with threats of firing their Houses, their persons with death and their goods with pillaging'. The complaint listed the soldiers' 'barbarous seizing of men's persons, and compelling them to ransom themselves with very great sums of money . . . their daily robberies of all Market people, killing and wounding men who resist . . . their contempt of all discipline, disobedience to all others . . . Their Insolencies, oppressions and Cruelties have already so disaffected and disheartened the people, that they are grown desperate and are already upon the point of rising everywhere and do not stick to say that they can find more justice in the Enemy's quarters than in the King's.'

When Goring, on one of his more sober days, exercising his ready charm, persuaded several Clubmen in the west to take up arms in the King's cause, it was feared that they might use those arms against him if his troops behaved as badly as they had been wont to do. Certainly Prince Rupert thought that this was quite likely. More anxious than ever now, the Prince rode off to Bristol, leaving Goring outside Taunton to deal with his problems as best he could.

The leaders of the New Model Army were now, by contrast, in full confidence of victory, though some of them were much concerned by the religious differences within the ranks. The self-satisfaction of the sectarians, their arrogation to themselves of the credit for the Army's success, naturally rankled with the Presbyterians. When Oliver Cromwell wrote an account of the battle of Naseby for Parliament he was careful to stress the part his own men had played in it and to make it clear to both Houses that one of their principal objects in fighting the war was liberty of conscience. 'There is none but the hand of God,' he declared; 'and to him alone belongs the glory . . . Honest men served you faithfully in this action. Sir, they are trusty . . . He that ventures his life for the liberty of his country, I wish he trust God for the liberty of his conscience, and you for the liberty he fights for.'

The House of Commons thought it advisable to leave out this last sentence when they had Cromwell's words printed. The House of Lords, however, printed them all; and, when the Commons' omission was noted, the squabbles between Presbyterians and Independents were renewed, causing almost as much indignation as the printing of the King's indiscretions in *The King's Cabinet Opened*.

Fairfax marching into the West Country gave little thought to these civilian imbroglios. Intent upon relieving Taunton and defeating Goring in Somerset, he paused in Dorset to talk to a delegation of the local Clubmen, assuring them that his men were not plunderers, that they would treat the countryside and its inhabitants with respect, and that only a Roundhead victory could ensure that England was not subjected to the foreign invasion which the King's letters amply demonstrated was his intent. They listened to him without interruption and with evident regard for his straightforward manner, some of them undertaking to concentrate only upon Royalist victims in future.

Two days after his meeting with the Clubmen, on 5 July 1645, Fairfax's troops entered Crewkerne after one of their by now famous fast marches. Here they were halted for a day of rest; but far as they had already come over rutted roads in the hot summer days, they declared their willingness to be taken on the further twenty-odd miles to Taunton. Taunton, however, was no longer in danger: Lord Goring had abandoned the siege and was now endeavouring to deceive Fairfax as to his intentions, to induce him to split his army so that, outnumbered as the Royalists were, he might have a chance of defeating him piecemeal. By a cunning manoeuvre, Goring did induce Fairfax to detach some four thousand men under Edward Massey with orders to ride towards Taunton and discover what the Cavaliers were up to. Massey came upon a party of Royalists at Ilminster, commanded by Goring's brother-in-law and drinking companion, Endymion Porter's son, George Porter, whose men were enjoying themselves by the banks of the river, some lying in the sun, others swimming, their horses unsaddled. Several of them managed to scamper off at Massey's approach but most were taken prisoner.

Lord Goring was now about fifteen miles from Ilminster at Langport where he had taken up a strong position in hilly countryside where the valleys were soggy after heavy summer rain and crisscrossed by narrow lanes running between tall hedges of hawthorn and hazel which in places met overhead. In one of these lanes, almost a tunnel of foliage, which led away from his position at Langport towards the Roundheads' quarters at Long Sutton, Goring had concealed company after company of musketeers, hidden by the branches and leaves of the hedges on either side. At the top of the lane he had placed two of his heavy guns. His cavalry, far outnumbering the enemy's, awaited the order to charge. He had reason to believe that he had made an attack on his position a suicidal venture.

All the same, Fairfax ventured it, trusting his men to obey their orders without question. His musketeers steadily made their way up the lane, drawing the fire of the enemy, answering it accurately, wounding and killing their opponents one by one, until they had cleared a path for the cavalry who then came clattering down after them, the red mud spattering at their horses' heels, riding close together four abreast since the narrowness of the passage allowed no more. At the first clash with the Cavalier cavalry at the end of the lane the Roundhead horse reeled back; but, while all attention had been concentrated on the lane, other troops of Roundhead cavalry, supported by infantry, trotted out into the open to fall upon the Royalists' flanks 'with the greatest gallantry imaginable'. The Cavaliers stood their ground for a time, but were soon forced to give way and sent galloping off the field towards Bridgwater. In an effort to prevent a pursuit, Goring gave orders that the wood-framed houses of Langport should be set alight. But this did not prevent Cromwell's horse from chasing after the fugitives, Cromwell himself, 'the fire flaming on both sides of him', galloping right through the burning village and onto the road to Bridgwater. 'To see this,' he said, 'is it not to see the face of God?'

Lord Goring rode into Barnstaple, having lost two thousand of his men as prisoners, together with well over a thousand of his horses. Scores of fugitives too weak to escape were cut down on the road by merciless Clubmen. His army had been virtually destroyed.

Scarcely a day passed that summer without reports of further disasters reaching the Royalist headquarters. On 22 July Bridgwater surrendered to Fairfax, after whole streets had been destroyed by flames and cannon shot. On the same day the Roundheads in the north, who had already taken Carlisle and Pontefract, occupied Scarborough where Sir John Meldrum, having survived both a shot in his codpiece and a fall of some two hundred feet from the top of the cliffs thanks to his billowing cloak, was at last killed by a bullet in his stomach. Several other smaller garrisons in the north now surrendered to the Roundheads. In the west, Bath also surrendered; and a Parliamentary force set about the reduction of Sherborne Castle whose plundered contents were soon to be sold by its pillagers in the local market. But before assaulting Sherborne Castle which was defended by the energetic Sir Lewis Dyve, Sergeant-Major-General of the County of Dorset, Cromwell decided that the Clubmen, so active in that county, must be dealt with first. Scores of these Clubmen had assembled at Shaftesbury, some twenty miles east of Sherborne; and Cromwell sent Charles Fleetwood, one of his most trustworthy officers, to confront them there. Fifty of them were captured, the rest dispersed. Two days later, Cromwell's scouts discovered another party of Clubmen encamped on Duncliff Hill, 'a place full of wood and almost inaccessible'. Cromwell himself climbed up the hill and, after speaking to them for some time, persuaded these men also to disperse. He was not, however, so successful in dealing with two thousand more of these 'poor silly creatures' who had assembled on Hambledon Hill, a Stone Age earthwork near Iwerne Courtney. Three times messages were sent up the hill urging the men to lay down their arms and to go home; and three times the Clubmen, led by two local parsons, 'vile Ministers', as Cromwell called them, refused a peaceful settlement. At length Cromwell decided upon assault. The first direct charge was repulsed; but when Colonel John Desborough, a farmer and attorney in civilian life, attacked the Clubmen in their rear, 'some were slain, many wounded, and the rest slid and tumbled down the steep hillside, to the hazard of their necks'. Many more were taken prisoner and marched off to be herded into Iwerne Courtney church where, after being severely lectured, they confessed to the errors of their ways, according to a Parliamentary report, 'and saw themselves misled'. Certainly, in that area at least, the Clubmen were persuaded by the relative good behaviour of the New Model Army to regard the Royalists as the greater threat to their livelihood.

Meanwhile in Wales, Rowland Laugharne drove a Royalist force off Colby Moor in Pembrokeshire and took Haverfordwest. Further south the Welsh levies refused to serve so long as the violent and widely disliked Charles Gerard remained in command of them. The King relieved him of his command but to soften the blow created him Lord Gerard of Brandon, an ennoblement which deeply angered others more deserving.

Worried by these reverses, the King, hoping to fare better elsewhere, decided to march north, leaving Prince Rupert to defend Bristol, his main hope of survival in the west. The Prince was dismayed by this proposal. 'It is now in everybody's mouth that the King is going for Scotland,' he wrote to the Duke of Richmond, knowing that the King would be shown the letter. 'I must confess it to be a strange resolution, considering not only in what condition he will leave all behind him, but what probability there is for him to get thither. If I were desired to deliver my opinion, which your Lordship may declare to the King, His Majesty hath no way left to preserve his posterity, kingdom and nobility, but by a treaty. I believe it a more prudent way to retain something than to lose all.'

'If I had any other quarrel but the defence of my religion, crown and friends, you had full reason for your advice,' the King replied, 'for I confess that speaking either as a mere soldier or statesman, I must say there is no probability but of my ruin. Yet as a Christian I must tell you that God will not suffer rebels and traitors to prosper, nor this cause to be overthrown . . . I know my obligation to be, both in conscience and honour, neither to abandon God's cause, injure my successors, nor forsake my friends.'

In this spirit, the King set out for the north accompanied by his Life Guards. He paused at Brecon to send instructions to the Prince of Wales to sail for France if he found himself in danger of falling into rebel hands; but otherwise he displayed little concern at his predicament. He seemed, indeed, to enjoy the march in the fine summer weather, taking his meals outside in the fields or in some country house like the one at Radnor where, as Sir Henry Slingsby reported:

> The King lay in a poor low Chamber, and my Ld of Linsey and others by the Kitching fire on hay; no better were we accomodated for victuals, which makes me remember this passage: When the King was at his supper eating a pullet and a peice of Cheese, the room without was full, but the men's stomacks empty for want of

meat; the good wife troubl'd with continual calling upon her for victuals, and having it seems but one cheese, comes into the room where the King was, and very soberly asks if the King had done with the cheese, for the Gentlemen without desired it.

Passing through Lichfield, the King, in less easygoing mood, ordered the arrest of Lord Loughborough, a man who had served him faithfully for months, for having been obliged to surrender Leicester after Naseby. He then carried on through Staffordshire and Derbyshire into Yorkshire, arriving in Doncaster on 11 August, collecting two thousand horsemen on the way, and considering his situation now 'miraculously good' again. Yorkshire, however, was as far as he reached; for near Rotherham he was warned of a large Scottish army approaching and he was constrained to move southeast instead. The countryside was almost bereft of troops, for the New Model Army was still campaigning in the West Country; and the King was able to enter Huntingdon without opposition. Many of the inhabitants, belying their traditions and professing that they were delighted to see him, came out to greet him 'with much compliment, all halting and bowing', though here as elsewhere, they were soon much disgusted by the behaviour of the Royalist troops who, after drinking bucketfuls of ale in the taverns, plundered the town and the surrounding farms to such an extent that the King's hanging of two of the worst offenders amongst his soldiers seemed to them not punishment enough.

From Huntingdon the King rode west again for Hereford, driving Parliamentary patrols out of the wayside villages *en route*, forcing the Earl of Leven's Scotsmen to abandon their siege of the town which the Royalists then entered in triumph. It was almost their last success. Thereafter one disaster followed upon another. Lord Goring, now drunk for days on end and quarrelling interminably with Sir Richard Grenville and Sir John Berkeley, showed no sign of being able to raise the new levies he had promised. Towards the end of the month Prince Rupert's position in Bristol was rumoured to be untenable.

Rupert had brought large stores into Bristol, ammunition, corn and cattle, as well as food for the inhabitants and heavy cannon to defend the walls. He had expressed the hope that he could hold out for four months. He had not had time to destroy the hedges in the surrounding countryside or to fill up the hollow lanes which would provide cover for the enemy's approach; but his patrols were tireless in their attacks on Fairfax's outposts and in one raid Colonel John Okey, the formidable commander of the Roundhead dragoons at Naseby, was captured. But morale in the town was low; plague was rife; and the citizens soon showed themselves prepared to betray the defenders for the sake of their trade. Prince Rupert's soldiers were disheartened by the death of Sir Richard Crane, the popular Colonel of his guards.

On 3 September, Fairfax wrote to the Prince in the politest terms asking him to surrender: 'I take into consideration your royal birth and relation to the Crown of England, your honour, courage and the virtue of your person . . . Sir, we fight to maintain [the Crown of England]; but the King, misled by evil counsellors, hath left his Parliament and his people . . . Sir, if God makes this clear to you, as he has to us, I doubt not, but he will give you a heart to deliver this place . . . It would be an occasion glorious in itself and joyful to us, for the restoring of you to the endeared affection of the Parliament and people of England.'

Prince Rupert responded by making a vague offer to negotiate; but when it became clear that he was merely playing for time, Fairfax decided upon immediate assault; and, on 10 September, at two o'clock in the morning, Fairfax's four huge siege pieces opened up on the walls of Prior's Hill Fort and soon afterwards the assault began.

Six hours later Prince Rupert's garrison in the castle were separated from the troops still fighting on the walls by Cromwell's cavalry which had come charging through the shattered defences. Hopelessly outnumbered, Prince Rupert felt obliged to surrender, and, under the generous terms which Fairfax allowed him, he marched away to Oxford with his men and his horses, his colours flying, his sword by his side. Followed by angry shouts of 'Give him no quarter! Give him no quarter!' he was miserably aware that, with the loss of Bristol, the King's last hope had gone.

While Prince Rupert was still on his way to Oxford, Cromwell wrote to Parliament, as he had done after Naseby, stressing the vital part his men had taken in the capture of Bristol and reminding Members that they had fought, and some had died, for freedom of conscience. As before this report was published with the contentious sentences omitted. But the Independents' printing presses issued copy after copy of the full version and, again as after Naseby, religious differences in London were deepened and exacerbated.

The King was convinced that he had been betrayed. Rupert's surrender, he wrote to his Secretary of State Sir Edward Nicholas in Oxford, was 'strange and most inexcusable'. Digby had always warned him of his nephew's unreliability; now there seemed proof of it. In his bitter disappointment at the fall of Bristol into the hands of the rebels, he began to believe all the stories he had ever been told about Rupert. There was surely something sinister in his being allowed to march out of the town with all his men and, except for cannon and muskets, all his weapons and baggage; and there was surely something alarming in Rupert's move on Oxford where the Governor, Colonel William Legge, was a close friend of his and where the King's second son, the Duke of York, lay open to the Prince's schemes to wrest power from the ashes of defeat.

Convinced that Rupert was about to stage some sort of coup, Charles issued orders to Sir Edward Nicholas for the immediate dismissal of Colonel Legge, and for the revocation of the Prince's commission. In a personal letter to Rupert he commanded him to consider himself expelled from the country. The surrender of Bristol, Charles wrote, 'is the greatest trial of my constancy that hath yet befallen me; for what is to be done, after one that is so near to me as you are both in blood and friendship, submits himself to so mean an action (I give it the easiest terms)? I have so much to say, that I will say no more of it, less rashness of judgement be laid to my charge . . . You assured me that, if no mutiny happened, you would keep Bristol for four months. Did you keep it four days? Was there anything like a mutiny? More questions might be asked, but now I confess to little purpose. My conclusion is, to desire you to keep your subsistence (until it shall please God to determine of my condition) somewhere beyond the sea, to which end I send you herewith a pass.'

'Wherever I am,' Rupert replied, 'or how unhappy so ever, and by your will made so, yet I shall ever retain that duty to Your Majesty which I have ever entertained as Your Majesty's most obedient nephew and faithful, humble servant.' He asked to be allowed to come to the King to defend his conduct. To this plea he received no immediate reply.

The King was once more marching north. With Bristol lost and with Rowland Laugharne triumphant in south Wales, he could remain no longer either in Hereford or at Raglan Castle, and so rode off through the Welsh hills in the vague hope of reaching Montrose. He did not even reach the Cheshire Plain, for hearing that Chester – so vital if help from Ireland were ever to reach him – was on the point of collapse, he turned to its assistance.

On 19 September the Roundheads had made a determined assault upon the city, breaking into the suburbs with the help of scaling ladders, killing the officer of the watch, scattering his guard, and sending the Mayor – who abandoned his wife as well as his mace – racing for the safety of the city's ancient walls. Having set fire to his house as well as several others in the suburbs to prevent the enemy using them as cover, the garrison hastily withdrew within the walls, blocking the archway through the East Gate with timber, earth and dung. It was, however, by the New Gate, also in the eastern wall, that a storming party made the first assault. Here they poured through a breach and into the city where the garrison, encouraged by news that the King had reached Chirk Castle less than twenty-five miles to the south, were ready to receive them. After savage fighting, the Roundheads were pushed back both here and by another breach opened in the wall further north; and the next day the King with an escort of cavalry rode into Chester across the bridge which spanned the river Dee, while the rest of his army under Sir Marmaduke Langdale took up position two miles to the south-east on the wide expanse of heath around the little village of Rowton. Here Langdale's cavalry clashed with the horsemen of the New Model Army commanded by Sydenham Poyntz, a former London tradesman's apprentice who had run away from his master to join the Dutch army; and after several hours of confused and savage fighting on the afternoon and evening of 24 September, the Royalists were overwhelmed and the King's cousin, Lord Bernard Stuart, the Duke of Richmond's younger brother, was killed. 'O Lord! O Lord!' the King lamented in his loss of the man who had been his dearest friend since the death of the Duke of Buckingham, more precious to him than anyone other than the Queen, 'What have I done that should cause my people to deal with me thus?'

The Royalist survivors of the battle on Rowton Heath ran off in all directions, most into Wales, some across the river Gowy by Stamford Bridge, a few into Chester which was immediately called upon to surrender by the victorious Roundheads. But Lord Byron, left in command of the city with orders to hold out for a few more days if he could, rejected the summons and called upon the citizens to continue its defence. They responded with a will, women as well as men helping to put out fires and repair damage to the walls, as the besiegers' cannon hurled shot after shot into Chester from four separate emplacements. The pounding was relentless. The shot came hurtling over the walls, crashing into houses and through church windows. On 8 October a wide breach was opened up in the northern wall and another storming party burst into the city. As in the month before they were thrown back after more fierce fighting, the garrison being encouraged in their defence by the heroic antics of a French volunteer, the Comte de St Pol, who charged at the enemy brandishing his sword, clothed in nothing but his shirt.

Throughout that month and the next the siege continued, the Roundheads shooting arrows into the town, their shafts carrying leaflets promising leniency in the event of surrender. Meanwhile cannon relentlessly threw shot and stones over the walls, causing severe damage to buildings and the occasional death of a soldier or citizen. 'The Talbott, an house adjoining to the East Gate, flames outright,' one citizen recorded; 'our hands are busy quenching this, while the law of nature bids us leave and seek our own security. Being thus distracted, another Thunder-crack invites our eye to the most miserable [sight] could possibly present us with – two houses in the Watergate skippe joynt from joynt, the main posts jossell each other, while the frightened casements fly for feare. In a word the whole fabrick is a perfect chaos . . . The grandmother and three children are struck stark dead in the ruins.'

Their nerves frayed by the bombardment, a group of citizens called upon Lord Byron and urged him to surrender, pleading the likelihood of starvation. He invited them to dine with him, to share the repast of the garrison commander. They sat down to plates of boiled wheat and cups of water.

The besiegers' summons to surrender was met by a response that the city would be given up only if the entire garrison could march out unharmed with all their arms and their remaining ammunition, with drums beating, colours flying, and trumpets sounding. These terms being refused by Sir William Brereton, the siege continued into December. That month Lathom House surrendered, the redoubtable

Countess of Derby having left it for the Isle of Man; and soon afterwards Beeston Castle also fell. There the garrison commander's horse was so weak with hunger that it could scarcely bear his weight when it carried him away; and in the abandoned fortress was found 'neither meate, ale nor beare, save onelie a peece of a Turkey pye, Two bisketts, a lyve Peacock and a peahen'.

There was little more than this now in Chester: an inspection carried out on Lord Byron's orders revealed that the larders and store rooms of most houses were almost empty. Hundreds of people, as in other besieged towns, had died of the plague. Moreover, the troops besieging Lathom House and Beeston Castle had come to swell Sir William Brereton's forces outside Chester. So Byron decided he must submit at last. His officers and a few soldiers were permitted to march out with their arms; the rest were to pile their weapons in the shire hall and leave their horses in the castle courtyard. After holding out for twenty weeks since the King's departure, Lord Byron left Chester on 3 February 1646 and Sir William Brereton marched in.

Having watched the fighting on Rowton Heath in September the year before, first from Phoenix Tower in Chester's eastern wall, then from the cathedral tower, where an officer was shot dead by his side, the King had withdrawn disconsolately to Denbigh, planning to move south for Worcester which had been strongly fortified as an alternative headquarters to Oxford. But Prince Maurice was Governor of Worcester, and Lord Digby, who had not troubled to conceal his delight at Prince Rupert's disgrace, was anxious to keep the King away from his brother and from probable intercessions on his behalf. Besides, Worcester was only about sixty miles from Oxford and Prince Rupert himself might well come over from there to plead his cause on his own behalf. So Digby urged upon the King the inconveniences and dangers of going to Worcester; and, when the capture of Berkeley Castle by General Fairfax threatened the safety of the town, the King was persuaded to ride instead through the Derbyshire dales and Sherwood Forest to Newark.

Here reports of fresh disasters reached him from every side. He was told of Royalist garrisons falling to Cromwell in Wiltshire and Hampshire, of the surrender of Devizes and Winchester, then, and most cruelly, of Montrose's defeat at Philiphaugh on 13 September, and, in the middle of October, of Cromwell's assault on the Marquess of Winchester's enormous and strongly fortified mansion, Basing House, 'Loyalty House', as it was called by its owner, who with a diamond had scratched '*Aimez Loyauté*' on every window pane in the house.

Numerous Royalists and people under Royalist protection had withdrawn to Basing House for safety, including the etcher Wenceslaus Hollar, several Jesuit priests, a giant, said to be nine feet tall, and Inigo Jones, 'the famous surveyor' and 'contriver of scenes for the Queen's dancing barne', who had been 'gotten thither for help' in planning the defences of the house. The Marquess had claimed that his garrison, which had successfully resisted previous sieges, could hold out 'for ever'. Certainly it had held out stubbornly since 20 August, despite an outbreak of smallpox in its garrison and the efforts of the Roundhead besiegers under the Dutch engineer Jan Dalbier to batter it into submission. A summons to surrender, 'to avoid the effusion of Christian blood', received the reply, 'Sir, it is a crooked demand, and shall receive its answer suitable. I keep this House in the right of my Soveraigne and will do it in despight of your Forces. Your letter I will preservé in testimony of your Rebellion. Winchester.'

The Marchioness was equally defiant. 'A lady of great honour and alliance', in Edward Hyde's words, she was the granddaughter of Queen Elizabeth I's Secretary of State, Sir Francis Walsingham, and half-sister of the Parliamentary general the Earl of Essex. To an offer from the commander of the besieging force that she should take out all the women and children from the house to spare them the attention of his 'disorderly guns' – which were soon to kill a waiting-woman and a chambermaid in her lodgings – the Marchioness replied that she 'thanked God she was not in that condition to accept of fair quarter . . . being resolved to run the same fortune as her Lord, knowing that there was a just and all-seeing Judge above who, she hoped, would have an especial hand in this business'.

On 15 October, however, the outer walls of this 'nest of Romanists' were broken down by ceaselessly pounding shot from the heavy guns which Cromwell had brought with him, and the Roundheads poured into the gardens and courts, then into the house, firing in all directions without discrimination, lashing out with their swords at armed defenders and civilian refugees alike, killing several of the priests and a young woman who tried to protect her father, stripping Inigo Jones and leaving him to be carried away in a blanket, stripping the Marquess of Winchester, also, and abandoning him to the denunciations of Cromwell's Bible-quoting and pistol-carrying chaplain, 'the Reverend dragoon' Hugh Peters. They pulled down tapestries and hangings, burnt religious pictures and papist-looking books, carried off a hundred petticoats and gowns which were discovered in wardrobes, carted away furniture and plate, even roofing lead and window bars, to sell to London dealers, tore the cloaks from the backs of ladies who were otherwise treated 'uncivilly' but not 'coarsely', since Cromwell, who hanged men for plundering innocent people without leave, had let it be known that he would certainly hang a man for rape. 'The dispute was long and sharp,' a writer in the *Kingdome's Weekly Post* reported, 'the enemy, for ought I can learn, desired no quarter, and I believe they had but little offered them. You must remember what they were. They were most of them Papists, therefore our musquets and our swords did show but little compassion, and the House being at length subdued did now satisfy for her treason and rebellion by the blood of the offenders.' 'Cursed be he that doth the Lord's work negligently,' shouted Major Thomas Harrison as he shot a major who, before the war, had been a comedian at Drury Lane.

About a hundred men and women were killed in all and three hundred taken prisoner before the house caught fire as the last of the booty was brought out, including piles of cheese and bacon which were spread out upon the grass and offered for sale to the country people who flocked from miles around to buy them.

'We have had little loss,' reported Cromwell, who advised the destruction of the remains of the house rather than incurring the expense of holding a place which his chaplain described as having been 'fit to make an emperor's court'. 'Most of the enemy our men put to the sword, and some officers of quality. Most of the rest we have prisoners.'

With these and other military defeats a daily burden to him, the King soon had further problems with which to contend. For Prince Rupert, refusing to be dismissed from the King's service without a hearing, rode to Newark accompanied by his brother Maurice, several loyal officers and a troop of horse, to demand an inquiry. Skilfully evading the 1,500 Parliamentary horsemen sent out to capture him, the patrolling garrison of Burghley House and the cavalry besieging Belvoir Castle, Prince Rupert arrived at Newark on 16 October. Lord Digby, forewarned of his approach, arranged to leave, as Lieutenant-General of the Royalist army north of the Trent, shortly before Rupert arrived.

At Newark feeling ran strongly in Rupert's favour. No soldier with any claim to military competence doubted that the Prince had nearly always been right in his arguments with Lord Digby and that Digby had been almost invariably wrong. The Prince was sometimes irritating and overbearing, and his habit of speaking little in councils of war except 'with a pish to neglect all another said' had clearly been maddening to Digby. But there could be no doubt that Digby's influence over the King – whose military capacity was not in any case pronounced – had been a dangerous one, nor that Prince Rupert had been treated with gross unfairness after the surrender of Bristol. Sir Edward Nicholas had felt so at the time; and had written to the King to assure him that his nephew, far from living in luxury on the spoils of plunder and bribery, was in fact very poor. The Governor of Newark, Sir Richard Willis, agreed that Rupert had been unfairly treated. So did Lord Gerard, still smarting, despite his barony, from his dismissal from his command in Wales. Disobeying the King's orders, they went together to greet the Prince as he approached the town gate.

When the Prince arrived and unceremoniously went up to the King to say that he had come to render an account of the loss of Bristol, his uncle would not speak to him. The King went in to supper and ignored him throughout the meal. Later, although he was prepared to endorse a council of war's opinion that there was no evidence of lack of courage or fidelity at Bristol, he still insisted that Rupert might have done more to hold the place longer. Displeased with the findings of the council members who exonerated the Prince from all blame, and concerned by the effect which these unseemly disputes were having on the morale of the Newark garrison, the King dismissed Sir Richard Willis from the governorship, attempting to placate him with the offer of the command of his Life Guards, vacant since Lord Bernard Stuart's death.

But Willis was not to be placated; and accompanied by Lord Gerard, Princes Rupert and Maurice and several other officers who supported him, he burst in upon the King after church on Sunday.

Willis demanded an explanation; he had been dishonoured; his fate was being discussed all over Newark. Rupert interrupted him to say that the explanation was simple: Willis had been dismissed because he had shown him sympathy. Then Lord Gerard spoke: 'This is all Digby's doing, and Digby is a traitor, and I can prove him so.'

The King asked for silence and said that he would speak to Willis privately in the next room. But Willis 'would not, saying that he had received a publicke injury and therefore expected a publicke satisfaction'.

'Say no more,' the King rebuked him, angry as always when his dignity was endangered. 'This is a time unreasonable for you to command here.'

'All that Sir Richard desires is very reasonable,' Gerard audaciously persisted. 'For if gentlemen must be putt out upon every occasion and aspersion it will discourage all from serving Your Majesty.'

'What does this concern you?'

'I am sure and can prove that Digby was the cause for which I was outsted from my command in Wales.'

Then Rupert broke in again about his own complaint, 'whereat the King sighed and said, "O nephewe," and stopt. Then he would say no more.' And at last he told them all to leave the room.

They left to put Willis's complaint in writing and later returned to present it to the King in person. Someone, with a kind of apology which the others felt far from expressing, hoped that the King would not call this mutiny. Charles would not give it a name, he said, but to him it looked 'very like'. And very like mutiny it was next morning when Rupert and his men rode into Newark's market place to protest against the appointment of a new Governor. The King came out to them. Those who were dissatisifed, he told them, his anger well controlled, could leave for Belvoir Castle and disband themselves. He would not do anything to stop them; but on no account would he give way to their demands. Defeated, they rode away south to the Vale of Belvoir.

The King was soon forced to follow them. Digby's forces in the north had disintegrated and Digby himself had crossed over to the Isle of Man, where he wrote with irrepressible buoyancy of his intention of sailing to Ireland and hurrying up the Irish reinforcements which would change the whole course of the conflict. But not even the most sanguine of his friends could believe Digby any more. The remaining strongholds in the south-west were falling fast. The fall of Carmarthen was followed by the occupation of Chepstow, the occupation of Chepstow by the fall of Monmouth, the fall of Monmouth by Fairfax's capture of Tiverton where a well-aimed shot at its chain sent the drawbridge crashing down across the moat of the castle, allowing the Roundheads to rush in before it could be pulled up again. More threatening to the King's own person, two armies, one English, the other Scottish, were converging fast on Newark. With the remnants of his Life Guard, the King rode out of the town for Oxford.

Back at Oxford, the King was once more soothed by the decorous and deferential atmosphere of court life. 'Once or twice a week,' Sir Henry Slingsby recorded, 'he would take horse and go about the town, to view both within and without the works, and be among his ordinance where they stood upon their carryages; he kept his hours most exactly, both for his exercises and for his dispatches, as also his hours for admitting all sorts to come and speak with him. You might know where he would be at any hour from his rising, which was very early, to his walk he took in the Garden, and so to Chapple and dinner; so after dinner, if he went not abroad, he had his houres for writing and discourcing, or chess playing, or Tennis.' He comforted himself with the hope that his enemies' quarrels and dissensions were more rancorous and went deeper than those in his own party. He occupied himself with plans and plots to deepen the growing distrust between the rebels' political and religious factions. He envisaged ways of separating Presbyterians from Independents, Englishmen from Scotsmen, of negotiating with one side at the expense of the other, of winning present help by promises of future favours. He continued to seek help from abroad, from both Spain and France. But Parliament's representative, Sir Harry Vane, proved a far more astute and skilful diplomatist than his rivals and succeeded in persuading the governments of both countries that the King's cause was doomed; indeed, Spain now recognized Parliament as the *de facto* ruler of England. The King appealed to the Pope, Urban VIII's successor, Innocent X, who replied that he might consider offering help if his Majesty publicly announced his conversion to the Roman Catholic faith.

The King's schemes never worked out as he planned they should, since it was a sad, inescapable fact that his promises were not believed any more, either in the country or outside it; he was not trusted to stand by his word even if he had the power and the means to do what he promised to do. He was judged to be even more deceitful than most monarchs usually were.

Yet if he could persuade himself that diplomatic bargaining might even now save him from defeat, he could not ignore the succession of military disasters that rendered victory in the field inconceivable. Nor could the return of an apologetic Prince Rupert to Oxford alter that bleak prospect of military defeat, for not only was the Prince given no command by the King, who had been reluctant at first to receive his nephew back into favour at all, but there were scarcely any forces left for him to be given. The remaining Midland garrisons were being battered into submission one by one. In the west the Royalist armies, fighting each other for the best quarters, scarcely existed any more. Goring had abandoned them for the pleasures and peace of France; Sir Richard Grenville, having given up all hope of victory, recommended a negotiated peace. In Devon Fairfax's capture of Tiverton Castle had induced the Prince of Wales's custodians to take him even farther down the Cornish peninsula to Truro where he indignantly rejected a polite summons to surrender his troops and himself to Parliament with the explosive comment, 'Rogues and rebels! Are they not content to be rebels themselves but they must have me of their number?'

Shortly before Christmas, in biting cold weather that froze the Thames and Severn and crippled soldiers with frostbite, an army of volunteers from Parliamentary garrisons in Somerset and Gloucestershire marched upon Hereford under the command of Colonel John Birch. A party of them, dressed as labourers, went up to the gate soon after dawn to ask about getting work in the city. While they were talking to the guards and distracting their attention from the movements behind them, others of Birch's men suddenly appeared from a hollow and rushed forward into the city. The whole Roundhead force pushed after them, plundering houses and pouring into the cathedral where they knocked the heads off statues, damaged effigies on tombs in the nave and transepts and smashed memorial brasses, deriding the brave protests of the Dean who would have been shot as he was standing in the pulpit had not Birch himself protected him.

In hopes of saving Chester, the Governor, Lord Byron, sent his pretty young wife – later, according to Pepys, Charles II's 'seventeenth mistress' – to Oxford to beg for help and reinforcements; but nothing could be spared for her, and after Christmas the city surrendered. Then Dartmouth was taken by Fairfax who offered the Royalist troops half a crown to go home or three shillings to join the New Model Army. From Dartmouth, Fairfax moved on to Torrington where he was nearly killed when the Royalists' stores of gunpowder were fired in the parish church, blowing the roof into the sky from which its shattered fragments hurtled to the ground. Then Launceston and Bodmin fell; and Ralph Hopton was driven out of Truro from which the Prince of Wales had already fled to the Isles of Scilly and thence to Jersey. In south Wales, Laugharne occupied Cardiff; in the Midlands, Belvoir Castle, Lichfield and Ashby de la Zouch were all occupied by the besieging forces of the New Model Army. Hopton undertook to disband his army and go abroad. Then, at last, on 21 March 1646, Lord Astley, commanding the King's only surviving army in the field, was defeated near Stow-on-the Wold. Over 1,500 of his infantry, mostly Welsh recruits, surrendered after a half-hearted fight. The cavalry galloped away for the safety of Oxford. Sitting on a drum, old Astley, who had fought bravely for the King since the Battle of Edgehill three and a half years before, gave up his sword to a Parliamentary soldier. 'You have done your work, boys,' he said. 'You may go play, unless you fall out among yourselves.'

Three weeks later Fairfax captured Exeter, taking prisoner the little Princess Henrietta Anne who had been left there with a governess when her mother escaped to France. 'The Western War,' wrote Fairfax, 'I trust in the Lord, is finished.' Within a few days of the capture of Exeter, Barnstaple also surrendered and the only place left holding out for the King in Somerset was Dunster Castle, whose commanding site had once served as a Saxon frontier fortress against the Celts. Here Colonel Francis Wyndham had been under siege since November 1645, ignoring frequent summons to surrender from the Parliamentary commander, Colonel Robert Blake, although provisions and ammunition were running low and water was in extremely short supply. When Sir Thomas Fairfax arrived in January 1646 with reinforcements for Blake, it was decided to attempt an assault. Mines failed to blow up the castle; but the Roundheads' guns, pounding away at the walls from the deer park, opened up a breach. The garrison, urged on by Wyndham, still refused to surrender, encouraged by reports that relief was near. This relieving force of 1,500 cavalry and three hundred foot arrived when part of the besieging army had been called away to help in operations against Lord Goring, and it managed to slip through Parliamentary lines and up the steep hill to the castle with thirty cows, fifty sheep and several barrels of powder, before going back to Barnstaple, destroying Colonel Blake's mines and much of his fortifications on the way. So the siege dragged on. Winter passed, spring came and Colonel Wyndham remained defiant. But towards the end of April, his supplies all but exhausted, he offered to surrender at last. His men marched out of the castle, armed and with flags flying; and Colonel Blake's troops marched in. The civil war in Somerset was over.

At Oxford, Charles recognized now, as he told the Queen, that he had 'neither force enough to resist nor sufficient to escape to any secure place'. For months deserters in their hundreds had been abandoning his cause and going over to the New Model Army; and officers had been sailing overseas to serve in Continental armies. Hopton's forces at the end had been nothing but a 'dissolute, undisciplined, wicked' army; at Truro they had drunkenly welcomed the Roundheads and sat down with them to dinner. Everywhere Royalist officers and troopers were abandoning themselves to what pleasures could still be enjoyed or taking to a life of crime: in future years travellers on the roads of England were to be in constant danger from highwaymen who had once been in the service of the King, men like Zachary Howard, who had mortgaged his estate for £20,000 to raise a troop of horse, and Jemmy Hinde, a saddler's son, who held up carriages and passers-by on the roads of Oxfordshire and Gloucestershire, calling himself Captain Hinde and behaving towards his victims with elaborate courtesy. Everywhere, too, Royalists were taking advantage of Parliament's offer of a peaceful settlement by compounding for their estates, paying fines proportionate to their value, saving what they could of their property while they could.

The Northern Horse, reduced to barely a thousand men, made for Scotland as part of a scratch force under the general command of Lord Digby. They pushed their way past a few companies of Roundheads at Ferrybridge; but at Sherburn-in-Elmet, east of Leeds, their path was blocked by a larger force, almost twice as numerous as their own.

'Gentlemen you are gallant men,' their commander, Sir Marmaduke Langdale, told them, 'but there are some that seek to scandalize
your gallantry for the loss of Naseby field. I hope you will redeem
your reputation, and still maintain that gallant report which you
have ever had. I am sure you have done such business as never has
been done in any war with such a number.'

For a time it seemed as though Langdale's men would indeed
redeem their great reputation. They charged furiously at the Roundhead horse, scattering one troop after another, sending some galloping away to the north, others to the south through Sherburn's main
street with Langdale's men racing after them. Seeing the fugitives
emerging from the little town, Digby's cavalry in the fields to the
north of it supposed them to be Langdale's troopers in headlong
flight, and, believing the brief battle lost, they rode away. Left on
their own, Langdale's horse could not withstand the shock when
the fleeing cavalry wheeled about and turned upon them, while the
Roundheads to the south of Sherburn galloped back into the fight.
Langdale himself escaped though four times pistols were discharged
at him at point-blank range; but most of his men were killed or
wounded, only three hundred or so escaping to gallop away through
Yorkshire and across the Pennines into Cumberland. Having picked
up a few Royalist stragglers on the way, they reached the coast near
Carlisle; and on the evening of 24 October they were caught on
Carlisle Sands by a far larger Parliamentary force. Many were killed
on the shore; many more driven into the sea and drowned; two
hundred were taken prisoner. A few escaped and rode back home to
Yorkshire; Langdale, who lived to fight for the King again as well
as for the Doge of Venice, escaped to the Isle of Man in a ship's
small open boat. But the Northern Horse, which he had commanded
so well for so long, were no more.

15

OXFORD
ABANDONED

---

*' 'Twould grieve one's heart to see men drop
like ripe fruit in a strong wind, and never see
their enemy.'*

Richard Atkyns

Without an army left to fight for him in England, Charles turned
for help to the Scots. He knew that the Scottish Covenanters felt
themselves ill-used by the English Parliament, which had been thankful enough to enlist their help when the Royalists seemed likely to
triumph, but which now seemed as ready to neglect the unpaid
Scottish army as to go back upon the undertakings about Presbyterianism and the other promises contained in the Solemn League
and Covenant. If Charles could play on this dissatisfaction, if he
could aggravate Scottish fears of the growing influence of the Independents in the English Parliamentary army, if he could arouse their
sympathy for one who was, after all, a Scottish King and persuade
them to agree to defend his interests against his rebellious English
subjects, he might yet retrieve his fortunes.

He left Oxford in an attempt to do so in the early hours of 27
April 1646. He took with him but two companions; one of his chaplains who had gained a good knowledge of the roads and by-lanes
of East Anglia while serving in the army as a scoutmaster, and Jack
Ashburnham. With his long hair trimmed, wearing a false beard and
a suit of ordinary clothes, the King travelled disguised as his companions' servant. 'Farewell, Harry,' the Governor called to him loudly
as the party clattered over Magdalen Bridge and the gates were shut

behind them, a clock in the distance striking three. Riding by night, eating and sleeping in strange taverns and alehouses, they passed through Dorchester and Henley, then, taking a circuitous route to the headquarters of the Scottish army near Newark, they went on through Slough and St Albans to Market Harborough and Stamford, then to Downham Market in Norfolk where they aroused the suspicions of the landlord of the Swan Inn by having a fire lit in their room, burning papers in the hearth, then, having tried to cut their hair with knives, sending for a barber.

Left behind in Oxford, the Governor, Sir Thomas Glemham, a tough gentleman from Little Glemham, Suffolk, and a grandson of the Earl of Dorset, undertook to defend the place as determinedly as he had held Carlisle where he was said to have been 'the first man that taught soldiers to eat cats and dogs'. He was, however, told by such members of the Privy Council as remained in Oxford that further resistance was useless and that he must be prepared to surrender.

All over the country Royalist strongholds which had been stubbornly holding out against their besiegers now fell one after the other. Most of these castles were of little strategic importance, but they were symbols of resistance which had given hope and spirit to the Royalist cause, and some had tied down large numbers of enemy troops for long periods and had cost the besiegers disproportionate casualties as they had attempted to storm the defences, running across open ground in face of an unseen enemy and falling 'like ripe fruit in a strong wind' or, as another officer said, 'like leaves from a tree in a winter storm'. Sudeley Castle in Gloucestershire, for example, had withstood a hard and lengthy siege, so had Donnington Castle in Berkshire, Pontefract Castle in Yorkshire and Raglan Castle which was surrendered after a close investment of over three months during which the garrison's horses, starved for want of hay, had been reduced to eating their own halters. Orders were given for the castle to be 'totally demolished'. Its enormous bulk saved it from this fate, though it was rendered utterly uninhabitable, its library being destroyed, its furniture dispersed, the lead from its roof being sold for £6,000, the trees in its park cut down and sent to Bristol, and those parts of the structure which resisted all ordinary methods of demolition being undermined and propped up by huge wooden beams the 'burning of which,' in the words of the nineteenth-century historian of Herefordshire, 'reduced it to the condition in which it excites the wonder and the pity of the stranger's eye. For many years the materials of this princely residence served for the common repairs of the neighbourhood; and no less than 23 staircases were at different times removed by a single workman.'

Bridgnorth Castle in Shropshire also underwent a long siege and suffered a similar fate. Here the chatelaine, Lady Beeston, after being rescued by Prince Rupert and dining with him in celebration, was unceremoniously told that she had better be out of the castle with her belongings the next morning as the Prince intended to have the place blown up in case it fell into enemy hands. At Scarborough Castle, Lady Cholmley, the Governor's wife, had stood by her husband throughout the siege, nursing the sick and wounded. 'She would not forsake me for any danger,' Sir Hugh Cholmley said. 'My dear wife endured much hardship,' he added later, 'and yet with little show of trouble; and though by nature, according to her sex, timorous, yet in greatest danger would not be daunted.' Wardour Castle in Wiltshire was also defended stubbornly. Here Lady Blanche Arundell, during her husband's absence in Oxford, defied a summons to surrender, though she had only twenty-five men against a besieging force of 1,300. No, she would not give in, she declared: she was commanded by her lord to keep the castle, and keep it, therefore, she would; and no, she would not accept quarter for the women and children if the offer were not to be extended to the men also. After prolonged battering, during which maidservants loaded their muskets for the men of the garrison, a mine was sprung beneath the fortress and its surrender thus obtained. The garrison was spared, but the contents of the castle, including its pictures and books, were pillaged and ransacked and a 'splendid carved chimney-piece, valued at £2,000, hacked to pieces with pole-axes'. The castle's outbuildings were burned, deer were killed, fish dragged from the ponds, fruit trees dug up or cut down. Even the castle's lead water pipes, two miles long, were cut into short lengths and sold at tuppence a foot. However, the women and children were not harmed.

At Grafton House near Stony Stratford they were not so fortunate. Here, after the stronghold had surrendered, they were all 'stripped to their naked skins'. The Roundhead stronghold Brampton Bryan, on the mid-Wales border, was treated even more harshly. Here Brilliana, Lady Harley, whose husband was at Westminster, refused to surrender with as much spirit as Lady Blanche Arundell. She did not know, she replied caustically to the summons to give the place up, that it was her husband's wish that she 'should entertain soldiers in his house'. And she remained steadfast in her defiance as the Royalist soldiers shouted insults at her and her household from the earthworks, as the bombardment increased in intensity, wounding two of her friends, and as shot crashed through the windows from the church steeple, shattering part of her precious collection of Venetian glass. During the course of the siege, the castle's cook was said to have been shot 'by a poisoned bullet, which murdered him with great torment, and noisomeness to the whole family'. The castle's park was laid waste; Brampton village was reduced to ruins, together with the castle's outbuildings; the parish church was ransacked and all its memorials to the Harley family were defaced before it was set on fire. After the death of Lady Harley from what she described in her last letter as 'a very greate coold', the castle also was burned down. So, too, was the nearby Hopton Castle, the home of the Wallop family, confirmed Parliamentarians like Sir Robert Harley.

For long periods castles like these had been able to withstand the onslaught of all that the besiegers' guns could throw against them. Their immensely thick medieval walls had been dented and crumbled on the surface rather than cracked and broken, even under the battering of the heaviest guns, including those borrowed from the fleet and lent for these purposes most reluctantly by the Earl of Warwick. More often than not, heavy siege guns were not available. The Earl of Essex set great store by them – and was often slowed down in his marches because he insisted upon taking them with him – but Waller and Fairfax refused to be burdened with cumbersome cannon, insisting that they were more trouble than they were worth.

Guns, heavy or light, were irrelevant now, however, as the last fortresses surrendered and the garrisons and besiegers marched away.

On the morning of 6 May, the King rode into the courtyard of the Saracen's Head at Southwell close by the Scottish army headquarters between Nottingham and Newark. The Scots, anxious to get him out of the way of the English, took him north to Newcastle where day in and day out for almost eight months they tried to persuade him to accept the Presbyterian system as outlined in the Solemn League and Covenant, to reform religion in England 'according to

In January 1644 Roundhead cavalry trounced the Cavaliers at Nantwich in Cheshire

Roundhead propaganda condemning the 'cruelties of the Cavaliers, 1644'

CRUELTIES OF THE CAVALIERS, 1644.

Donnington Castle, a mediaeval stronghold north of Newbury, garrisoned by Royalists in 1642, resisted repeated attacks and was relieved by the King in 1644

ABOVE: An eighteenth-century print depicting 'Prince Rupert summoning the Garrison of Leicester to surrender to the Army of Charles the First, May 30th 1645'

BELOW: The King rode out of Oxford wearing a false beard and with his long hair trimmed on 27 April 1646

General FAIRFAX with his FORCES before the City of OXFORD

Negotiations for the surrender of the Royalist garrison at Oxford to Parliament were concluded in June 1646

A plan of Newark showing the defences and dispositions at the time of the town's last siege in 1646

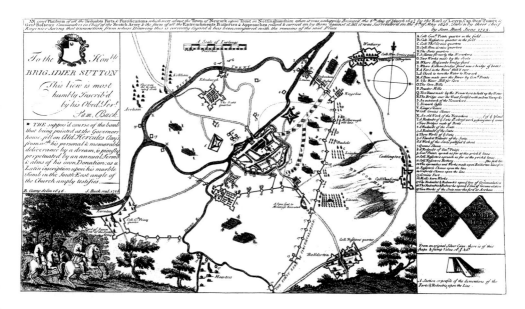

A contemporary woodcut depicting
Sir Thomas Fairfax and the Council
of the Army, 1647

The Royalist Sir Charles Lucas at
the siege of Colchester in 1648

A great and bloudy
FIGHT
AT
COLCHESTER
AND

The ſtorming of the Town by the Lord Generals Forces, with the manner how they were repulſed and beaten off, and forced to retreat from the Walls, and a great and terrible blow given at the ſaid ſtorm, by Granadoes and Gunpowder. Likewiſe their hanging out the Flag of Defiance, and their ſallying out upon Tueſday laſt, all the chief Officers ingaging in the ſaid Fight, and Sir *Charles Lucas* giving the firſt onſet in the Van, with the number killed and taken, and Sir *Charles Lucas* his Declaration.

Christ Church Coll: Ox. Canterbury Minster Trinn: Colledge Camb.

MERCURIUS RUSTICUS

Countess of Rivers plundered pag: 11.

Sᵗ John Lucas house plundered pag: 3.

Sᵗ Rich Mynshuls hous plundered pag: 31.

A Bonfire for the voting downe Episcopacy pag: 26.

Mᵗ Jones a Miniſ: carried on a Beare pag: 9.

Edge hill Battle

THE COUNTRYS COMPLAINT Recovnting the sad Events of the late unparalleld REBELLION

Warder Castle defended by a Lady. pag: 41.

ABOVE: The title page of an account of the 'great and bloudy Fight at Colchester' published in 1648

RIGHT: The engraved title page of *Mercurius Rusticus*, the Royalist newspaper. 'The sad Events of the late unparalleld Rebellion' include the plundering of Sir John Lucas's house, the siege of Wardour Castle and, at the bottom, the 'hedgehogs' of pikemen at Edgehill

Behold your King

THE ILE OF WAIT

LEFT: A broadsheet of 1648 showing the King imprisoned in Carisbrooke Castle where he remained from November 1647 until his removal to Hurst Castle in December 1648

OPPOSITE: A contemporary engraving of the trial of the King in Westminster Hall in January 1649

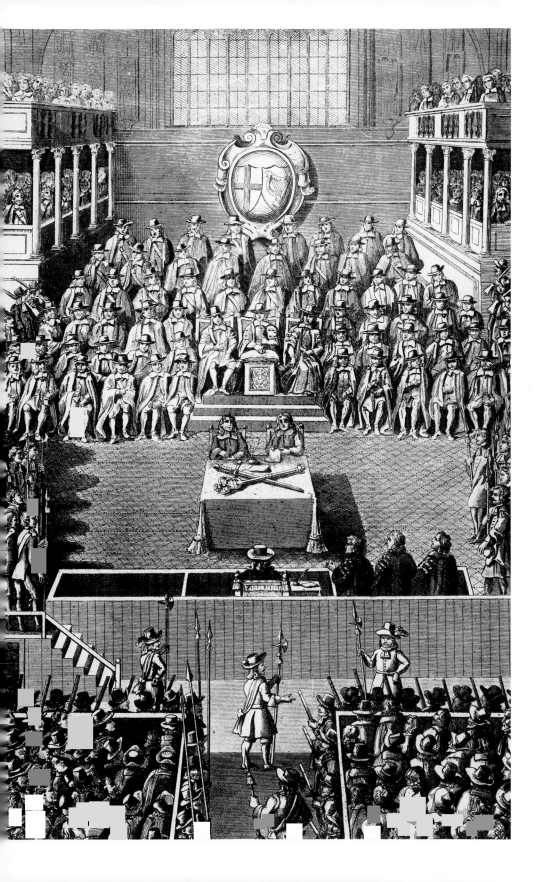

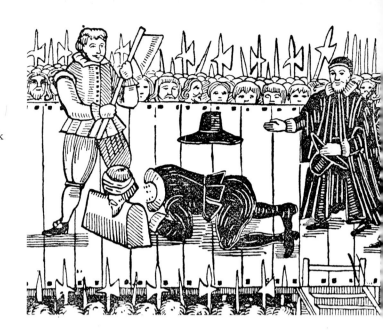

RIGHT: The title page of *The Confessions of Richard Brandon*, 'printed in the Year of the Hang-man's downfall, 1649'. It was later rumoured by Royalists that Brandon, the City's principal executioner, had refused to perform his task and that Hugh Peter, the Army chaplain, or even Cromwell himself had taken his place

BELOW: 'The apotheosis or death of the King', a Royalist depiction of Charles I being borne to Heaven by angels and cherubs

the Word of God' and 'the example of the best reformed Churches'. Every conceivable argument was advanced to him by an assortment of Scottish ministers who, singly and together, pleaded with him, argued with him, quarrelled with him, pitied his ignorance, flattered his intellect, condemned his stubbornness in an attempt to break down his intractable resistance, his obstinate beliefs. They could not believe that he had come to the Scottish camp without intending to support the Scots on the Presbyterian issue, and they refused to be defeated by his obduracy.

Deprived of the reassuring comfort and consoling, attentive flattery of his gentlemen and courtiers, deserted even by his chaplain and Jack Ashburnham who had come with him to Newcastle but had been advised to leave him there to avoid being handed over as prisoners to the English, the King was quite alone. He was permitted to go out to 'the Shield Field without the Walls' to play an occasional game of golf, watched by Scottish sentinels; but golf and chess were almost his only relaxations from the tedious discussions with the Presbyterian divines who hung about him so persistently that he was 'never wanting new vexations'. He remained placid, only once showing a flash of anger when he abruptly cut short a long extempore grace of more than usual tedium by falling to his meat with the comment that he did not intend to let it grow cold while the minister 'stood whistling for the spirit'. Normally, however, the King reserved his complaints for his wife, and in the letters that he managed to send her he told her that he had never known what it was to be 'barbarously baited before'. The only comfort he had left was in her love and his own 'clear conscience'.

The Queen had little sympathy with his tiresome conscience; any promises he gave need not be permanently binding. She agreed with Lord Jermyn: surely it was better in the end to be a Presbyterian King than no sort of King at all. It was not as if he were a Catholic.

But the King would not give way. His 'clear conscience' would not let him abandon the Church which he loved; and even now there might be hope. Admittedly the news from England continued to be bad: the few towns that remained in Royalist hands were all falling fast. Only a few scattered strongholds were left: Worcester, Wallingford, Lichfield Cathedral and its close, Conway in north Wales, Pendennis in Cornwall. Towards the end of June the storekeeper at Oxford announced that he had provisions for only twelve more days and that supplies of powder were all but exhausted. The town's garrison was on the verge of mutiny, threatening to kill the Royal councillors unless they were paid. Hurriedly the councillors came to terms with the Parliamentary commanders, and in an effort to quieten the tumult in the garrison's ranks over their arrears of pay, agreed to pawn to a Roundhead officer the King's insignia of the Order of the Garter which Charles had left behind. On 20 June the articles of capitulation were signed. Sir Thomas Fairfax marched into the city and, living up to his reputation as a bibliophile, immediately placed a guard upon the Bodleian Library. Prince Rupert and the Duke of York were taken prisoner, the Prince sent into exile, the Duke taken to London to join Princess Henrietta Anne and his six-year-old brother Prince Henry under guard at St James's Palace. But the Prince of Wales had escaped, sailing from Jersey to France on the very day that Oxford capitulated; and from France or from Ireland help might yet come.

The King also took comfort from reports of continuing quarrels among the Parliamentary leaders. Their peace terms had now been drafted. They were so harsh upon the Royalists that when Hyde read them he decided that if his Majesty accepted them there would in future be no 'seeds left for monarchy to spring out of'. The King was required to abolish the episcopal Church, to agree to severe penalties being imposed upon Roman Catholics and to the education of their children by Protestants, to hand over control of the army and navy to Parliament for twenty years, to consent to all titles created since the beginning of 1642 being declared void, and to certain of his most loyal supporters being exempted from pardon.

When Parliament's representatives came to Newcastle the King knew that he must reject their terms. Had they any authority to discuss them with him? he asked the Earl of Pembroke, head of the mission. No, he was told, they had come merely to take back his answer. In which case, the King retorted, their mission might just as well have been entrusted to 'an honest Trumpeter'.

Yet Charles did not want to give them an immediate reply. Delay meant a prolongation of hope; he studied how to make an 'honest denying answer'; he persuaded himself that at least the terms contained clauses that might bring about an open breach between the Scots and the English. But all Charles's hopes, in the end, were disappointed and his prevarications of no avail. The Scots, as it turned out, urged him to accept the terms. If he did not do so he would lose all his friends in both Houses of Parliament, the Scottish Chancellor bluntly warned him. 'England will join against you as one man. They will depose you and set up another government. They will charge us to deliver your Majesty to them.' And this, at last, was what happened.

Understandably refusing to consider the King's proposition that he should agree to the establishment of Presbyterianism for three years – since Charles admitted it would go against his conscience not to use that period to 'lay a ground for a perfect recovery' – the Scots entered into negotiations with the English for the payment of the money due to them for their army's services in the recent war. When this money was paid the Scots prepared to withdraw across the border, leaving the King to fall into the hands of the English Parliamentarians.

Once he had resigned himself to the inevitability of this fate, the King appeared quite tranquil once more. When he was told that the Scots had definitely decided not to receive him in their country, he went on calmly with a game of chess; when he tried and failed to escape he appeared not unduly perturbed; when he heard the figure – £400,000 – which the Scots had agreed, after a good deal of haggling, to accept for their military help, he teased them on the poor bargain they had made in selling him; and when the Earl of Pembroke came to Newcastle again as Parliament's messenger to discuss the arrangements for the King's removal south, Charles greeted him politely and consented to go with him to Holdenby, the huge house in Northamptonshire which Sir Christopher Hatton had built in the previous century in the vain hope that Queen Elizabeth I would favour him there with a visit.

On his journey south Charles was welcomed as though on a triumphal progress. Church bells rang in greeting; civic dignitaries came forward to offer speeches of respectful welcome; people sank to their knees as he rode by; voices cried out, 'God bless your Majesty!' Men and women suffering from scrofula came forward to seek the age-old cure of touch by royal hands. The guards riding with him made no effort to keep the people back, allowing them to approach as close as they wished, 'a civility which his Majesty was well pleased with'. On his arrival at Holdenby 'very many country gentlemen, gentle-women and others of ordinary rank, stood ready there to welcome their King with joyful countenance and prayers, counting him as only able to restore to them their peace and settlement'. Once more the King, impressionable and complacent as always in momentary success, began to hope that all would yet be well.

16

SOLDIERS AND
LEVELLERS

'I do think that the poorest man in England is
not at all bound . . . to that government that
he hath not had a voice to put himself under.'

Colonel Thomas Rainsborough

A few days after the battle of Naseby, Richard Baxter, the loquacious
Presbyterian preacher and army chaplain, had gone to talk to Cromwell's soldiers and had been appalled by the language of the 'hot-
headed sectaries' amongst them, their wild religious views and coarse
jokes, their insulting references to the King, their demands for the
'liberty of all'. Since then, disgruntled by evasive responses to their
demands for their arrears of pay and having few military activities
to occupy their time, the soldiers of the New Model Army had
become increasingly restive and argumentative, debating amongst
themselves the most revolutionary political propositions and airing
religious views which horrified the more conservative of the Presbyterians, let alone those who clung to the beliefs and traditions of the
Anglican Church of their lamented Archbishop Laud. Officers and
soldiers alike took to preaching sermons in churches and from the
mounting steps outside village alehouses. Upper-class officers who
had fought under the Earl of Manchester derided such 'godly, precious men [who] had filled dung-carts before they were captains',
who were turning the areas where they were stationed into 'a mere
Amsterdam' in which churches rang with their ravings, while honest
clergymen chased from their pulpits were obliged to listen to them,
to their ranting about 'visions and revelations'.

Although sharing the social conservatism of the old Presbyterians like the Earl of Manchester and Sir William Waller, Oliver Cromwell was still in broad sympathy with the religious views of the Independents amongst his soldiers. When Richard Baxter, appointed chaplain to the regiment commanded by Cromwell's cousin, Edward Whalley, announced his plans to impose a far more strict religious conformity upon the Army, Colonel William Purefoy warned him that if 'Noll Cromwell' heard about that he 'would cleave his crown'. Yet Cromwell was undoubtedly distressed by the soldiers' demands for political reform which threatened the stability of the country and by the spreading among the troops of the extreme doctrines of the republican Levellers who demanded the abolition of social distinctions. When one of the leading Levellers, John Lilburne – whose political tracts continued to demand religious liberty and manhood suffrage – failed to obtain the arrears of pay he was entitled to as an officer in Parliament's army, Cromwell interceded with the House of Commons on his behalf, urging them to be careful not to ignore the claims of men who had fought against their mutual enemies. But soon afterwards Cromwell was thumping on the table in denunciation of the Levellers. 'I tell you, sir,' he shouted, 'You have no other way to deal with these men but to break them or they will break you; yea, and bring all the guilt of the blood and treasure shed and spent in this kingdom upon your heads and shoulders, and frustrate and make void all that work that, with so many years' industry, toil and pains, you have done, and so render you to all rational men in the world as the most contemptible generation of silly, low-spirited men in the earth to be broken and routed by such a despicable, contemptible generation of men as they are . . . I tell you again, you are necessitated to break them.'

'We are full of faction and worse,' Cromwell complained to Fairfax. From all over the country there were reports of desertions from the Army, threats that whole regiments would disband themselves, mutinies and attacks upon Parliamentary agents and local government officials. In Nantwich victims of 'the desperate soldiers' had recently recorded that 'ffyve Companyes of our Garrison Soldyers, being about ffive hundred unreasonable men without either Captyns or Commanders, in a most outragious maner fell upon us and with great fury did throwe us into the Comon prison amongst prisoners, Cavaliers and Horstealers, neither sufferinge any to relieve us with

meate drinke or any necessaryes but what the parsons or some weo-
men did privatlie convaye unto us, where wee (being Ancyent men)
did lye upon the boards . . . The Governor of the Towne and his
man they wounded and abused most cruelly.'

Later, from King's Lynn there came another characteristic report:
'The miseric of our Towne is growne unto such a highet, and our
souldiers for want of pay are growne so mutinous [that there] will
be noe livinge for us.' At York, Major-General Sydenham Poyntz
was arrested by his men and taken to Pontefract. He was 'carried
away in his slippers,' his wife said, 'not suffered to Express any
congugall comefort or courtesie to me at his departing, & what wil
be the dooms they will pass on him I cannot tell'. From Plymouth,
the Governor wrote, 'Souldiers who were to relieve the guards came
to the Parade on Saturday morning last but absolutely refused to goe
uppon duty and would also forcibly have carried away their colours.
Amonge whom I resolved to make some Examples, but Famine
seemed to appear in most of their faces . . . uppon which grounds
I forbore to proceed against them and to allay this mutiny I was
inforced to take five hundred pounds out of the Custome howse for
their present supply with bread.'

In the immediate aftermath of Naseby, Cromwell had been full of
confidence. Convinced that God had been on Parliament's side, he
had looked upon his soldiers as God's faithful servants; and while
strict in maintaining discipline, publicly hanging a man for plundering, he had been prepared to indulge them. He was seen to laugh
at their occasional antics and would sit down to joke with them as
they sat around their camp fires, smoking their pipes, playing their
recorders, singing their rude songs.

Samuel Carrington, whose biography of Cromwell was published
in 1695, said that his hero 'loved his soldiers as his children, and his
greatest care was to see them provided with all necessaries requisite'.
He did all he could to persuade Parliament to settle their arrears of
pay which were now standing at some £2¾ million and were a constant source of complaint and agitation.

Cromwell himself, in acknowledgement of his 'unwearied and
faithful services', was voted £2,500 a year by Parliament, mostly
from the Duke of Buckingham's estate, as well as a capital sum of
£500, Fairfax getting £5,000 and other Parliamentary commanders,

including Waller, far less. Cromwell was thus enabled to move from his modest lodgings in Long Acre to a house in Drury Lane and from there to a large house in King Street, Westminster, closer to the House of Commons in whose affairs he was now playing a much more obtrusive part. He was also now able to provide dowries for two of his daughters, for his favourite, Elizabeth, who married John Claypole, the twenty-two-year-old son of a friend of her father, and for Bridget who married Henry Ireton after a protracted courtship befitting the bridegroom's temperament.

These days had been relatively happy ones for Cromwell, despite his concern over the Army whose men, after several further outbreaks of violence, were forbidden by Parliament to come within fifty-five miles of London where there were troubles enough as it was, with crucifixes and popish books being burned by rowdy crowds in Cheapside and with frequent demonstrations by mobs of apprentices and by such fanatics as those who protested at the honours done to the memory of the Earl of Essex.

Essex's death on 14 September was followed by a vote in Parliament, inspired by the Independents, that his brother-in-law the Marquess of Hertford, who had fought for the King, together with all others who had done so, should be banned from the funeral. At the ceremony in Westminster Abbey a Presbyterian was allowed to preach the sermon. 'He was the man to break the ice and to set his first footing in the Red Sea,' the preacher said, referring with 'some confusion of metaphor' to Essex's early attachment to the Parliamentary cause. 'He was a man resolved, when others hung in suspense . . . No proclamation of treason could cry him down, nor threatening standard daunt him that, in that misty morning when men knew not each other, whether friend or foe, by his arising dispelled the fog, and, by his very name, commanded thousands into your service.'

An effigy of the Earl, as though clothed for battle, with his baton in his hand, was afterwards brought into the church and placed upon a hearse. It did not remain there long before it was hacked to pieces by a religious maniac who, mutilating also the figure of the antiquary William Camden, explained that an angel had commanded him to beat down all images in God's church.

Soon after Essex's funeral, Oliver Cromwell, whom the Earl had condemned as 'an Incendiary', fell ill and for weeks on end, unable to attend the Commons, was deeply depressed and, by his own account, close to death. Dismayed by the influence which Lilburne and his friends were exercising over the Army, distressed by their attacks on him for criticizing a petition which the ordinary soldiers had presented to Parliament and for assuring Members that 'the Army would disband and lay down their arms at their door, whensoever they should command them', Cromwell for a time even considered going abroad to fight in a Protestant army on the Continent. When he did appear in the Commons and spoke of the nation's new troubles, he would weep bitterly, so Clarendon said, 'and appear the most afflicted man in the world'.

By the beginning of May, Cromwell had sufficiently recovered to be appointed one of the commissioners sent by Parliament to hear the complaints of the Army. He and Philip Skippon set out accordingly for Saffron Walden where they were to meet two hundred officers in the parish church. The grievances of the soldiers, their demands for pay and for a cessation of unwarranted attacks upon their conduct, were not unreasonable, though Skippon felt it necessary to rebuke some of the speakers for the vehement manner of their protests. Cromwell, while accepting that the grievances were not unjustified, urged the officers to be patient and circumspect, to lend their support to Parliament rather than to blame it unequivocally for their misfortunes, to respect the authority under which they all now served. They evidently listened to his words in gloomy silence, many of them believing that Parliament would shortly issue orders to disband the Army in the hope of ridding themselves once and for all of the monster they had created.

On 25 May it was learned that the Presbyterians in the House of Commons, bent on denying the soldiers' demands for liberty of conscience, had carried the day and the Army was, indeed, to be disbanded.

Cromwell, the 'great Independent', had now to make a fateful decision. He had strongly pleaded the Army's cause, but, never in sympathy with its wilder spirits, he had always tried earnestly to reconcile it with Parliament; and in doing so he had satisfied neither side. Lilburne accused him of being under the malign influence of those 'two unworthy covetous earthworms', Vane and St John, and of betraying the Army. Parliament distrusted him and blamed him for the Army's unrest. At last, recognizing the impossibility of reconciliation, he decided to throw in his lot with the Army.

Before taking any step, however, he appears to have decided that the Army must secure the person of the King who, in Fairfax's words, had become 'the Golden Ball cast between the two parties'; and it seems that at Cromwell's house in Drury Lane – where the fare served by the parsimonious lady of the house was said to be nothing more appetizing than 'small beer and bread and butter' – plans to seize the King were made.

On 1 June a young man named George Joyce, in civilian life a tailor, who had served as a junior officer in the Eastern Association, set out for Oxford with some five hundred troopers. At Oxford he took over the arsenal before moving on to Holdenby. On his arrival there he was asked by the guards at the gatehouse what his business was. He replied that he had come to arrest Colonel Charles, the King's gaoler, and 'to prevent a plot to convey the King to London'.

The King, who had been in bed when Joyce arrived, was awakened by the sound of voices raised in argument below his room. He rang the silver bell which always stood on the table beside his bed and when a servant came into the room he asked what the disturbance was about. Joyce himself gave the answer: he had come, he said, to take the King away for his own good, assuring him that no harm would come to him, that his servants could accompany him, and that he would be required to do nothing against his conscience.

'Sir, we have secured the King,' Joyce reported in a letter to Lieutenant-General Cromwell to be opened in his absence by either Sir Arthur Haselrig or Charles Fleetwood, Member of Parliament for Marlborough, who had commanded a regiment of horse at Naseby and who, on Henry Ireton's death, was to marry Cromwell's daughter Bridget. 'We are resolved to obey no orders but the General's . . . I humbly beseech you to consider what is done, and act accordingly with all the haste you can. We shall not rest night nor day till we hear from you.'

By six o'clock that morning the King was standing on the lawn in front of the house where Joyce's troopers were drawn up on parade. Joyce called upon them to swear that they all promised to observe the assurances which he had given to the King. They shouted their agreement, 'All! All!'

'And now, Mr Joyce,' the King said conversationally, 'what commission have you to secure my person?' Joyce made some evasive reply to which the King responded, 'Have you nothing in writing from Sir Thomas Fairfax?'

Joyce hesitated for a moment, evidently reluctant to admit under whose orders he was acting. Then, turning round in his saddle, he stretched out his arm to the troopers behind him.

'It is,' the King commented ironically, 'as fair a commission and as well written as any I have seen in a long while.'

Soon afterwards the prisoner and his captors rode off towards Hinchinbroke, then to Newmarket, Fairfax's headquarters, and finally to a house at Childerley near Cambridge. And here, for the first time, the King met Cromwell who had hurriedly left London early on the morning of 4 June on learning that the Presbyterians planned to arrest him as soon as he made his next appearance in the House of Commons.

On his ride to Childerley, Cromwell was accompanied by Fairfax and by Henry Ireton. When taken in to see the prisoner, Fairfax kissed the King's offered hand. Neither Ireton nor Cromwell felt able to offer him this courteous respect, but both 'behaved themselves with good manners towards him'.

He was allowed to have his chaplains back, to have visits from his friends, to have the Duke of Richmond to attend him, to have his former servants wait upon him. Profoundly reassured, he clearly felt a resurgence of hope as the country seemed to be tottering ever closer to chaos. Recent poor harvests had nearly doubled the price of wheat; beggars roamed the streets of almost every town; local officials were being attacked by disgruntled, unpaid soldiers; there were increasing numbers of reports from several towns of lord mayors, aldermen and senior officers of the New Model Army being manhandled in the streets, insulted in their homes and even dragged away to imprisonment. The King well knew how weary people had become of such violence after four years of bitter quarrelling, fighting, plundering, loss of rents and wages, disruption of trade and profits, desolation of homes and pleasures; how they longed for peace and the order of the past. Changes in the manners and structures of society, the breaking down of social conventions, the denial of old allegiances, were far from being universally acclaimed. The demands for the reformation of society provoked by the propaganda of the war, and by the experiences of those who had fought in it, were vociferous enough; but, as the King had good cause to believe, they were not shared by many of those whom he continued to regard as his people. Gerrard Winstanley, who in addition to a wholesale reform of the legal system and an immediate end to all prerogative taxes, demanded that all men should have an 'equal share in the earth', had ardent supporters; so too had John Lilburne; so had Colonel Thomas Rainsborough, the New Model Army officer, who preached the necessity of manhood suffrage; but they horrified those anxious to return to the calm of their former lives. Their more extreme pronouncements also dismayed Cromwell who was unable to conceal the sympathy he felt personally for the King, ill-advised, faithless and wrongheaded though he was.

When the King's children were brought from St James's Palace to see their father at the Greyhound Inn, Maidenhead, his joy at being with them again was as touching as it was unaffected; and the deeply emotional Cromwell, a loving father himself, was much moved by the scene. His own eldest son had died, probably of smallpox, when a seventeen-year-old schoolboy at Felsted, and he had never fully recovered from the grief of it. 'It went as a dagger to my heart,' he was to say when his own health was failing, 'indeed it did.' His second son, Oliver, handsome and brave, a 'civil young gentleman and the joy of his father', had left Cambridge to fight in the war as an officer in his father's own regiment, and had also died of smallpox. Their deaths made Cromwell all the more sympathetic towards those who had suffered in the same way. After the battle on Marston Moor he had written to his brother-in-law Valentine Walton, whose son had been killed, 'Sir, you know my trials this way; but the Lord supported me . . . God give you His comfort . . . [He] hath taken away your eldest son by a cannonshot. It brake his leg. We were necessitated to have it cut off, whereof he died . . . At his fall, his horse being killed with the bullet, and as I am informed three horses more, I am told he bid them open on the right and left that he might see the rogues run. Truly he was exceedingly beloved in the Army, of all that knew him. But few knew him, for he was a precious young man, fit for God. You have cause to bless the Lord. He is a glorious saint in heaven, wherein you ought exceedingly to rejoice. Let this drink up your sorrow . . . You may do all things by the strength of Christ.'

No doubt remembering his own family's losses as he watched the King, who was clearly so happy to be with his two younger sons and his little daughter Elizabeth, and seeing them all having dinner together at a big table in the tavern parlour, Cromwell's eyes, as he afterwards confessed, filled with tears.

On the day that the King had been taken as Joyce's prisoner from Holdenby House, Thomas Fairfax had addressed his assembled regiments on Kentford Heath outside Newmarket. Urging upon them the need for discipline in these critical times, he had induced the 'agitators' – the elected representatives of the militant soldiers – to sign a *Solemn Engagement*, a moderate document which, while declaring that the Army would not disband until its demands for pay and indemnity were met, contented itself with unexceptionable requests for an early settlement of religious and political disputes. At the same time the formation was announced of a General Council of the Army consisting of two representatives, one an officer, the other a man, from every regiment.

Five days later, with some sense of discipline restored, the Army moved south, so much alarming Parliament that a new Committee of Public Safety was hastily appointed and London's fortifications were manned with such armed citizens as could be brought to their defence. At St Albans the Army halted to deliver a severe rebuke to Parliament, a Declaration which called upon it to remember that the New Model Army was not a 'mere mercenary army hired to serve any arbitrary power of a state, but called forth . . . to the defence of the people's just rights and liberties'. 'And so we took up arms,' the Declaration continued, 'and here so continued them, and are resolved . . . to assert and vindicate the just power and rights of this Kingdom . . . against arbitrary power, violence and oppression, and against all particular parties or interests whatsoever.' All Members of Parliament hostile to the Army were to be immediately expelled from its Houses and the remainder, having satisfied the Army's demands, were then to vote for their own dissolution and to make arrangements for a new election.

Parliament tried to buy time by sending a month's pay to St Albans, but the General Council of the Army responded by naming eleven Members of Parliament who were to be expelled as opposed to the Army's interests. The Commons did not reply to this demand, but the eleven Members thought it as well to withdraw of their own accord, and by the end of the month Parliament had undertaken to 'make provision' for the Army's maintenance. Fairfax accordingly withdrew his men from St Albans to the Midlands.

No sooner had he left, however, than London was again in uproar. For months there had been growing resistance to the weekly assessments and to the excise tax which fell even on such essential commodities as meat and ale. Why, it was asked, should Londoners be so mercilessly squeezed for the pay of an army whose existence seemed increasingly unnecessary? At the same time hundreds of workers and apprentices were demanding an end to the present state of affairs and a return to those untroubled days when their livelihood had been relatively secure. Most of them had supported the Parliamentary cause at the beginning of the war, but now they were deeply divided, many of them vociferously urging a negotiated peace and a settlement with the King. On 21 July a large crowd of apprentices, watermen and disbanded soldiers poured into Skinners' Hall to sign a *Solemn Engagement* pressing for the King's restoration to power. This was immediately denounced by the House of Lords and a sparsely-attended House of Commons which, for the safety of the capital, proposed that the command of London's Trained Bands should be vested in a Parliamentary Committee. For almost a week the rioting continued. The House of Lords was invaded and forced to withdraw its objection to the *Solemn Engagement*. Then the House of Commons was attacked, the mob pouring through the lobby, bursting open the doors and shouting to the Members to do as the Lords had done. From two o'clock in the afternoon until six in the evening the Members resisted the mob's demands, while outside the chamber men pounced upon as the servants of Army officers were roughly handled and pulled about by their noses and ears.

At length the House of Commons submitted; but the demonstrators were still not satisfied. Holding the Speaker, William Lenthall, down in his chair, they refused to allow the Members to adjourn until they had voted on a resolution inviting the King to return to London.

Three days later it was learned that General Fairfax was marching back towards London; and soon afterwards that the Speaker, Lenthall, and the Speaker of the House of Lords, the Earl of Manchester, together with eight peers and nearly sixty Members of the Commons, had gone to seek Fairfax's protection at St Albans, protesting that London was in such tumult that they could no longer conduct the business of Parliament in safety.

Fairfax, therefore, decided that he must march into London with his men. On 6 August he did so, riding at the head of sixteen thousand troops who passed through the streets with laurel leaves in their hats as though parading after a victory. He entered Parliament, from which the eleven proscribed Members – who had returned during the recent rioting – had fled; and he was received with respect. He then rode on to the Tower where he installed himself as Constable in place of the Lord Mayor, and, sending for a copy of Magna Carta, the document so often cited by John Lilburne, he pronounced his own benediction upon it by declaring, 'This is what we have fought for, and with God's help must maintain.' The Lord Mayor, one of the Sheriffs and three Aldermen were arrested; the Trained Bands of the City were separated from those of the suburbs and placed under City authorities; and orders were given for the reduction of London's military strength by the demolition of its fortifications, to the pleasure and amusement of a Royalist ballad writer:

> Is this the end of all the toil
> And labour of the Town?
> And did our true works rise so high
> Thus low to tumble down?

Fairfax's show of force had its desired effect. Parliament, subdued, turned its attention to the relief of wounded and crippled soldiers, of widows and orphans, to indemnities for soldiers convicted of various offences in civilian courts and – limited as resources were at a time when people all over the country were refusing to meet their tax demands – to the Army's grievances over pay.

At the same time the Army commanders, advised by the lawyer Henry Ireton and by a group of Members of the House of Lords, helped to draw up a document known as the *Heads of the Proposals* in an attempt to come to terms with the King. These *Proposals*, accepted by the Council of the Army, were a generous attempt at compromise. There was little in them to which the King could have raised reasonable objections. 'A crown so near lost,' said his friend Sir John Berkeley, advising him to accept them, 'was never so near won.' But the King characteristically hesitated; and believing that delay would favour him, that the uneasy relations between the Army and Parliament would soon erupt into a violent quarrel which could be manipulated in his favour, and knowing that many influential citizens in London, in their fear and hatred of the revolutionary Army, would welcome his return to the throne, he chose to wait and to intrigue. He had good reason to believe that many Londoners were becoming increasingly exasperated by the pretensions of the New Model Army, the usurpation of the 'pulpits of divers godly ministers' by 'preaching soldiers and others who infect their flock with strange and dangerous errors'. He knew that leading citizens had warmly welcomed plans to disband most of the Army, and that he had many friends amongst the unskilled and semi-skilled workers of London, among porters and watermen, as well as shopkeepers, whose trades and businesses had been badly damaged by the with-drawal of the court to Oxford.

Fairfax was ill; so the protracted negotiations with the King were conducted by Cromwell and Ireton at Hampton Court where the King was treated as though his rights as a monarch were not in dispute. Cromwell's cousin, the tactful Colonel Edward Whalley, charged with the King's security, allowed it to seem that the soldiers of his guard were at the palace for his Majesty's protection rather than for his confinement. He was permitted to go out hunting and to play billiards and tennis in 'a new tennis suit of wrought coloured satin lined with taffeta', and to visit his children, now staying with the Earl of Northumberland at Syon House. He was allowed to attend his chapel and worship there as he pleased, to write to his wife, to talk to visitors in the privacy of his bedchamber, to entertain guests. Cromwell and Ireton brought their wives to dinner and Jack Ashburnham exercised upon them the easy, cheerful charm which so endeared him to the King.

The negotiations dragged on, Cromwell becoming exasperated as much by the prevarications of the King as by the objections of Parliament whom he threatened to 'purge and purge and purge, and never leave purging' until they were 'of such a temper', as to endorse the *Proposals*. He was equally exasperated by the Levellers, whose pamphlet, *The Case of the Army Truly Stated*, required the dissolution of the Long Parliament within a matter of months and a more representative one elected, and demanded to know when the Army was going to be true to the words of its former Declaration, when its leaders were going to pay more regard to the wishes of the soldiers, when they were going to oblige the King to come to a settlement more in keeping with the desires of the people than those of 'the unworthy Crown'.

In the past the Levellers had had little influence with the Army, which they saw as largely responsible for the country's sorry pass and which, in turn, was inclined to regard the political opinions of Lilburne and his friends as scarcely relevant to their immediate and pressing demands. Yet, once the Army had appeared to be incontestably in control of the country's destiny, the Levellers recognized the necessity of gaining influence over its policies. Fairfax, for his part, thought it advisable to call for a series of debates about their differences between the Army leaders, the 'agitators' elected by the regiments, and various representatives of the London Levellers. The debates were to be held in Putney, in the medieval parish church of St Mary's at the end of October and the beginning of November; and, since Fairfax himself had not yet fully recovered from his illness, they were to be supervised by Cromwell and Ireton.

At the first meeting the Levellers predictably changed the ground rules by bringing forward for discussion a far more radical document than their *Case of the Army Truly Stated*, a paper entitled the *Agreement of the People* which proposed a republican constitution with a single chamber exercising legislative and executive power. Since this would inevitably involve another civil war, both Cromwell and Ireton firmly opposed it, pointing out that the proposition was far more extreme than any previously considered by the Army. There was worse to come. The next day Colonel Thomas Rainsborough once more made an impassioned plea for manhood suffrage in direct opposition to the belief expressed by Cromwell and Ireton that voters should be limited to owners of property. 'I think that the poorest he that is in England hath a life to live, as the greatest he,' Rainsborough declared, the passion of his conviction heightened rather than diminished by the clumsiness of his oratorical style, 'and therefore truly, Sir, I think it's clear that every man that is to live under a government ought first by his own consent to put himself under that government; and I do think that the poorest man in England is not at all bound in a strict sense to that government that he hath not had a voice to put himself under.'

Cromwell, addressing the delegates in those rambling and abstruse declamations which often made his arguments so difficult to follow, was hard put to it to bring the noisy discussions to an end that Friday;

and on the Monday next tempers were lost again when the role of the King came under discussion. All that week the arguments raged until on the tenth day of what became known as the Putney Debates, Fairfax prevailed upon the contestants to depart on the understanding that the various regiments of the Army, at present dispersed, would meet at a general rendezvous towards the end of November.

To forestall the expected trouble from the Levellers at this rendezvous, Fairfax later arranged for three separate meetings on three different dates and issued a firmly worded denunciation of the Levellers' doctrines entitled *Remonstrance concerning the late Discontents and Distractions in the Army*. In this publication Fairfax threatened to resign unless the 'agitators' obeyed his orders given through the Council of the Army. If, on the contrary, the soldiers undertook to follow and trust him, he in turn would undertake to do all he could to get them their arrears of pay, to have the Long Parliament dissolved, and to work for the assembly of a new Parliament 'as near as may be' representative of the people who were to elect it.

Within the next few days Fairfax showed how ruthless he was prepared to be with soldiers who were still intent upon resisting his authority. On the day appointed for the first rendezvous, on Corkbush Field near Ware, two regiments whose men had expelled their officers marched onto parade with green ribbons and Leveller mottoes in their hats. One of these regiments, described as 'the most mutinous in the whole army', had formerly been commanded by Robert Lilburne, John Lilburne's elder brother, the other by the excitable colonel from Staffordshire Thomas Harrison, who, at the battle of Langport, 'with a loud voice had broken out into praises of God with fluent expressions as if in a rapture'. The provocation of both regiments was swiftly dealt with: ribbons and mottoes were snatched from the hats of the rebellious soldiers who were forced at gunpoint to tear up the copies of the Levellers' *Agreement of the People* which they had brought with them. Two officers who sympathized with the protesters were arrested and marched away under guard; ringleaders were dragged from the ranks and one of them was shot on the spot. When the other regiments were marched off, they did so to shouts of 'The King and Sir Thomas!' At the other two subsequent rendezvous there were no such disturbances: the soldiers obediently swore to obey the commands of General Fairfax.

17

THE SECOND
CIVIL WAR

'I should have thought myself a happy person
if I could live . . . to see the King, my master,
on his throne again.'

Sir George Lisle

Although the soldiers had linked the name of the King with that of Fairfax as they marched off Corkbush Field, the negotiations between the two parties had been brought to a sudden end. Four days before that rendezvous, on the afternoon of Thursday 11 November 1647, the King had disappeared from Hampton Court. He had told his secretary that he had a very long letter to write before evensong at six o'clock, and had accordingly retired to his room. He had also said that he was not feeling very well, so that when he did not appear at evensong Colonel Whalley was not at first too concerned. As the evening wore on, however, and the King did not come down to supper, Whalley became increasingly worried. Some days before, it seems, he had received a letter from his cousin Cromwell warning him that there were 'rumours abroad of some intended attempt on his Majesty's person'. He had shown this letter to the King who had also evidently received a warning to the effect that certain Levellers had 'resolved for the good of the Kingdom' to take his life away. The King was known to be a man of courage not afraid of death, but, like his father and his father's predecessor Queen Elizabeth, he did fear the sudden indignity of assassination by an unseen and perhaps unsuspected hand. He might well, it was suspected, have fled from a place where he no longer felt safe.

By eight o'clock Colonel Whalley, 'extreme restless in his thoughts', decided to investigate. He looked through the keyhole of the King's room and seeing no sign of him tried the door. It was locked on the inside. He forced an entrance by another door and found the room empty. He immediately sent out patrols, but his prisoner had long since crept down a back stairway and along an underground passage to the river where Ashburnham and Berkeley were waiting with horses on which they and the King had galloped away to the Hampshire coast. They crossed the Solent to the Isle of Wight and made their way to Carisbrooke Castle where they were welcomed by the island's Governor, Colonel Robert Hammond, a known enemy of the Levellers in the Army, a nephew of Henry Hammond, one of the King's Anglican chaplains, and a distant relative of the Royalist Marquess of Winchester. While in Hammond's care, Charles hoped that he would be able to continue his clandestine negotiations with the Scots – with whose help he still believed he could regain his throne – and from Carisbrooke he could always if necessary escape to the Continent.

With some relief Cromwell and Ireton now broke off their negotiations with a man whom they had always found it as difficult to trust as to dislike. Parliament continued their own negotiations for a time; but, when the King abruptly rejected their proposals, they too decided to stop talking to him, having good reason to believe that he was merely using the prolonged discussions to come to terms with Scottish envoys at their expense. Indeed, while still in correspondence with Parliament, the King at Carisbrooke had signed a secret treaty, an *Engagement*, with the Scots whereby he agreed to establish Presbyterianism in England for at least three years, to suppress 'the opinions and practices of Independents and all such scandalous doctrines', and to appoint to the Privy Council in London a 'considerable and competent number of Scotsmen'. If Parliament declined to disband the Army and refused to allow the King to return to London to negotiate a peace treaty in cooperation with Scottish commissioners, a Scottish army was to restore him to his erstwhile powers by force. The *Engagement* was enclosed in lead and buried in the garden at Carisbrooke Castle.

As it happened, though, the raising of an adequate army north of the border proved a far more difficult undertaking than the Scottish Commissioners at Carisbrooke had expected. One of the principal

Commissioners was James Hamilton, second Earl of Cambridge in the English peerage and first Duke of Hamilton in the Scottish. Married at thirteen to a niece of the Duke of Buckingham, whom he succeeded as Master of the Horse at the English court, he had been educated at Exeter College, Oxford and was considered by the Scots, if not more English than Scottish, a firm friend of the English and their ways. This could scarcely be said of his colleague John Maitland, second Earl of Lauderdale, a Scotsman through and through; but he, too, was believed in Scotland, in particular by the radical Kirk party, to be too friendly towards the King and to have his interests at heart rather than the establishment of Presbyterianism in England in accordance with the terms of the Solemn League and Covenant. Hamilton and Lauderdale were also distrusted by the tough and shrewd, cross-eyed and long-nosed Archibald Campbell, Marquess of Argyll, who warmly supported the Kirk and, through his great influence as chieftain of Clan Campbell and owner of hundreds of thousands of acres in western Scotland, successfully opposed in Argyll the enlistment and collection of taxes for the army of forty thousand men which the so-called 'Engagers' were endeavouring to raise on behalf of the King and his friends the Duke of Hamilton and Lord Lauderdale.

Having signed the *Engagement*, the King prepared to leave Carisbrooke Castle; but he now found it impossible to do so, for his deceitful intrigues had resolved all doubts in Colonel Hammond's mind as to the manner of his treatment. From now on, for the next nine months, he was kept as close a prisoner on the Isle of Wight as ever he had been at Holdenby House. His personal attendants and chaplains were dismissed and replaced by four 'Conservators' whose instructions were never to leave his side 'in their courses two at a time, to be always in his presence, except when he retires into his bedchamber, and then they are to repair, the one to one door, and the other to the other, and there to continue till the King comes forth again'.

While the King was closely constrained on the Isle of Wight, his friends on the mainland were once more active on his behalf. The twenty-third anniversary of his accession to the throne, 27 March 1648, was celebrated by riots in several towns throughout the country. In London bonfires were lit in the streets and the crowds singing and dancing around them forced passers-by and the occupants of coaches to stop and drink the health of the King. In other towns there were riots provoked not only by Royalists but also by Parliamentarians angered by what they took to be the machinations of the Army. In Wales, from Pembroke to Chepstow, garrisons refused orders to disband and barricaded themselves within the walls of their fortresses. There were violent scenes in Norwich and in Bury St Edmunds where a riot erupted at the hoisting of a maypole and where, next day, crowds marched through the streets shouting 'For God and King Charles!' and chased known supporters of Parliament out of the town.

In London the riots of 27 and 28 March were followed by further disturbances in the City the following month when mobs paraded through the streets shouting 'Now for King Charles!' until Cromwell's troopers were ordered to disperse the troublemakers, two of whom were killed. Undeterred, the rioters came out the next day when the Lord Mayor was forced to flee to the Tower. Fairfax was still Constable here but, impatient with the petty wrangling over religion in the City and depressed by its cantankerous political squabbles, he was glad to get away with the Army into the country, leaving London in the keeping of the Trained Bands under the veteran Sir Philip Skippon.

No sooner had the Army left London than there were further disturbances. A petition appealing for the disbandment of the Army and bearing the signatures of numerous people from the county of Surrey was borne to Parliament through streets crowded with demonstrators, most shouting in support of the petitioners, some hooting in derision. A similar petition from the people of Essex had been presented three weeks before. On that occasion the demonstration had passed off without too much trouble; but when the men from Surrey appeared there was savage fighting and over a hundred people were seriously injured and ten were killed.

By this time violence was also threatened again in Norfolk where apprentices in Norwich, protesting against the repressive measures of the Puritan city fathers, demanded that they be allowed to celebrate their traditional festivals as of old. Crowds of men wielding sticks and pitchforks attacked the houses of leading Puritan aldermen, smashed the Sheriff's windows, broke down his doors, 'drank his beer and devoured his brawn and his pies'. They broke into several other houses of unpopular citizens and prominent Parliamentarians, carrying off what they fancied and handing out arms to their friends in the streets outside.

Troops were sent for; but at reports of their approach the rioters made for the headquarters of the County Committee where large stores of ammunition and weapons were known to be stored, swords and pikes and armour as well as muskets and pistols. Pushing aside the guard, the crowd stormed into the building and were emerging armed from the Committee House when the Parliamentary troopers arrived from East Dereham. Outnumbered by the rioters, they were endeavouring to disperse them and fighting running battles in the streets, while those inside the Committee House were still searching for powder, one man scooping it up in his hat, another, so it was afterwards reported, 'very busy with a lantern in his hand'. Suddenly there was a deafening explosion and the whole building disintegrated, as powder casks flew through the shattered walls and parts of the roof shot away towards the church of St Peter Mancroft whose windows, together with those of other churches, were blown apart. Several people lay dead among the fallen debris and many more were wounded.

Violence had also by now erupted in Kent, where on Christmas Day the year before there had been a riot at Canterbury in protest against a Puritan attempt to abolish the celebrations usually held in honour of the Nativity. Windows were smashed; shots were fired; city officials and 'busy prating' Puritans were chased about the streets, locked up or laid in irons; the city magazine was seized, its gate shut and barred against approaching trained bands; the city gaol was broken open; shouts of 'For God, King Charles and Kent!' filled the air. People 'set up holly-bushes at their doors like your country alehouses, and gave entertainment with Nothing to Pay and Welcome Gentlemen'. The Mayor, 'a man of rough and unkind nature', 'made strict proclamation that every man depart to his own house', at which the multitude, 'hollowing thereat', jeered at the aldermen and constables. 'Soon after issued forth the commanders of this rabble, with an addition of soldiers into the High Street, and brought with them two footballs.' This 'drew together on a sudden great numbers of rude persons not only of the city but of country-fellows, strangers from the parts adjacent, whereby they speedily grew into a tumult'.

When the rioters were brought to trial and were acquitted there were celebrations all over the county; and when Sir Anthony Weldon, the 'malicious-minded author' who was one of the leaders of the Parliamentary committee in Kent, tried to prevent signatures being subscribed to a petition he described as seditious, there were renewed riots against the authorities not only in Canterbury but in nearly all the principal towns of the county from Rochester to Sandwich. Over ten thousand protesters assembled on Burham Heath near Maidstone and put themselves under the command of Lord Goring's elderly father, the Earl of Norwich, who had just returned from France to see how the troubles in England could be turned to his advantage. As Master of the Queen's Horse, he had formerly been one of the jolliest men at court, renowned for his jokes and fooleries and good nature but hardly such a one to command an army of rebels, 'fitter', as Clarendon observed, 'to have drawn such a body together by his frolic and pleasant humour, which reconciled people of all constitutions wonderfully to him, than to form and conduct them towards any enterprise'. All the same, news of the advance of so large a body of men upon Blackheath naturally caused alarm in London, an alarm aggravated by reports of a mutiny aboard several ships in the Downs whose crews demanded that their captains take them against the King's enemies.

Trouble had been threatening in the fleet ever since April 1645 when the Earl of Warwick had had to resign under the terms of the Self-Denying Ordinance. A highly talented sailor, and a reminder of those days when Parliament's cause was in the hands of such worthy men as Hampden and Pym, he was well liked by sailors who were mostly still unaffected by the radical notions which had spread so fast throughout the Army. The officer who succeeded him, Vice-Admiral William Batten, was certainly no radical. A hardbitten old seafarer of long experience, he had been a Surveyor of the Navy before the war and after it was to return to that office, much to the chagrin of Pepys, who recorded at length in his diary his numerous acts of knavery, his incompetence and – a practice Pepys himself was scarcely in a position to condemn – the relentless feathering of his nest. Batten, however, did not last long in command; his unconcealed political sympathies soon got him into trouble with Parliament which summoned him to Westminster to explain himself. He promptly resigned and was replaced by that arch-Radical, Colonel

Thomas Rainsborough, who, the son of a mariner, had been a sea captain himself before joining the Army. But the dour Rainsborough was no more to the taste of the fleet than Batten was to Parliament. On 27 May the squadron lying in the Downs unequivocally declared for the King and declined to allow Rainsborough aboard. He was rowed ashore in an open boat while the ships of which he was normally in command secured various ports along the Kentish coast and laid siege to Dover. Parliament felt constrained to cancel Rainsborough's appointment and to call back the Earl of Warwick to the command of such ships as remained at their disposal.

Parliament's survival now seemed as uncertain on land as it did at sea. The redoubtable Royalist Sir Marmaduke Langdale had captured Berwick; another staunch Royalist, Sir Philip Musgrave, who represented Westmorland in the Long Parliament, had taken Carlisle; Cromwell, ordered to South Wales with about five thousand men, had become involved in a prolonged siege of Pembroke, battering at the immensely thick medieval walls of the castle with guns from a man-of-war, his own siege artillery having slipped its ropes and sunk when being towed across the Severn. Fairfax, facing the rebels in Kent with scarcely more than six thousand men, asked urgently for reinforcements; but the Derby House Committee – as the Committee for Both Kingdoms had become since the Scottish members had left it – felt unable to help him so long as important strongholds in the West Country were threatened by Royalists.

Depleted as his regiments were, however, Fairfax was expected to have little trouble with the old prankster, the Earl of Norwich. Nor did he. Moving from Blackheath to Gravesend, detaching part of his force to relieve Dover, marching briskly towards Rochester, until hearing how strongly the castle there was held, he then attacked Lord Norwich's men at Maidstone on 2 June. Here the Royalists were well placed in the shops and houses of the narrow streets with cannon ready to fire from the crossroads in the middle of the town; and, just before Fairfax's attack, messengers sent galloping off to Rochester and the village of Aylesford returned with reinforcements which brought up the Royalists' strength in Maidstone to about two thousand men. The subsequent fighting was as violent as any Fairfax had experienced. As his troops broke into the town and the townspeople shouted 'For God, King Charles and Kent!' a violent storm broke out, soaking the struggling soldiers as they lashed out at each other in the dense smoke from the guns. Before nightfall the town was in Parliament's hands; and the Royalist reserves still on Burham Heath were so alarmed that they ran away in all directions through the woods and fields and orchards, some rowing out from Channel ports to the ships of the mutinous fleet.

Fairfax now moved on to Canterbury – where the defenders, warned by what had happened in Maidstone, soon surrendered under easy terms – then back towards London, leaving detachments to take those Channel ports remaining in Royalist hands, to deal with any landing parties which might come ashore from the warships standing off the coast, and to guard the numerous prisoners who were locked up in local churches since Leeds Castle and Westenhanger House, Lord Strangford's moated home, were already packed with Kentish rebels.

As Fairfax approached London with Colonel Whalley's regiment riding ahead of him, most of Lord Norwich's remaining soldiers fled east and west. Norwich himself, with a few of his more resolute companions, tried to get into London; but, finding Sir Philip Skippon had closed the gates against him, he rode to Colchester, joining forces on the way with other Royalists, among them Sir Charles Lucas, Lord Capel, Sir George Lisle and Bernard Gascoigne, who were hoping that there would be an uprising in East Anglia when supplies and men reached Colchester from the Royalist fleet by way of the River Colne.

Pursued closely by Fairfax and Whalley, whose horsemen clattered after them through village after village, the Royalists reached the outskirts of Colchester on the afternoon of 13 June just as their enemies caught up with the rearguard, falling on them 'like madmen, killing and slaying them in a terrible manner, even in the cannon mouths'. It was an appallingly ferocious encounter, both sides losing hundreds of men in the slaughter until the Royalists managed to get into the town and the gates were slammed shut behind them.

Secure for the moment inside the walls of Colchester, Lord Norwich's Royalists could deny Fairfax who, with too few men left to conduct a proper siege, was told by the Derby House Committee that he could not expect reinforcements with uprisings threatening them elsewhere all over the south and west and a Scottish army likely to cross the border at any moment. Already there was serious trouble in Surrey where the Earl of Holland – who had returned to England with Lord Norwich and, through the Queen's influence, been ludicrously appointed to high command – had called for men to fight for the King at Kingston upon Thames. Holland was joined here by the twenty-year-old second Duke of Buckingham, son of the King's dear friend, by the Duke's brother, Lord Francis Villiers, and by Jan Dalbier, the Dutch engineer who had previously served in the Parliamentary army but felt an obligation to change sides because of his friendship with the Duke's father. For a time the Earl of Holland considered marching upon London, but since no more than four or five hundred men rallied to his call, he decided upon a more modest objective, the capture of Reigate Castle. Even this he was not able to achieve, since the Derby House Committee had sent an urgent summons to Sir Michael Livesey, an arrogant, quarrelsome, pusillanimous though influential baronet who had once commanded the Kentish horse. Livesey, supported by a regiment brought up from Dover, sent the Earl of Holland hurtling back from Kingston through Harrow and St Albans to St Neots, followed by the Duke of Buckingham whose brother, Lord Francis Villiers, was killed in a skirmish at Surbiton. At St Neots, Holland was captured by Colonel Adrian Scrope, 'a comely gentleman', and led away a prisoner to Warwick Castle and thence to London where he was beheaded, despite the protests of both his brother, the Earl of Warwick, and of Sir Thomas Fairfax. Dalbier was killed by Scrope's men; the Duke of Buckingham contrived to escape, made his way to the coast, and took ship for Holland.

St Neots was fortunate in having been taken so quickly. Colchester was now forced to face a long and painful siege conducted by Sir Thomas Fairfax with exceptional thoroughness. Extensive earthworks were built around the town and manned by over five thousand of the Essex and Suffolk Trained Bands; no less than ten forts were constructed, as well as a wide ditch and high rampart on the London side of the town; supplies were prevented from reaching the town from the sea by men of war at the river's mouth. Inside Colchester, as the heavy summer rain poured down, food became so scarce that permission was sought for women and children to leave it. Fairfax refused to consider the request; and a party of women who managed to slip away were stopped by the besiegers, stripped naked and sent back again. The water supply was cut; the suburbs were burned; but week after week the garrison held out, though reduced to eating horses and dogs. The possibility of making a sally was discussed but the idea had to be dismissed since the horses which had been left uneaten 'were too few for that enterprise'. And then in the last week of August calamitous news came from the north and the Earl of Norwich surrendered. He and Lord Capel were sent as prisoners to London.

But both Sir Charles Lucas, whose father was one of Colchester's leading citizens, and Sir George Lisle, who had served with distinction at Cheriton, Newbury and Naseby, were condemned to death by a council of war which, assembled as hastily as it was to pass judgement, described them as 'mere soldiers of fortune'. Both Lisle and Lucas, a man so arrogant and cantankerous that he had been considered in Colchester 'more intolerable than the siege', died bravely. 'I should have thought myself a happy person,' said Lisle, who was shot in the castle yard at Colchester the day after the surrender, 'if I could live to have a longer time of repentance and to see the King, my master, on his throne again.' Lucas was equally defiant. Protesting against Parliament's declaration that all who fought against it were guilty of high treason, and against Ireton's use of this declaration to justify the council of war's sentences of death, he said, 'I am no traitor but a true subject to my King and the laws of the Kingdom . . . I have fought with a commission from those that were my sovereigns, and from that commission I justify my action.'

Sir Bernard Gascoigne was also condemned to be shot as a traitor; but he was reprieved at the last moment when it was discovered that he was a Florentine military adventurer, Bernardo Guasconi who had been an *uomo d'arme* in the Grand Duke of Florence's service before coming over to fight in the English Civil War. The Council's verdict was overthrown on the grounds that should this Italian be shot, those who had condemned him to death, 'their family and friends, might pay dear for many generations'.

At the beginning of the previous month, July 1648, the Duke of Hamilton had crossed the border into England with about nine thousand men in the worst summer weather that any of them had ever known. The rain poured down in torrents, flooding rivers, carrying away bridges, swirling over fords and stepping-stones, turning roads into bogs. The cavalry and infantry, soaked to the skin, struggled through the mud, the ill-trained pikemen exhausted by their unaccustomed loads, the musketeers unable to keep their matches alight, the wagoners tugging at the slipping wheels of their carts. Behind them came hundreds of women, so many women, indeed, that the people of the northern counties through which the Scottish army so slowly stumbled told each other that these unwelcome visitors had come to settle in England. Unwelcome they most undoubtedly were, even amongst the most dedicated Royalists in whose cause they had come to fight. They pushed their way into the poor dwellings of the English villagers, helping themselves to what food they could find in a bleak countryside, 'this barren and undone country', which had been stricken by a meagre harvest the year before and was faced by a worse in this. They took away everything of value that they were able to carry; they rounded up sheep and cattle and drove them off; they dragged away children and forced their families to buy them back.

The sodden army lumbered on, joined by three thousand-odd men, mostly infantry, whom Sir Marmaduke Langdale had managed to raise after taking Berwick. They came south through Penrith to Appleby, forcing General John Lambert's horsemen back by sheer weight of numbers, halting for a time at Kirkby Thore so that the regiments still being raised in Scotland when they left could catch up with them. Reinforced by another five thousand or so men but still short of provisions and ammunition and with very few guns, the Duke of Hamilton moved on south again at the end of July to Kendal, the Parliamentary army withdrawing on the other side of the Pennines, through Richmond and Ripon to Knaresborough.

At Kendal, Hamilton was joined by Sir George Monro, a veteran of King Gustavus II Adolphus's army and commander of the Scottish troops in Ireland. He had been ordered to bring some three thousand of these troops over from Ulster across the Irish Sea; and, although pursued by two of the English Parliament's men of war, he had succeeded in ferrying them over in small boats sailing by night. When he arrived at Kendal, however, Monro refused to take orders from the Duke of Hamilton's second-in-command, James Livingstone, Earl of Callander, a crotchety, autocratic officer who, having been long in the Dutch service, did not bother to disguise his disdain of those who had not been trained in that exacting school. Having as little regard for Monro as Monro had for him, Callander sent him off to Kirby Lonsdale, with two infantry regiments under Sir Philip

Musgrave and Sir Thomas Tyldesley, to wait for the expedition's artillery to come down from Scotland. At the same time Hamilton and the rest of the army moved south to Hornby where they still were at the end of the second week in August.

By now Cromwell, having at last brought about the surrender of Pembroke Castle, was on his way north to block the further progress of the Scottish army. He sent some of his cavalry regiments ahead and took the rest, together with his infantry, to join forces with General Lambert, going by way of Northampton and Leicester to pick up new shoes and stockings which had been ordered for his men by the Derby House Committee, and collecting also several hundred additional men from the trained bands of the Midland counties. Arriving in Doncaster on 8 August, and halting there briefly for some wagonloads of ammunition expected from Hull, he went on to Pontefract where he took away with him the more experienced of the soldiers who were besieging the Royalist garrison there, leaving the men of the Midland trained bands in their place. South of Knaresborough on 12 August his vanguard came upon John Lambert's men. The combined forces of the two generals were now, as one of their young officers said, 'a fine smart army, fit for action'. There were, however, still fewer than nine thousand of them, whereas Hamilton's and Langdale's forces, scattered though they were, numbered over seventeen thousand, with 4,500 more men in reserve under Sir George Monro, Musgrave and Tyldesley. Cromwell would have to be most wary in his approach.

He was so. Advancing cautiously from Otley to Skipton and from Skipton to Gisburn, one of his patrols came upon a party of Hamilton's horse near Clitheroe before the Duke was aware of his approach.

At a council of war in the Scottish camp at Hornby, there had been an argument as to whether the advance south should be continued through Lancashire or by the more direct route to London across the Pennines into Yorkshire. Both General John Middleton, who was in command of the cavalry, and Sir James Turner, the Scottish Adjutant-General, a 'soldier to the backbone', though 'mad when he was drunk and that was very often', seem to have argued for the army's crossing the Pennines and moving south through Yorkshire, since the country there offered better opportunities for the use of the cavalry. The infantry commander, William Baillie, however, suggested that it would be better to stay in Lancashire where the army might not only attract Royalist recruits from Wales but also have an opportunity of capturing the important town of Manchester.

So Hamilton, persuaded by Baillie's arguments, gave orders for the march continuing south through Lancashire to Preston, sending most of his cavalry far ahead towards Wigan in deference to Middleton's suggestion that it would be much easier for the men to find decent quarters if they were not all bunched up together. Thus it was that when Cromwell's troops, having spent the night in the grounds of Stonyhurst Hall, the home of a Mr Sherbourne, a 'Papist', came upon their enemy near Longbridge on the morning of 17 August, Hamilton's forces were perilously extended. Hamilton himself was with his main body on Preston Moor, just over a mile north of Preston; most of his cavalry were sixteen miles to the south at Wigan; Sir George Monro, with Musgrave and Tyldesley's regiments, were even further away to the north. Langdale's troops were over ten miles to the east, drawn up on Ribbleton Moor across the road from Longbridge to Preston.

It was here that Cromwell's men struck. 'The General comes to us, and commands us to march,' one of his officers recorded. 'We not having half our men come up, desired a little Patience. He gives out the word, "March!" And so we drew over Ribbleton Moor and came to a ditch, and the enemy let fly at us, a company of Langdale's men . . . The Major orders me to march to the next hedge, and I bid him order the men to follow me . . . and we came up to the hedge end, and the enemy, many of them, threw down their arms, and run to their party where was their stand of pikes and a great body of colours.'

Cromwell's vanguard kept Langdale's men engaged for long enough on Ribbleton Moor for a proper attack to be mounted. As more and more of his men came up, he hastily formed them into a rough order of battle, cavalry regiments on either flank, the infantry in the centre 'coming to push of pike and to close firing', in Cromwell's words, slowly forcing Langdale's now outnumbered men to give ground, driving them from hedge to hedge. 'There was nothing but fire and smoke,' Captain Hodgson wrote. 'The bullets flew freely . . . I met with [an officer of Colonel Ashton's regiment] and about three hundred men, and I ordered him to march. But he said he

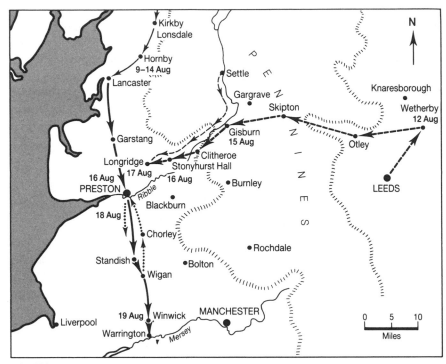

N

P E N I N E S

Kirkby
Lonsdale

Hornby
9–14 Aug

Lancaster

Settle

Gargrave

Knaresborough

Skipton

Wetherby
12 Aug

Garstang

Gisburn
15 Aug

Otley

Longridge

Clitheroe
Stonyhurst Hall

LEEDS

16 Aug
17 Aug
16 Aug

PRESTON

Burnley

Ribble

Blackburn

18 Aug

Chorley

Rochdale

Standish

Bolton

Wigan

Liverpool

19 Aug

Winwick

MANCHESTER

Warrington

Mersey

0   5   10

Miles

ROUTES

———▶ Duke of Hamilton   ·······▶ John Middleton

------▶ Oliver Cromwell   -----▶ Sir Marmaduke Langdale

The Preston Campaign

would not till [the rest of] his men were come up. A sergeant belonging to them asked me where they should march? I showed him . . . and he, like a true-bred Englishman marched, and I caused the soldiers to follow him . . . Presently they fell upon the enemy.'

Langdale's men held their ground bravely as long as they could, at times counter-attacking and retaking lost ground before being driven back again across the upturned, muddy earth, some of them, wounded or stumbling, being trampled underfoot by the enemy horses.

Still on Preston Moor, the Duke of Hamilton was persuaded to withdraw into Preston and across the River Ribble in the hope that Middleton's cavalry might be brought back from Wigan in time to present a united front to Cromwell's attack. So General Baillie took the infantry over the river to the rising ground by Walton Hall, while Hamilton himself, having sent off the cavalry rearguard north along the Lancaster road to join Sir George Monro, made for a ford to the east of Preston with Langdale and a few other officers and men. They found the ford; but it was deep under water and the enemy was now close upon their heels. Hamilton and the small party with him turned at bay, charged their pursuers and beat them back from the river bank. Twice more the enemy charged at them; twice Hamilton charged back, and after the third counter-charge Cromwell's troopers were driven away far enough for the Duke and his companions to plunge into the river, swim to the far bank and join Baillie by Walton Hall.

North of the Hall, the two Scottish brigades which Baillie had left to defend the bridge were now under fierce attack. Reinforcements were sent from the Hall to stiffen the resistance; but these came under such heavy musket fire from the hedges and houses in front of them as they approached the river that they were forced back. And after two hours' fighting the Scottish brigades whom they had tried to help were driven back too.

Cromwell's men, both horse and foot, came after them in the gathering darkness, pressing on through the grounds of Walton Hall in the still-falling rain, capturing several wagons from one of which, overturned in the mud, slid the Duke of Hamilton's plate. With his army in disarray, the Duke called another council of war. Night had now fallen, and it seemed to most of his officers that their only hope lay in endeavouring to creep away unobserved to the south, dark as it was and clogged with mud as were the sunken lanes that led to Wigan. Somewhere along those lanes Middleton's cavalry would be coming up to meet them; and at least, when they met, the army would be more or less of a piece again. The orders were given: the strictest silence was to be observed; all the powder, apart from what the soldiers could carry with them in their bags, was to be blown up by a long fuse after the last soldier had stolen away.

In the darkness and rain, Cromwell's scouts failed to notice the Scots' withdrawal. Cromwell himself had been principally concerned that they did not escape north to join forces with the cavalry which had fled from Preston Moor and with Sir George Monro's regiments, last reported at Kirkby Lonsdale. Despatching several troops of horse to prevent this possible movement, Cromwell allowed the rest of the army to settle down for what remained of the night by the river banks where they had fought or in the relative comfort of the houses of Preston.

As soon as he learned that the enemy were not preparing to move north but had already gone south, Cromwell sent three regiments of cavalry after them under one of his most reliable officers, Colonel Thornhaugh. But instead of coming upon the Scottish rearguard withdrawing, Thornhaugh's men rode into General Middleton's cavalry advancing towards them; for Middleton had taken a different road from that along which Hamilton's men were marching: they had accordingly missed each other in the dark; and now, instead of meeting each other as planned, were marching away from each other on parallel roads. As soon as he realized what had happened, Middleton turned away sharply and took his men splashing back through the mud to find the Scottish infantry on the other road behind him. Colonel Thornhaugh pursued them hard; he himself was killed in one of the bitter skirmishes when Middleton's troopers turned round to fight; and, by the time Cromwell had brought five thousand men together to join in the pursuit, Scottish and English dead lay scattered on every side.

As dawn approached the retreating army was drawn up on rising ground at Standish, just north of Wigan, as if prepared to make a stand. Cromwell approached them cautiously. Although the Scots had lost far more men outside Preston than he had, and although he had taken four thousand prisoners, Hamilton's army still out-numbered his own. Besides, he had had to leave a garrison in Preston to guard against a possible attack from Sir George Monro, while some of his best cavalry troops had not returned from their foray from Preston Moor.

Cromwell's men, however, were mostly experienced soldiers, the Scottish recruits were not. Hamilton was little respected as a general; Cromwell was highly regarded. What were they fighting for anyway? one Scottish soldier was heard to ask. He had no stomach for it. Nor, it seemed, did most of his comrades as they stood, wet, hungry and dispirited on that hill outside Wigan. Their powder was as wet as their clothes, and they could get no more. The supplies left behind to be blown up at Preston had now fallen into Cromwell's hands, since the long fuse had been extinguished by the rain.

The bedraggled Scottish army was not put to the test of holding their ground. Orders were given for them to continue their withdrawal to Wigan and then to retreat by night to Warrington where the River Mersey would provide a more secure defensive line and where help might reach them from the Royalists in north Wales. On their retreat they continued to plunder the houses on the line of march as they had done ever since they had arrived in England. So hungry were they that they stopped to pillage even though the enemy were close upon their heels, breaking down doors, clambering in through windows with the musket balls whistling about their ears, seeming not to care whether or not they were killed, as many of them were.

At Winwick, just north of Warrington, they turned at bay again. As though conscious that they had nothing now to lose but their miserable lives, they fought with desperation. Cromwell's men, as he himself described them the day before, were 'very dirty and weary, having marched twelve miles over such ground' as he had never ridden over in all his life before. They closed upon the Scots, however, and for over three hours the struggle raged, pike against pike, first one side giving ground, then the other stumbling back, until, after a determined attack in their flank, the Scots were driven back towards Winwick Church. On a green outside the church the fierce hand-to-hand fighting continued until, with scores of their fellow-countrymen dead and wounded around them, hundreds of the surviving Scotsmen fled to surrender in the church; the rest ran away to Warrington where many were killed by the local people, many others taken prisoner and happy to be so, making no attempt to run away for there was nowhere safe to go. 'Two men will keep a thousand from running away,' said Cromwell, who was prevailed upon to give passes to his own men so that they should not be mistaken for Scotsmen and mishandled accordingly.

It was the end of the fighting and the end of the war. The Scottish troops – scarcely a thousand of them still in arms and all covered in mud and with empty stomachs – were completely broken. The surviving cavalry rode away with the Duke of Hamilton and the Earl of Callander. General Baillie, left to come to what terms he could with Cromwell, asked his officers to shoot him to spare him the humiliation of surrender; but eventually he met his adversary on the bridge at Warrington and agreed that his men would hand over all such arms as they still carried. 'Surely,' Cromwell wrote the next day, expressing a familiar sentiment, 'this is nothing but the hand of God.' His cavalry, riders and horses alike, were too exhausted to pursue the Duke of Hamilton. 'If I had five hundred fresh horses and five hundred nimble foot,' he said, 'I could destroy them all. But we are so weary, we shall scarce be able to do more than walk after them.' As it was, he could feel satisfied that he had finished 'the business of Scotland'.

The vanquished went their separate ways. General Baillie disappeared into obscurity; the Earl of Callander contrived to escape to Holland; Langdale was captured in an alehouse near Nottingham and taken to Nottingham Castle whence he, too, managed to escape to the Continent. Sir George Monro retreated across the border into Scotland; General John Middleton was taken prisoner and kept in gaol at Newcastle before being allowed to live at Berwick where he seems to have broken his parole and escaped to Scotland. Back in England in 1651, he was again taken prisoner and sent to the Tower of London from which he escaped in his wife's clothes and made his way to Paris. The Duke of Hamilton was taken prisoner by John Lambert at Stafford. He tried to escape but failed and was tried and executed. He was allowed to see the King before he died.

18

THE DEATH OF
THE KING

'I am not suffered for to speak. Expect what
justice other people will have.'

Charles I

At the time of the fighting in Lancashire, the King was still on the
Isle of Wight. In the hope that terms might be agreed with him before
the Army returned from the north, Parliament, in contravention of
their Vote of No Addresses, had sent representatives to Newport to
hold discussions with him at an inn in the town. The negotiations
were utterly fruitless. The Parliamentary delegates, fearing an imminent military dictatorship, urged the King to come to terms without
delay. But the King would not be hurried. Choosing to suppose that
the Scottish defeat at Preston was not so much an end to the war as
a reason for a new one, he played for time while still hoping and
plotting for help from France. Contesting every point at issue, he
exhausted the Parliamentary delegates, who had hoped the negotiations would not last for more than forty days at the most. Day after
day they dragged inconclusively on until, at the end of October,
they were brought to an end, the two sides as far apart as ever.
    Cromwell had by now concluded that a satisfactory agreement
with the King would never be reached. A year before he had hoped
for such an agreement, not sharing the republicans' distaste for the
monarchy as an institution. But the enlistment of Scottish troops –
as foreign to him as French and Spaniards were – was unforgivable.
Before the fighting had started again, he had attended a prayer meet-

ing of Army officers at Windsor Castle and had decided with the others, many of them in tears, that it was their duty, 'if ever the Lord brought [them] back in peace, to call Charles Stuart, that Man of Blood, to an account for the blood he had shed, and the mischief he had done to his utmost against the Lord's cause and people in these poor nations'. To have further dealings with such a man now was 'to meddle with an accursed thing'.

Cromwell himself was still in the north when the conference at Newport broke up, having pursued the Scots across the border then settled down before the Royalist fortress of Pontefract, 'one of the strongest inland garrisons in the Kingdom'. Here he was maliciously said to have connived at the murder of that tiresome Leveller Thomas Rainsborough, who was mortally wounded in the streets of Doncaster when an attempt was made by a party of Cavaliers to carry him off in order to exchange him for Sir Marmaduke Langdale.

But Cromwell's son-in-law Henry Ireton was at Windsor where, having failed to persuade Fairfax to reoccupy London and purge the House of Commons, he was preparing a *Remonstrance of the Army*, elaborating the King's conduct and demanding that he be brought to trial and that the Monarchy be abolished. Faithless as he recognized the King to be, Fairfax refused to accept so radical a document; and he summoned a Council of Officers to consider it. Rather than modify it, Ireton chose to make it more radical than ever after a meeting at the Nag's Head tavern in the Strand with various prominent Levellers. The final *Remonstrance*, a verbose document which was eventually to cover nearly eighty printed pages, demanded not only the abolition of the Monarchy but also the dissolution of Parliament, and the election of a new House of Commons by a revised electoral system. Extreme as it had now become, Fairfax and his Council of Officers felt obliged to accept the *Remonstrance* once yet another set of proposals sent by them to the King had been rejected.

The *Remonstrance* was accordingly sent to the House of Commons on 20 November. A few days later Fairfax – having issued orders for the King to be brought over from the Isle of Wight to Hurst Castle, a gloomy fortress on a long strip of sand and shingle by the west entrance to the Solent – reoccupied London and repeated his demands for money to pay his troops. The House of Commons, after lengthily debating the crisis, sitting up all night for the first time in their history, responded on the morning of 5 December by declaring the King's removal illegal.

Ireton, who had long been calling for the forcible dissolution of Parliament, now decided to take the matter into his own hands. With the agreement of some Independent Members but evidently without consulting Fairfax and in the absence of Cromwell – who was prudently lingering in the north until the problem was resolved – Ireton decided that, if he could not dissolve Parliament, he would certainly purge the House of Commons.

On 6 December this was done. Early on the morning of that day, Colonel Thomas Pride, the former brewer's drayman, marched towards the House with a party of soldiers. Posting himself before the doors with a list of names in his hand and Lord Grey of Groby, long a firm opponent of the King, by his side, he awaited the arrival of the Members. Nearly two hundred were turned away on this and subsequent days; others, protesting at their treatment, were arrested; some were locked up in a convenient chamber, some required to spend the night confined in a tavern. The 'Rump' which survived numbered about 150 Members. Fairfax expressed his anger at this illegal outrage; but Cromwell, who arrived in London within a matter of hours of its perpetration, declared that while he had not 'been acquainted with this design; yet, since it was done, he was glad of it, and would endeavour to maintain it'. And when the 'Rump' passed an ordinance setting up a High Court of Justice to try the King and naming 150 Commissioners to serve on it, he assured his fellow Commissioners that the time had come to act decisively. 'I tell you,' he cried in a terrible and memorable phrase, 'we will cut off the King's head with the crown on it.'

'Charles Stuart, the now King of England', was accused of having entertained 'a wicked design totally to subvert the ancient and fundamental laws and liberties of this nation, and in their place to introduce an arbitrary and tyrannical government; and that, besides all other evil ways and means to bring his design to pass, he hath prosecuted it with fire and sword, levied and maintained a cruel war in the land.' The House declared that a King who prosecuted such a war against his subjects was guilty of treason.

This was more than many, even of the King's opponents, could stomach. The Presbyterians, their voice in Parliament stilled by Colonel Pride, were strongly opposed to the trial. So were the Levellers, whose leader John Lilburne denounced it as a plot by the 'Grandees' and the 'silken Independent', Oliver Cromwell, to use the proceedings as a means of turning attention away from the far more urgent problems of social reform. So, too, was Thomas Fairfax, who was not to be found when the King was brought to London on the bitingly cold morning of 18 January 1649 to appear before the High Court. His wife, a high-spirited daughter of a gallant old soldier, was there, though; and when her husband's name was called she cried out from the gallery as one of the guards threatened her with his musket, 'He has more wit than to be here!' Later, Fairfax was to regret that he had not done more to save the King, whose trial – he seems to have persuaded himself to believe – was engineered in an effort to force the stubborn man to yield. He quarrelled with Cromwell for the first time in his opposition to the trial; but he left London when it was under way, afterwards maintaining that any action to stop it might have plunged the country into a third civil war.

Many others shared the General's qualms. The two Chief Justices and the Lord Chief Baron of the Exchequer all refused to appear in court, though all three were opponents of the King and had only recently been appointed. Other legal luminaries withdrew into the country or, like the Attorney General, pleaded illness. Eventually the little-known and not notably distinguished Chief Justice of Chester, John Bradshaw, described by a contemporary as 'a strict man and learned in his profession, no friend of monarchy', was appointed President of the Court; and John Cook, a devoutly religious republican barrister of Gray's Inn, was delegated to conduct the prosecution.

The trial was opened on 21 January before 135 judges, few of whose names were known to general fame and none of whom was a peer, since the House of Lords had rejected the ordinance for the trial. But it was, as one of the judges said, 'not a thing done in a corner'. The proceedings were held in Westminster Hall which was so crowded with spectators that several of them were forced to clamber up the walls to sit in the embrasures of the windows. The President was so exposed to public view in his crimson velvet chair that he thought it as well to reinforce his hat with steel plates.

Opposite him sat the prisoner in a black velvet cloak, the embroidered silver star of the Order of the Garter gleaming on his sleeve. He was forty-eight years old but his appearance was that of an old man; his cheeks were sunken, his hair grey, his eyes deeply shadowed. Between the fingers of one of his small white hands he carried a silver-headed cane.

He listened in silence as the fervent John Cook, staring him intently in the face, accused him of 'high treason and high misdemeanours'. But when Cook said he would read out the charge, and began to unroll the long scroll of parchment upon which it was written, the King spoke for the first time: 'Hold a little.'

Cook, affecting not to hear him, continued to unroll the parchment; and the King, in an effort to attract his attention, tapped him on the arm with his cane. The silver knob fell off. The King made no effort to retrieve it; and then, as though suddenly remembering that he had no page now to pick it up for him, he bent down and picked it up himself. He sat back in his chair, making no further attempt to interrupt Cook's reading of the charge, looking about him, seeming to 'be indifferent to the words', once laughing quickly and sardonically when described as a 'tyrant, traitor and murderer'. But when Cook had at last finished and the President told him that the court required an answer to the charges, he replied calmly, confidently and quite without the impediment that normally hampered his speech, that he knew not by what lawful authority he was required to make any answer, that the court had no right to try him, that he declined to submit to its jurisdiction.

Day after day he stubbornly refused to recognize the authority of the court, reminding its members that he was their lawful King, contemptuously rejecting the President's warning that a prisoner who would not plead was regarded as guilty, glancing towards the gallery when, in response to Bradshaw's urging him to remember that his accusers were 'the people of England', a woman stood up to answer for him, 'Not a quarter of them! Oliver Cromwell is a traitor!' 'Upon which,' so Edward Hyde related, 'one of the officers bade the soldiers fire into that box whence those presumptuous words were uttered. But it was quickly discerned that it was the general's wife, the lady Fayrefax, who had uttered both those sharp sayings; who was presently persuaded or forced to leave the place to prevent any new disorder. She was of a very noble extraction, one of the daughters and heirs of Horace Lord Vere of Tilbury, who, having been bred in Holland, had not that reverence for the Church of England as she ought to have had, and so had unhappily concurred in her husband's entering into rebellion, never imagining what misery it would bring upon the kingdom; and now abhorred the work in hand as much as any body could do, and did all she could to hinder her husband from acting any part in it. Nor did he ever sit in that bloody court.'

Even among those who hoped to see him condemned to death there were many who could not but admire the King's spirit, and felt obliged to conclude that, traitor or not, here was a man of resolution, conviction and courage. Exasperating those who, believing him to be pliable, had come upon the ultimate bedrock of his obstinacy, angering those who condemned his calm manner as impudence in a man 'guilty of the blood that hath been shed in this war', he refused to betray his conscience. Always impressionable and, in the past, readier to accept the advice of others than to trust in his own opinions, he was not afraid of his judgement now. It was not until 27 January, when Charles Stuart was condemned to be put to death as 'a public enemy' 'by the severing of his head from his body' – a verdict with which all sixty-seven judges concurred – that the King momentarily lost control of himself. Shocked by the sudden ending of the trial, he called out loudly, 'Will you hear me a word, Sir?'

'You are not to be heard after the sentence.'

'No, Sir?'

'No, Sir, by your favour, Sir. Guard, withdraw your prisoner.'

'I may speak after the sentence, by your favour, Sir, I may speak after the sentence. By your favour, hold! The sentence, Sir – I say, Sir, I do –'

For the first time in the trial he was incoherent. The soldiers moved in on him to drag him away if necessary. 'I am not suffered for to speak,' he said resignedly, once more in control of his emotions. 'Expect what justice other people will have.' As he was led out of the Hall, some of the guard called out at a signal from their colonel, 'Execution! Justice! Execution!' as they breathed tobacco smoke in his face. He commented wryly, 'Poor creatures! For sixpence they will say as much of their own commanders.' He was carried away in a sedan chair towards Whitehall Palace. The crowds of people looking down upon the parade from the windows and roofs of King Street were silent.

★

The King asked to see his children Elizabeth and Henry for the last time, and his request was granted. They had been separated for over a year; and when the thirteen-year-old Elizabeth came into the room she burst into tears. She sank to her knees before him and could not stop crying. The King bent down to help her to her feet and told her to try to listen carefully and to remember the important things he had to say. She was still weeping so bitterly as her father talked to her that he said to her in gentle reproach, 'Sweetheart, you will forget this.'

'No,' she said, 'I will never forget it whilst I live'; she would write it all down that night. And so she did:

'He told me he was glad I was come. He wished me not to grieve and torment myself for him, for what would be a glorious death that he should die, it being for the laws and liberties of this land, and for maintaining the true Protestant religion . . . He should die a martyr. He told me he had forgiven all his enemies, and hoped God would forgive them also, and commanded us, and all the rest of my brothers and sisters to forgive them. He bid me tell my mother that his thoughts had never strayed from her, and that his love should be the same to the last . . . He doubted not but the Lord would settle his throne upon his son, and that we should be all happier than we could have expected to have been if he had lived.'

When he had finished speaking to Elizabeth he turned to Henry and, sitting down, took the eight-year-old boy on his knee. 'Heed, my child, what I say,' he said to him. 'They will cut off my head and perhaps make thee a king.' The boy looked up at his father 'very steadfastly'; and Charles went on, 'But mark what I say, you must not be a king so long as your brothers Charles and James do live; for they will cut off your brothers' heads (when they can catch them) and cut off thy head too, at last; and therefore I charge you, do not be made a king by them.'

Henry promised that he would rather be 'torn in pieces first'. Charles put the boy down and kissed him. He kissed Elizabeth, too, and blessed them both. Then he asked them to go away with Bishop Juxon, and was himself leaving the room for the bedroom next door when a fresh outburst of sobbing from Elizabeth, who was herself to die at Carisbrooke the following year, made him come back to give her a last kiss. He turned away, walked quickly into the bed-chamber, and lay down on the bed; his legs were trembling.

At ten o'clock on the morning of 30 January 1649 he was told it was time to leave St James's for the black-draped scaffold which had been built outside the Banqueting House in Whitehall. It had been decided that the execution should take place here and not on Tower Hill since the space in front of Inigo Jones's handsome building was small and easily guarded.

The King walked through the Banqueting House beneath Rubens's splendid ceiling, then out through one of the building's specially enlarged windows. He walked, so one observer wrote, with 'the same unconcernedness and motion, that he usually had, when he entered into it on a Masque-night'. The executioner and his assistant were standing by the block, both of them masked and wearing false hair and beards. He asked the executioners what he should do about his own hair and was advised to tuck it up under a cap; he also asked if the block could be raised higher so that he could kneel in front of it instead of having to lie down. But it had been set low so that it would be easier to kill him should he struggle. 'It can be no higher, Sir,' the executioner said.

The King stood praying for a short time, looking up at the sky, then he lay down with his neck on the block. The axe fell and the King's head was severed by a single stroke.

'The blow I saw given,' said a young spectator, 'and can truly say with a sad heart, at the instant whereof I remember well, there was such a grone by the thousands then present as I never hear before and desire I may never hear again.'

There was a short scramble round the scaffold as people ran forward to dip their handkerchiefs in the spilled blood or to grab some sort of memento of the scene they had witnessed; but the space around the scaffold was soon cleared by cavalry, and by the late afternoon London had fallen into a kind of shocked silence. There were no disturbances that night. The wars had caused much suffering; trade had been badly hit; the poor were as poor as they ever had been; crippled soldiers and beggars wandered everywhere. Men had been dismissed from workshops all over the north, in the Midlands and in the West Country; country town markets had been almost deserted at times; cloth workers in Gloucestershire, miners in Durham and Northumberland, cattle drovers in north Wales had all feared starvation; parts of large towns subjected to long sieges were virtually derelict, their populations decimated by plague and sickness. To pay for the costs of war, taxation had risen almost seven times higher than it had been in the 1630s.

Almost two hundred thousand lives had been lost in a population which probably numbered rather less than one and a half million males between the ages of sixteen and fifty. Well over eighty thousand had been killed in the fighting and more than a hundred thousand had died from accidents and disease in plague-ridden towns. Perhaps the death of the King would lead to better times. Certainly it was true that no one in the whole of the teeming, rambling town had risked his life to save him, and many Londoners felt sure that those who had brought him to his death had done their duty to their country and to God.

EPILOGUE

*'Nobody can tell what we have fought about
all this while.'*

The Earl of Berkshire

The Prince of Wales, now recognized by his supporters as King Charles II, was eighteen years old. Tall and dark, slim and graceful, he was already remarkable for the charm of his manner, his courteous affability, his courage and his love of pleasure. He was, as yet, less well known for his deviousness, his talent for dissimulation and deceit, the mocking cynicism sometimes to be glimpsed in the set of his ugly mouth. Recognized as their King by the Scots, who had naturally not taken kindly to the execution of his father by the English without consulting them, Charles agreed to take the Covenant, swearing to establish the Presbyterian Kirk. He also undertook to repudiate the Marquess of Montrose, his Lieutenant-General in Scotland, who had, unknown to him, been defeated in Sutherland on 27 April 1650, the very day upon which Charles himself set sail from the Continent for Scotland and, avoiding the ships of the Commonwealth, as the republican Government of England was now known, landed at the mouth of the River Spey.

In London the Council of State, of which Cromwell was first chairman, determined to invade Scotland before a Scottish army marched into England. So that summer an army raised by the Commonwealth advanced from Newcastle across the border. Cromwell was in command; Charles Fleetwood and John Lambert were both with him; so, in command of the infantry, was George Monck, son of a Devonshire landowner who had fought in the Low

Countries and for the Royalists before changing sides after two years' imprisonment in the Tower following his capture at Nantwich in 1644. The Commonwealth army was a well-trained force of some fifteen thousand men; and, although the Scottish army under David Leslie was far larger – and the English ranks became much thinned by sickness – at Dunbar in the early morning of 3 September 1650, the ground underfoot sodden by heavy rain, Cromwell's army won a decisive victory.

Four months later Charles II was crowned at Scone near Perth where the Kings of Scotland had been enthroned for centuries; and in July he marched south with an army of thirteen thousand men, English as well as Scottish, to lay claim to his inheritance in London. He advanced as far as Worcester, recruiting more men on the way, losing others by desertion, attempting to cheer up his General, David Leslie, who, gloomy and dispirited, grumbled that 'how well, soever' their army looked, 'it would not fight'.

It did fight; but, outnumbered by the army of the Commonwealth, it was overwhelmed at Worcester on the anniversary of the defeat at Dunbar. The King escaped after the battle through the northern gate of the city and made his circuitous way to Boscobel in Shropshire, the house of a Roman Catholic family, in whose grounds he hid for a time in an oak tree, the fame of which has been preserved in the name of so many of England's public houses, over twenty of them in London alone. From Boscobel the King, described by his enemies as that 'malicious and dangerous Traitor, Charles Stuart, son of the late Tyrant', 'a tall black man over two yards high', made his way towards the Sussex coast at Brighton, then known at Brightelmstone, disguised in rough country clothes, with a price of £1,000 on his head, his once long, curly hair cut short and crammed beneath a greasy hat. After more than six weeks on the run he was carried ashore from a cock-boat at Fécamp in Normandy in the middle of October.

In England, where the Monarchy and the House of Lords had already been abolished, Cromwell's soldiers forcibly ejected the so-called 'Rump', those Members of the Commons of the Long Parliament who had been allowed to keep their seats after the purge of Colonel Pride. Cromwell himself became Lord Protector; and, with Scotland subdued and Ireland largely in the hands of the Protestant ascendancy, he set about reducing the size of the Army and endeavouring to give his government a civilian rather than military aspect, encouraging his garrison commanders to take part in local government. In March 1655 an abortive Royalist uprising led by Colonel John Penruddock, a Wiltshire squire, induced Cromwell to extend the power of these military commanders by dividing the country into eleven districts, each commanded by a major-general; but two years later the Protector felt able to accede to the wishes of his new Parliament and the rule of the major-generals, together with the tax levied to support them, came to an end. By the time of Cromwell's last illness in September 1658 the Protectorate, a generally benevolent despotism which allowed a large measure of intellectual freedom and religious toleration, seemed secure.

But as the Protector lay dying in Whitehall Palace a fierce gale, 'as loud as his immortal fame', swept across England: trees, huge oaks even, were uprooted; roofs were torn from houses; ships were sunk; church steeples and parapet walls were sent crashing into the streets as the wind came 'howling over Thames-side palace stones . . . echoing dying Cromwell'. As always in such times, men saw the havoc wreaked by the gale as a portent of disasters yet to come, and within months the country was, indeed, in turmoil.

As the Lord Protector's chosen successor, his son Richard Cromwell, 'Tumbledown Dick', was quite unsuited to the task. At odds with the Army, he was dismissed, and, once arrangements had been made for the settlement of his debts, sailed without regret for Paris, where he lived for a time as Clarke before retiring to private life in Hertfordshire. The Army soon expelled Parliament in its turn, and a Committee of Safety was established to assert control over the country after rebels, led by Sir George Booth, a Cheshire landowner, had succeeded in taking Chester and other towns in the north and west before being defeated by John Lambert.

General Monck, still in command of the army in Scotland, now made up his mind to put an end to the lawlessness and to restore the Long Parliament. When Monck was joined by Fairfax, who came out of retirement to lend him his support, all resistance collapsed. Monck's army entered London; the Long Parliament was recalled; and, in accordance with the wishes of its Members, and with those of the people at large, King Charles II was invited to come home.

John Evelyn, who had gone abroad in 1643 to 'evade the doing of very unhandsome things', watched the celebrations and rejoiced:

This day [29 May 1660] came in his Majestie Charles the 2d to London after a sad, and long Exile, and Calamitous Suffering both of the King and Church: being 17 yeares: This was also his Birthday [thereafter to be celebrated as Oak-Apple Day] and with a Triumph of above 20000 horse and foote, brandishing their swords and shouting with unexpressable joy: The wayes strew'd with flowers, the bells ringing, the streetes hung with Tapissry, fountaines running with wine: The Mayor, Aldermen, all the Companies in their liver[ie]s, Chaines of Gold, banners; Lords and nobles, Cloth of Silver, gold and vellvet every body clad in, the windos and balconies all set with Ladys, Trumpets, Musick, and [myriads] of people flocking the streetes . . . I stood in the Strand and beheld it, and blessed God: And all this without one drop of bloud, and by that very Army, which rebell'd against him but it was the Lords doing for such a Restauration was never seene in the mention of any history, antient or modern, nor so joyfull a day.

By the end of the century the returning King's father, Charles Stuart, 'Man of Blood', had been recreated in the national consciousness as the Blessed King Charles the Martyr. Prints depicted him surrounded by angels, rays of light emanating from his shiny locks, his hands raised in benediction. The anniversary of his execution was commemorated by a day of fasting; in a regular church service held in his memory the congregation thanked God for the 'abundant grace bestowed upon our martyred Sovereign'. The Church congratulated itself that the restored Monarchy had brought about its own salvation, that religious extremism had perished with the regicides, that men once described as Presbyterians were now, outwardly at least, content to become Anglicans and that the Anglican clergy were seen to be the natural allies of the squire in the maintenance of the social order. Admittedly a new Act of Uniformity of 1662, which required church services to be conducted in accordance with a revised prayer book and liturgy, drove over two thousand clergy from their livings; but this permanent breach between Anglicanism and Noncomformity did little damage either to the influence of the Church or to the fabric of lay society. The Levellers disappeared with the Puritans; Oliver Cromwell was blamed for all the ills of those times of 'late unhappy troubles' until rehabilitated in the nineteenth century by

Thomas Carlyle; and the Monarchy became once more a real power in the land.

To be sure the Monarchy could no longer act outside the Common Law, impose taxes without Parliamentary consent, or have its enemies imprisoned without due cause. But the command of the Army and Navy remained in the hands of the King; and by an Act of 1661 it was decreed that neither 'Parliament nor the People . . . nor any persons whatever [had] any coercive power over the persons of the Kings of this realm'. It was as though Parliament, horrified by what had happened in the immediate past, had accepted not only the restoration of the Monarchy but the enhancement of its prestige; and in its dread of further strife was prepared to submit to such provocations as Charles II's dissolution of Parliament in 1681 after a sitting of no longer than a week.

After the 'Glorious Revolution' of 1688 in which, with so little violence, Charles II's Roman Catholic brother James II was driven from the throne to be replaced by his niece Mary and her husband, Charles I's grandson, William of Orange, England fell under the rule of an oligarchy whose members came to regard the Great Rebellion in contrasting lights. Certainly, so it was now held, King Charles I had behaved tyranically and with stubborn irresponsibility; but equally to be condemned were the religious fanaticism and political extremism of his times. The demands of the radicals for the extension of the right to vote were no more acceptable to those in power when put forward by the Chartists of the 1840s than they had been when advanced by the Levellers two hundred years before. For most English people, indeed, the thousands of men who had died in the Civil Wars had given their lives to little discernible effect. As the Royalist Earl of Berkshire said when the wars were almost over, 'Nobody can tell what we have fought about all this while.'

The Fate of Characters Whose End is Not Recorded in the Text

An Act of Indemnity and Oblivion passed in 1660 confirmed Charles II's Declaration of Breda in which a free pardon was offered to those who had acted against the monarchy in the Civil War and during the Commonwealth. The Act excluded fifty individuals, among them the regicides who had signed King Charles I's death warrant. The bodies of certain of the leading regicides who had died before 1660 were disinterred and gibbeted at Tyburn, their heads being displayed at Westminster Hall. Ten surviving regicides were executed, but their bravery on the scaffold was such that the Government thought it as well to hang no more.

Earl of Argyll (Archibald Campbell, eighth Earl of Argyll, created Marquess in 1641): At the Restoration he presented himself at Court but Charles II refused to see him and he was escorted to the Tower. From there he was sent to face trial in Scotland for collaborating with Cromwell's regime. He was sentenced to death and in May 1661 beheaded.

Lady Blanche Arundell: Went to Salisbury after the fall of Wardour Castle to seek the protection of Lord Hertford. She died at Winchester in 1649.

John Ashburnham: After his flight with the King from Oxford, Ashburnham escaped to the Continent, returning to attend upon the King in 1647. He was arrested at the beginning of 1648 and imprisoned at Windsor.

Released in exchange for a Parliamentarian, he was thereafter closely watched and occasionally held in custody until the Restoration when he was reappointed Groom of the Bedchamber. He died in 1671.

Sir Jacob Astley (created Lord Astley in 1644): After his defeat at Stow-on-the-Wold, he was for a time imprisoned in Warwick Castle, then held in London before being allowed to return on bail to his home in Kent where he died in retirement in 1652.

Sir Arthur Aston: The widely disliked Governor of Oxford was invalided out of the Royalist army after losing his leg 'to the great rejoycing of the soldiers'. He subsequently served in Ireland, however, and was hacked to pieces in 1649 at Drogheda where the garrison of the town was massacred, his brains being beaten out of his skull with his wooden leg.

Sir William Balfour: Having served with distinction at Edgehill, in the West Country and at the Second Battle of Newbury, Balfour, by then an elderly man, retired from the Army in 1644 and died in the year of the Restoration.

Praise-God Barebone: 'The leather-seller of Fleet Street', as he was commonly known, was summoned by Cromwell in June 1653 to take upon himself 'the trust of Member for the City of London'. The short-lived 'Little Parliament' of 140 'godly men' was also known as 'Barebone's Parliament' though he was far from being its most distinguished Member and seems never to have spoken in it. An opponent of the Restoration of King Charles II, he was arrested and imprisoned in the Tower in 1661, but survived to die at home in 1679.

William Batten: Reappointed Surveyor of the Navy at the Restoration, he became one of the leading characters in Pepys's diary. 'Sir W. Batten is so ill that it is believed he cannot live till tomorrow,' Pepys wrote on 4 October 1667, 'which troubles me and my wife mightily, partly out of kindness, he being a good neighbour, and partly because of the money he owes us.' He died the next day.

Richard Baxter: Left Parliament's army before the end of the war and devoted his time to writing. He was appointed a royal chaplain at the Restoration; but, having refused a bishopric, he was forced out of the

Church by the Act of Uniformity in 1662. Returning to London when the Act of Indulgence was passed in 1672, he became a popular preacher. Accused of sedition, he was brought before Judge Jeffreys who treated him harshly and saw that he was sent to prison. He was released in November 1686, and died in 1691.

John Belasyse (created Baron Belasyse of Worlaby in 1644): Fought for the King at Edgehill, Brentford, Newbury and Naseby. At the Restoration he was appointed Lord Lieutenant of the East Riding. King James II, as a fellow-Roman Catholic, appointed him First Lord Commissioner of the Treasury in 1687. He died two years later.

Sir John Berkeley (created Baron Berkeley of Stratton in 1658): After accompanying the King on his flight to Hampshire in November 1647, Berkeley went abroad, served for a time in the Duke of York's household, then in the army of Marshal Turenne. Returning to England at the Restoration, he was appointed a Commissioner of the Navy and later Lord Lieutenant in Ireland. He acquired extensive lands to the north of Piccadilly and built himself a great house on the site of the later Devonshire House. After his death in 1678 his widow sold strips of land on either side of the garden for building Berkeley Street and Stratton Street. He was succeeded in the title by each of his three sons in turn.

Robert Blake: Left the land service for the navy in 1649 and became one of the greatest of England's admirals. After brilliant victories over the Dutch and Spanish fleets, he died aboard his flagship as she was sailing into Plymouth harbour in 1657. He was buried in Westminster Abbey on Cromwell's orders but his body was dug up at the Restoration and reburied with others in a pit outside the Abbey walls.

Sir Henry Blount: Served on various commissions on law and trade during the Commonwealth and after the Restoration, retiring in the 1670s to Tittenhanger in Hertfordshire where he died in 1682.

George Booth: After his defeat by Lambert, Booth, disguised as a woman, attempted to escape to the Continent; but an innkeeper, whose suspicions were aroused by the purchase of a razor, reported the arrival of his curious guest to the authorities. Released on bail, he was raised to the peerage as Lord Delamere at the Restoration. He died in 1684.

Sir John Boys: The defender of Donnington Castle was imprisoned in Dover Castle in 1659 for signing a petition for a free Parliament. Soon released, he died at Bonnington in Kent in 1664.

John Bradshaw: After serving as President of the Commission which tried King Charles I, Bradshaw presided over the trials of other lesser Royalist prisoners, several of whom were also sentenced to death. He sat on the Council of State in the early years of the Commonwealth but his relations with Cromwell grew increasingly unfriendly. He did not long outlive him, dying in October 1659 in the Deanery at Westminster which had been handed over to him when appointed to conduct the King's trial.

Shortly before his death he declared 'that if the King were to be tried and condemned again, he would be the first man that would do it'. At the Restoration it was ordered that his body, which had been buried in Westminster Abbey, should be exhumed and hanged in its coffin at Tyburn before being buried beneath the gallows. His head, together with those of Cromwell, Pride and Ireton, was afterwards put on display at Westminster Hall.

Sir William Brereton: Having defeated the only significant forces in the field at Stow-on-the-Wold in 1646, Brereton was rewarded with the palace of the Archbishop of Canterbury at Croydon. He was described as 'a notable man at a thanksgiving dinner, having terrible long teeth and a prodigious stomach, to turn the Archbishop's chapel at Croydon into a kitchen; and to swallow up that palace and lands at a morsel'. He died at Croydon in 1661.

Richard Browne: Having fallen out with his former friends, Browne was expelled from the House of Commons, deprived of his offices as Alderman and Sheriff, cast into prison and, so he maintained, 'used worse than a cavalier, taken away and sent prisoner to Wales [where he was treated] with more cruelty than if in Newgate [and] in a worse prison than common prisoners'. Knighted at the Restoration, he was elected Lord Mayor in October 1660. He died in Essex in 1669.

Duke of Buckingham (George Villiers, second Duke of Buckingham). Escaped abroad after the battle of Worcester, returning secretly to England and marrying Mary, the only daughter of Lord Fairfax to whom the larger part of his confiscated estates had been assigned. At the Restoration he became one of the most notorious of 'the Merry Gang' at court of which the rake and poet the Earl of Rochester was another leading member. Buckingham was also in the Cabal, the group of Charles II's advisers so known because of the initials of its members, Clifford, Arlington, Buckingham, Ashley Cooper and Lauderdale. Much of his land was sold to pay his debts and 'worn to a thread with whoring', he died at Kirkby Moorside in 1687, 'in the worst inn's worst room' according to Alexander Pope, actually in the house of one of his tenants.

Sir John Byron (created Baron Byron of Rochdale in 1643): After the surrender of Chester, Byron held out in Carnarvon Castle for some time before that, too, had to be given up. He then sailed for the Continent where he was appointed Superintendent General of the Duke of York's household. He died in exile in 1652, the title passing to Richard, the eldest of six brothers who fought for the King. Richard was Governor of Newark in 1643–45. The poet was the sixth Lord Byron.

Earl of Callander (James Livingstone, first Earl of Callander): Escaped to Holland after the Royalist defeat at Preston. He returned in 1654 to Scotland where his estates were later confiscated and he himself was imprisoned. At the Restoration he was recompensed for his losses. He died in 1674.

Lord Capel (Arthur Capel, created Lord Capel of Hedham in 1641): After the surrender of Colchester, Capel was imprisoned, first at Windsor, then in the Tower whence he escaped only to be betrayed by a waterman. Imprisoned again, he was tried, condemned and executed in March 1649. His eldest son was created Earl of Essex at the Restoration.

Earl of Carnwarth (Robert Dalyell, second Earl of Carnwarth): Served with Lord Digby after the Royalist defeat at Naseby and sailed with him to the Isle of Man, and thence to Ireland, after Digby's defeat in Yorkshire. Returning to England, he fought for Charles II at Worcester where he was taken prisoner and escorted to the Tower of London. He died in 1654.

Sir Hugh Cholmley: Deserted Parliament after the Queen's return to England in 1643. Having spurned the Marquess of Newcastle's pleas to accompany him to the Continent after the Royalist defeat at Marston Moor, Cholmley was obliged to surrender Scarborough in July 1645. He then went abroad but in 1649 returned to England where he died in 1657.

James Chudleigh: Taken to Oxford after his capture at Stratton, he was killed while serving with Prince Rupert's army in the West Country in October 1643.

Sir John Clotworthy: Accused of embezzling funds and of making trouble between Parliament and the Army, Clotworthy was arrested and imprisoned in 1651. Released, he returned to Ireland where he served the King so well that he was created Viscount Massereene in November 1660. He died five years later.

William Compton: Knighted in 1643, he greatly distinguished himself during the siege of Banbury which was eventually raised by his brother, the Earl of Northampton, in October 1644. He also fought bravely at Colchester in 1648. He and his companions became known as 'The Sealed Knot' because of the secrecy in which they managed their attempts to restore Charles II to the throne. When the Restoration eventually took place, Compton was appointed Master-General of the Ordnance. He died in 1663.

John Cook: Appointed Chief Justice of Munster, Cook left for Ireland in 1651. He was arrested in 1660 and brought back to England to face trial. He was executed on 16 October.

Anthony Ashley Cooper (first Earl of Shaftesbury): Having changed sides in the war, he withdrew his support from Cromwell after it was over and was one of the commissioners who invited King Charles II to return home from the Continent. He was appointed Chancellor of the Exchequer in 1661 and later Lord Chancellor. After attempting to exclude Charles's brother James from the throne, he was sent to the Tower accused of high treason. Released, he fled abroad and died in Amsterdam in 1683.

John Corbet: After the war became rector of Bramshot, Hampshire from which living he was ejected in 1662 because of his nonconformist views. He then moved to London and afterwards lived with his second wife in the Hertfordshire house of Richard Baxter. He died awaiting an operation for stone in 1680.

Lawrence Crawford: Killed in August 1645 during the siege of Hereford.

Richard Cromwell: Died in retirement at Cheshunt in 1712. His wife had died in 1675, his son Oliver at the age of nine. Three daughters survived him.

Sir John Culpeper: The King's leading supporter in the House of Commons was appointed Chancellor of the Exchequer in 1642 and raised to the peerage in 1644. He accompanied Prince Charles to Scilly and thence to France. Returning to England at the Restoration, he died soon afterwards.

Sir Bernard de Gomme: Appointed Quartermaster-General at the Restoration, and Surveyor-General of Ordnance in 1682. He died in 1685, having married an Englishwoman as his second wife in 1667.

Lord Denbigh (Basil Feilding, 2nd Earl of Denbigh): Despite the pleas of his mother, Denbigh remained uncertainly committed to the Parliamentary cause after the death of his father from wounds received while fighting for the Royalists at Birmingham. By 1651, however, he was known to be seeking an accommodation with the Royalists. He succeeded in doing so and died in 1674. He was married four times but had no children.

Earl of Derby (James Stanley, seventh Earl of Derby): Sailed for Castle Rushen on the Isle of Man after the Royalists' defeat at Marston Moor and the loss of the north to Parliament. He remained on the island for six years, returning to the mainland in 1651 to join King Charles II at Worcester. After the Royalists' defeat there he accompanied Charles to Boscobel but on his way north he was captured at Nantwich, court-martialled, sentenced to death and executed at Bolton. The Countess, who was still on the Isle of Man at the time of her husband's death, returned to Knowsley where she characteristically petitioned that her husband's 'murderers might be brought to condign punishment'. She died at Knowsley in 1664. Charles, the eldest of her nine children, was restored as eighth Earl of Derby on the reversal of his father's attainder. The thirteenth Earl became Prime Minister in 1852.

John Desborough: As Cromwell's brother-in-law he expected and obtained various responsible appointments during the Commonwealth. He was arrested on attempting to escape overseas at the Restoration but eventually succeeded in reaching Holland where he entered into republican conspiracies which came to the notice of the English Government. Obeying a summons to return home, he was imprisoned in the Tower, but at his trial was allowed his freedom on condition that he retired from public life. He died in 1680. The body of his wife, mother of his eight children, which had been buried in Westminster Abbey, was exhumed and removed from the Abbey.

Lord Digby (George, Lord Digby, succeeded his father in 1653 as second Earl of Bristol): After his defeat on Carlisle Sands, this brave, inconsistent, able and unreliable man fled with Sir Marmaduke Langdale to the Isle of Man and thence to Ireland before going to France where he joined the French Army as a volunteer, later becoming a Lieutenant-General. Cashiered for his part in a plot against Cardinal Mazarin, he left France to join the Spanish Army in the Netherlands. While on the Continent he was converted to Roman Catholicism which prevented his being appointed to any of the offices of state to which he might otherwise have felt himself entitled at the Restoration. He died at Chelsea in 1677 at Beaufort House, formerly the home of Sir Thomas More.

William Dowsing: At the Restoration, Dowsing disappeared into the obscurity from which he had emerged, and died about 1679.

Sir Lewis Dyve: Captured when Fairfax besieged and took Sherborne Castle in 1645, Dyve was sent a prisoner to the Tower of London whence he was removed to the King's Bench Prison. He escaped from here to fight at Preston. Taken prisoner, he escaped again and made his way to Paris where John Evelyn described him as 'indeed a valiant gentleman, but not a little given to romance when he spake of himself'.

Lord Eythin (James King, created Lord Eythin and Kerrey in 1643): Having gone to the Continent with the Marquess of Newcastle after the battle of Marston Moor, he died at Stockholm in 1652.

Sir Thomas Fairfax (later third Baron Fairfax): After the King's execution, Lord Fairfax, who had succeeded to the Barony on his father's death in 1648, lived mostly in retirement in Yorkshire, collecting coins and engravings, writing verse, ecclesiastical history and a treatise on the breeding of horses, and translating works from the French and Latin. His relationship with Cromwell grew increasingly strained; and after Cromwell's death he helped General Monck in the restoration of the Monarchy. He then returned, however, to his quiet life in Yorkshire. For most of the rest of his life he was in poor health. His spirited wife died in 1665, Fairfax himself six years later.

Nathaniel Fiennes: Exonerated from blame by Cromwell for his surrender of Bristol, Fiennes was appointed a member of the Council of State in 1654. He disappeared into obscurity at the Restoration and died in Wiltshire in 1669. His son succeeded as third Viscount Saye and Sele in 1674.

Charles Fleetwood: Having fought at Dunbar and Worcester, Fleetwood was appointed Commander-in-Chief in Ireland in 1652. A warm supporter of Cromwell, whose eldest daughter, Bridget, he married after Ireton's death, he nevertheless escaped punishment at the Restoration since he had taken no part in the King's trial. He retired into obscurity and died in 1692 in a house which had belonged to his third wife, who predeceased him.

Earl of Forth (Patrick Ruthven, Earl of Forth and Brentford): Aged, deaf, 'much decayed in his parts, and, with the long-continued custom of immoderate drinking, dozed in his understanding', Forth nevertheless remained active in support of the King after being superseded in command by Prince Rupert. He accompanied the Prince of Wales to Jersey in 1646.

Returning to Scotland in 1650, he died at Dundee the following year.

Sir Bernard Gascoigne (Bernardo Guasconi): Returned to Florence, having been spared execution after the fall of Colchester. After the Restoration, however, he came back occasionally to England where he was rewarded for his services to the Crown. Elected a Fellow of the Royal Society in 1667, he was appointed English envoy in Vienna during the unsuccessful negotiations for the marriage of the Duke of York to the daughter of the Archduke of Austria in 1672–73. He died in London in 1687.

Sir John Gell: After the battle of Hopton Heath, Gell was given command of a force of cavalry. He was accused by Parliament of neglecting to intercept the flight of the King after his defeat at Naseby. Subsequently accused of plotting against the Commonwealth, he was arrested and incarcerated in the Tower. Released in 1652, he died in 1671 in his seventy-ninth year.

Charles Gerard (created first Baron Gerard of Brandon in 1645 and Earl of Macclesfield in 1679): Wounded three times in various engagements. His successful campaign in Wales was followed by his appointment as Commander of the King's bodyguard. Wounded for a fourth time at Rowton Heath, he left for the Continent after the surrender of Oxford. He returned to England where his sequestered estates were returned to him, and commanded Charles II's Life Guards on the King's progress to Whitehall. Twenty-eight years later, he commanded William of Orange's bodyguard during the Prince's progress from Devon to London. He lived on until 1694.

Earl of Glamorgan (Edward Somerset, sixth Earl and second Marquess of Worcester, was styled Lord Herbert from 1628 to 1644): Went into exile in France, having failed in his mission to raise troops for the King in Ireland. He lived in Paris for four years. At the Restoration he managed to recover most of his sequestered estates and to recoup some of the immense fortune he had bestowed upon the King's cause. The last years of his life were largely occupied with mechanical studies and inventions. His *Century of Inventions* describes numerous ingenious devices including an instrument for 'driving up water by fire', the idea for which is believed to have occurred to him while watching the lid of a saucepan raised by the pressure of steam. He died in 1667. His son became the first Duke of Beaufort.

Sir Thomas Glemham: Imprisoned after the surrender of Oxford, Glemham was soon released and fought in the Second Civil War. He died some time in 1649.

Lord Goring (George Goring, eldest son of the first Earl of Norwich): After his defeat at Langport, Goring retreated into north Devonshire where he made little effort to oppose Fairfax's advance and ignored the King's order summoning him to Oxford. In poor health because of his extremely heavy drinking and a wound in his leg which he had received at the siege of Breda in 1637, he asked for permission to sail for the Continent, left without receiving it, obtained a military command, and died in poverty in Madrid in 1657.

Sir Richard Grenville: Sailed for France in 1646 pleading that, if he fell into the hands of Fairfax's army, he 'had no reason to expect the least degree of mercy'. He continued at first to make trouble on the Continent as he had done in England, but the last years of his life, until his death in 1658, were spent in retirement.

Henry Grey (first Earl of Stamford): Condemned by Parliament for his conduct in the West Country in 1643, he declared for the King in 1659, was arrested and sent to the Tower. At the Restoration he was received with favour at court. He died in 1673, the father of nine children by a daughter of the Earl of Exeter.

Lord Grey of Groby: One of the King's judges, he signed the death warrant. Thereafter, he took no significant part in public life, dying in 1657.

Sir Richard Gurney: For his support of the King, Gurney was committed to the Tower in July 1642 by Parliament and dismissed as Lord Mayor of London. He was released only a short time before his death in 1647.

Robert Hammond: Found employment by Cromwell in Ireland during the Protectorate, Hammond left for Dublin in August 1654 but died a few weeks later.

Thomas Harrison: One of the commissioners appointed for the King's trial, he signed the death warrant and thereafter maintained that he 'did it all according to the best of [his] understanding, deciding to make the revealed will of God in His holy scriptures a guide to me'. He declined to run away at the Restoration, was arrested at his house in Staffordshire, tried, condemned and executed. On the scaffold he declared, 'By God, I have leaped over a wall; by God, I have run through a troop; and by God I will go through this death, and He will make it easy for me.'

Sir Arthur Haselrig: Although he supported Cromwell in his quarrel with the Earl of Manchester and served under Cromwell in Scotland in 1650, Haselrig became and remained highly critical of him after 1653 when Cromwell forcibly dissolved the so-called 'Rump', what remained of the Long Parliament after Pride's purge. A convinced republican to the end of his days, Haselrig was sent to the Tower at the Restoration and soon after died there.

Henrietta Anne: Fifth daughter and youngest child of Charles I. Born at Exeter in 1644, she was taken to France soon afterwards by her mother and brought up in Paris. She was married at the age of sixteen to the duc d'Orléans, the homosexual brother of King Louis XIV. After a brief affair with the King, she settled down to a more regular intimacy with the comte de Guiche. She died at Saint-Cloud in 1670. One of her daughters married King Charles II of Spain.

Henrietta Maria: An exile in France from July 1644, she paid visits to England after the Restoration of her son as King Charles II but did not return to live there, complaining of the climate. She died at her château at Colombes near Paris in August 1669.

Prince Henry, Duke of Gloucester: Third son of King Charles I. Sent to Penshurst, Kent after his father's execution, and thence to Carisbrooke where his sister Elizabeth died, he was granted permission to go abroad by Cromwell in 1652. Having quarrelled with his mother over his refusal to abandon Protestantism, he served bravely in the Spanish army. At the Restoration he accompanied his brother Charles II to England but died of smallpox a few months later. He was twenty-one.

Lord Herbert: *see* **Earl of Glamorgan**.

Earl of Hertford (William Seymour, second Earl of Hertford, created Marquess in 1640): He became Duke of Somerset in 1660 by the reversal of the attainder of his ancestor, the Lord Protector, and died a few months later. His first wife, James I's cousin, the former Lady Arabella Stuart, had died in 1615.

Lord Holland (Henry Rich, Baron Kensington, first Earl of Holland): Captured at St Neot's after the failure of the Royalist insurrection, he was sent a prisoner to Warwick Castle and, despite the protests of both Fairfax and his elder brother, the Earl of Warwick, he was beheaded with the Duke of Hamilton on 9 March 1649.

Denzil Holles: Accused of treason for proposing the disbanding of the army in 1647, he fled to France. Granted a pass by Cromwell, he returned to England during the Protectorate. After the Restoration he was created Baron Holles of Ifield, and was English Ambassador in Paris from 1663 to 1666. He died in 1680.

Ralph Hopton: Raised to the peerage as Lord Hopton of Stratton in 1643, he accompanied Prince Charles to Scilly and thence to Jersey, after being wounded at Torrington and forced to surrender at Truro. He died, still in exile, at Bruges in 1652.

Sir John Hotham: A 'rough and rude man', in Clarendon's opinion, he was arrested when it was discovered that, as Governor of Hull, he was carrying on clandestine negotiations with the Royalist commander, the Earl of Newcastle. He was brought to London, condemned to death and, attended on the scaffold by Hugh Peters, was executed on 2 January 1645.

Captain John Hotham: The son of the above. He was said by Sir Thomas Fairfax to have had a 'peevish humour' and by Lucy Hutchinson to have had 'a great deal of wicked wit [as] he made sport with the miseries of the poor country'. It was mainly through him that negotiations were carried on with the Earl of Newcastle. He was arrested with his father, tried by court-martial and sentenced to be beheaded. He and his father were executed on the same day.

James Hutchinson: Signed the King's death warrant with marked reluctance and retired from public life after the expulsion of the Long Parliament in 1653 until taking his seat again in 1659. He escaped execution as a regicide at the Restoration, but would have offered his life with the others had not his wife dissuaded him. He was imprisoned in the Tower in 1663 and died, still a prisoner, in Sandown Castle, Kent the next year. His wife survived him and spent the years between 1664 and 1671 writing his biography.

Edward Hyde, First Earl of Clarendon: After the execution of Charles I, became one of Charles II's chief advisers and was confirmed in his office as Lord Chancellor at the Restoration and appointed Chancellor of Oxford University. Widely disliked as a statesman, he was the victim of a court intrigue. Impeached, he went abroad and settled first at Montpellier, then at Moulins. While in exile he wrote his great work, *The True Historical Narrative of the Rebellion and Wars in England*. The copyright of this was presented to Oxford University by his son, and helped to pay for the Clarendon Building for the University Press. Still in exile, Clarendon, described as 'a fair, ruddy, fat, middle-statured, handsome man', died at Rouen aged sixty-five in 1674.

Henry Ireton: Having regularly attended the King's trial and signed the warrant for his execution, Ireton was appointed Cromwell's deputy in Ireland where he showed himself to be as severe as he was hard-working. He was so diligent in the public service 'it was said of him that he never regarded what clothes or food he used, what hour he went to rest, or what horse he mounted'. After the capture of Limerick he contracted a fever from which he died in November 1651 at the age of forty. His widow, Cromwell's daughter Bridget, by whom he had one son and four daughters, married Charles Fleetwood. In 1661 her first husband's body, together with those of Cromwell, Bradshaw and Pride, was ordered to be dug up and hanged in its coffin at Tyburn before being buried there beneath the gallows.

Prince James, Duke of York: Second son of King Charles I. He escaped to Holland shortly before his father's execution and served in the army on the Continent. When his brother was restored to the throne as Charles I in 1660, the Duke of York was appointed Lord High Admiral, an office which he had to relinquish under the Test Act as an avowed Roman Catholic. In 1659 he married Anne Hyde, daughter of the Earl of Clarendon; and, after her death, Mary, daughter of the Duke of Modena. He ascended the throne on the death of his brother in 1685, but was thrown off it by the Revolution of 1688 when his sister's son, William of Orange, became King William III and his elder daughter, who was married to William, became Queen Mary II. Princess Anne, his other daughter by Anne Hyde, succeeded to the throne as Queen Anne in 1702. His descendants by his second wife, Mary of Modena, became the Jacobite Pretenders to the English throne.

Henry Jermyn, Earl of St Albans: Much favoured at the Restoration, as he had been before it because of his intimacy with Queen Henrietta Maria, Jermyn was granted large tracts of land north of Pall Mall on which were laid out Jermyn Street, St James's Square and the streets leading off them which were named after himself, members of the royal family and household. He died in his house in St James's Square, blind and almost eighty, yet still enjoying his food and gambling, in 1684.

George Joyce: Appointed Governor of the Isle of Portland in 1650, he was also granted lands worth £100 a year in 1651. He fled to the Continent at the Restoration and lived in Amsterdam until 1670 when orders were given to Sir William Temple, English Ambassador at the Hague, to have him arrested. The Dutch authorities seem to have connived at his escape and no more was heard of him.

William Juxon: After attending the King on the scaffold, Juxon was deprived of his see as Bishop of London and went to live in seclusion at Little Compton, Gloucestershire, where his pack of hounds was said to exceed all others in England. At the Restoration he was appointed Archbishop of Canterbury by the new King with whom, however, he did not get on as well as he had done with Charles's father. The Archbishop died in London in 1663.

John Lambert: Fought bravely with Cromwell at Dunbar and became one of the Protector's closest supporters until 1657, when he realized that he would not be named his successor. After the overthrow of Richard Cromwell, he was for a time virtual ruler of England as the leading member of the Committee of Safety. Sent to the Tower at the Restoration, he was kept a prisoner until his death, insane, on St Nicholas Isle off the Cornish coast in 1683.

Sir Marmaduke Langdale (created Baron Langdale of Holme in 1658): Having escaped from Nottingham Castle after the defeat of the Royalists at Preston, he fled to the Continent where, his estates confiscated by Parliament, he lived in such poverty that he was constrained to retire to a monastery in Germany. Pleading that he was too poor to attend King Charles II's coronation, he died a few months later.

Earl of Lauderdale (John Maitland, second Earl and first Duke of Lauderdale): Taken prisoner at Worcester in 1651, he was imprisoned for nine years. At the Restoration he was appointed Scottish Secretary of State. He died in 1682.

Rowland Laugharne: Outraged by the treatment of his soldiers, some of whom had received no pay for over two years and many of whom he supported out of his own pocket, Laugharne changed sides in 1648. Defeated and badly wounded by the Parliamentarians at St Fagans in May that year, he was, together with two other Royalist commanders, court-martialled and sentenced to death. The three officers were allowed to draw lots to determine which one of them should be executed. Laugharne was lucky. At the Restoration he was granted a pension.

Colonel William Legge: Having shared Prince Rupert's disgrace after the fall of Bristol, Legge was readmitted to the King's favour and helped to bring about a reconciliation between his Majesty and the Prince. A faithful attendant upon the King thereafter, he was accused of high treason in 1649 and imprisoned in Exeter Castle and subsequently in the Tower. At the Restoration he was appointed Lieutenant-General of the Ordnance and offered an earldom, which he declined. He died in 1670. His son was created Lord Dartmouth in 1682.

William Lenthall: Remained Speaker of the House of Commons until the Long Parliament was forcibly dissolved by Cromwell in 1653. 'I went to the Speaker,' recorded Thomas Harrison who was ordered by Cromwell to remove Lenthall, 'and told him, Sir, seeing things are brought to this pass, it is not requisite for you to stay there; he answered he would not come down unless he was pulled out; Sir, said I, I will lend you my hand, and he putting his hand into mine came down without any pulling, so that I did not pull him.'

Returned for Oxford county in Cromwell's first Parliament as Protector, Lenthall was unanimously voted Speaker again. At the Restoration he retired into private life at Burford Priory and died in 1662.

Alexander Leslie (first Earl of Leven): Defeated by Cromwell at Dunbar in 1650, Leven retreated to Edinburgh and thence to Stirling. He was spared the blame for his defeat because of 'all his former employments and service with ample approbatione for his fidelitie thairin'. He died at Balgonie, Fifeshire in 1661.

David Leslie (first Baron Newark): Fought with the Earl of Leven at Dunbar and, like him, was exonerated 'of all imputation anent the miscarriage'. At the Restoration, as well as being created Lord Newark, he was granted a pension. He died in 1682.

John Lilburne: After his release from the Tower in 1648, Lilburne continued his career as a political agitator and pamphleteer, vehemently attacking the Army leaders, demanding constitutional reforms and championing the rights of the people. Repeatedly in and out of prison, he was banished into exile in 1652, returning in 1653 without the pass he had requested from Cromwell. Arrested again, he was tried again, eventually being removed to the Channel Islands where the Governor of

Guernsey complained that he caused more trouble than ten Cavaliers. Brought back to the mainland in 1655, he announced that he had become a Quaker and seemed intent thenceforth on living more quietly, which he did until his death at Eltham in 1657.

Earl of Lindsey (Montague Bertie, second Earl of Lindsey): Imprisoned for a time in Warwick Castle after attending to his dying father at Edgehill, he was exchanged for another prisoner, joined the King at Oxford and fought at Newbury, Cropredy Bridge, Lostwithiel and Naseby where he was wounded. He lived quietly in England until the Restoration when he became Lord High Chamberlain. He died at Kensington in 1666 shortly before the Great Fire.

Sir Michael Livesey: Having signed the warrant for the King's execution, he fled abroad at the Restoration. His estates were assigned to the Duke of York. He is believed to have died, still in exile, in 1663.

Lord Loughborough (Henry Hastings, created Lord Loughborough in 1643): Went abroad after the defeat of the Royalist forces in Leicestershire, returning in the Second Civil War to take part in the defence of Colchester. Taken prisoner when Colchester surrendered, he was held for a time in Windsor Castle from which he contrived to escape to Holland. At the Restoration he was appointed Lord Lieutenant of Leicestershire. He died in 1667.

Edmund Ludlow: Served in the army until his election as Member for Wiltshire in 1646. Having signed the King's death warrant, he was sent as a Commissioner for the Government of Ireland. He fled to France in 1660 and lived on the Continent, where he adopted his mother's maiden name of Phillips, until 1689 when he returned to London. Threatened with arrest he went back to Switzerland, where he died in 1692.

Colonel Thomas Lunsford: Knighted after his removal as Lieutenant of the Tower, he was with the King at Hull and served in several engagements of the Civil War, including Edgehill where he was taken prisoner. Released, he was soon after captured again at Hereford and imprisoned in the Tower where he was accused of treason. The next year, however, he turned up in Holland whence he took ship for America where he died, probably in Virginia, in 1653.

Earl of Manchester (Edward Montagu, second Earl of Manchester): Condemned by Cromwell for his unwillingness to fight and deprived of his command by the Self-Denying Ordinance, Manchester remained active politically but was relieved of his offices in 1650 after declining to take the Engagement, the oath of allegiance to a government without King or House of Lords which had been imposed by the English Commonwealth on all men over eighteen. Having opposed the King's trial, he was much favoured at the Restoration, appointed Lord Chamberlain and a Knight of the Garter. He died in 1671.

Henry Marten: Expelled from the House of Commons because of his extreme views, he was in 1644 appointed Governor of Aylesbury, an appointment which he held for the rest of the war. Readmitted to Parliament, he reasserted his extremist opinions and strongly advocated the King's trial and execution. At the Restoration he gave himself up and, although convicted, was not executed. He was imprisoned at first in the Tower, then at Windsor whence, being such 'an eyesore to his Majesty', he was sent to Chepstow Castle where he died in 1680.

Princess Mary: The eldest daughter of King Charles I, she was born at St James's Palace in 1631. She was married to William, Prince of Orange in 1641 and was taken by her mother to Holland the following year. Her son, William, became King William III of England in 1689.

Edward Massey: As a Presbyterian opponent of the army, he was arrested and imprisoned with William Waller in 1648. He escaped to Holland and thereafter worked and fought for the Royalists. Knighted at the Restoration, he was elected Member of Parliament for Gloucester in 1661 and remained in the Commons until his death in 1675.

Prince Maurice: Sailed from Dover to Holland after the surrender of Oxford. He served for a time in the Prince of Orange's army, then took to piracy. He was drowned in a storm off the Virgin Islands in 1652.

Sir John Meldrum: Commanded troops in numerous engagements in the West Country as well as in Yorkshire and Lancashire before being mortally wounded during the siege of Scarborough in 1645.

John Middleton (created Earl of Middleton in 1656): Returned to England in the company of Charles II in 1660 and appointed Commander-in-Chief in Scotland. Accused of all manner of offences by his rival and enemy Lord Lauderdale, he was summoned to London and deprived of his several offices in Scotland. In 1674 he was appointed Governor of Tangier, where he died, having fallen over when drunk.

George Monck: Rewarded at the Restoration by being created Duke of Albemarle, granted a large pension and appointed Master of the Horse. He later commanded the English fleet against the Dutch. He died in 1670. Albemarle Street off Piccadilly is named after his son, the second Duke, whose mother was the daughter of a farrier. Having bought Clarendon House from the Earl of Clarendon, he sold it and its extensive ground to a group of developers, including the financier Sir Thomas Bond; hence Bond Street.

Sir George Monro: Withdrew to Scotland after the battle of Preston, then sailed for Holland. Returning to Scotland in 1650, he became a Member of Parliament after the Restoration and supported the 1688 Revolution which brought William and Mary to the throne. He died in 1693.

Earl of Montrose (James Graham, fifth Earl and first Marquess of Montrose): After his several victories in Scotland, Montrose was defeated by David Leslie at Philiphaugh in 1645. He sailed for the Continent the following year. Swearing to avenge the death of Charles I, he returned to Scotland, was captured, and taken to Edinburgh where he was hanged in May 1650 and his body dismembered.

Sir Philip Musgrave: Left England after the King's death but soon afterwards returned. He was arrested and imprisoned in 1653 after taking part in various Royalist plots. At the Restoration he was appointed Governor of Carlisle. He died in 1678.

Earl of Newcastle (William Cavendish, Viscount Mansfield (1620), Earl of Newcastle (1628), Marquess (1643)): Set sail from Scarborough for the Continent after the defeat of the Royalist forces at Marston Moor. Returning to England, greatly impoverished, at the Restoration, he was restored to his former offices at court and created Duke of Newcastle in 1665. He retired from public life, however, concentrating upon the recruitment of his estate and wealth and writing works on horsemanship as well as plays and poetry. He died in 1676.

Sir Edward Nicholas: Remained Secretary of State in name until the King's execution, but Henrietta Maria's dislike of him prevented his being taken into Charles II's confidence, and he lived in poverty on the Continent. Thereafter he had little influence, and soon after the Restoration was succeeded by a friend of the King's mistress, Lady Castlemaine. He was offered a peerage but could not afford to accept it. He retired to Surrey and died there in 1669.

Earl of Norwich (George Goring, created Baron Goring in 1628 and Earl of Norwich in 1644): Imprisoned in Windsor Castle after the fall of Colchester, he was tried for his life, pardoned and released. Rejoining Charles II on the Continent, he was appointed Captain of the King's Guard at the Restoration although by then nearly eighty. He died at Brentford in 1663.

John Okey: Having been regular in attendance at the King's trial and having signed the death warrant, he fled to Germany at the Restoration. Arrested in Holland in 1662 he was brought back to England and, with two other regicides who had been apprehended with him, executed on 9 April. He had been sentenced to death by hanging, drawing, and quartering, but public sympathy for the brave man was such that the more revolting parts of the sentence were omitted.

Earl of Ormonde (James Butler, twelfth Earl of Ormonde, created Duke of Ormonde in 1661): Left Ireland in 1650 and became one of Charles II's principal advisers on the Continent. He was well rewarded for his services at the Restoration and lived until 1688.

Sir Isaac Penington: Sir Richard Gurney's successor as Lord Mayor of London, he displayed throughout his term of office his strong Puritan sympathies. As Lieutenant of the Tower, he conducted Archbishop Laud to the scaffold. He was one of the commissioners for the King's trial, though he did not sign the death warrant. He was, however, accused of treason at the Restoration and committed to the Tower where he soon died.

John Penruddock: Taken prisoner at South Molton, Penruddock was condemned to death and beheaded at Exeter in 1655.

Hugh Peters: A keen supporter of Cromwell during the Protectorate, Peters was arrested at the Reformation and imprisoned in the Tower. He was 'an enthusiastical buffoon preacher', in the words of Gilbert Burnet, 'though a very vicious man who had been of great use to Cromwell and had been very outrageous in pressing the King's death with the cruelty and rudeness of an inquisitor'. He was executed at Charing Cross in October 1660.

George Porter: Condemned for his negligence at Ilminster by Lord Goring who described him as 'the best company but worst officer that ever served the King', Porter deserted the King's cause for Parliament's in 1645. He nevertheless intrigued for the Restoration of Charles II and was eventually rewarded by being appointed to an office at court. He died in 1683.

Sydenham Poyntz: Went to live in Holland in 1648, and from there sailed to the West Indies where he became Governor of the Leeward Islands. On the arrival of a Parliamentary fleet in West Indian waters, he fled from St Christopher's to Virginia and died there in about 1650.

Thomas Pride: One of the Commissioners appointed for the trial of the King, he signed the death warrant. He fought at both Dunbar and Worcester and subsequently made so much money from contracts to supply the navy that he was able to buy Nonsuch Park in Surrey which had been built by Henry VIII. He strongly opposed the suggestion that Cromwell should accept the crown, but took a seat in Cromwell's House of Lords. He died in 1658. At the Restoration Nonsuch was returned to the Crown.

Duke of Richmond (James Stuart, fourth Duke of Lennox and first Duke of Richmond): A steadfast supporter and generous benefactor of the King, he died in 1655 'with the good liking of all and without the hate of any'.

Prince Rupert: After an adventurous life as soldier and sailor, Prince Rupert returned to England at the Restoration and was granted a large annuity by Charles II. He served for a time in the navy against the Dutch, then settled down at Windsor Castle of which he was appointed Constable. A prematurely old man with 'a dry hard-favoured visage and a stern look', his last years were spent in chemical and mechanical researches, writing long letters to friends in Germany and receiving visits from his mistresses. He died at his house in Spring Garden, London, in 1682.

Oliver St John: Appointed Chief Justice of the Common Pleas in 1648, he remained in that post during the Commonwealth, though without exercising much influence. Excluded from office at the Restoration, he went to live in retirement in Northamptonshire. Leaving the country for the Continent in 1662, he died, still in exile, in 1673.

Lord Saye and Sele (William Fiennes, first Viscount Saye and Sele): Became a leading member of the Committee for

Both Kingdoms and sided with the Army in its quarrel with Parliament. Thereafter he endeavoured to come to terms with the King having, as Edward Hyde put it, 'not the least thought of dissolving the monarchy, and less of levelling the ranks and distinctions of men. He was as proud of his quality, and of being distinguished from other men by his title, as any man alive.' After the King's death he retired into relative obscurity and died at his country house in 1662.

Adrian Scrope: Signed the warrant for the King's execution, but, having taken no part in the upheavals which followed the death of Cromwell, he surrendered himself at the Restoration in the hope of mercy. However, Richard Browne deposed that Scrope had told him in conversation that he thought the King's death justified. The court accordingly condemned him to death and he was executed at Charing Cross in October 1660.

Philip Skippon: Having distinguished himself in the first Civil War, he was made commander-in-chief of the London Militia at the outbreak of the second. After the war he was appointed one of the King's judges, but did not attend the sittings of the court. Nor, as Member for Lyme in the Parliaments of 1654 and 1656, did he take any significant part in their debates. After Cromwell's death he signed the proclamation appointing the Protector's son, Richard Cromwell, his successor. The restored Long Parliament, regarding him as a soldier rather than a politician, did not, however, hesitate to appoint him commander of the London Militia in 1659. He survived this appointment by only a few months.

Sir Philip Stapleton: A brave soldier until deprived of his commission by the Self-Denying Ordinance, Stapleton was one of the eleven Members of Parliament whose expulsion was demanded by the General Council of the Army in June 1647. He sailed for Calais in August and died, supposedly of the plague, in an inn there later that month.

Richard Swanley: Remained at sea until 1647 when he retired to his house by the Thames at Limehouse where he died in 1650.

James Turner: Released from imprisonment after the Royalist defeat at Preston on condition that he went abroad, he took ship for Germany. He returned to Scotland in 1650, and fought at Worcester, where he was taken prisoner. He escaped and again went abroad. Knighted at the Restoration, he was subsequently granted a pension. He died about 1686.

Sir John Urry: Having deserted to the Royalists in 1643, he changed sides again in 1644 after fighting at Marston Moor and then served in Scotland before returning once more to the Royalists. Taken prisoner after the battle of Preston, he escaped only to be captured again. He was beheaded at Edinburgh in 1650.

Sir Henry Vane, the Elder: Dismissed by the King as Secretary of State in 1641, Vane was appointed Lord Lieutenant of Durham by Parliament later that year. A member of the Committee for Both Kingdoms from its inception, he became Member for Kent in Cromwell's first Parliament. He died in 1655.

Sir Henry Vane, the Younger: Although he took no part in the King's trial and declined to take the oath approving of his execution, Vane was extremely busy during the Commonwealth both with home and foreign affairs. But after the ejection of 'The Rump' he lived for a time in retirement, composing his *Healing Question* (1656), a publication so hostile to the Protectorate that he was imprisoned in Carisbrooke Castle. Returning to Parliament after Cromwell's death, he opposed the Restoration. Considered 'too dangerous to live', he was sent to the Tower and beheaded on Tower Hill on 14 June 1662.

John Venn: Until the summer of 1645 Venn remained Governor of Windsor Castle where he removed or destroyed several ornaments and much furniture in St George's Chapel. Thereafter he served assiduously on an army committee of the House of Commons and just as sedulously as a commissioner during the trial of the King. He died, reportedly by his own hand, the year after the King's execution.

Sir Edmund Verney: Third son of Sir Edmund Verney, King Charles I's standard-bearer who was killed at Edgehill. Unlike his elder brother Sir Ralph, he fought for the King as his father did. He was knighted in 1644 and appointed Lieutenant-Governor of Chester. He was 'sought out and killed in cold blood' while serving against Cromwell's troops in Ireland in September 1649.

Sir Ralph Verney: Eldest son of Sir Edmund, whom he much distressed by

fighting for Parliament. As a devoted member of the Church of England he went abroad in 1643 rather than sign the Covenant. He travelled widely on the Continent, returning to England in 1653, but was unhappy under the rule of his erstwhile companions in arms. After the Restoration he was created a baronet and thereafter lived for the most part quietly upon his estate at Claydon in Buckinghamshire until his death, aged eighty-three, in 1696.

Edmund Waller: Banished to France after the failure of his conspiracy, he published his collected poems in 1645. His banishment was revoked in 1651, and he returned to England where, in characteristic fashion, he wrote *A Panegyric to my Lord Protector*, a eulogy of Cromwell, in 1655, and, in 1660, a poem of praise to Charles II in *To The King upon His Majesty's Happy Return* (1660). He died at his country house, Hall Barn, Beaconsfield in 1687.

Sir William Waller: An outspoken critic of the pretensions of the Army, Waller was arrested in December 1648 and imprisoned for three years. Released, he was again arrested on the well-grounded suspicion that he was in touch with Royalist agents and brought before Cromwell who, so he said, examined him 'as a stranger, not as one whom he had aforetime known and obeyed'. At the Restoration he was not rewarded for such help as he had given in bringing it about, and he lived in relative obscurity until his death in 1668.

Earl of Warwick (Robert Rich, second Earl of Warwick): After his dismissal as Lord High Admiral in 1648 he refused to recognize the

Commonwealth, while remaining an admirer of Cromwell whose daughter, Frances, married Warwick's grandson and heir in 1657. This grandson died the following year and Warwick himself two months later.

Edward Whalley: Having fought in the second Civil War, he was appointed one of the commissioners for the trial of the King and signed the death warrant. Wounded at Dunbar in 1650, he fought also at Worcester in 1651. A strong supporter of Cromwell during the Protectorate, he sailed for America at the Restoration and disappeared into oblivion, dying probably in 1675.

Bulstrode Whitelocke: Having endeavoured to negotiate peace throughout the war, Whitelocke refused to take any part in the King's trial. He was appointed Ambassador to Queen Christina of Sweden in 1653. He also served as Keeper of the Great Seal and Lord President of the Council. When Charles II was restored to the throne Whitelocke not only evaded punishment but was frequently consulted on both legal and religious matters. He retired to his estate in Wiltshire, which had been purchased by his rich third wife. By this and his previous wives he had seventeen children.

John Williams: On the outbreak of the war, Williams, who had been enthroned as Archbishop of York shortly before, fled from his archiepiscopal palace at Cawood when it came under threat of Parliamentary attack and went to promote the King's cause in his native Wales. Convinced that Cromwell had 'the properties of all evil beasts', he was

steadfast in the Royalist cause until he died of a peritonsillar abscess at Gloddaeth in 1650.

Henry Wilmot (created Baron Wilmot of Adderbury in 1643, succeeded his father as second Viscount Wilmot of Athlone in 1644 and became first Earl of Rochester in 1652): In Paris he fought a duel with his old adversary Lord Digby who wounded him. He became one of Charles II's principal advisers in France. He was with him at Worcester, and, having accompanied him on his subsequent journeys, returned with him to France where his influence over him became stronger than ever. He died at Sluys in 1658. The poet and rake John Wilmot was his son and succeeded him as second Earl of Rochester.

Marquess of Winchester (John Paulet, fifth Marquess of Winchester): After the fall of Basing House, he was brought a prisoner to London, protesting that 'if the King had no more ground in England but Basing House, he would adventure it as he did, and so maintain it to the uttermost'. A prisoner in the Tower, accused of high treason, he was joined there by his wife who was granted a small allowance for the support of her children provided they were brought up as Protestants. At the Restoration he received little compensation for his losses and went to live in Berkshire in a house which had belonged to his second wife, daughter of the Earl of St Albans and Clanricarde. He enlarged this now demolished house, the front of which was said to have much resembled a church organ. He died in 1675. His son, an early supporter of King William III, was created first Duke of Bolton in 1689.

Sir Francis Windebank: Condemned by Parliament for his Roman Catholic sympathies, he fled in 1640 to France where he was reported to be 'as merry as if he were the contentedest man living'. He died at Paris in 1646 having been received into the Roman Catholic Church.

Sir John Winter: Left for France in 1644, returning in 1646 to England where he was later arrested and imprisoned. In 1660 he went back to France where he became Queen Henrietta Maria's secretary until her death in 1669. Thereafter he devoted himself to his ironworks in Gloucestershire.

Some of the Principal Civil War Sites, Buildings, Memorials and Museums in England

Abingdon, Oxfordshire: Museum, North Street

Alton, Hampshire: Church (St Laurence's)

Ampthill, Bedfordshire: Ruins of Houghton House (English Heritage)

Arundel, West Sussex: Castle besieged

Ashby de la Zouch, Leicestershire: Museum; Castle ruins (English Heritage)

Bamburgh Castle, Northumberland: Arms and armour collection

Banbury, Oxfordshire: Town Museum

Barthomley, Cheshire: Church (St Bartoline's)

Basing House, Hampshire: Excavations; earthworks; tithe barn

Beeston Castle, Cheshire: Besieged (English Heritage)

Belvoir Castle, Rutland (Leicestershire): Besieged

Bickleigh Castle, Devon: Besieged

Bishop's Waltham, Hampshire: Palace ruins (English Heritage)

Boscobel, Shropshire: Boscobel House and grounds and the descendant of the Royal Oak (English Heritage)

Brampton Bryan, Hereford and Worcester: Castle ruins

Brandon Hill, Bristol, Avon: Earthworks

Bridgnorth, Shropshire: Castle ruins; museum

Bridgwater, Somerset: Robert Blake Museum

Broughton Castle, near Banbury, Oxfordshire: Home of Viscount Sale and Sele

Cambridge: Sidney Sussex College, burial place of Cromwell's head

Canons Ashby House, Northamptonshire: Arms and armour (National Trust)

Carisbrooke Castle, Isle of Wight: Charles I's prison

Carlisle, Cumbria: Castle besieged

Chalgrove, Oxfordshire: John Hampden Memorial

Chester, Cheshire: King Charles Tower; city walls

Colchester, Essex: Museum

Corfe Castle, Dorset: Castle ruins (National Trust)

Coughton Court, Alcester, Warwickshire: Besieged (National Trust)

Coxwold, North Yorkshire: Newburgh Priory, reputed burying place of Cromwell's headless body

Cropredy, Oxfordshire: St Mary's Church

Dartmouth Castle, Devon: Besieged (English Heritage)

Devizes, Wiltshire: Museum

Donnington Castle, Berkshire: Castle ruins (English Heritage)

Edgehill, Warwickshire: Edgehill Battle Museum at Farnborough Hall

Exeter, Devon: Royal Albert Museum; city walls

Farnborough Hall: *see* **Edgehill**

Gloucester: Folk Museum, Westgate Street; East Gate

Goodrich Castle, Hereford and Worcester: Besieged (English Heritage)

Hambledon Hill, near Blandford Forum, Dorset: Fight with Clubmen (National Trust)

Hartlebury Castle, near Kidderminster, Hereford and Worcester: Besieged

Helmsley, North Yorkshire: Castle ruins (English Heritage)

Hereford: Old House Museum; Churchill Gardens Museum

Holdenby House Gardens, Northamptonshire: Charles I's prison

Hull: City Museum; Beverley Gate

Huntingdon, Cambridgeshire: Cromwell Museum

Hurst Castle, Hampshire: Charles I held here, 1648

Landsdown, Bath, Avon: Sir Bevil Grenville's Monument (English Heritage)

Leicester: Newarke Houses Museum

Lichfield, Staffordshire: St Mary's Centre Museum

Lincoln: City and County Museum

Littlecote, near Hungerford, Berkshire: Roundhead arms and armour collection

London: Banqueting House, Whitehall; Putney Parish Church; Royal Armouries; Museum of London; National Army Museum; Le Sueur's equestrian statue of Charles I, Trafalgar Square; Thornycroft's Cromwell outside Westminster Hall

Middle Claydon, Buckinghamshire: Claydon House, the Verney family home; parish church

Moreton Corbet, Shropshire: Castle ruins (English Heritage)

Morpeth, Northumberland: Castle ruins

Moseley Old Hall, Staffordshire:

Charles II's hiding place after the battle of Worcester

Nantwich, Cheshire: Museum, Pillory Street

Naseby, Northamptonshire: Museum, Purlieu Farm

Newark-on-Trent, Nottinghamshire: Castle ruins and museum and best surviving earthworks of the period

Newbury, Berkshire: District Museum, the Wharf

Northampton: Museum of Leathercraft

Nottingham: Castle museum

Nunney Castle, Somerset: Besieged (English Heritage)

Oxford: Museum of Oxford; Ashmolean

Pendennis Castle, Cornwall: Besieged (English Heritage)

Pontefract Castle, North Yorkshire: Besieged

Powderham Castle, Devon: Besieged

Preston, Lancashire: Harris Museum

Ripley, North Yorkshire: Castle, and parish church where prisoners believed to be killed

Rockingham Castle, Leicestershire: Besieged

Rousham House, near Steeple Aston, Oxfordshire: Attacked 1645

Saffron Walden, Essex: Museum; castle ruins

Scarborough Castle, North Yorkshire: Besieged (English Heritage)

Sherborne Castle, Dorset: Digby family home

Sherborne Old Castle, Dorset: Besieged

Shrewsbury, Shropshire: Castle and Rowley's House Museum

Skipton Castle, North Yorkshire: Besieged

Stokesay Castle, Shropshire: Attacked

Stow-on-the-Wold, Gloucestershire: Portraits in St Edward's Hall

Stratton, Cornwall: Relics in St Andrew's Church

Sudeley Castle, Gloucestershire: Besieged

Taunton, Somerset: Castle museum

Tisbury, Wiltshire: Wardour Old Castle ruins

Tiverton Castle, Devon: Armoury

Warwick: Castle, arms and armour collection

Windsor, Berkshire: Charles I's grave in St George's Chapel

Woodstock, Oxfordshire: Oxfordshire County Museum

Worcester: Royalist headquarters in Commandery

York: City walls; Castle museum; Yorkshire Museum; St Mary in Castlegate

BIBLIOGRAPHY

ABBOT, W.C., *Writings and Speeches of Oliver Cromwell* (4 vols, Cambridge, Mass., 1937–47)

ABELL, Henry Francis, *Kent and the Great Civil War* (Ashford, 1901)

ACTON, Mrs F. S., *The Garrisons of Shropshire During the Civil War* (Shrewsbury, 1867)

ADAIR, John, *Roundhead General: A Military Biography of Sir William Waller* (London, 1969)

—— *Cheriton 1644: The Campaign and the Battle* (London, 1973)

—— *By the Sword Divided: Eyewitness Accounts of the English Civil War* (London, 1983)

ADAMSON, John, 'The English Nobility and the Projected Settlement of 1647', *Historical Journal*, 1987

—— 'The Baronial Context of the English Civil War', *Transactions of the Royal Historical Society*, 1990

AMUSSEN, Susan Dwyer, *An Ordered Society* (Oxford, 1988)

ANDRIETTE, Eugene A., *Devon and Exeter in the Civil War* (Newton Abbot, 1971)

ARCHER, E., *A True Relation of the Red Trained Bands of Westminster* (London, 1643)

ASHFORD, L. J., *History of the Borough of High Wycombe* (London, 1960)

ASHLEY, Maurice, *Cromwell's Generals* (London, 1954)

—— *Prince Rupert of the Rhine* (London, 1976)

—— *The English Civil War* (new edition, Gloucester, 1990)

—— *The Battle of Naseby and the Fall of Charles I* (Gloucester 1992)

ASHTON, Robert, *The English Civil War: Conservatism and Revolution, 1603–1649* (2nd edition, London, 1989)

ATKYNS, Richard, *Military Memoirs of the Civil War* (ed. Peter Young, London, 1967)

AYLMER, G. E. (ed.), *The Levellers in the English Revolution* (London, 1975)

—— *Rebellion or Revolution?* (Oxford, 1986)

AYLMER, G. E. and MORRILL, J. S., *The Civil War and Interregnum: Sources for Local Historians* (London, 1979)

BAILLIE, Robert, *Letters and Journals* (ed. David Laing, Edinburgh, 1841)

BAKER, Anthony, *A Battlefield Atlas of the English Civil War* (Shepperton, 1986)

BARNETT, CORRELLI, *Britain and her Army 1509–1970: A Military, Political and Social Survey* (London, 1970)

BAXTER, RICHARD (*see also* J. M. L. Thomas), *Reliquiae Baxterianae* (London, 1696)

BAYLEY, A. R., *The Great Civil War in Dorset* (Taunton, 1910)

BIRCH, Colonel John, *Military Memoir* (ed. T. W. Webb, London, 1873)

BLACKWOOD, Gordon, 'The Cavalier and Roundhead Gentry of Suffolk' (*Suffolk Review*, No. 5, 1985)

—— *The Lancashire Gentry and the Great Rebellion, 1640–1660* (Manchester, 1978)

BOND, Brian and ROY, Ian (eds), *War and Society* (London, 1975)

BRETT, S. Reed, *John Pym, 1583–1643* (London, 1940)

BRIGHTON, J. T., *Royalists and Roundheads in Derbyshire* (London, 1981)

BROXAP, Ernest, *The Great Civil War in Lancashire* (Manchester, 1973)

BULSTRODE, Sir Richard, *Memoirs* (London, 1971)

BURNE, A. H., *The Battlefields of England* (London, 1951)

CAPP, Bernard, *Cromwell's Navy: The Fleet and the English Revolution, 1648–1660* (Oxford, 1990)

CARLTON, Charles, *Charles I: The Personal Monarch* (London, 1983)

—— *Archbishop William Laud* (London, 1988)

—— *Going to the Wars: The Experience of the British Civil Wars* (London, 1992)

CHOLMLEY, Sir Hugh, *Memoirs* (London, 1787)

CLARENDON, Edward Hyde, Earl of, *History of the Rebellion and Civil Wars in England* (ed. W. D. Macray, 1888)

CLARKE, D. T. D., *The Siege of Colchester, 1648* (Colchester, 1976)

CLIFFE, J. T., *Yorkshire Gentry from the Reformation to the Civil War* (London, 1969)

CLIFFORD, D. J. H. (ed.), *The Diaries of Lady Anne Clifford* (Gloucester, 1990)

COATE, Mary, *Cornwall in the Great Civil War and Interregnum, 1642–1660* (Oxford, 1933)

COATES, W. H. (ed.), *The Journal of Sir Simonds D'Ewes from the First Recess of the Long Parliament to the withdrawal of King Charles from London* (New Haven, 1942)

COCKERILL, *see* Woodward

COGSWELL, Thomas, *English Politics and the Coming of War, 1621–1624* (Cambridge, 1989)

COLEBY, A. M., *Central Government and the Localities: Hampshire, 1649–1659* (Cambridge, 1987)

COLLINSON, Patrick, *The Birthpangs of Protestant England: Religious and Cultural Change in the Sixteenth and Seventeenth Centuries* (London, 1989)

CRAWFORD, Patricia, *Denzil Holles* (London, 1979)

DAVIES, Godfrey, *The Restoration of Charles II, 1658–60* (San Marino, Cal., 1955)

DENTON, Barry, *Crisis in the Army, 1647* (Leigh-on-Sea, 1984)

—— *Naseby Fight* (Leigh-on-Sea, 1985)

D'EWES, *see* Coates and Notestein

DONAGAN, Barbara, 'Prisoners in the English Civil War', *History Today*, March 1991

DONALD, Peter, *An Uncounselled King: Charles I and the Scottish Troubles, 1637–1641* (Cambridge, 1990)

DORE, R. N., *The Civil War in Cheshire* (Chester, 1966)

—— *The Great Civil War in the Manchester Area* (Manchester, 1972)

—— (ed.), *The Letter Books of Sir William Brereton* (Manchester, 1984)

—— (with John Lowe), 'The Battle of Nantwich', *Transactions of the*

Historical Society of Lancashire and Cheshire, CXIII, 1961

DOW, F. D., *Radicalism in the English Revolution* (Oxford, 1985)

DOWNING, Taylor and MILLMAN, Maggie, *Civil War* (London, 1991)

DUGDALE, Sir William, *A Short View of the Late Troubles in England* (Oxford, 1681)

DURSTON, Christopher, *The Family in the English Revolution* (Oxford, 1989)

EALES, Jacqueline, *Puritans and Roundheads: The Harleys of Brampton Bryan and the Outbreak of the English Civil War* (Cambridge, 1990)

EDGAR, F. T. R., *Sir Ralph Hopton* (Oxford, 1968)

ELTON, Richard, *Complete Body of the Art Military* (London, 1650)

EVANS, J. T., *Seventeenth-Century Norwich* (Oxford, 1979)

EVELYN, John, *The Diary of John Evelyn* (6 vols., ed. E. S. de Beer, Oxford, 1955)

EVERITT, Alan, *The Community of Kent and the Great Rebellion, 1640–60* (Leicester, 1966)

—— *Suffolk and the Great Rebellion, 1640–60* (Ipswich, 1961)

FARROW, W. J., *The Great Civil War in Shropshire, 1642–1649* (Shrewsbury, 1926)

FERGUSSON, Bernard, *Rupert of the Rhine* (London, 1952)

FIRTH, C. H., *Cromwell's Army* (4th edition, London, 1962)

—— *Oliver Cromwell* (London, 1900)

—— and DAVIES, Godfrey, *The Regimental History of Cromwell's Army* (2 vols, Oxford, 1940)

FLETCHER, Anthony, *A Country Community in Peace and War: Sussex, 1600–1660* (London, 1976)

—— *The Outbreak of the English Civil War* (London, 1981)

FORSTER, John, *Sir John Eliot* (London, 1865)

FOSTER, Sergeant Henry, *A True and Exact Relation of the Marching of the Trained Bands of the City of London* (1643, reprinted Leigh-on-Sea, 1990)

FRASER, Antonia, *Cromwell: Our Chief of Men* (London, 1973)

—— *King Charles II* (London, 1979)

—— *The Weaker Vessel: Woman's Lot in Seventeenth-Century England* (London, 1989)

FULLER, Thomas, *History of the Worthies of England* (ed. J. Freeman, London, 1952)

GARDINER, D. (ed.), *The Oxinden Letters, 1607–1642* (London, 1933)

GARDINER, S. R., *History of the Great Civil War, 1642–9* (4 vols, London, 1893)

GAUNT, Peter, *The Cromwellian Gazetteer: An Illustrated Guide to Britain in the Civil War and Commonwealth* (Gloucester, 1987)

GENTLES, Ian, 'The Arrears of Pay of the Parliamentary Army', *Bulletin of the Institute of Historical Research*, 1975

—— 'The Struggle for London in the Second Civil War', *Historical Journal*, xxvi, 2 (1983)

—— *The New Model Army in England, Ireland and Scotland* (London, 1991)

GIBB, M. A., *The Lord General* (London, 1938)

GILLINGHAM, John, *Cromwell: Portrait of a Soldier* (London, 1976)

GODWIN, G. N., *The Civil War in Hampshire (1642–45) and the Story of Basing House* (Southampton, 1904)

GOUGH, Richard, *The History of Myddle* (ed. D. Hey, London, 1981)

GREGG, Pauline, *Free-Born John: A*

Biography of John Lilburne (London, 1961)
—— *King Charles I* (London, 1981)
—— *Oliver Cromwell* (London, 1988)
GWYNN, Captain John, *Military Memoirs* (ed. Norman Tucker, London, 1967)

HARRIS, R. W., *Clarendon and the English Revolution* (London, 1983)
HEXTER, J. H., *The Reign of King Pym* (Cambridge, Mass., 1941)
HILL, Christopher, *The English Revolution, 1640* (3rd edition, London, 1955)
—— *Puritanism and Revolution* (London, 1958)
—— *God's Englishman: Oliver Cromwell and the English Revolution* (London, 1970)
—— *The World Turned Upside Down: Radical Ideas During the English Revolution* (London, 1972)
—— *The Century of Revolution, 1603–1714* (revised edition, Oxford, 1980)
HIRST, Derek, *Authority and Conflict: England, 1603–58* (London, 1986)
HOBBY, Elaine, *Virtue of Necessity* (London, 1988)
HODGSON, Captain J., *Memoirs* (Bradford, 1902)
HOLLINGS, J. F., *The History of Leicester During the Great Civil War* (Leicester, 1840)
HOLMES, Clive, *The Eastern Association and the English Civil War* (Cambridge, 1974)
—— *Seventeenth-Century Lincolnshire* (Lincoln, 1980)
HOPTON, Sir Ralph, *Bellum Civile* (ed. Alan Wicks, Leigh-on-Sea, 1988)
HOWARD-FLANDERS, W., *King, Parliament and Army: More Particulars relating to that honourable . . . expedition of Kent, Essex and Colchester in 1648* (London, 1905)

HOWELL, Roger, *Newcastle upon Tyne and the Puritan Revolution* (Oxford, 1974)
—— *Cromwell* (1977)
—— *Puritans and Radicals in North England* (Lanham, 1984)
HUGHES, Ann, *The Causes of the English Civil War* (London, 1991)
—— *Politics, Society and Civil War in Warwickshire, 1620–1662* (Cambridge, 1987)
HULME, Harold, *The Life of Sir John Eliot, 1552–1632* (London, 1957)
HUNT, W. A., *The Puritan Movement: The Coming of Revolution in an English County* (Harvard, 1983)
HUTCHINSON, Lucy, *see* Sutherland
HUTTON, Ronald, *The Royalist War Effort, 1642–6* (London, 1982)

Information How to Train or Drill a Foot Company (Clarke MSS, Worcester College, Oxford)
IVES, E. W. (ed.), *The English Revolution 1600–1660* (London, 1968)

JEFFERSON, S., *An Historical Account of Carlisle during the Civil War* (Carlisle, 1840)
JOHNSON, D. A. and VAISEY, D. G. (eds), *Staffordshire and the Great Rebellion* (Stafford, 1964)
JOHNSON, G. W., *The Fairfax Correspondence* (2 vols, London, 1848)
JOSSELIN, Ralph, *The Diary of Ralph Josselin* (ed. A. Macfarlane, London, 1976)
Journal of the Siege of Lathom House (1823, ed. E. Halsall, London, 1902)

KEELER, M. F., *The Long Parliament* (Philadelphia, 1954)
KELLY, Rosemary and Tony, *A City at War: Oxford 1642–46* (Leckhampton, 1987)
KELTON-CREMER, R. W., *Norfolk*

in the Civil War: A Portrait of a Society in Conflict (London, 1969)

KENYON, J. P., The Stuarts: A Study in English Kingship (London, 1958)

—— The Stuart Constitution, 1603–88 (Cambridge, 1966)

—— Stuart England (London, 1978)

—— The Civil Wars of England (London, 1988)

KINGSTON, Alfred, Hertfordshire During the Great Civil War (London, 1877)

—— East Anglia and the Great Civil War (London, 1897)

KISHLANSKY, Mark, The Rise of the New Model Army (Cambridge, 1979)

LAMPLOUGH, Edward, Yorkshire Battles (1891)

LEE, Ross, Law and Local Society in the Time of Charles I: Bedfordshire and the Civil War (London, 1956)

LEWIS, T. T. (ed.), 'Letters of the Lady Brilliana Harley', Camden Society, 1st Series, LI, 1853

LISTER, John, The Autobiography of John Lister of Bradford (ed. T. Wright, 1842)

LITHGOW, William, The Present Surveigh of London and England's State (1643, reprinted in Somers Tracts, iv, 538)

LOCKYER, Roger, The Early Stuarts: A Political History of England, 1603–1642 (London, 1990)

LUDLOW, Edmund, The Memoirs of Edmund Ludlow, 1625–1672 (ed. C. H. Firth, London, 1894)

MALCOLM, Joyce Lee, Caesar's Due: Loyalty and King Charles, 1642–6 (London, 1983)

MANNING, Brian, Politics, Religion and the English Civil War (London, 1973)

—— The English People and the English Revolution, 1640–1649 (London, 1976)

MARKHAM, Clements, The Great Lord Fairfax (London, 1870)

MARSHALL, Rosalind K., Henrietta Maria: The Intrepid Queen (London, 1990)

MATHEW, David, The Age of Charles I (London, 1951)

MELLING, Elizabeth (ed.), Kent and the Civil War (Maidstone, 1960)

MILLER, Amos C., Sir Richard Grenville and the Civil War (London, 1979)

MILLMAN, Maggie, see Downing

MILWARD, R. J., Wimbledon in the Time of the Civil War (Epsom, 1976)

MORRILL, J. S., Cheshire, 1630–1660: County Government and Society During the English Revolution (Oxford, 1974)

—— The Revolt of the Provinces: Conservatives and Radicals in the English Civil War, 1630–1650 (London, 1976)

—— Seventeenth-Century Britain, 1603–1714 (Folkestone, 1980)

—— (ed.), Reactions to the English Civil War (London, 1982)

—— 'Mutiny and Discontent in the English Provincial Armies, 1645–7', Past and Present, 56, 1982

—— (ed.), Oliver Cromwell and the English Revolution (London, 1990)

—— (ed.), The Impact of the English Civil War (London, 1991)

NEWMAN, P. R., Royalist Officers in England and Wales 1642–60: A Biographical Dictionary (New York, 1981)

—— Marston Moor (London, 1981)

—— Atlas of the English Civil War (London, 1985)

NICHOLAS, Donald, Mr Secretary Nicholas, 1593–1669: His Life and Letters (London, 1955)

NOTESTEIN, Wallace (ed.), The Journal of Sir Simonds D'Ewes from the

Beginning of the Long Parliament to the Opening of the Trial of the Earl of Strafford (New Haven, 1923)

OGLANDER, Sir John, *A Royalist's Notebook* (ed. F. Bamford, 1936)
OLLARD, Richard, *This War Without an Enemy: A History of the English Civil Wars* (London, 1976)
—— *The Image of the King: Charles I and Charles II* (London, 1979)
—— *Clarendon and his Friends* (London, 1987)
OMAN, Carola, *Henrietta Maria* (London, 1936)
O'NEILL, B. H. St J., *Castles and Cannon* (Oxford, 1960)

PARKER, Geoffrey, *The Military Revolution: Military Innovation and the Rise of the West 1500–1800* (Cambridge, 1988)
PARRY, R. H. (ed.), *The English Civil War and After* (London, 1970)
PARSONS, Daniel (ed.), *The Diary of Sir Henry Slingsby of Scriven* (London, 1836)
PEARL, Valerie, *London and the Outbreak of the Puritan Revolution* (London, 1961)
PENNINGTON, Donald and THOMAS, Keith, *Puritans and Revolutionaries: Essays in Seventeenth-Century History presented to Christopher Hill* (Oxford, 1978)
PENNINGTON, Donald and ROOTS, Ivan, *The Committee at Stafford 1643–1645* (Manchester, 1957)
PHILIP, I. G. (ed.), *The Journal of Sir Samuel Luke* (3 vols, Oxfordshire Society, 1947–53)
PHILLIPS, John Roland, *Memoirs of the Civil War in Wales and the Marches, 1642–1646* (2 vols, London, 1874)
POTTER, Lois, *Secret Rites and Secret Writing: Royalist Literature, 1641–1660* (Cambridge, 1990)
POWELL, J. R., *The Navy in the English Civil War* (Hamden, 1962)

RALPH, P. L., *Sir Humphrey Mildmay, Royalist Gentleman* (London, 1947)
RECKITT, Basil N., *Charles the First and Hull, 1639–1645* (London, 1952)
RICHARDSON, R. C., *The Debate on the English Revolution Revisited* (London, 1977)
ROBERTS, Keith, *London and Liberty: Ensigns of the London Trained Bands* (Leigh-on-Sea, 1987)
ROOTS, Ivan, *The Great Rebellion 1642–1660* (London, 1966)
—— *The Speeches of Oliver Cromwell* (London, 1989)
ROWSE, A. L., *Reflections on the Puritan Revolution* (London, 1986)
RUSHWORTH, John (ed.), *Historical Collections* (7 vols, 1659–1701)
RUSSELL, Conrad (ed.), *The Origins of the English Civil War* (London, 1973)
—— *The Causes of the English Civil War* (Oxford, 1990)
—— *The Fall of the British Monarchies, 1637–42* (Oxford, 1991)
—— *Unrevolutionary England, 1603–1642* (Hambledon, 1991)

SCHOFIELD, B. (ed.), *The Knyvett Letters* (London, 1979)
SHARPE, Kevin (ed.), *Faction and Parliament: Essays on Early Stuart History* (Oxford, 1978)
—— *Politics and Ideas in Early Stuart England* (London, 1989)
—— *The Personal Rule of Charles I* (London, 1992)
SHARPE, Reginald R., *London and the Kingdom* (London, 1894)
SHERWOOD, R. E., *Civil Strife in the Midlands, 1642–1651* (Chichester, 1974)

SLACK, Paul (ed.), *Rebellion, Popular Protest and the Social Order in Early Modern England* (Cambridge, 1984)

SMITH, Steven R., 'Almost Revolutionaries: The London Apprentices During the Civil War', *Huntington Library Quarterly*, vol. 42, 1978–9

SNOW, Vernon F., *Essex the Rebel* (Lincoln, Nebraska, 1970)

SPALDING, Ruth, *The Improbable Puritan: A Life of Bulstrode Whitelock, 1605–1675* (London, 1975)

—— (ed.), *The Diary of Bulstrode Whitelocke, 1605–1675* (London, 1990)

SPRIGGE, Joshua, *Anglia Rediviva: England's Recovery* (London, 1647)

STEVENSON, David, *The Scottish Revolution, 1637–1644* (Newton Abbot, 1973)

STONE, Lawrence, *The Causes of the English Revolution 1529–1642* (London, 1972)

SUTHERLAND, James (ed.), *Memoirs of the Life of Lucy Hutchinson* (London, 1973)

SYMMONDS, Captain Richard, *Diary of the Marches of the Royal Army During the Great Civil War* (1859, reprinted Leigh-on-Sea, 1990)

TAYLOR, Philip A. M. (ed.), *The Origins of the English Civil War: Conspiracy, Crusade or Class Conflict* (London, 1960)

TENNANT, Philip, *Edgehill and Beyond* (Stroud, 1992)

THOMAS, J. M. L. (ed.), *Autobiography of Richard Baxter* (London, 1925)

THOMAS, Keith, *Religion and the Decline of Magic* (London, 1971)

THOMSON, Gladys Scott, *Life in a Noble Household, 1641–1700* (London, 1937)

TOMLINSON, Howard and GREGG, David, *Politics, Religion and Society in Revolutionary England, 1640–60* (London, 1989)

TOWNSEND, Henry, *Diary* (Worcester, 1920)

TOYNBEE, Margaret and YOUNG, Peter, *Strangers in Oxford* (London, 1973)

TREASE, Geoffrey, *Portrait of a Cavalier: William Cavendish, First Duke of Newcastle* (London, 1979)

TREVOR-ROPER, H. R., *Archbishop Laud* (2nd edition, London, 1962)

TURNER, Sir James, *Memoirs* (Edinburgh, 1829)

TURNER, J. Horsfall, *The Autobiography of Captain John Hodgson* (Brighouse, 1882)

TWIGG, John, *A History of Queen's College, Cambridge* (Woodbridge, 1987)

UNDERDOWN, David, *Pride's Purge: Politics in the English Revolution* (Oxford, 1971)

—— *Somerset in the Civil War and Interregnum* (Newton Abbot, 1973)

—— *Revel, Riot and Rebellion: Popular Politics and Culture in England, 1603– 1660* (Oxford, 1985)

VARLEY, F. J., *Cambridge During the Civil War, 1642–1646* (Cambridge, 1935)

—— *The Siege of Oxford: Oxford During the Civil War, 1642–1646* (London, 1932)

VERNEY, F. P. (ed.), *Memoirs of the Verney Family* (vols 1 and 2, London, 1892)

VICARS, John, *God in the Mount, or England's Remembrances* (London, 1642)

Victoria County Histories

WALFORD, E. A., *Edgehill: The Battle and Battlefield* (Banbury, 1886)

WALKER, Sir Edward, *Historical Discourses* (1705)

WALLINGTON, Nehemiah, *Historical Notes of Events Occurring Chiefly in the Reign of Charles I* (2 vols, London, 1869)

WARWICK, Sir Philip, *Memoirs of the Reign of King Charles* (1813)

WASHBURN, J. (ed.), *Biblioteca Gloucesterensis: A Collection of Scarce and Curious Tracts relating to the County and City of Gloucester* (1825)

WEBB, John, *Memorials of the Civil War in Herefordshire* (London, 1879)

WEDGWOOD, C. V., *Oliver Cromwell* (London, 1939)

—— *The Great Rebellion: The King's Peace, 1637–1641* (London, 1958)

—— *The Great Rebellion: The King's War, 1641–1647* (London, 1961)

—— *Thomas Wentworth, First Earl of Strafford, 1593–1641* (London, 1961)

—— *The Trial of Charles I* (London, 1964)

WENHAM, Peter, *The Great and Close Siege of York* (Kineton, 1970)

WHARTON, Nehemiah, 'Letters from a Subaltern Officer in the Earl of Essex's Army', *Archaeologia*, vol. xxxv, 1853, ed. S. L. Ede Borrett, Leigh-on-Sea, 1983

WILLIS-BUND, J. W., *The Civil War in Worcestershire, 1642–1646* (Birmingham, 1905)

—— (ed.), *The Diary of Henry Townshend* (Worcester, 1920)

WILSON, John, *Fairfax* (1985)

WOOD, Alfred C., *Nottinghamshire in the Civil War* (Oxford, 1937)

WOOD, Anthony, *Historia et Antique Universitatis Oxoniensis* (2 vols, 1674)

WOODHOUSE, A. S. P., *Puritanism and Liberty* (London, 1938; new edition 1974 with introduction by Ivan Roots)

WOODWARD, Daphne and COCKERILL, Chloë, *The Siege of Colchester, 1648. A History and Bibliography* (2nd edition, Colchester, 1979)

WOOLRYCH, Austin, *Battles of the English Civil War* (London, 1961)

—— *Soldiers and Statesmen: The General Council of the Army and its Debates, 1647–8* (London, 1987)

WORDEN, Blair, *The Rump Parliament* (Cambridge, 1974)

—— (ed.), *Stuart England* (Oxford, 1986)

WORMALD, B. H. G., *Clarendon* (Cambridge, 1951)

WROUGHTON, John, *The Civil War in Bath and North Somerset* (Bath, 1973)

YOUNG, Peter (with A. H. Burne), *The Great Civil War* (London, 1959)

—— *Edgehill, 1642: The Campaign and the Battle* (London, 1967)

—— *Marston Moor, 1644* (1967)

—— (with Margaret Toynbee), *Cropredy Bridge* (London, 1970)

—— *Armies of the English Civil War* (London, 1973)

—— (with Wilfred Pemberton), *The Cavalier Army* (London, 1974)

—— (with Richard Holmes), *The English Civil Wars, 1642–51* (London, 1974)

—— *Oliver Cromwell and His Times* (new edition, London, 1975)

—— (with Wilfred Pemberton), *Sieges of the Great Civil War* (London, 1978)

—— *Naseby, 1645: The Campaign and the Battle* (London, 1985)

—— *The Civil War Papers of Brigadier Peter Young* (National Army Museum manuscripts)

ILLUSTRATION CREDITS

INDEX

The abbreviation CR is used to denote King Charles I